Supreme Court DRAMA

Cases That Changed America

Supreme Court DRAMA

Cases That Changed America

Daniel E. Brannen, &
Dr. Richard Clay Hanes

Elizabeth Shaw, Editor

VOLUME 3

AFFIRMATIVE ACTION

ASSISTED SUICIDE AND
THE RIGHT TO DIE

CIVIL RIGHTS AND
EQUAL PROTECTION

GENDER DISCRIMINATION

REPRODUCTIVE RIGHTS

RIGHTS OF IMMIGRANTS, GAYS,
AND THE DISABLED

VOTING RIGHTS

AN IMPRINT OF THE GALE GROUP

DETROIT · NEW YORK · SAN FRANCISCO
LONDON · BOSTON · WOODBRIDGE, CT

Supreme Court Drama:
Cases That Changed America

DANIEL E. BRANNEN
RICHARD CLAY HANES

Staff

Elizabeth M. Shaw, U•X•L Editor
Carol DeKane Nagel, U•X•L Managing Editor
Thomas L. Romig, U•X•L Publisher

Shalice Shah-Caldwell, Permissions Associate (Pictures)
Maria Franklin, Permissions Manager
Robyn Young, Imaging and Multimedia Content Editor

Rita Wimberley, Senior Buyer
Evi Seoud, Assistant Manager, Composition Purchasing and Electronic Prepress
Dorothy Maki, Manufacturing Manager
Mary Beth Trimper, Production Director
Michelle DiMercurio, Senior Art Director

Pamela A. Reed, Imaging Coordinator
Randy Basset, Image Database Supervisor
Barbara Yarrow, Imaging and Multimedia Content Manager

Linda Mahoney, LM Design, Typesetting

Cover photographs: Reproduced by permission of the Library of Congress and the Supreme Court of the United States.

Library of Congress Cataloging-in-Publication Data
Brannen, Daniel E., 1968-
    Supreme Court drama: cases that changed the nation / Daniel E. Brannen, Jr. and Richard Clay Hanes ; Elizabeth M. Shaw, editor.
        p. cm.
    Includes bibliographical references and index.
    ISBN 0-7876-4877-9 (set) – ISBN 0-7876-4878-7 (v.1) – ISBN 0-7876-4879-5 (v.2) –ISBN 0-7876-4880-9 (v.3) – ISBN 0-7876-4881-7 (v.4)
      1.Constitutional law–United States–Cases–Juvenile literature. 2. United States. Supreme Court–Juvenile Literature. [1. Constitutional law–United States–Cases. 2. United States. Supreme Court.] I. Hanes, Richard Clay, 1946- II. Shaw, Elizabeth M., 1973- III. Title.

    KF4550.Z9 B73 2001
    347.73'26'0264–dc21

                                                00-056380

Printed in Canada

10 9 8 7 6 5 4 3 2

Contents

VOLUME 1: INDIVIDUAL LIBERTIES

FREEDOM OF ASSEMBLY

Contents

Contents

VOLUME 2: CRIMINAL JUSTICE AND FAMILY LAW

CAPITAL PUNISHMENT

CRIMINAL LAW AND PROCEDURE

Contents

VOLUME 3: EQUAL PROTECTION AND CIVIL RIGHTS

AFFIRMATIVE ACTION

ASSISTED SUICIDE/ RIGHT TO DIE

CIVIL RIGHTS AND EQUAL PROTECTION

Contents

Contents

VOLUME 4: BUSINESS AND GOVERNMENT LAW

ANTITRUST, BUSINESS, CORPORATE AND CONTRACT LAW

FEDERAL POWERS AND SEPARATION OF POWERS

times to justify presidential initiatives in foreign affairs and contributed greatly to the growth of the power of the presidency in modern times.

Contents

Contents

Trials Alphabetically

A

B

Trials Alphabetically

F

G

H

I

N

O

P

**Trials
Alphabetically**

T

U

V

W

**Trials
Alphabetically**

Y

Trials Chronologically

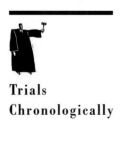

**Trials
Chronologically**

**Trials
Chronologically**

**Trials
Chronologically**

1960

1961

1962

1963

1964

1965

1966

**Trials
Chronologically**

1973

1974

1975

1976

1977

1978

**Trials
Chronologically**

1986

1987

1988

1989

1990

**Trials
Chronologically**

1998

1999

2000

**Trials
Chronologically**

Reader's Guide

U.S. citizens take comfort and pride in living under the rule of law. Our elected representatives write and enforce the laws that cover everything from family relationships to the dealings of multi-billion-dollar corporations, from the quality of the air to the content of the programs broadcast through it. But it is the judicial system that interprets the meaning of the law and makes it real for the average citizen through the drama of trials and the force of court orders and judicial opinions.

The four volumes of *Supreme Court Drama: Cases that Changed America* profile approximately 150 cases that influenced the development of key aspects of law in the United States. The case profiles are grouped according to the legal principle on which they are based, with each volume covering one or two broad areas of the law as follows:

- **Volume : Individual Liberties** includes cases that have influenced such First Amendment issues as freedom of the press, religion, speech, and assembly. It also covers the right to privacy.

- **Volume 2: Criminal Justice and Family Law** covers many different areas of criminal law, such as capital punishment, crimnal procedure, family law, and juvenile law.

- **Volume 3: Equal Protection and Civil Rights** includes cases in the areas of affirmative action, reproductive rights segregation, and voting rights, as well as areas of special concern such as immigrants, the disabled, and gay and lesbian citizens. Sexual harassment and the right to die are also represented in this volume.

- **Volume 4: Business and Government Law** also encompasses two major spheres of the law. Monopolies, antitrust, and labor-related cases supplement the business fundamentals of corporate law. The government cases document the legal evolution of the branches of the federal government as well as the federal government's relation to state power. Separate topics address military issues, taxation, and legal history behind some Native American issues.

- **Appendixes** to all volumes also present the full text of the U.S. Constitution and its amendments and a chronological table of Supreme Court justices.

Coverage

Issue overviews, averaging 2,000 words in length provide the context for the case profiles that follow. Case discussions range from 750 to 2,000 words according, to their complexity and importance. Each provides the background of the case and issues involved, the main arguments presented by each side, and an explanation of the Supreme Court's decision, as well as the legal, political, and social impact of the decision. Excerpts from the Court's opinions are often included. Within each issue section, the cases are arranged from earliest to most recent.

When a single case could be covered under several different areas—the landmark reproductive rights decision in *Roe v. Wade,* for example, is also based upon an assertion of privacy rights—the case is placed with the issue with which it is most often associated. Users should consult the cumulative index that appears in each volume to find cases throughout the set that apply to a particular topic.

Additional Features

- The issues and proceedings featured in *Supreme Court Drama* are presented in language accessible to middle school users. Legal terms must sometimes be used for precision, however, so a Words to Know section of more than 300 words and phrases appears in each volume.

- A general essay providing a broad overview of the Supreme Court of the United States and the structure of the American legal system.

- **Bolded** cross-references within overview and case entries that point to cases that appear elsewhere in the set.

- Tables of contents to locate a particular case by name or in chronological order.

- A cumulative index at the end of each volume that includes the cases, people, events and subjects that appear throughout *Supreme Court Drama.*

Suggestions Are Welcome

We welcome your comments on *Supreme Court Drama: Cases That Changed America.* Please write, Editors, *Supreme Court Drama,* U•X•L, 27500 Drake Road, Farmington Hills, MI 48331-3535; call toll-free: 1-800-877-4253; fax to 248-414-5043; or send e-mail via http://www.galegroup.com.

Advisors

The editor is grateful for all the assistance and insight offered by the advisors to this product.

- Mary Alice Anderson, Media Specialist, Winona Middle School, Winona, Minnesota

- Sara Brooke, Librarian, Ellis School, Pittsburgh, Pennsylvania

- Marolynn Griffin, Librarian, Desert Ridge Middle School, Albuquerque, New Mexico

- Dr. E. Shane McKee, Instructor, The Putney School at Elm Lea Farm, Putney, Vermont

The editor and writers would also like to acknowledge the tireless review and copy editing work done by:

- Aaron Ford, The Ohio State University, Columbus, Ohio

- Kathleen Knisely, Franklin County Courts, Columbus, Ohio

- Courtney Mroch, Freelance Writer, Jacksonville, Florida

- Melynda Neal, Franklin County Courts, Columbus, Ohio

- Berna Rhodes-Ford, Franklin County Courts, Columbus, Ohio

- Gertrude Ring, Freelance Writer, Los Angeles, California

- Lauren Zupnic, Franklin County Courts, Columbus, Ohio

Guide to the Supreme Court of the United States

The United States Supreme Court is the highest court in the judicial branch of the federal government. That means the Supreme Court is equal in importance to the president, who heads the executive branch, and Congress, which heads the legislative branch. Congress makes laws, the president enforces them, and the Supreme Court interprets them to make sure they are properly enforced.

The Supreme Court's main job is to review federal (national) and state cases that involve rights or duties under the U.S. Constitution, the document outlining the laws and guidelines for lawmaking and enforcement in the United States. The Court does this to make sure that all federal and state governments are obeying the Constitution.

For example, if Congress passes a law that violates the First Amendment freedom of speech, the Supreme Court can strike the law down as unconstitutional. If the president violates the Fourth Amendment by having the Federal Bureau of Investigation search a person's home without a warrant, the Supreme Court can fix the violation. If a state court violates the Constitution by convicting someone of a crime in an unfair trial, the Supreme Court can reverse the conviction.

As the highest court in the United States government, the Supreme Court also has the job of interpreting federal law. Congress creates law to regulate crimes, drugs, taxes, and other important issues across the nation. When someone is accused of violating a federal law, a federal court must interpret the law to decide whether the accused has broken the law. In this role, the Supreme Court makes the final decision about what a federal law means.

The Federal Court System

The Supreme Court was born in 1789, when the United States adopted the Constitution. Article III of the Constitution says, "The judicial Power of the United States, shall be vested in one supreme Court, and in such inferior Courts as the Congress may from time to time ordain and establish." With this sentence, the Constitution made the Supreme Court the highest Court in the judicial branch of the federal government. It also gave Congress the power to create lower courts.

Congress used that power to create a large judicial (court) system. The system has three levels. Trial courts, called federal district courts, are at the lowest level. There are ninety-four federal district courts covering different areas of the country. Each federal district court handles trials for cases in its area.

Federal district courts hold trials in both criminal and civil cases. Criminal trials involve cases by the government against a person who is accused of a crime, like murder. Civil trials involve cases between private parties, such as when one person accuses another of breaking a contract or agreement.

When a party loses a case in federal district court, she usually may appeal the decision to a U.S. court of appeals. Federal courts of appeals are the second level in the federal judicial system. There are twelve courts of appeals covering twelve areas, or circuits, of the country. For example, the district courts in Connecticut, New York, and Vermont are part of the Second Circuit. Appeals from district courts in those states go to the U.S. Court of Appeals for the Second Circuit.

During an appeal, the losing party asks the court of appeals to reverse or modify the trial court's decision. In essence, she argues that the trial court made an error when it ruled against her.

The party who loses before the court of appeals must decide whether to take her case to the U.S. Supreme Court. The Supreme Court is the third and highest level of the federal judicial system. The process of taking a case to the U.S. Supreme Court is described below.

State Court Systems

Most states have a judicial system that resembles the federal system. Trial courts hold trials in both criminal and civil cases. Most states also have special courts that hear only certain kinds of cases. Family, juvenile, and traffic courts are typical examples. There also are state courts, such as justices of the peace and small claims courts, that handle minor matters.

Appeals from all lower courts usually go to a court of appeals. The losing party there may take her case to the state's highest court, often called the state supreme court. When a case involves the U.S. Constitution or federal law, the losing party sometimes may take the case from the state supreme court to the U.S. Supreme Court.

Bringing a Case to the U.S. Supreme Court

There are three main ways that cases get to the U.S. Supreme Court. The most widely used method is to ask the Supreme Court to hear the case. This is called filing a petition for a writ of *certiorari*. The person who files the petition, usually the person who lost the case in the court of appeals, is called the petitioner. The person on the other side of the case is called the respondent. The Court only grants a small percentage of the writ petitions it receives each year. It usually tries to accept the cases that involve the most important legal issues.

The second main way to bring a case to the Supreme Court is by appeal. An appeal is possible only when the law that the case involves says the parties may appeal to the Supreme Court. The losing party who files the appeal is called the appellant, while the person on the other side of the case is a called the appellee.

The third main way to bring a case to the Supreme Court is by filing a petition for a writ of habeas corpus. This petition is mainly for people who have been imprisoned in violation of the U.S. Constitution. For example, if an accused criminal is convicted and jailed after the police beat him to get a confession (a police act that is illegal), the prisoner may ask the Supreme Court to release him by filing a petition for a writ of habeas corpus. The person who files the petition is called the petitioner, while the person holding the petitioner in jail is called the respondent.

The process of arguing and deciding a case in the Supreme Court is similar no matter how the case gets there. The parties file briefs that explain why they think the lower court's decision in their case is either right or wrong. The Supreme Court reviews the briefs along with a record of the evidence presented during trial in the federal district court or state trial court. The Supreme Court also may allow the parties to engage in oral argument, which is a chance for the lawyers to explain their clients' cases. During oral argument, the Supreme Court justices can ask questions to help them make the right decision.

After the justices read the briefs, review the record, and hear oral argument, they meet privately in chambers to discuss the case. Eventually, the nine justices vote for the party they think should win the case. A party must receive votes from five of the nine justices to win the case. The justices who cast the votes for the winning party are called the majority, while the justices who vote for the losing party are called the minority.

After the justices vote, one justice in the majority writes an opinion to explain the Court's decision. Other justices in the majority may write concurring opinions that explain why they agree with the Court's decision. Justices in the minority may write dissenting opinions to explain why they think the Court's decision is wrong.

The Supreme Court's decision is the final word in a case. Parties who are unhappy with the result have no place to go to get a different ruling. The only way to change the effect of a Supreme Court decision is to have Congress change the law, have the entire nation change, or amend, the Constitution, or have the president appoint a different justice to the Court when one retires or dies. This is part of the federal government's system of checks and balances, which prevents one branch from becoming too strong.

Supreme Court Justices

Supreme Court justices are among the greatest legal minds in the country. Appointment to the job is usually the high point of a career that involved some combination of trial work as a lawyer, teaching as a professor, or service as a judge on a lower court.

Under the Constitution, the president appoints Supreme Court justices with the advice and consent of the Senate when one of the nine justices retires, dies, or is removed from office. Supreme Court justices cannot be removed from office except by impeachment and conviction by Congress for serious crimes. That means the process of appointing a new justice usually begins when one of the justices retires or dies.

The president begins the process by nominating someone to fill the empty seat on the Court. The president usually names someone who he thinks will interpret the Constitution favorably to his political party's wishes. In other words, democratic presidents typically nominate liberal justices, while republican presidents nominate conservative justices.

The next step in the process is for the Senate Judiciary Committee to review the president's recommendation. If the Senate is controlled by the president's political party, the review process usually results in Senate approval of the president's selection.

If the president's political opposition controls the Senate, the review process can be fierce and lengthy. The Judiciary Committee calls the nominee before it to answer questions. The Committee's goal is to determine whether the nominee is qualified to be a Supreme Court justice. The Committee also uses the investigation to try to figure out how the nominee will decide controversial cases, such as cases involving abortion. After its investigation, the Committee recommends whether the Senate should confirm or reject the president's nomination. Two-thirds of the senators must vote for the nominee to confirm him as a new Supreme Court justice.

The Supreme Court has changed greatly over the years. One of the Court's greatest liberal periods was when Chief Justice Earl Warren headed the Court from 1953 to 1969. In 1954, the Warren Court decided one of its most famous cases, *Brown v. Board of Education,* in which it forced public schools to end the practice of separating black and white students in different schools.

The Warren Court was followed by one of the Court's greatest conservative periods, under Chief Justice Warren E. Burger from 1969 to 1986, followed by Chief Justice William H. Rehnquist from 1986 onward. In one of the Rehnquist Court's most important decisions, *Clinton v. Jones* (1997), the Court said the president may be sued while in office for conduct unrelated to his official duties. The decision allowed Paula Jones to sue President William J. Clinton for sexual harassment.

Unfortunately, the justices on the highest court in a nation of diversity have not been very diverse themselves. Until 1916, all Supreme Court justices were white, Christian men. That year, Louis D. Brandeis became the first Jewish member of the Supreme Court. In 1967, Thurgood Marshall became the first African American justice. Clarence Thomas became just the second in 1991. In 1981, President Ronald Reagan nominated Sandra Day O'Connor to be the first woman on the Supreme Court. Ruth Bader Ginsburg joined her there in 1993.

Research and Activity Ideas

Activity 1: New School Rule

Assignment: Imagine that your school principal has just announced a new school rule for detention. Students who get detention are not allowed to explain themselves, even if they did nothing wrong. Instead, they must sit in the principal's office during lunch. They are not allowed to eat lunch, not allowed to talk at all, and must listen to Frank Sinatra music during the entire period. Your teacher has asked you to prepare a written report on whether this new rule violates the U.S. Constitution.

Preparation: Begin your research by reading the Bill of Rights, which contains the first ten amendments to the U.S. Constitution, along with the Fourteenth Amendment. These amendments contain many rights that might apply to the principal's new rule. Do you see any that might help? Continue your research by looking in *Supreme Court Drama: Cases That Changed America* for essays and cases on the freedom of speech, cruel and unusual punishment, and students' rights in school. Consult the library and Internet web sites for additional research material. Does it seem to matter whether you are in a public or private school?

Presentation: After you have gathered your information, prepare a report that explains what you found. Does the principal's new rule violate the Constitution? Why or why not? Explain your conclusions by referring to specific amendments from the Constitution and specific cases from *Supreme Court Drama*.

**Research
and Activity
Ideas**

Activity 2: Taking a Case to Court

Assignment: Pretend you were in a bookstore that was being robbed. When the police arrived to arrest the criminal, they accidentally arrested you. During the arrest they treated you roughly and broke your arm. Your lawyer has informed you that you may sue the police to recover damages in either state or federal court. Before deciding which court system to use, you must do some research about both systems.

Preparation: Begin by reading the Introduction to *Supreme Court Drama: Cases That Changed America* so you can learn about the federal and state court systems in general. Continue with library and Internet research for more information about these systems. Then figure out which courts you need to use for your case. For the state system, use the library and Internet to find your local trial court for civil cases. Then find your state court of appeals and supreme courts in case you lose in the trial court. For the federal system, find the federal district court and U.S. court of appeals for your area. Write to the state supreme court and the U.S. court of appeals to find out what percentage of cases make it from those courts to the U.S. Supreme Court each year.

Presentation: Write a letter to your attorney explaining what you found. Tell her where you need to file your case if you choose the state system, and where you need to take appeals in that system. Do the same for the federal system. Tell her what your chances are of getting to the U.S. Supreme Court with your case.

Activity 3: Oral Argument

Activity: Imagine that a new religious group called Planterism has moved into your community. Planters are a group of men who worship trees, flowers, and other plant life. Once every week they hold an all-night ceremony during which they burn a tree as a sacrifice for all living plants. The ceremony disturbs neighbors who are trying to sleep and threatens to eliminate rare trees in your town.

Your mayor or other local leader decides he does not like Planters, so he enacts the following law:

> **Everyone in this town must follow Christianity, Judaism, or some other popular religion. Anyone who follows a false religion, including Planterism, is guilty of a felony. Anyone who burns a tree as a**

sacrifice during a religious ceremony is guilty of a felony. Anyone who disturbs the peace with a religious ceremony at night is guilty of a felony.

Violation of this law by men is punishable by life in prison without a trial. If the local police suspect a man is violating this law, they shall enter his house immediately without a warrant, arrest him, and take him to jail for imprisonment. Violation of this law by women is punishable by thirty days in jail only after a jury finds the woman guilty in a fair trial.

Research
and Activity
Ideas

Your teacher has instructed the class to convene a Supreme Court to determine whether this law violates the U.S. Constitution.

Preparation: Select nine members of your class to be justices on the Court. The rest of your class should divide into three teams. One team will represent the mayor, who will argue in favor of the law. The second team will represent a group of Planters who want to challenge the law. The third team will represent a group of Christians, who want to burn palms on Palm Sunday, a religious holiday that happens once a year.

The justices and all three teams should begin by reading the Bill of Rights and the Fourteenth Amendment of the U.S. Constitution. Continue by reading *Supreme Court Drama: Cases That Changed America* for essays and cases on the freedom of religion, the establishment clause, search and seizure, cruel and unusual punishment, governmental power, due process of law, and gender discrimination. Supplement this with research from library materials and Internet web sites. You may want to assign small groups from each team to handle specific issues.

Presentation: When everyone has completed the research, all three teams should prepare to argue before the Supreme Court. The team representing the mayor should explain why the law should be upheld. The teams representing the Planters and the Christians should explain why the law should be struck down as unconstitutional. During the argument, the justices are allowed to ask questions of each team. After every team has made its argument, the justices should meet to discuss the case and to make a ruling. Is the law unconstitutional? Which parts are valid and which are not?

Words to Know

A

Accessory Aiding or contributing in a secondary way to a crime or assisting in or contributing to a crime.

Accomplice One who knowingly and voluntarily helps commit a crime.

Acquittal When a person who has been charged with committing a crime is found not guilty by the courts.

Admissible A term used to describe information that is allowed to be used as evidence or information in a court case.

Adultery Voluntary sexual relations between an individual who is married and someone who is not the individual's spouse.

Affidavit A written statement of facts voluntarily made by someone in front of an official or witness.

Affirmative action Employment programs required by the federal government designed to eliminate existing and continuing discrimination, to remedy lingering effects of past discrimination, and to create systems and procedures to prevent future discrimination; commonly based on population percentages of minority groups in a particular area. Factors considered are race, color, sex, creed (religious beliefs), and age.

Age of consent The age at which a person may marry without parental approval.

Age of majority The age at which a person, formerly a minor or an infant, is recognized by law to be an adult, capable of managing his or her own affairs and responsible for any legal obligations created by his or her actions.

Aggravated assault A person is guilty of aggravated assault if he or she tries to cause serious bodily injury to another or causes such injury purposely, knowingly, or recklessly without any concern for that person or without remorse.

Alien Foreign-born person who has not been naturalized to become a U.S. citizen under federal law and the Constitution.

Alimony Payment a family court may order one person in a couple to make to the other when the couple separates or divorces.

Amendment An addition, deletion, or change to an original item, such as the additions to the Constitution.

Amicus curiae Latin for "friend of the court"; a person with strong interest in, views on, or knowledge of the subject matter of a case, but is not a party to the case. A friend of the court may petition the court for permission to file a statement about the situation.

Amnesty The action of a government by which all persons or certain groups of persons who have committed a criminal offense—usually of a political nature that threatens the government (such as treason)—are granted immunity from prosecution.

Appeal Timely plea by an unsuccessful party in a lawsuit to an appropriate superior court that has the power to review a final decision on the grounds that the decision was made in error.

Appellate court A court having jurisdiction to review decisions of a lower court.

Apportionment The process by which legislative seats are distributed among those who are entitled to representation; determination of the number of representatives that each state, county, or other subdivision may send to a legislative body.

Arbitration Taking a dispute to an unbiased third person and agreeing in advance to comply with the decision made by that third person, after both parties have had a chance to argue their side of the issue.

Arraignment The formal proceeding where the defendant is brought before the trial court to hear the charges against him or her and to enter a plea of guilty, not guilty, or no contest.

Arrest The taking into custody of an individual for the purpose of answering the charges against him or her.

Arrest warrant A written order issued by an authority of the state and commanding that the person named be taken into custody.

Arson The malicious burning or exploding of a house, building, or property.

Assault Intentionally harming another person.

Attempt Unsuccessfully preparing and trying to carry out a deed.

B

Bail An amount of money the defendant needs to pay the court to be released while waiting for a trial.

Bankruptcy A federally authorized procedure by which an individual, corporation, or municipality is relieved of total liability for its debts by making arrangements for the partial repayment of those debts.

Battery An intentional, unpermitted act causing harmful or offensive contact with another person.

Beneficiary One who inherits something through the last will and testament (will) of another; also, a person who is entitled to profits, benefits, or advantage from a contract.

Bigamy The offense of willfully and knowingly entering into a second marriage while married to another person.

Bill A written declaration that one hopes to have made into a law.

Bill of rights The first ten amendments to the U.S. Constitution, ratified (adopted by the states) in 1791, which set forth and guaranteed certain fundamental rights and privileges of individuals, including freedom of religion, speech, press, and assembly; guarantee of a speedy jury trial in criminal cases; and protection against excessive bail and cruel and unusual punishment.

Black codes Laws, statutes, or rules that governed slavery and segregation of public places in the South prior to 1865.

Bona fide occupational qualification An essential requirement for performing a given job. The requirement may even be a physical condition beyond an individual's control, such as perfect vision, if it is absolutely necessary for performing a job.

Brief A summary of the important points of a longer document.

Burden of proof The duty of a party to convince a judge or jury of their position, and to prove wrong any evidence that damages the position of the party. In criminal cases the party must prove their case beyond a reasonable doubt.

Burglary The criminal offense of breaking and entering a building illegally for the purpose of committing a crime.

Bylaws The rules and regulations of an association or a corporation to provide a framework for its operation and management.

C

Capacity The ability, capability, or fitness to do something; a legal right, power, or competency to perform some act. An ability to comprehend both the nature and consequences of one's acts.

Capital punishment The lawful infliction of death as a punishment; the death penalty.

Cause A reason for an action or condition. A ground of a legal action.

Censorship The suppression of speech or writing that is deemed obscene, indecent, or controversial.

Certiorari Latin for "to be informed of"; an order commanding officers of inferior courts to allow a case pending before them to move up to a higher court to determine whether any irregularities or errors occurred that justify review of the case. A device by which the Supreme Court of the United States exercises its discretion in selecting the cases it will review.

Change of venue The removal of a lawsuit from one county or district to another for trial, often permitted in criminal cases in which the court finds that the defendant would not receive a fair trial in the first location because of negative publicity.

Charter A grant from the government of ownership rights of land to a person, a group of people, or an organization, such as a corporation.

Circumstantial evidence Information and testimony presented by a party in a civil or criminal case that allows conclusions to be drawn about certain facts without the party presenting concrete evidence to support their facts.

Citation A paper commonly used in various courts that is served upon an individual to notify him or her that he or she is required to appear at a specific time and place.

Citizens Those who, under the Constitution and laws of the United States, owe allegiance to the United States and are entitled to the enjoyment of all civil rights awarded to those living in the United States.

Civil law A body of rules that spell out the private rights of citizens and the remedies for governing disputes between individuals in such areas as contracts, property, and family law.

Civil liberties Freedom of speech, freedom of press, freedom from discrimination, and other rights guaranteed and protected by the Constitution, which were intended to place limits on government.

Civil rights Personal liberties that belong to an individual.

Class action A lawsuit that allows a large number of people with a common interest in a matter to sue or be sued as a group.

Clause A section, phrase, paragraph, or segment of a legal document, such as a contract, deed, will, or constitution, that relates to a particular point.

Closing argument The final factual and legal argument made by each attorney on all sides of a case in a trial prior to the verdict or judgment.

Code A collection of laws, rules, or regulations that are consolidated and classified according to subject matter.

Collective bargaining agreement The contractual agreement between an employer and a labor union that controls pay, hours, and working conditions for employees which can be enforced against both the employer and the union for failure to comply with its terms.

Commerce Clause The provision of the U.S. Constitution that gives Congress exclusive power over trade activities between the states and with foreign countries and Native American tribes.

Words to Know

Words to Know

Commercial speech The words used in advertisments by commercial companies and service providers. Commercial speech is protected under the First Amendment as long as it is not false or misleading.

Common law The principles and rules of action, embodied in case law rather than legislative enactments, applicable to the government and protection of persons and property, Common laws derive their authority from the community customs and traditions that evolved over the centuries as interpreted by judicial tribunals (types of courts).

Common-law marriage A union of two people not formalized in the customary manner but created by an agreement by the two people to consider themselves married followed by their living together.

Community property The materials and resources owned in common by a husband and wife.

Complaint The possible evidence that initiates a civil action; in criminal law, the document that sets in motion a person's being charged with an offense.

Concurring opinion An opinion by one or more judges that provides separate reasoning for reaching the same decision as the majority of the court.

Conditional Subject to change; dependent upon the occurrence of a future, uncertain event.

Confession A statement made by an individual that acknowledges his or her guilt of a crime.

Conflict of interest A term used to describe the situation in which a public official exploits his or her position for personal benefit.

Consent Voluntary agreement to the proposal of another; the act or result of reaching an agreement.

Conspiracy An agreement between two or more persons to engage in an unlawful or criminal act, or an act that is innocent in itself but becomes unlawful when done by those participating.

Constituent A person who gives another person permission to act on his or her behalf, such as an agent, an attorney in a court of law, or an elected official in government.

Constitution of the United States A document written by the founding fathers of the United States that has been added to by Congress over the centuries that is held as the absolute rule of action and decision for all branches and offices of the government, and which all subsequent laws and ordinances must be in accordance. It is enforced by representatives of the people of the United States, and can be changed only by a constitutional amendment by the authority that created it.

Contempt An act of deliberate disobedience or disregard for the laws or regulations of a public authority, such as a court or legislative body.

Continuance The postponement of an action pending (waiting to be tried) in a court to a later date, granted by a court in response to a request made by one of the parties to a lawsuit.

Corporations Business entities that are treated much like human individuals under the law, having legally enforceable rights, the ability to acquire debt and pay out profits, the ability to hold and transfer property, the ability to enter into contracts, the requirement to pay taxes, and the ability to sue and be sued.

Counsel An attorney or lawyer.

Court of appeal An intermediate court of review that is found in thirteen judicial districts, called circuits, in the United States. A state court of appeal reviews a decision handed down by a lower court to determine whether that court made errors that warrant the reversal of its final decision.

Covenant An agreement, contract, or written promise between two individuals that frequently includes a pledge to do or refrain from doing something.

Criminal law A body of rules and statutes that defines behavior prohibited by the government because it threatens and/or harms public safety, and establishes the punishments to be given to those who commit such acts.

Cross-examination The questioning of a witness or party during a trial, hearing, or deposition by the opposing lawyer.

Cruel and unusual punishment Such punishment as would amount to torture or barbarity, any cruel and degrading punishment, or any fine, penalty, confinement, or treatment so disproportionate to the offense as to shock the moral sense of the community.

Custodial parent The parent to whom the court grants guardianship of the children after a divorce.

Words to Know

D

Death penalty See Capital punishment.

De facto Latin for "in fact"; in deed; actually.

Defamation Any intentional false communication, either written or spoken, that harms a person's reputation; decreases the respect, regard, or confidence in which a person is held; or causes hostile or disagreeable opinions or feelings against a person.

Defendant The person defending or denying; the party against whom recovery is sought in an action or suit, or the accused in a criminal case.

Defense The forcible reaction against an unlawful and violent attack, such as the defense of one's person, property, or country in time of war.

De jure Latin for "in law"; legitimate; lawful, as a matter of law. Having complied with all the requirements imposed by law.

Deliberate Willful; purposeful; determined after thoughtful evaluation of all relevant factors. To act with a particular intent, which is derived from a careful consideration of factors that influence the choice to be made.

Delinquent An individual who fails to fulfill an obligation or otherwise is guilty of a crime or offense.

Domestic partnership laws Legislation and regulations related to the legal recognition of nonmarital relationships between persons who are romantically involved with each other, have set up a joint residence, and have registered with cities recognizing said relationships.

Denaturalization To take away an individual's rights as a citizen.

Deportation Banishment to a foreign country, attended with confiscation of property and deprivation of civil rights.

Deposition The testimony of a party or witness in a civil or criminal proceeding taken before trial, usually in an attorney's office.

Desegregation Judicial mandate making illegal the practice of segregation.

Disclaimer The denial, refusal, or rejection of a right, power, or responsibility.

Discrimination The grant of particular privileges to a group randomly chosen from a large number of people in which no reasonable difference exists between the favored and disfavored groups. Federal laws prohibit discrimination in such areas as employment, housing, voting rights, education, access to public facilities, and on the bases of race, age, sex, nationality, disability, or religion.

Dismissal A discharge of an individual or corporation from employment.

Dissent A disagreement by one or more judges with the decision of the majority on a case before them.

Divorce A court decree that terminates a marriage; also known as marital dissolution.

Double jeopardy A second prosecution for the same offense after acquittal or conviction or multiple punishments for the same offense. The evil sought to be avoided by prohibiting double jeopardy is double trial and double conviction, not necessarily double punishment.

Draft A mandatory call of persons to serve in the military.

Due process of law A fundamental, constitutional guarantee that all legal proceedings will be fair and that one will be given notice of the proceedings and an opportunity to be heard before the government acts to take away one's life, liberty, or property. Also, a constitutional guarantee that a law shall not be unreasonable, random, or without consideration for general well-being.

Duress Unlawful pressure exerted upon a person to force that person to perform an act that he or she ordinarily would not perform.

E

Emancipation The act or process by which a person is liberated from the authority and control of another person.

Entrapment The act of government agents or officials that causes a person to commit a crime he or she would not have committed otherwise.

Equal Pay Act Federal law that commands the same pay for all persons who do the same work without regard to sex, age, race, or ability.

Equal protection The constitutional guarantee that no person or class of persons shall be denied the same protection of the laws that is enjoyed by other persons or other classes in like circumstances in their lives, liberty, property, and pursuit of happiness.

Establishment Clause The provision in the First Amendment that provides that there will be no laws created respecting the establishment of a religion, inhibiting the practice of a religion, or giving preference to any or all religions. It has been interpreted to also denounce the discouragement of any or all religions.

Euthanasia The merciful act or practice of terminating the life of an individual or individuals inflicted with incurable and distressing diseases in a relatively painless manner.

Exclusionary rule The principle based on federal constitutional law that evidence illegally seized by law enforcement officers in violation of a suspect's right to be free from unreasonable searches and seizures cannot be used against the suspect in a criminal prosecution.

Executive agreement An agreement made between the head of a foreign country and the president of the United States. This agreement does not have to be submitted to the Senate for consent, and it supersedes any contradicting state law.

Executive orders When the president uses some part of a law or the Constitution to enforce some action.

Executor The individual legally named by a deceased person to administer the provisions of his or her will.

Ex parte Latin for "on one side only"; done by, for, or on the application of one party alone.

Expert witness A witness, such as a psychological statistician or ballisticsexpert, who possesses special or superior knowledge concerning the subject of his or her testimony.

Ex post facto laws Latin for "after-the-fact laws"; laws that provide for the infliction of punishment upon a person for some prior act that, at the time it was committed, was not illegal.

Extradition The transfer of a person accused of a crime from one state or country to another state or country that seeks to place the accused on trial.

F

Family court A court that presides over cases involving: (1) child abuse and neglect; (2) support; (3) paternity; (4) termination of custody due to constant neglect; (5) juvenile delinquency; and (6) family offenses.

Federal Relating to a national government, as opposed to state or local governments.

Federal circuit courts The twelve circuit courts making up the U.S. Federal Circuit Court System. Decisions made by the federal district courts can be reviewed by the court of appeals in each circuit.

Federal district courts The first of three levels of the federal court system, which includes the U.S. Court of Appeals and the U.S. Supreme Court. If a participating party disagrees with the ruling of a federal district court in its case, it may petition for the case to be moved to the next level in the federal court system.

Felon An individual who commits a felony, a crime of a serious nature, such as burglary or murder.

Felony A serious crime, characterized under federal law and many state statutes as any offense punishable by death or imprisonment in excess of one year.

First degree murder Murder committed with deliberately premeditated thought and malice, or with extreme atrocity or cruelty. The difference between first and second degree murder is the presence of the specific intention to kill.

Fraud A false representation of a matter of fact—whether by words or by conduct, by false or misleading allegations, or by concealment of what should have been disclosed—that deceives and is intended to deceive another so that the individual will act upon it to her or his legal injury.

Freedom of assembly See Freedom of association.

Freedom of association The right to associate with others for the purpose of engaging in constitutionally protected activities, such as to peacefully assemble.

Freedom of religion The First Amendment right to individually believe and to practice or exercise one's religious belief.

Freedom of speech The right, guaranteed by the First Amendment to the U.S. Constitution, to express beliefs and ideas without unwarranted government restriction.

Freedom of the press The right, guaranteed by the First Amendment to the U.S. Constitution, to gather, publish, and distribute information and ideas without government restriction; this right encompasses

freedom from prior restraints on publication and freedom from censorship.

Fundamental rights Rights that derive, or are implied, from the terms of the U.S. Constitution, such as the Bill of Rights, the first ten amendments to the Constitution.

G

Gag rule A rule, regulation, or law that prohibits debate or discussion of a particular issue.

Grandfather clause A portion of a statute that provides that the law is not applicable in certain circumstances due to preexisting facts.

Grand jury A panel of citizens that is convened by a court to decide whether it is appropriate for the government to indict (proceed with a prosecution against) someone suspected of a crime.

Grand larceny A category of larceny—the offense of illegally taking the property of another—in which the value of the property taken is greater than that set for petit larceny.

Grounds The basis or foundation; reasons sufficient in law to justify relief.

Guardian A person lawfully invested with the power, and charged with the obligation, of taking care of and managing the property and rights of a person who, because of age, understanding, or lack of self-control, is considered incapable of administering his or her own affairs.

Guardian ad litem A guardian appointed by the court to represent the interests of infants, the unborn, or incompetent persons in legal actions.

H

Habeas corpus Latin for "you have the body"; a writ (court order) that commands an individual or a government official who has restrained another to produce the prisoner at a designated time and place so that the court can determine the legality of custody and decide whether to order the prisoner's release.

Hate crime A crime motivated by race, religion, gender, sexual orientation, or other prejudice.

Hearing A legal proceeding in which issues of law or fact are tried and evidence is presented to help determine the issue.

Hearsay A statement made out of court that is offered in court as evidence to prove the truth of the matter asserted.

Heir An individual who receives an interest in, or ownership of, land or tenements from an ancestor who died through the laws of descent and distribution. At common law, an heir was the individual appointed by law to succeed to the estate of an ancestor who died without a will. It is commonly used today in reference to any individual who succeeds to property, either by will or law.

Homicide The killing of one human being by another human being.

Hung jury A trial jury selected to make a decision in a criminal case regarding a defendant's guilt or innocence that is unable to reach a verdict due to a complete division in opinion.

I

Immunity Exemption from performing duties that the law generally requires other citizens to perform, or from a penalty or burden that the law generally places on other citizens.

Impeachment A process used to charge, try, and remove public officials for misconduct while in office.

Inalienable Not subject to sale or transfer; inseparable.

Incapacity The absence of legal ability, competence, or qualifications.

Income tax A charge imposed by government on the annual gains of a person, corporation, or other taxable unit derived through work, business pursuits, investments, property dealings, and other sources determined in accordance with the Internal Revenue Code or state law.

Indictment A written accusation charging that an individual named therein has committed an act or admitted to doing something that is punishable by law.

Indirect tax A tax upon some right, privilege, or corporation.

Words to Know

Individual rights Rights and privileges constitutionally guaranteed to the people as set forth by the Bill of Rights; the ability of a person to pursue life, liberty, and property.

Infant Persons who are under the age of the legal majority—at common law, twenty-one years, now generally eighteen years. According to the sense in which this term is used, it may denote the age of the person, the contractual disabilities that nonage entails, or his or her status with regard to other powers or relations.

Inherent rights Rights held within a person because he or she exists.

Inheritance Property received from a person who has died, either by will or through state laws if the deceased has failed to execute a valid will.

Injunction A court order by which an individual is required to perform or is restrained from performing a particular act. A writ framed according to the circumstances of the individual case.

In loco parentis Latin for "in the placeof a parent"; the legal doctrine under which an individual assumes parental rights, duties, and obligations without going through the formalities of legal adoption.

Insanity defense A defense asserted by an accused in a criminal prosecution to avoid responsibility for a crime because, at the time of the crime, the person did not comprehend the nature or wrongfulness of the act.

Insider Relating to the federal regulation of the purchase and sale of stocks and bonds, anyone who has knowledge of facts not available to the general public.

Insider trading The trading of stocks and bonds based on information gained from special private, privileged information affecting the value of the stocks and bonds.

Intent A determination to perform a particular act or to act in a particular manner for a specific reason; an aim or design; a resolution to use a certain means to reach an end.

Intermediate courts Courts with general ability or authority to hear a case (trial, appellate, or both) but are not the court of last resort within the jurisdiction.

Intestate The description of a person who dies without making a valid will.

Involuntary manslaughter The act of unlawfully killing another human being unintentionally.

Irrevocable Unable to cancel or recall; that which is unalterable or irreversible.

J

Judicial Relating to courts and the legal system.

Judicial discretion Sound judgment exercised by a judge in determining what is right and fair under the law.

Judicial review A court's authority to examine an executive or legislative act and to invalidate (cancel) that act if it opposes constitutional principles.

Jurisdiction The geographic area over which authority (such as a cout) extends; legal authority.

Jury In trials, a group of people selected and sworn to inquire into matters of fact and to reach a verdict on the basis of evidence presented to it.

Jury nullification The ability of a jury to acquit the defendant despite the amount of evidence against him or her in a criminal case.

Just cause A reasonable and lawful ground for action.

Justifiable homicide The killing of another in self-defense or in the lawful defense of one's property; killing of another when the law demands it, such as in execution for a capital crime.

Juvenile A young individual who has not reached the age whereby he or she would be treated as an adult in the area of criminal law. The age at which the young person attains the status of being a legal majority varies from state to state—as low as fourteen years old, as high as eighteen years old; however, the Juvenile Delinquency Act determines that a youthful person under the age of eighteen is a juvenile in cases involving federal jurisdiction.

Juvenile court The court presiding over cases in which young persons under a certain age, depending on the area of jurisdiction, are accused of criminal acts.

Juvenile delinquency The participation of a youthful individual, one who falls under the age at which he or she could be tried as an adult, in illegal behavior.

Words to Know

L

Larceny The unauthorized taking and removal of the personal property of another by a person who intends to permanently deprive the owner of it; a crime against the right of possession.

Legal defense A complete and acceptable response as to why the claims of the plaintiff should not be granted in a point of law.

Legal tender All U.S. coins and currencies—regardless of when coined or issued—including (in terms of the Federal Reserve System) Federal Reserve notes and circulating notes of Federal Reserve banks and national banking associations that are used for all public and private debts, public charges, taxes, duties, and dues.

Legislation Lawmaking; the preparation and enactment of laws by a legislative body.

Liability A comprehensive legal term that describes the condition of being actually or potentially subject to (responsible for) a legal obligation.

Libel and slander The communication of false information about a person, a group, or an entity, such as a corporation. Libel is any defamation that can be seen, such as in print or on a film or in a representation such as a statued. Slander is any defamation that is spoken and heard.

Litigation An action brought in court to enforce a particular right; the act or process of bringing a lawsuit in and of itself; a judicial contest; any dispute.

Living will A written document that allows a patient to give explicit instructions about medical treatment to be administered when the patient is terminally ill or permanently unconscious; also called an advance directive.

Lobbying The process of influencing public and government policy at all levels: federal, state, and local.

M

Magistrate Any individual who has the power of a public civil officer or inferior judicial officer, such as a justice of the peace.

Majority Full age; legal age; age at which a person is no longer a minor. The age at which, by law, a person is capable of being legally responsible for all of his or her acts (i.e., contractual obligations) and is entitled to manage his or her own affairs and to the enjoy civic rights (i.e., right to vote). Also the status of a person who is a major in age.

Malice The intentional commission of a wrongful act, without justification, with the intent to cause harm to others; conscious violation of the law that injures another individual; a mental state indicating a disregard of social responsibility.

Malpractice When a professional, such as a doctor or lawyer, fails to carry out their job correctly and there are bad results.

Mandate A judicial command or order from a court.

Manslaughter The unjustifiable, inexcusable, and intentional killing of a human being without deliberation, premeditation, or malice.

Material Important; significant; substantial. A description of the quality of evidence that possesses such value as to establish the truth or falsity of a point in issue in a lawsuit.

Mediation Settling a dispute or controversy by setting up an independent person between the two parties to help them settle their disagreement.

Minor An infant or person who is under the age of legal competence. In most states, a person is no longer a minor after reaching the age of eighteen (though state laws might still prohibit certain acts until reaching a greater age; i.e., purchase of liquor).

Misdemeanor Offenses lower than felonies and generally those punishable by fine, penalty, or imprisonment other than in a penitentiary.

Mistrial A courtroom trial that has been ended prior to its normal conclusion. A mistrial has no legal effect and is considered an invalid trial. It differs from a new trial, which recognizes that a trial was completed but was set aside so that the issues could be tried again.

Mitigating circumstances Circumstances that may be considered by a court in determining responsibility of a defendant or the extent of damages to be awarded to a plaintiff. Mitigating circumstances do not justify or excuse an offense but may reduce the charge.

Monopoly An economic advantage held by one or more persons or companies because they hold the exclusive power to carry out a particular business or trade or to manufacture and sell a particular task or produce a particular product.

Moratorium A suspension (ending) of activity or an authorized period of delay or waiting. A moratorium is sometimes agreed upon by the interested parties, or it may be authorized or imposed by operation of law.

Motion A written or oral application made to a court or judge to obtain a ruling or order directing that some act be done in favor of the applicant.

Motive An idea, belief, or emotion that causes a person to act in a certain way, either good or bad.

Murder The unlawful killing of another human being without justification or excuse.

N

National origin The country in which a person was born or from which his or her ancestors came. One's national origin is typically calculated by employers to provide equal employment opportunity statistics in accordance with the provisions of the Civil Rights Act.

Naturalization A process by which a person gains nationality and becomes entitled to the privileges of citizenship. While groups of individuals have been naturalized in history by treaties or laws of Congress, such as in the case of Hawaii, typically naturalization occurs on the individual level upon the completion of a list of requirements.

Necessary and Proper Clause The statement contained in Article I, Section 8, Clause 18 of the U.S. Constitution that gives Congress the power to pass any laws that are necessary and proper to carrying out its specifically granted powers.

Negligence Conduct that falls below the standards of behavior established by law for the protection of others against unreasonable risk of harm.

Nonprofit A corporation or an association that conducts business for the benefit of the general public rather than to gain profits for itself.

Notary public A public official whose main powers include administering oaths and witnessing signatures, both important and effective ways to minimize fraud in legal documents.

O

Obscenity An act, spoken word, or item tending to offend public morals by its indecency or lewdness.

Ordinance A law, statute, or regulation enacted by a municipality.

P

Palimony The settlement awarded at the end of a non-marital relationship, where the couple lived together for a long period of time and where there was an agreement that one partner would support the other in return for the second making a home and performing domestic duties.

Pardon When a person in power, such as a president or governor, offers a formal statement of forgivenss for a crime and takes away the given punishment.

Parental liability A statute (law), enacted in some states, that makes parents responsible for damages caused by their children if it is found that the damages resulted from the parents' lack of control over the acts of the child.

Parole The release of a person convicted of a crime prior to the end of that person's term of imprisonment on the condition that they will follow certain strict rules for their conduct, and if they break any of those rules they will return to prison.

Patents Rights granted to inventors by the federal government that permit them to keep others from making, using, or selling their invention for a definite, or restricted, period of time.

Peremptory challenge The right to challenge the use of a juror in a trial without being required to give a reason for the challenge.

Perjury A crime that occurs when an individual willfully makes a false statement during a judicial proceeding, after he or she has taken an oath to speak the truth.

Petition A formal application made to a court in writing that requests action on a certain matter.

Petit larceny A form of larceny—the stealing of another's personal property—in which the value of the property that is taken is generally less than $50.

Plaintiff The party who sues in a civil action.

Plain view doctrine In the context of searches and seizures, the principle that provides that objects that an officer can easily see can be seized without a search warrant and are fair to use as evidence.

Plea The phase in a court case where the defendant has to declare whether they are guilty or not guilty.

Police power The authority that states to employ a police force and give them the power to enforce the laws and protect the community.

Poll tax A specified sum of money to be paid by each person who votes.

Polygamy The offense of having more than one wife or husband at the same time.

Precedent A court decision that is cited as an example to resolve similar questions of law in later cases.

Preponderance of evidence A rule that states that it is up to the plaintiff to convince the judge or the jury of their side of the case in or to win the case.

Prima facie [*Latin,* On the first appearance.]A fact presumed to be true unless it is disproved.

Prior restraint Government violating freedom of speech by not allowing something to be published.

Privacy In constitutional law, the right of people to make personal decisions regarding intimate matters; under the common law, the right of people to lead their lives in a manner that is reasonably secluded from public scrutiny, whether such scrutiny comes from a neighbor's prying eyes, an investigator's eavesdropping ears, or a news photographer's intrusive camera; and in statutory law, the right of people to be free from unwarranted drug testing and electronic surveillance.

Privilege An advantage or benefit possessed by an individual, company, or class beyond those held by others.

Privileges and immunities Concepts contained in the U.S. Constitution that place the citizens of each state on an equal basis with citizens of other states with respect to advantages resulting from citizenship in those states and citizenship in the United States.

Probable cause Apparent facts discovered through logical inquiry that would lead a reasonably intelligent person to believe that an accused person has committed a crime.

Probate court Called Surrogate or Orphan's Court in some states, the probate court presides over wills, the administration of estates, and, in some states, the appointment of guardians or approval of the adoption of minors.

Probation A sentence whereby a convict is released from confinement but is still under court supervision; a testing or a trial period. It can be given in lieu of a prison term or can suspend a prison sentence if the convict has consistently demonstrated good behavior.

Procedural due process The constitutional guarantee that one's liberty and property rights may not be affected unless reasonable notice and an opportunity to be heard in order to present a claim or defense are provided.

Property A thing or things owned either by government—public property—or owned by private individuals, groups, or companies—private property.

Prosecute To follow through; to commence and continue an action or judicial proceeding to its conclusion. To proceed against a defendant by charging that person with a crime and bringing him or her to trial.

Prosecution The proceedings carried out before a court to determine the guilt or innocence of a defendant. The term also refers to the government attorney charging and trying a criminal case.

Punitive damages Money awarded to an injured party that goes beyond that which is necessary to pay for the individual for losses and that is intended to punish the wrongdoer.

Q

Quorum A majority of an entire body; i.e., a quorum of a legislative assembly.

Quota The number of persons or things that must be used, or admitted, or hired in order to be following a rule or law.

R

Rape A criminal offense defined in most states as forcible sexual relations with a person against that person's will.

Ratification The confirmation or adoption of an act that has already been performed.

Reapportionment The realignment of voting districts done to fulfill the constitutional requirement of one person, one vote.

Referendum The right reserved to the people to approve or reject an act of the legislature, or the right of the people to approve or reject legislation that has been referred to them by the legislature.

Refugees Individuals who leave their native country for social, political, or religious reasons, or who are forced to leave as a result of any type of disaster, including war, political upheaval, and famine.

Rehabilitation Work to restore former rights, authority, or abilities.

Remand To send back.

Replevin A legal action to recover the possession of items of personal property.

Reprieve The temporary hold put on a death penalty for further review of the case.

Rescind To declare a contract void—of no legal force or binding effect—from its beginning and thereby restore the parties to the positions they would have been in had no contract ever been made.

Reservation A tract of land under the control of the Bureau of Indian Affairs to which a Native American tribe retains its original title of ownership, or that has been set aside from the public domain for use by a tribe.

Reserve Funds set aside to cover future expenses, losses, or claims. To retain; to keep in store for future or special use; to postpone to a future time.

Resolution The official expression of the opinion or will of a legislative body.

Retainer A contract between attorney and client specifying the nature of the services and the cost of the services.

Retribution Punishment or reward for an act. In criminal law, punishment is based upon the theory that every crime demands payment.

Reverse discrimination Discrimination against a group of people that is generally considered to be the majority, usually stemming from the enforcement of some affirmative action guidlelines.

Revocation The recall of some power or authority that has been granted.

Robbery The taking of money or goods in the possession of another, from his or her person or immediate presence, by force or intimidation.

S

Sabotage The willful destruction or impairment of war material or national defense material, or harm to war premises or war utilities. During a labor dispute, the willful and malicious destruction of an employer's property or interference with his or her normal operations.

Search warrant A court order authorizing the examination of a place for the purpose of discovering evidence of guilt to be used in the prosecution of a criminal action.

Second degree murder The unlawful taking of human life with malice, but without premeditated thought.

Sedition A revolt or an incitement to revolt against established authority, usually in the form of treason or defamation against government.

Seditious libel A written communication intended to incite the overthrow of the government by force or violence.

Segregation The act or process of separating a race, class, or ethnic group from a society's general population.

Self-defense The protection of one's person or property against some injury attempted by another.

Self-incrimination Giving testimony in a trial or other legal proceeding that could subject one to criminal prosecution.

Sentencing The post-conviction stage of a criminal justice process, in which the defendant is brought before the court for penalty.

Separate but equal The doctrine first accepted by the U.S. Supreme Court in *Plessy v. Ferguson* establishing that different facilities for blacks and whites was valid under the Equal Protection Clause of the Fourteenth Amendment as long as they were equal.

Separation of church and state The separation of religious and government interest to ensure that religion does not become corrupt by government and that government does not become corrupt by religious conflict. The principle prevents the government from supporting the practices of one religion over another. It also enables the government to do what is necessary to prevent one religious group from violating the rights of others.

Separation of powers The division of state and federal government into three independent branches.

Words to Know

Words to Know

Settlement The act of adjusting or determining the dealings or disputes between persons without pursuing the matter through a trial.

Sexual harassment Unwelcome sexual advances, requests for sexual favors, and other verbal or physical conduct of a sexual nature that tends to create a hostile or offensive work environment.

Share A portion or part of something that may be divided into components, such as a sum of money. A unit of stock that represents ownership in a corporation.

Shield laws Statutes that allow journalists not to disclose in legal proceedings confidential information or sources of information obtained in their professional capacities.

Statutes that restrict or prohibit the use of certain evidence in sexual offense cases, such as evidence regarding the lack of chastity of the victim.

Shoplifting Theft of merchandise from a store or business establishment.

Small claims court A special court that provides fast, informal, and inexpensive solutions for small claims.

Solicitation The criminal offense of urging someone to commit an unlawful act.

Statute An act of a legislature that declares, or commands something; a specific law, expressed in writing.

Statute of limitations A type of federal or state law that restricts the time within which legal proceedings may be brought.

Statutory law A law which is created by an act of the legislature.

Statutory rape Sexual intercourse by an adult with a person below a designated age.

Subpoena Latin for "under penalty"; a formal document that orders a named individual to appear before an officer of the court at a fixed time to give testimony.

Suffrage The right to vote at public elections.

Summons The paper that tells a defendant that he or she is being sued and asserts the power of the court to hear and determine the case. A form of legal process that commands the defendant to appear before the court on a specific day and to answer the complaint made by the plaintiff.

Supreme court The highest court in the U.S. judicial system.

Surrogate mother A woman who agrees under contract to bear a child for an infertile couple. The woman is paid to have a donated fertilized egg or the fertilized egg of the female partner in the couple (usually fertilized by the male partner of the couple) artificially placed into her uterus.

Suspended sentence A sentence that states that a criminal, in waiting for their trial, has already served enough time in prison.

Symbolic speech Nonverbal gestures and actions that are meant to communicate a message.

T

Testify To provide evidence as a witness in order to establish a particular fact or set of facts.

Testimony Oral evidence offered by a competent witness under oath, which is used to establish some fact or set of facts.

Trade secret Any valuable commercial information that provides a business with an advantage over competitors who do not have that information.

Trade union An organization of workers in the same skilled occupation or related skilled occupations who act together to secure for all members favorable wages, hours, and other working conditions.

Treason The betrayal of one's own country by waging war against it or by consciously or purposely acting to aid its enemies.

Treaty A compact made between two or more independent nations with a view to the public welfare.

Trespass An unlawful intrusion that interferes with one's person or property.

Trial A judicial examination and determination of facts and legal issues arising between parties to a civil or criminal action.

Trial court The court where civil actions or criminal proceedings are first heard.

Truancy The willful and unjustified failure to attend school by one required to do so.

U

Unenumerated rights Rights that are not expressly mentioned in the written text of a constitution but instead are inferred from the language, history, and structure of the constitution, or cases interpreting it.

Unconstitutional That which is not in agreement with the ideas and regulations of the Constitution.

Uniform commercial code A general and inclusive group of laws adopted, at least partially, by all of the states to further fair dealing in business.

V

Valid Binding; possessing legal force or strength; legally sufficient.

Vandalism The intentional and malicious destruction of or damage to the property of another.

Venue A place, such as a city or county, from which residents are selected to serve as jurors.

Verdict The formal decision or finding made by a jury concerning the questions submitted to it during a trial. The jury reports the verdict to the court, which generally accepts it.

Veto The refusal of an executive officer to approve a bill that has been created and approved by the legislature, thereby keeping the bill from becoming a law.

Voir dire Old French for "to speak the truth"; the preliminary examination of possible jurors to determine their qualifications and suitability to serve on a jury, in order to ensure the selection of a fair and impartial jury.

Voluntary manslaughter The unlawful killing of a person where there is no malice, premeditation or deliberate intent but too near to these standards to be classified as justifiable homicide.

W

Waive To intentionally or voluntarily give up a known right or engage in conduct that caused your rights to be taken away.

Ward A person, especially an infant or someone judged to be incompetent, placed by the court in the care of a guardian.

Warrant A written order issued by a judicial officer commanding a law enforcement officer to perform a duty. This usually includes searches, seizures and arrests.

White collar crime Term for nonviolent crimes that were committed in the course of the offender's occupation.

Will A document in which a person explains the management and distribution of his or her estate after his or her death.

Workers' compensation A system whereby an employer must pay, or provide insurance to pay, the lost wages and medical expenses of an employee who is injured on the job.

Writ An order issued by a court requiring that something be done.

Z

Zoning Assigning different areas within a city or county different uses, whereby one area cannot be used for any other purpose other than what it is designated. For example, if an area is assigned as residential, an office building could not be built there.

Words to Know

AFFIRMATIVE
ACTION

Racial and gender (sex) discrimination in the United States have a long history. Discrimination is defined as giving privileges to one group but not another. Throughout the eighteenth, nineteenth, and at least until the mid-twentieth century, racial and gender discrimination denied black Americans and women opportunities in the most basic aspects of their lives including work, education, and voting rights.

Following the American Civil War (1861–65), Congress passed and the states approved amendments to guarantee rights to former slaves. One of the amendments, the Fourteenth Amendment approved in 1868, made it unlawful to "deprive any person of life, liberty, or property" and promised "equal protection of the laws." Congress also found it necessary to pass laws to make sure the amendments were enforced. However, more often than not, the U.S. Supreme Court handed down rulings on these laws that allowed discrimination to continue. Blacks and women experienced little "equal protection of the laws."

Not until the 1950s and 1960s during the Civil Rights Movement did the Supreme Court begin to strike down laws that discriminated against individuals on the basis of race and sex. Through the Court's decisions in

Brown v. Board of Education (1954) and *Reed v. Reed* (1971), the Court ruled that black Americans and women must have equal protection rights as guaranteed by the Fourteenth Amendment. During the same time period Congress passed the Civil Rights Act of 1964 prohibiting discrimination on the basis of race, color, religion, sex, or national origin. The Supreme Court in *Heart of Atlanta Motel v. United States* (1964) ruled on the 1964 act. The Court upheld the act finding Congress has the constitutional power to promote equality of opportunity and to prevent discrimination. Black Americans and women finally had a law under which they could claim equal protection rights when they were discriminated against in such areas as education and employment.

How Could Negative Effects of Discrimination Be Overcome?

Although jubilant over the civil rights successes, forward thinking leaders for black Americans and women knew the successes would not be enough to overcome two and a half centuries of discrimination. Organizations such as the National Association for the Advancement of Colored People (NAACP) and the National Organization of Women (NOW) proposed programs to give a degree of preferential (preferred) treatment to individuals of groups long discriminated against. The name *affirmative action* was given to these programs. "Affirm" means in this case to support an individual's civil rights by taking positive "action" to protect individuals from the lasting effects of discrimination. The goals of these action programs are increased job opportunities, employment promotions, and increased admissions to universities.

As early as 1961, three years before the landmark Civil Rights Act, President John F. Kennedy seemed to already be aware of the need. Actually using the term "affirmative action," he signed Executive Order 10925 requiring federal contractors (private companies who do work for the government) to hire more minority employees. Likewise, President Lyndon Johnson believed that the scars caused by years of legal discrimination could not be easily erased. In a commencement speech he delivered at Howard University on June 4, 1965, President Johnson showed a wise understanding of the problem saying, "You do not take a person who, for years, has been hobbled by chains and liberate him, bring him up to the starting line of a race and then say, 'You're free to compete with all the others,' and justly believe that you have been completely fair."

Johnson asserted that simply freedom from discrimination was not enough, opportunity had be provided as well. Johnson continued, "not just equality as a right and a theory, but equality as a fact."

Backing up his words that same year, President Johnson signed Executive Order 11246 providing a practical way to carry out affirmative action plans. The order required federal contractors to file written affirmative action plans with the Office of Federal Contract Compliance Programs (OFCCP) under the Department of Labor.

U.S. presidents continued to support affirmative action programs. President Richard M. Nixon was the first to require specific number goals or quotas and timetables for hiring minorities and women. For example, a federal contractor might be required to hire at least twelve minority or women workers for every one hundred workers and to hire those twelve within six months. Government set-asides also appeared. Set-aside programs have a goal that a certain percentage, such as five percent, of all government contracts should be given to minority and women-owned businesses. In 1977 President Jimmy Carter supported affirmative action by signing the Public Works Employment Act. The act required that at least ten percent of federal funds in each grant awarded by the Department of Commerce to state or local governments for local public works projects must be used to contract for services or supplies from businesses owned by minorities.

Characteristics of Affirmative Action Programs

Affirmative action programs have four general characteristics. First, they may be begun and supported by either government agencies or set up voluntarily by private organizations such as private universities or vocational schools, businesses, or labor unions.

Second, when considering an individual for a job, promotion, or admission to a school, the program must look at personal factors such as race or gender. However, the individual must also be qualified for the job or education program they apply to. Therefore, the individual may not receive job or education opportunities based solely on their race or gender.

Third, a program must clearly be designed to make up for unfair treatment in the past of the race or gender group to which the individual belongs. Fourth, affirmative action plans are to be only temporary solutions and are not meant to continue forever.

Affirmative Action as a Jump Start

Supporters claim only with these positive action programs can black Americans and women achieve equality of opportunity. The reason, which President Johnson referred to in his Howard University speech, lies in the fact that both blacks and women were prevented by long term discrimination from gaining education and job skills, pushing them into and keeping them in the lowest levels of employment. Whether required by the government or voluntarily begun by private employers or schools, affirmative action programs are the best means to overcoming the negative outcomes of discrimination. In effect, they serve as a "jump start" to put the discriminated groups on a more level playing field with those who traditionally have not suffered discrimination. Affirmative action programs are widely established in government agencies, businesses, and schools.

But What About the Fourteenth Amendment?

By the late 1970s public sentiment was growing against affirmative action programs. Whatever happened to "equal protection of the laws" under the Fourteenth Amendment? Does it allow certain kinds of preferential treatment typical of affirmative action plans for specific groups of persons? Similarly, what about the Civil Rights Act of 1964 prohibiting discrimination on the basis of race, color, religion, sex, and national origin? Cries of reverse discrimination began to be heard. Reverse discrimination is the lessening of opportunity for a group of people not traditionally discriminated against, such as white adult males.

To many, there seemed to be conflict between civil rights laws and affirmative action. The civil rights laws basically forbid individuals and organizations, such as businesses and schools, to consider race and gender as factors for making decisions. Affirmative action policies, however, require that race and gender be taken into account when hiring or admitting to school individuals and that preference be given to minorities or women to make up for past discrimination. As affirmative action cases began to reach the Supreme Court in the mid-1970s, the Court wrestled with these questions of equal protection and fairness.

Affirmative action disputes eventually became the main form of civil rights cases before the Court. Between 1974 and 1987 the Court's record was mixed on affirmative action cases and in no case were more than six justices in agreement.

Cases Challenging Affirmative Action

The first case challenging affirmative action to be decided by the Supreme Court was *Regents of the University of California v. Bakke* in 1978. The case involved the charge of "reverse discrimination" in which a California university medical school had set aside sixteen slots out of one hundred solely for minority applicants. Allan Bakke, a non-minority applicant, was twice turned down by the medical school yet minorities with lower entrance scores were accepted. In reaction, Bakke charged he was discriminated against by the school in violation of the Fourteenth Amendment's Equal Protection Clause and Title VI of the 1964 Civil Rights Act. After hearing the arguments presented by Bakke and the University of California, the Court agreed with Bakke that the school had discriminated against him. The Court ruled that setting quotas (requiring that a predetermined number of openings be filled by minorities) was not an acceptable form of addressing past injustices. On the other hand, the Court also ruled that affirmative action programs could be appropriate under certain circumstances. Consideration of race would not violate the Equal Protection Clause if race is one of several factors considered, not the only factor considered. The Court said that for the government to treat citizens unequally the government must show a very important need, such as making up for past specific instances of discrimination, and that the program must be very carefully applied.

The Court's next affirmative action case was *United Steelworkers v. Weber* (1979). The case simply asked the question whether or not the Civil Rights Act prohibited an employer from voluntarily establishing a temporary affirmative action training program which favored blacks over whites. The Court decided to permit the program which would lead to better, more skilled jobs for black Americans in an industry which historically they had been under represented. Following the *United Steelworkers* case, *Fullilove v. Klutznick* (1980) led the Court to uphold the government set-aside program established by the 1977 Public Works Employment Act.

During the 1980s, President Ronald Reagan's administration was openly opposed to affirmative action and was pleased by two Supreme Court rulings. The Court determined in *Firefighters Local Union No.*

1784 v. Stotts (1984) and *Wygant v. Jackson Board of Education* (1986) that affirmative action policies could not be used by companies when laying off workers. Seniority, not race, should be a key factor in deciding who should be let go. But by 1987 the Court had established in *Johnson v. Transportation Agency* a firm stance in favor of affirmative action. The Court supported a county agency's action in promoting a woman ahead of a male with slightly higher test scores. Correcting the under representation of women in the agency was a suitable goal to justify the agency decision. In *United States v. Paradise* (1987) the Court upheld a temporary quota system to promote black state troopers in Alabama. The "one black, one white" promotion quota corrected employment discrimination long present in the Alabama state police.

Affirmative action cases continued into the 1990s. In *Adarand Constructors, Inc. v. Pena* (1995) the Court tightened requirements on affirmative action programs. Writing for the Court, Justice Sandra Day O'Connor commented, "Government may treat people differently because of their race only for the most compelling [very important] reasons." To ensure that all persons receive equal protection of the laws affirmative action programs could only be considered legal if they were designed to correct specific instances of past discrimination.

Becoming one of the most controversial social issues of the day, the affirmative action debate continued. President Bill Clinton delivered his "Mend it, but don't end it" speech in July of 1995. Summarizing the overall picture of affirmative action, he commented,

> **We had slavery for centuries before the passage of the Thirteenth, Fourteenth, and Fifteenth Amendments. We waited another hundred years for the civil rights legislation. Women have had the vote for less than a hundred years. We have always had difficulty with these things, as most societies do. But we are making more progress than many other nations. Since, based on the evidence, the job is not done, here is what I think we should do. We should reaffirm the principle of affirmative action and fix the practices.**

Despite the call to fix, not abandon affirmative action programs, in 1996 Californians voted to ban existing state government affirmative action programs. Supporters of the ban claimed that by eliminating preferences racial and gender equality under state law would be reestablished in education, contracting, and employment. Believing the initiative likely violated the Equal Protection Clause of the Fourteenth Amendment, a federal court judge stopped the ban from taking effect and allowed affirmative action programs to continue. A federal appeals court in 1997 reversed the judge's decision and allowed the ban to take effect.

To Be Fair and Equal—the Debate Continues

Fairness and equal protection are central questions in the affirmative action debate. White males and middle-class white females have strongly opposed affirmative action policies. White males commonly argue that they are being unfairly discriminated against for past injustices they had no personal responsibility for. Supporters of affirmative action, on the other hand, have contended that white males continue to directly benefit from past discrimination. They point to a 1995 study showing that white males still held 95 percent of top management positions in major companies and that men earned up to 45 percent more money than women or minorities. Critics of affirmative action also argue that the tradition of rewarding a job well done or hard work is lessened with a lessening in standards for hiring and promotion. Supporters counter that any influence in the reward system, if any, is minimal.

Aside from public debates, the courts have given their approval to affirmative action programs. However, the courts have sent a clear message that for a company to impose preferences to individuals based on their race or sex, they must be able to show the preferential treatment is directly related to making up for specific past discrimination. Likewise, government programs giving special consideration to previously disadvantaged groups must show their programs are very carefully designed and serve a compelling public purpose of making up for past injustices.

Suggestions for further reading

Chavez, Lydia. *The Color Bind: California's Battle to End Affirmative Action.* Berkeley: University of California Press, 1998.

Edley, Christopher, Jr. *Not All Black and White: Affirmative Action, Race, and American Values.* New York: Hill & Wang Pub., 1996.

Guernsey, Joan Bren. *Affirmative Action: A Problem or a Remedy?* (Pro/Con Series). Minneapolis, MN: Lerner Publications Co., 1997.

Regents of the University of California v. Bakke
1978

Petitioner: The University of California at Davis Medical School

Respondent: Allan Bakke

Petitioner's Claim: That the University of California Medical School's special admission affirmative action program violated Bakke's civil rights when he was denied admission.

Chief Lawyer for Petitioner: Archibald Cox, Paul J. Mishkin, Jack B. Owens, Donald L. Reidhaar

Chief Lawyer for Respondent: Reynold H. Colvin

Justices for the Court: Chief Justice Warren Burger, Lewis F. Powell, Jr., William H. Rehnquist, John Paul Stevens, Potter Stewart

Justices Dissenting: Harry A. Blackmun, William J. Brennan, Jr., Thurgood Marshall, Byron R. White

Date of Decision: June 28, 1978

Decision: Ruled in favor of Bakke by finding the school's special admissions program unconstitutional because of its use of quotas and that Bakke should be admitted.

Significance: The Court ruled that race could be one factor among several considered for admissions, but it could not be the only factor considered. Since race could be considered, the ruling was the first court approval of affirmative action.

On October 12, 1977 a long line wound its way up the marble staircase and between the towering columns of the U.S. Supreme Court building. Some had camped out all night to get a chance to hear the case to be argued that day, *Regents of the University of California v. Allan Bakke,* the first affirmative action case to reach the Supreme Court.

The courtroom was packed, yet most of the audience had obtained tickets through their connections to the court or through the parties to the case. Despite their special interest in the case, only a small number of people of color or women could be spotted in the select gathering. This alone was testimony (evidence) to the many years of gender (sex) exclusion in professional circles.

Demonstrators who marched in the streets that day were of a decidedly different makeup. Men and women of all colors marched not only outside the Court but from New York to Berkeley, California, raising banners and chanting slogans such as "We won't go back. We won't go back!" The crowds put the Court and world on notice that whatever the outcome in the case, the struggle to open the doors of universities to minorities would go on, never to return to the days when the same demonstrators' grandparents and parents could not gain admission. However, not all Americans supported these demonstrators. Many were opposed to giving increased opportunity at the expense of others through affirmative action programs.

What's All the Fuss About?

Affirmative action means making a special effort to provide opportunities in education and businesses for members of groups (people of color and women) that had been discriminated (giving privileges to one group but not to another) against in the past. In the mid-1970s, educational affirmative action programs often used "quotas." Quotas meant setting a goal that a certain number of minority students would be admitted.

The medical school at the Davis campus of the University of California had such a program in 1970. The program called for a quota of sixteen out of one hundred openings to be filled by disadvantaged students from minority groups. The medical school viewed minority groups as "Blacks," "Chicanos," "Asians," and "American Indians." Under special admission procedures, the minority applicants were evaluated by placing less focus on test scores and grade point average and more on the applicant's overall life and qualifications. The medical school did not

rate or compare special applicants against students applying under regular admission requirements, but recommended special applicants for admission until the sixteen places were filled. This enabled sixteen minority students to join Davis' freshman class of one hundred students.

Allan Bakke

Allan Bakke, a white, thirty-seven year old engineer, wanted to be a medical doctor. He applied in 1973 and again in 1974 through the regular admission process to the University of California at Davis Medical School. Although each year he appeared more qualified than several students admitted through the affirmative action special admissions program, Bakke was rejected both years. As a result, Bakke sued for admission to the Davis medical school. He claimed the medical school's special admission policy denied admission to him solely on the basis of his race thus violating his rights under the Equal Protection Clause of the Fourteenth Amendment. The trial court agreed with Bakke and ruled the special admissions procedure unconstitutional (not following the intent of the U.S. Constitution). Yet, the court refused to order the school to admit

There were many protests surrounding the Bakke *decision.* Reproduced by permission of AP/Wide World Photos.

Bakke. In 1976, the California Supreme Court agreed with the trial court's judgement, but also ordered the school to admit Bakke. The university appealed to the U.S. Supreme Court which agreed to hear the case.

The Arguments

As demonstrators chanted outside, Archibald Cox for the university and Reynold Colvin, Bakke's lawyer, argued the case. Cox, a Harvard law professor who had appeared before the Court many times, defended the university's affirmative action special admissions program. He claimed it was a fair and constitutional way of making up for past discrimination against minority groups. The program gave new opportunity to members of groups which had not had these opportunities in the past.

Colvin, in his first Supreme Court appearance, made several claims against the university. He argued that the admission policy was in conflict with Title VI of the Civil Rights Act of 1964. Title VI prohibits discrimination based on race, color, or national origin in programs which receive federal funds. All state university programs, including the Davis medical school, receive such funds. Furthermore, Colvin argued if Title VI was violated, then the Equal Protection Clause of the Fourteenth Amendment guaranteeing "equal protection of the laws" was also violated. Therefore, the special admission policy was unconstitutional. Continuing in Bakke's defense, Colvin suggested the program went too far in offering increased opportunities for minority groups and seemed to be "reverse discrimination." Reverse discrimination is the lessening of opportunity for a group of people not traditionally discriminated against such as white males.

Two Majority Opinions

More than eight months would pass before the Supreme Court delivered its decision. The Court was as sharply divided over the affirmative action issue as the nation was. Two majority opinions were presented. Each of the opinions was agreed to by a different grouping of five justices. Justice Lewis F. Powell was key to the Bakke decision being the only justice in both majorities.

The two 5–4 majority opinions delivered by Justice Powell were:

(1) The special admissions program with a fixed quota or number of places available only to minorities violated Title VI of the Civil Rights

AFFIRMATIVE ACTION

Act of 1964. Those places were denied to white applicants based only on their race. The university's policy was struck down and the university was ordered to admit Bakke.

(2) Admissions programs do not violate the Equal Protection Clause of the Fourteenth Amendment if they consider race as one of several factors used to decide admission. Therefore, race may be considered but it may not be the only factor considered.

Developing the Two Opinions

The two majority opinions developed in the following manner. In the first opinion four justices (John Paul Stevens, Warren Burger, Potter Stewart, and William Rehnquist) avoided completely the constitutional issue of Equal Protection and instead said it was "crystal clear" that the quota system violated Title VI of the Civil Rights Act. These four also agreed race could never be a factor in admissions. Although he reasoned differently, Justice Powell agreed the quota system violated Title VI. His agreement with the Title VI part added up to a five-justice majority, making quota systems illegal. However, he did not agree race could never be used in admission programs.

In the second opinion four different justices (William J. Brennan, Thurgood Marshall, Byron White, and Harry Blackmun) pointed out that "race conscious programs" do not violate the Equal Protection Clause as long as race was only one factor among many factors considered for admission to a program. Powell agreed, and his agreement made a five-justice majority on that point.

Allan Bakke was admitted to the medical school at the University of California Davis. He graduated in 1982.

Justice Marshall's Dissent

Justice Marshall, the first African American to serve on the Supreme Court and a strong supporter of affirmative action programs, commented in one of his most famous dissents,

> **The position of the Negro today in America is the tragic but inevitable (unavoidable) consequence of centuries of unequal treatment. Measured by any benchmark of comfort or achievement, meaningful equality remains a distant dream for the Negro. . .**

LEWIS FRANKLIN POWELL, JR.

Appointed by President Richard M. Nixon, Lewis Franklin Powell, Jr., served as an associate justice of the U.S. Supreme Court from 1972 until his retirement in 1987. Born into a distinguished Virginia family whose first American ancestor was an original settler of the Jamestown colony in 1607, Powell received his law degree from Washington and Lee University and his masters in law at Harvard in 1932. Powell became one of Virginia's most respected and honored lawyers as well as a strong community leader. While serving on the Richmond School Board and the Virginia State Board of Education, he oversaw the peaceful integration of the state's public schools in the late 1950s.

As an admired Supreme Court member, Powell generally held conservative views but was comfortable taking a middle stand. He often cast a deciding vote, or "swing vote," in cases where justices' opinions were split. Balancing the rights of a society against rights of individuals, Powell frequently cast decisive pro-civil rights votes. His most famous decisive vote came in *Regents of the University of California v. Bakke* (1978) where he prohibited quota systems in university admission policies but upheld the principle of "affirmative action."

> Now, we have the Court again stepping in, this time
> to stop affirmative action programs of the type
> [quota system] used by the University of California.

Impact

Based on the ruling, quota systems used in affirmative action programs were out but race could be considered if other factors were also considered. This concession that race could be used as a factor was at least a partial victory for affirmative action and demonstrators who had filled the streets. As is often the case, the divided or split decision seemed to

allow more room for differing applications across the country. For example, universities with strong affirmative action programs used the part that the race factor could continue to help them build strong multiracial communities. On the other hand, schools that had always been reluctant in racially integrating their campuses used the decision to abandon attempts at affirmative action.

Affirmative action continued to be a controversial topic in the 1990s. In 1995 demonstrators in California again took to the streets in support of affirmative action programs at the state universities. President Bill Clinton made his famous speech on affirmative action in July of 1995 saying to "mend it, but don't end it." However, in 1996 Californians voted to ban existing state government affirmative action programs. The issue remains controversial and complex.

Suggestions for further reading

Dreyfuss, Joel, and Charles Lawrence III. *The Bakke Case: The Politics of Inequality.* New York: Harcourt, Brace, Jovanovich, 1979.

Lawrence, Charles R., III, and Mari J. Matsuda. *We Won't Go Back: Making the Case for Affirmative Action.* Boston: Houghton Mifflin Company, 1997.

Welch, Susan, and John Gruhl. *Affirmative Action and Minority Enrollments in Medical and Law Schools.* Ann Arbor: University of Michigan Press, 1998.

United Steelworkers of America v. Weber 1979

Petitioner: United Steelworkers of America

Respondent: Brian Weber

Petitioner's Claim: That an affirmative action program started by Kaiser Aluminum, in voluntary partnership with the United Steelworkers, did not violate Title VII of the 1964 Civil Rights Act.

Chief Lawyers for Petitioner: Michael E. Gottesman

Chief Lawyers for Respondent: Michael R. Fontham

Justices for the Court: Harry A. Blackmun, William J. Brennan, Jr., Warren E. Burger, Thurgood Marshall, William H. Rehnquist, Potter Stewart, Byron R. White

Justices Dissenting: Warren E. Burger, William H. Rehnquist

Date of Decision: June 27, 1979

Decision: Ruled in favor of United Steelworkers and reversed the rulings of two lower courts by upholding the legality of the affirmative action plan.

Significance: The decision was the first Supreme Court ruling to address the issue of affirmative action in employment. Affirmative action programs were not in violation of Title VII of the Civil Rights Act as long as private parties entered into such programs voluntarily and on a temporary basis. The ruling encouraged private employers to experiment with affirmative action plans to open job opportunities for minorities.

AFFIRMATIVE ACTION

Between 1947 and 1962 the unemployment of black Americans compared to whites skyrocketed. In 1947 the non-white employment rate was 64 percent higher than the white rate. By 1962 it was 124 percent higher than the white rate. Determined to address long standing inequalities between blacks and whites in America and to help end discrimination (giving privileges to one group but not to another similar group) against blacks, Congress passed the Civil Rights Act of 1964. The act banned discrimination because of a person's color, race, national origin, or religion. Responding to questions like the one asked by Senator Hubert Humphrey, "What good does it do a Negro to be able to eat in a fine restaurant if he cannot afford to pay the bill?" Congress made sure the Civil Rights Act included sections dealing with employment. The language of subsection 703(a) of Title VII of the Civil Rights Act reads:

> **It shall be an unlawful employment practice for an employer (1) to fail to refuse to hire or to discharge [fire] any individual . . . because of such individual's race . . . or (2) to limit, segregate [separate into groups] or classify his employees or applicants for employment in any way which would deprive [take away] or tend to deprive any individual of equal opportunities . . . because of such individual's race. . .**

This wording was further supported in Section 703(d) which forbids employers, labor organizations, or any combination of the two to discriminate against any individual on the basis of race, color, religion, sex or national origin in apprenticeship (learning a craft or trade from an already skilled worker) or on-the-job training programs.

Despite the act's clear language, forward-thinking leaders in America believed more would be necessary to overcome two and a half centuries of discrimination and to promote equal opportunity. Together, black and political leaders began in the 1960s to fashion plans known as affirmative action plans. Affirmative action means making a special effort or taking a specific action to promote opportunities in education or employment for members of groups discriminated against in the past. The goals of these programs are increased job opportunities, employment promotions, and admissions to universities for minorities.

Kaiser's Affirmative Action Plan

In 1974 the United Steelworkers of America, a labor union, and Kaiser Aluminum and Chemical Company, a huge steel maker with fifteen plants nationwide, voluntarily agreed to set up an affirmative action plan. According to the plan, Kaiser would reserve 50 percent of the places in its craft-training (apprenticeship) programs for black workers. The plants would continue this policy until the percentage of black American craft workers in its plants was equal to the percentage of black Americans in the local population. The education provided in the craft-training programs turned unskilled workers into higher paid skilled workers.

At Kaiser's plant in Gramercy, Louisiana less than 2 percent of all skilled workers were black Americans despite the fact that 39 percent of the total labor force in the town was black. The low percentage of skilled black workers was a reflection of past discrimination. Black workers in the area had long been denied opportunities to become skilled craftworkers. The Gramercy plant's affirmative action plan, following the guidelines worked out between the steelworker's union and Kaiser, was to have approximately 39 percent of its skilled positions filled by black Americans. The plan was temporary and would be ended when they reached the goal.

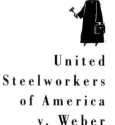

Brian Weber, Man of Steel

Brian Weber was a white unskilled union worker at Kaiser in Gramercy. He applied for a position in the craft-training program but was rejected although he had more seniority than several of the blacks selected. Seniority is a status or rank that an individual has attained based on the amount of time the individual has spent on the job. A common labor practice is to give better jobs or job training placements to those with more seniority. Before the affirmative action plan, Kaiser used seniority to decide who was admitted to training programs. However, under the affirmative action plan, to keep the training program at 50 percent blacks and 50 percent whites, the company had to choose some blacks with less seniority than some whites.

Weber charged that since his rejection was due to his race, he had been discriminated against in violation of the Civil Rights Act Title VII, sections 703(a) and (d). He filed a class action suit (lawsuit brought by a number of persons with a common interest) in U.S. District Court. Weber's argument was simple. Under Title VII an employer may not dis-

AFFIRMATIVE ACTION

criminate on the basis of race or color. Weber claimed Kaiser's affirmative action plan did just that. The plan actually was "reverse discrimination," discrimination against a group which has not historically been discriminated against such as white males. The district court and the Court of Appeals of the Fifth Circuit agreed with Weber. The courts ruled that race-based employment practices, even those designed to fix past discrimination, were themselves discriminatory in violation of Title VII. The United Steelworkers of America Union appealed to the U.S. Supreme Court.

Court Gives History Lesson

The Supreme Court reversed the two lower courts' rulings in a 5-2 vote. Justice William J. Brennan, Jr., writing for the majority, delivered a history lesson on discrimination in the United States. He also illustrated how the Court must carefully consider America's past in order to shape its future more fairly for all. Justice Brennan identified the question as:

> **Whether Title VII forbids private employers and unions from voluntarily agreeing upon . . . affirmative action plans that accord [give] racial preferences in the manner and for the purpose provided in the Kaiser-USWA plan.**

Recognizing that Weber's argument was understandable and had merit (value), Brennan examined the concerns Congress had when it passed the Civil Rights Act of 1964. Extensively quoting Senator Humphry's speeches made in the Senate in 1963, Brennan noted "'the plight of the Negro in our economy'" and how "blacks were largely relegated [assigned to a low ranking job] to 'unskilled and semi-skilled jobs.' . . . As a consequence the 'position of the Negro worker [was] steadily worsening.'" Brennan continued, "it was to this problem that Title VII's prohibition against racial discrimination in employment was primarily addressed."

Given the legislative history of the Civil Rights Act, Brennan wrote that the Court could not agree with Weber. Congress had not meant to prohibit the private business sector from voluntarily taking steps designed to meet the goals of Title VII. Brennan commented that to interpret 703(a) and (d) as forbidding "all race-conscious affirmative action would bring about an end completely at variance with [opposite to] the purpose of the statute [law] and must be rejected." The Court held, "Title VII's prohibition in 703 (a) and (d) against racial discrimination does not condemn all private, voluntary, race-conscious affirmative action plans."

UNDERSTANDING LABOR UNIONS

Before labor unions were formed, wage earners had no voice in their pay, work hours, or working conditions. Newly established labor unions allowed workers to gain some control over their employment conditions. A labor union is an organization of employees whose purpose is to gain, through legal bargaining with an employer, better working conditions, pay, and benefits (health insurance, retirement plan, etc.).

Workers in the United States have formed three main kinds of unions: (1) craft unions limited to skilled tradesmen such as carpenters; (2) industrial unions open to skilled and unskilled workers in mass-producing industries such as the automobile and steel industries; and, (3) public employee unions such as city workers, fire fighters, and police.

Unions in trades such as steelmaking, bricklaying, and printing provide apprentice programs in cooperation with employers to train persons to become skilled trade workers. The training combines on-the-job experience with individual and classroom instruction.

Banding together in a group gives workers more power than they would have as individuals. Numerous lawsuits brought by unions on behalf of their workers have reached the U.S. Supreme Court.

Where Was Weber's Equal Protection?

The Equal Protection Clause of the Fourteenth Amendment, often used in charges against affirmative action plans, did not apply in this case. The reason was that the Equal Protection Clause guarantees that "equal protection of the laws" shall not be denied by any state. The keyword here is "state." Kaiser is a private company. A year before *Weber*, the Court ruled that the Equal Protection Clause did apply in the affirmative action case of *University of California v. Bakke* (1978) because it involved a state-funded university. The United Steelworkers of America was a pri-

AFFIRMATIVE ACTION

vate union and Kaiser a private business, hence the Equal Protection Clause could not be applied.

Suggestions for further reading

American Federation of Labor and Congress of Industrial Organization. [Online] Website: http://www.aflcio.org (Accessed July 31, 2000).

Lynch, Frederick R. *Invisible Victims: White Males and the Crisis of Affirmative Action.* New York: Praeger, 1991.

Mosley, Albert G., and Nicholas Capaldi. *Affirmative Action: Social Justice or Unfair Preference.* Lanham: Rowman & Littlefield Publishers, 1996.

Skrentny, John David. *The Ironies of Affirmative Action: Politics, Culture, and Justice in America.* Chicago: The University of Chicago Press, 1996.

Fullilove v. Klutznick
1980

Petitioner: H. Earl Fullilove and others

Respondent: Philip M. Klutznick, U.S. Secretary of Commerce

Petitioner's Claim: That a provision in the law requiring that 10 percent of all federal funds for local public works projects go to minority-owned businesses violates the U.S. Constitution.

Chief Lawyers for Petitioner: Robert G. Benisch and Robert J. Hickey

Chief Lawyers for Respondent: Drew S. Days III

Justices for the Court: Harry A. Blackmun, William J. Brennan, Jr., Warren E. Burger, Thurgood Marshall, Lewis F. Powell, Byron R. White

Justices Dissenting: William H. Rehnquist, John Paul Stevens, Potter Stewart

Date of Decision: July 2, 1980

Decision: Affirmed lower court rulings rejecting the petitioners' claim that minority "set-asides" were unconstitutional.

Significance: The decision clarified the Court's position on the constitutionality of minority set-aside programs. Plus many state and local governments adopted set-aside programs for minority-owned businesses.

Congress had long struggled with the fact that when various government agencies, including state and local governments, contracted for construction of public works projects rarely did they contract with minority-owned businesses. Public works projects are projects that receive money from the federal government for such things as construction of schools, courthouses, post offices, roads, bridges, dams, power projects, water systems, and waste treatment plants. Federal money received by governmental agencies to pay for the projects almost never reached minority business enterprises (companies).

In May of 1977, President Jimmy Carter signed the Public Works Emplyment Act, making it a law.
Courtesy of the Library of Congress.

According to Representative Mitchell of Maryland, speaking on the floor of the House of Representatives on February 23, 1977, " . . . every agency of the Government has tried to figure out a way to avoid doing this very thing. Believe me, these bureaucracies can come up with 10,000 ways to avoid doing it."

Minority Business Enterprise Provision

Representative Mitchell pointed out that in 1976 less than one percent of federal funds for these projects found their way to minority companies, yet minorities made up 15-18 percent of the general population. Representative Mitchell's efforts ended with passage of the Public Works Employment Act of 1977. The act authorized an additional $4 billion for federal grants [money from the federal government for projects] to be awarded by the Secretary of Commerce to state and local governments for use in local public works projects. But there was a "catch" to these dollars. The catch was a section of the act, Section 103 (f) (2) called the "minority business enterprise" or MBE provision. The MBE provision required that,

> **. . . no grant shall be made under the Act for any local public works project unless the applicant gives satisfactory assurance to the secretary [of Commerce] that at least 10 per cent of the amount of each grant shall be expended [spent] for [services from] minority business enterprises.**

So 10 percent of the federal grant money provided for each project had to go to minority-owned businesses. This forced governments to contract with those businesses for at least some work on each project. Minority group members were defined as citizens of the United States who are "Negroes, Spanish-speaking, Orientals, Indians, Eskimos, and Aleuts."

Public Works Employment Act Challenged

Signed into law by President Jimmy Carter in May of 1977, the Public Works Employment Act was an affirmative action plan designed to increase opportunities for businesses owned by groups traditionally discriminated against in U.S. history. This plan was a "set-aside" program, that is, 10 percent of federal grant money directed to public works projects had to be "set-aside" and awarded to MBE's. This was the first federal law, since the mid-1800s, to establish a specific class of persons based on race to which special treatment was to be given.

As expected after only six months the act was challenged in court. H. Earl Fullilove and several associations of non-minority construction contractors filed suit against Philip M. Klutznick, U.S. Secretary of Commerce. They complained the 10 percent MBE requirement had hurt their companies incomes because of lost business—business which now went to the MBEs. They charged the MBE provision was unconstitutional (the law did not follow the intent of the U.S. Constitution) because it violated the Equal Protection Clause of the Fourteenth Amendment of the U.S. Constitution and also the equal protection promised under the Due Process Clause of the Fifth Amendment. The Equal Protection Clause guarantees that no person or class of persons will be denied the

same protection of the laws enjoyed by other persons or classes in similar circumstances in their lives, liberty, property, and pursuit of happiness. Due process is also a constitutional guarantee that before the government acts to take away a person's life, liberty, or property fair legal proceedings must take place. They demanded that no more federal monies be given to minority contractors pending the outcome of their lawsuit.

First the district court and then the U.S. Court of Appeals for the Second Circuit ruled against Fullilove and affirmed (supported) the MBE program as constitutional. The court of appeals cited the many years of governmental attempts to remedy (fix) past racial and ethnic (groups of various races) discrimination. The Court found it "difficult to imagine" any other purpose for the MBE provision.

Fullilove's group appealed to their last avenue of hope, the U.S. Supreme Court who agreed to hear the case.

Congress Need Not Be Color-Blind

On July 2, 1980, the U.S. Supreme Court issued its 6-3 plurality ruling (a majority agrees on the decision but for different reasons). The justices again affirmed the constitutionality of the Public Works Employment Act and rejected Fullilove's claims. Chief Justice Warren Burger wrote that Congress had frequently used the Spending Power provision of Article I of the Constitution to hold back federal money until "governments or private parties [agreed] to cooperate voluntarily with federal policy." The Spending Power provision, the Court recognized, allowed Congress to "provide for the . . . general Welfare" and the MBE provision does that. Furthermore Justice Burger commented that in attempting to right past discrimination, Congress need not act in a wholly "color-blind" fashion. The set-asides were a "reasonably necessary means of furthering the compelling [important] governmental interest in redressing [to make up for] the discrimination, that affects minority contractors." Even though groups were receiving preferential treatment under the law, the Equal Protection Clause was not violated because the preferential treatment was necessary to boost the opportunities of those groups.

Chief Justice Burger also wrote that Due Process was not violated. While Congress, in debating passage of the act, had not actually held hearings on set-asides, they nevertheless had acted in a knowledgeable and reasonable manner to correct long recognized discrimination practices in the construction industry. Yet another reason for the plurality rul-

THE HOT CONTROVERSY OVER REVERSE OR BENIGN DISCRIMINATION

Affirmative action programs to correct past discrimination against minorities and women have led to a new form of discrimination known as reverse or benign (with good intentions) discrimination. White males generally are thought of as being the victims by losing jobs or educational opportunities to minorities or women.

Supporters of affirmative action say the programs were never suppose to be painless. The group which historically did not suffer but rather benefitted greatly from its privileged status must now suffer. Yet, supporters point to statistics showing white males are suffering little. Any setbacks suffered by white male reduced opportunities are more likely results of the U.S. economy and job markets. Critics say the cost to those who are being required to pay for historical wrongs are paying too much. They point to reverse discrimination in college admissions, scholarships, government contracts, and jobs in the private and public sectors.

The second main argument is over the idea of merit. Critics claim that better qualified candidates lose out as a result of affirmative action. They contend that only individual qualities should determine who is hired or granted admission. Supporters say those who question merit miss the point. Affirmative action merely gives a jump start and does not ignore merit. Besides, merit can not be precisely ranked in individuals. Additionally, there are many "no merit" situations in American society such as the children of the rich attend the best schools regardless of their qualifications

ing was the MBE, when highly scrutinized (examined by the Court), still passed as constitutional.

Burger concluded simply with, "The MBE provision of the Public Works Employment Act of 1977 does not violate the [U.S.] Constitution."

The act was reasonably debated then well written, had the honest and important goal to right past discriminations, and Congress had the constitutional power to enforce the set-asides.

Because of *Fullilove,* many state and local governments adopted set-aside programs for minority owned businesses. Some withstood court tests while less flexible ones did not. By the late 1980s the Court had reinforced its position in upholding affirmative action in three cases, *Local Number 28 of the Sheet Metal Workers' International v. Equal Employment Opportunity Commission* (1986); *Local Number 93, International Association of Firefighters, AFL-CIO C.L.C. v. City of Cleveland, et al.* (1986); and, *Johnson v. Transportation Agency* (1987).

Reverse Discrimination

Fullilove, along with **University of California v. Bakke** (1978) and **United Steelworkers of America v. Weber** (1979), all tested the problem of "reverse discrimination." Reverse discrimination is discrimination against a group not historically discriminated against as white males. With all three cases, the Court showed a tendency to protect affirmative action even at the expense of what appeared to be injustice to equally qualified white contractors, students or workers.

Suggestions for further reading

Mills, Nicolaus, ed. *Debating Affirmative Action: Race, Gender, Ethnicity, and the Politics of Inclusion.* New York: Dell Publishing, 1994.

Minority Business Development Agency. [Online] Website: http://www.mbda.gov (Accessed on July 31, 2000).

McWhiter, Darien A. *The End of Affirmative Action: Where Do We Go From Here?* New York: Carol Publishing Group, 1996.

Zelnick, Bob. *Backfire: A Reporter's Look at Affirmative Action.* Washington, DC: Regnery Publishing, Inc., 1996.

Metro Broadcasting, Inc. v. Federal Communications Commission 1990

Petitioner: Metro Broadcasting, Inc.

Respondent: Federal Communications Commission

Petitioner's Claim: That FCC programs designed to increase minority ownership of broadcast licenses violate the principle of equal protection.

Chief Lawyer for Petitioner: Gregory H. Guillot

Chief Lawyer for Respondent: Daniel M. Armstrong

Justices for the Court: Harry A. Blackmun, William J. Brennan, Jr., Thurgood Marshall, John Paul Stevens, Byron R. White

Justices Dissenting: Anthony M. Kennedy, Sandra Day O'Connor, Chief Justice William H. Rehnquist, Antonin Scalia

Date of Decision: June 27, 1990

Decision: Ruled in favor of the FCC by finding that its minority ownership policies did not violate equal protection.

Significance: For the first time the Court endorsed a federal program intended to promote increased minority participation, rather than merely remedy past racial discrimination. The opportunity to broadcast opinions of racial minorities benefits not only minorities, but the public in general.

Historically in the United States, the broadcasting or media communications industry (newspapers, radio, television) reflected the white American's world. For example, little appreciation or understanding of black American culture, thought, or history was communicated. A 1968 report by the National Advisory Commission on Civil Disorders noted, "The world that television and newspapers offer to their black audience is almost totally white." Minorities, including not only black Americans but also Hispanics, Orientals, and Native Americans, rarely saw their viewpoints expressed over the airways.

Policies of the FCC

In the Communication Act of 1934, Congress assigned authority to the Federal Communication Commission (FCC) to grant licenses to persons wishing to construct and operate radio broadcast stations in the United States. The act also encouraged the FCC to promote diversification (a variety of viewpoints representing all citizens) of programming. The FCC used various strategies to attract minority participation but little broadcast diversity resulted. To try harder, the FCC in 1978 adopted a "Statement of Policy on Minority Ownership of Broadcast Facilities." Intended to increase minority ownership of broadcast licenses, the statement outlined two FCC policies, known as the minority preference or ownership policies. First, in selecting companies applying for licenses, the FCC would give special consideration to radio or television stations owned or managed by minority groups. Race would be one of several factors looked at. Secondly, the FCC would permit a broadcaster in danger of losing its license, known as a "distressed" broadcaster, to transfer that license through a "distress sale" to an FCC-approved minority company thereby avoiding a FCC hearing on their suitability. The license sale price could not exceed 75 percent of its fair market value. Despite these FCC's efforts, by 1986 minorities still only owned just over 2 percent of the more than 11,000 radio and television stations. Many of these served limited geographic areas with relatively small audiences.

The FCC's minority preference policies were considered affirmative action policies. Affirmative action means making a special effort or taking a specific action to promote opportunities in business or education for members of groups historically discriminated against. The FCC policies were intended to increase opportunities in the broadcasting industry for minorities. Two cases challenging the constitutionality of the FCC's minority preference policies reached the U.S. Supreme Court in 1990.

Metro Broadcasting

Metro Broadcasting, Inc. and Rainbow Broadcasting each applied for a license to construct and operate a new television station in Orlando, Florida. Metro was a non-minority business, but Rainbow was 90 percent Hispanic-owned. In 1983, the license was granted Metro. However, the FCC reviewed the decision the following year and awarded the license to Rainbow instead. Metro appealed to the U.S. Court of Appeals for the District of Columbia Circuit which agreed with the FCC decision. Metro, challenging FCC's policy awarding preferences to minority-owned businesses, appealed to the U.S. Supreme Court. The Court agreed to hear the case.

Metro
Broadcast-
ing, Inc.
v. FCC

Shurberg Broadcasting—Second Case

In 1980, the Faith Center, Inc., a licensee in Hartford, Connecticut, sought permission to transfer its license under the distress-sale policy. After several attempts to transfer to minority-owned companies fell through, Faith Center finally sold its license to Astroline Communications Company, a minority-owned business. Shurberg Broadcasting was also seeking a license but because it was a non-minority business, Shurberg could not buy Faith Center's license. Shurberg challenged the transfer to Astroline on several grounds including that the FCC's distress-sale policy violated its constitutional right to equal protection. Equal protection is a constitutional guarantee that no person or group of persons will be denied the same treatment of the laws as another person or group under similar circumstances. The FCC rejected Shurberg's challenge, but the U.S. Court of Appeals for the District of Columbia agreed with Shurberg. The FCC had violated its right of equal protection under the Fifth Amendment.

The case was examined under equal protection of the Fifth Amendment instead of under the Equal Protection Clause of the Fourteenth Amendment because the Fourteenth applies only to questions involving laws of state government. The Fifth applies to federal government laws and policies. The decision was appealed to the U.S. Supreme Court which agreed to hear the case.

To Promote Diversity

The Supreme Court combined the two cases and heard them at the same time since both considered whether or not the minority preference poli-

**AFFIRMATIVE
ACTION**

cies of the FCC were constitutional under the equal protection guarantee of the Fifth Amendment. Justice William J. Brennan, Jr. delivered the 5-4 decision of the Court ruling in favor of FCC in both cases. In making its decision, the Court considered several key factors.

First, the Court examined whether the policies were designed to make up for past specific acts of discrimination. Previous Court decisions on affirmative action policies strongly emphasized that preferential treatment had to remedy (make up for) specific past discrimination. For example, in *United Steelworkers of America v. Weber* (1979) Kaiser Aluminum's affirmative action policy was upheld. Kaiser's program specifically made up for the fact that throughout the company's history black Americans had been denied opportunities to become highly paid skilled workers. Kaiser's policy was designed to remedy or fix its past discrimination against blacks. The policy was "remedial." However, in a far-reaching conclusion, Brennan wrote in the FCC case,

> **Congress and the Commission [FCC] do not justify the minority ownership policies strictly as remedies for victims of this discrimination [under representation of minorities in broadcasting], however. Rather, Congress and the FCC have selected the minority ownership policies primarily to promote programming diversity, and they urge that such diversity is an important governmental objective [goal] that can serve as a constitutional basis for the preference policies. We agree.**

The key phrase is "to promote . . . diversity." With this statement, the Court for the first time upheld an affirmative action policy designed not to remedy specific past discrimination but to promote diversity.

An Important Governmental Objective

The Court found that program diversity is an important governmental objective because underrepresentation of minorities in broadcasting not only hurts minority audiences but also the entire viewing and listening public. The public has a right to receive a diversity of views and information over the airwaves, therefore the FCC had to encourage minorities to enter broadcasting. Justice Brennan wrote, "Minority viewpoint in programming serves not only needs and interests of minority but enriches and educates the non-minority audience." Justice Brennan concluded, "

FEDERAL COMMUNICATIONS COMMISSION

The Federal Communications Commission (FCC) is an independent U.S. government agency, established by the Communication Act of 1934. The FCC is directly responsible to Congress. It is charged with regulating interstate and international communication by radio, television, wire, satellite, and cable in the United States. The FCC's seven operating bureaus are Cable Services, Common Carrier, Consumer Information, Enforcement, International, Mass Media, and Wireless Communications. These bureaus are responsible for regulatory programs, processing licenses, aiding in emergency alerts, national defense, analyzing complaints, conducting investigations, and taking part in FCC hearings. As the United States entered the digital age, the FCC is committed to creating a competitive marketplace in Internet connections, phone service, and assuring choices in video entertainment.

The FCC is dedicated to making certain the "Information Age" technologies reach all Americans from business districts to the poorest neighborhoods. While controlling the access and flow of information has become increasingly vital to business success, only approximately 3 percent of commercial broadcast stations has minority ownership. In early 2000 the FCC announced one thousand new low-power non-commercial FM radio stations for community groups, churches, and educational organizations to aid in broadening the range of interests and ideas.

. . . the interest in enhancing broadcast diversity is, at the very least, an important governmental objective, and is therefore a sufficient basis for the Commission's [FCC's] minority ownership policies."

Will FCC's Policies Achieve the Objective?

If diversity of programming is the objective of the government, will increased minority ownership opportunities be, in fact, a good way to

achieve diversity? First, Justice Brennan examined in detail the "historical evolution of current federal policy" regarding the broadcasting industry. Congress had required diversity since 1934 and the FCC had developed policies to carry out the requirement. But, previous approaches had not produced adequate diversity. Both Congress and the FCC after "long study, painstaking consideration of all available alternatives [programs tried] came to the conclusion that "minority ownership policies [best] advance the goal of diverse programming." The FCC's minority preference policies take direct aim "at the barriers that minorities face in entering the broadcasting industry." Similarly, the distress-sale policy addresses a common minority company problem of too little capital (money) with which to purchase licenses. It effectively lowers the sale price of existing stations plus provides an incentive for distressed stations to seek out minority buyers.

Turning Point

Justice Brennan summarized:

> **FCC policies do not violate equal protection . . . since they [the policies] bear the imprimatur [mark] of longstanding Congressional support and direction and are substantially related to the achievement of important governmental objectives [directly work to achieve the goal] of broadcasting diversity.**

More importantly, the ruling marked a turning point in American social history. With this decision the Court for the first time approved the constitutionality of affirmative action policies designed to promote minority diversity, rather than to just remedy past discrimination.

Suggestions for further reading

Federal Communications Commission. [Online] Website: http://www.fcc.gov (Accessed on July 31, 2000).

National Association of Broadcasters. [Online] Website: http://www.nab.org (Accessed on July 31, 2000).

Torres, Sasha, ed. *Living Color: Race and Television in the Unites States.* Duke University Press, 1998.

THE RIGHT TO DIE AND ASSISTED SUICIDE

Death is the end of life and the process of dying involves choices and actions. By the end of the twentieth century not only has life become more complicated, but so has the process of dying. No longer do many Americans die early from infectious diseases (strep throat, pneumonia, etc.), but life expectancies run well into the seventies with heart disease and cancer being primary killers. Medical technology can keep terminally ill (dying) patients alive much longer than ever before. Patients who previously would have died quickly from an inability to eat and drink or other complications now can be sustained for days, weeks, even years. Intravenous (IV) feeding and hydration (watering), artificial blood circulating and respiratory systems, antibiotics, and chemotherapy (treatment for cancer) enable life to be prolonged.

Die Nobly and at the Right Time

The Roman's philosophy about dying was, "To live nobly also means to die nobly and at the right time." Figuring out what is the "right time" is the key problem, especially toward the end of the twentieth century. In the 1990s the courts wrestled with ethical (moral codes) and legal controversies. When should an artificial respirator or feeding tube be removed from a person in a coma? When should chemotherapy be discontinued for a cancer patient? Not only when, but who has the right to make the call? Patient's rights groups and physician's organizations as well as religious groups battle for control over decisions about how and when an individual dies. Laws and court decisions began to establish rules and standards to apply to the dying. For example, the right of an individual to refuse medical procedures—sometimes referred to as the right to die—has been affirmed. Before considering court decisions, the difference between right to die and assisted suicide must be clear.

The Right to Die

The right to die generally refers to allowing a patient to die by natural causes when life-sustaining treatment is taken away. The cause of death is considered, therefore, the illness. A competent person may refuse medical treatment. A competent patient is considered by the courts one who can give consent (agree) to be treated or not be treat. The ability to accept or refuse medical treatment is often referred to as bodily self-determination or patient autonomy (self-reliance). On the other hand, an incompetent patient does not have the ability to make such decisions.

A competent person, realizing that he may become incompetent as time passes, may leave instructions to others about desired medical decisions. These directions are called an advance directive or living will. Another option is for the person to appoint a trusted individual to make decisions when he becomes unable to do so. This individual would be called a proxy directive or durable power of attorney. In the 1990s most states had living will laws and all fifty had durable power-of-attorney laws. More people chose to use proxy directives or power-of-attorney than living wills.

Assisted Suicide

Assisted suicide, generally referred to as physical-assisted suicide, is when a doctor helps individuals take their own lives. Generally, the physician helps a patient to take his own life by prescribing a drug that the doctor knows will be used by the patient to commit suicide. The patient dies not by natural causes, but by human action. Assisted suicide is a felony offense in most states. Only in Oregon has physician-assisted suicide been legalized. Oregon voters approved the Oregon Death with

Dignity Act in November of 1994 and, in a repeat voter referendum in 1997, refused to repeal (cancel) the act. The Oregon law is crafted with many requirements and restrictions.

The most famous individual associated with physician-assisted suicide through the 1990s was Dr. Jack Kervorkian, also known as the "suicide doctor." With questionable screening procedures, the retired pathologist assisted in numerous suicides using a machine that allows the patient to decide when to deliver a lethal (killing) poison. Charged numerous times with murder, Kervorkian was found guilty in 1997 of second degree murder in a Michigan trial.

By the 1990s the difference in the meaning of the two terms, right to die and assisted suicide, became clouded in the general public's mind. This is because organizations promoting assisted-suicide legislation began to refer to their effort as the right-to-die movement.

The Controversy Over Assisted Suicide

Supporters of assisted suicide say it is not really different from withholding life supporting medical care and that it is a merciful and dignified option for individuals whose quality of life has become intolerable due to illness. It is a more visible and more easily regulated decision.

On the other side is the American Medical Association whose Code of Medical Ethics considers assisted suicide very different from removal of life sustaining medical care. Although accepting that removal of life support is sometimes necessary to honor a patient's wishes, it holds that assisted suicide is against professional ethics. Others in opposition see a "slippery slope" where legalizing assisted suicide could lead to abuses of the chronically ill, handicapped, and elderly. The Catholic Church, arguing that human life should not be destroyed for any reason, is one of many religious organizations opposed to assisted suicide.

Vital Decisions

Approximately fifteen years before most cases considering life-and-death medical decisions began working their way through the legal system, the 1975 case of Karen Ann Quinlan was decided in the New Jersey Supreme Court. For the first time Americans focused on the right to die. Quinlan, a twenty-one year old woman in a coma from apparent ingestion of tranquilizers and alcohol. She was on life support and her condition was considered hopeless. Her parents asked that life-sustaining medical care be stopped. In a unanimous decision, the New Jersey Supreme Court ruled that Quinlan had a constitutional right to privacy to refuse medical treatment. Under the circumstances, her father's decision to end care should be honored. The *Quinlan* decision established the first legal guidelines for withholding life supporting medical treatment.

In 1990 the U.S. Supreme Court jumped into the right to die argument with a decision in ***Cruzan v. Director, Missouri Department of Health.*** Nancy Cruzan, permanently unconscious from brain injuries sustained in an automobile accident, had previously made informal statements to her roommate about never wanting to be kept in a "vegetative" state. Her parents contended that these statements were enough to indicate her wishes and the life preserving medical treatment should stop. The Court ruled that when a competent person issues "clear and convincing" instructions as to medical care including food and water, it is their constitutional right to have those directions followed. The right has been rooted in common law for centuries. However, the Court decided Cruzan's statements to her roommate were not clear and convincing instructions. In the absence of "clear and convincing" instructions from what became an incompetent person, the Court recognized the state of Missouri's interest in protecting life and safeguarding against potential abuses. The Court refused to require Missouri to honor the "substituted judgement" of Cruzan's family as had been honored in the Quinlan case. The Court left it up to states to adopt "clear and convincing" evidence standards. A key result of the ruling was that it encouraged people to leave advance instructions since the courts will honor them. This ruling was an affirmation of an individual's control of their right to die. The Court, reflecting general public opinion, was comfortable in allowing a competent person to refuse treatment, even if it meant their death. However, that same level of comfort for many people and the courts has not been reached for assisted suicide.

Is Assisted Suicide a Right?

Justice Sandra Day O'Connor had commented in *Cruzan* that the country was only beginning to address questions of medical ethics and that the crafting of procedures should be left to the states. In ***Washington v. Glucksberg*** (1997) the Supreme Court was asked to review the constitutionality of a Washington state statute prohibiting physician-assisted suicide. The law made it a crime to assist, aid or cause the suicide of another person. Many other states have similar laws. Four physicians, three seriously ill patients, and a non-profit counseling organization asked that the law be negated claiming assisted suicide was a constitutional right. The Court in examining U.S. history, tradition, and legal practice and finding no support for assisted suicide as a fundamental right, upheld the Washington law. The Court commented that the state of Washington had a real interest in preserving life, preventing suicide, and safeguarding the poor, sick, and elderly from relatives that might encourage assisted suicide.

On the same day in 1997, the Court also released its decision in a similar case, *Vacco v. Quill.* A New York law prohibits helping another person commit suicide while allowing competent adult patients to terminate (stop) life sustaining measures. Three doctors and three terminally ill patients claimed this was inconsistent and in violation of "equal protection of the laws" guaranteed in the Fourteenth Amendment. The Court concluded that physician-assisted suicide is very different from refusing medical treatment. States may treat each practice differently without being in conflict with equal protection.

A Matter of States

Through *Washington v. Glucksberg* and *Vacco v. Quill* the Court rejected the idea that assisted suicide was a constitutional right and confirmed that states could draft laws banning assisted suicide.

Through 1999 no cases involving the Oregon Death With Dignity Act had reached the Supreme Court. However, the U.S. Senate was considering passage of the Pain Relief Promotion Act. This bill would prevent use of federally controlled medications in assisting suicide and, if passed, would in effect outlaw the procedures of the Oregon law.

Suggestions for further reading

Bender, David L., and Bruno Leone, eds. *Euthanasia: Opposing Viewpoints.* San Diego: Greenhaven Press, Inc., 1989.

Cox, Donald W. *Hemlock's Cup: The Struggle for Death with Dignity.* Buffalo, NY: Prometheus Books, 1993.

Delury, George E. *But What If She Wants to Die? A Husband's Diary.* New York: Carol Publishing Group, 1997.

Cruzan v. Director, Missouri Department of Health 1990

Petitioner: Nancy Beth Cruzan, by her parents and co-guardians

Respondent: Director, Missouri Department of Health

Petitioner's Claim: That the state of Missouri had no legal authority to interfere with parents' wish to remove a life-sustaining feeding tube from their daughter's comatose body.

Chief Lawyer for Petitioner: William H. Colby

Chief Lawyer for Respondent: Robert L. Presson, Attorney General of Missouri

Justices for the Court: Anthony Kennedy, Sandra Day O'Connor, Chief Justice William H. Rehnquist, Antonin Scalia, Byron R. White

Justices Dissenting: Harry A. Blackmun, William J. Brennan, Jr., Thurgood Marshall, John Paul Stevens

Date of Decision: June 25, 1990

Decision: Ruled in favor of Missouri by determining the state did not violate the Fourteenth Amendment guarantee of liberties of the comatose patient.

Significance: The case marked the first time the U.S. Supreme Court ruled in a right-to-die case. The Court ruled that rejection of life preserving medical treatment by a competent person is a liberty protected by the Constitution.

Right-to-die is a general term referring to a patient's right to die by natural causes when refusing life sustaining treatment. The refusal can be made by a competent (able to make decisions on their own) patient realizing that their decision may mean death.

Even before the birth of America, right-to-die had been considered a liberty in English common law (legal based on practices rather than laws). As under the U.S. Constitution, such liberties are fundamental freedoms in which a person may participate relatively free from government interference.

Right-to-die is quite different from assisted suicide which was prominent in news in the 1990s. Assisted suicide is when a doctor helps individuals to take their own lives. The patient dies not by natural causes, but by human action.

The first case involving right-to-die that come to the nation's attention was that of Karen Ann Quinlan in 1975. The case involved a young woman in a permanent vegetative state and her family's legal battle to remove life support from her. The case was decided in the New Jersey Supreme Court with a ruling to honor the family's wishes. Not until 1983 did a right-to-die case reach the U.S. Supreme Court.

Cruzan v. Director, Missouri Department of Health

An Accident on an Icy Missouri Road

Twenty-five year old Nancy Beth Cruzan, driving on an icy Missouri road in January of 1983, lost control of her car. The accident left Cruzan brain damaged and in what doctors described as a "permanent vegetative state." She could not move, speak, or communicate, and showed no indication of thinking abilities, but was able to breath on her own. About a month after the accident a feeding tube was inserted into her stomach through which she received all her nutrition and fluids (food and water). Doctors estimated with this life support she could be kept alive another thirty years.

Clear and Convincing Evidence

By 1988, Lester and Joyce Cruzan had lost all hope that their daughter could ever emerge from her vegetative state. They asked the Missouri state hospital to remove the feeding tube. Hospital officials refused, so the parents sought a court order to have the tube removed. The trial court

THE RIGHT
TO DIE AND
ASSISTED SUICIDE

ordered removal of the tube by finding that a person in Nancy's condition had a right to direct the removal of her life supporting feeding tube.

At issue with this decision was that Nancy could not actually relate her wishes. Before the accident as a healthy active, competent young woman, Nancy had neither made a living will nor appointed anyone to make health care decisions for her if she ever became incompetent (unable to make decisions on her own). However, she had apparently once remarked that she would not want to live in a "vegetative state." Similarly, she stated "that if she couldn't do things for herself 'even halfway, let alone not at all,' she wouldn't want to live that way." The trial court had decided these statements indicated Nancy would not desire to be kept in her vegetative condition and that her parent's wishes to remove the feeding tube should be honored.

The state of Missouri appealed to the Missouri Supreme Court which reversed (changed) the lower court's ruling. A majority of members of the Missouri Supreme Court believed Nancy's remarks about her future care were general and made in a casual way. For a parent or guardian to make a decision for an incompetent patient to remove life support, under Missouri law, the patient must have left "clear and con-

vincing . . . reliable evidence" of her wishes. The court concluded that such evidence was not available from Nancy.

The Cruzans appealed to the U.S. Supreme Court which agreed to hear the case.

The Arguments

Lawyers for the Cruzan family argued before the Supreme Court that "forced . . . medical treatment, and even . . . artificially-delivered food and water [as in the case of Nancy's feeding tube]" would be a violation of a competent person's liberty. Likewise, "an incompetent person should possess the same right in this respect as is possessed by a competent person." A "substituted judgement" of close family members must be accepted, they argued, even if no proof existed that their views reflected the views of the patient. The lawyers contended that Missouri's refusal to allow the parents to direct the removal of their incompetent daughter's feeding tube was in violation of Nancy's constitutional liberty.

The state of Missouri argued that in the interest of protecting an individual's liberty to have their wishes carried out, the State requires that "clear and convincing evidence" be available and that this "rule of decision" is not prohibited by the U.S. Constitution.

U.S. Supreme Court's First Right-to-Die Ruling

In a 5-4 ruling, Chief Justice Rehnquist wrote the opinion for the majority. Rehnquist first affirmed (supported) that "the right of a competent individual to refuse medical treatment" (the right-to-die) is a "constitutionally protected liberty interest" under the Fourteenth Amendment. [The] Fourteenth Amendment provides that no State shall "deprive any person of life, liberty, or property, without due process of law." The Court clearly agreed that to deny a person the right to refuse medical treatment resulting in prolonged misery would deprive the person of their constitutional liberty.

Rehnquist described the problem before the Court, "In this Court, the question is simply and starkly whether the United States Constitution prohibits Missouri from choosing the rule of decision [using the clear evidence rule]" in such instances. Rehnquist recognized that Missouri

honestly sought to safeguard against potential abuses in such situations where persons are incompetent. The state worries that family members would not always make the decision that the incompetent person might make if they were competent. Rehnquist asked, "Does Missouri have the right to put state interests to protect life above all else when the choice between life and death is a deeply personal decision of obvious and overwhelming finality [the final ending]?"

The Supreme Court, agreeing with the Missouri Supreme Court, ruled that Missouri's law requiring clear evidence of a person's wishes for the removal of life-saving treatment was, in fact, not prohibited by the Constitution's Fourteenth Amendment. Lacking such clear wishes, the state had an honest interest in preserving human life at all costs.

Four Justices Disagree with the Majority

Justice William J. Brennan, Jr., wrote for the dissenting justices,

> **Dying is personal . . . For many, the thought of an ignoble end [not noble] steeped in decay, is abhorrent [horrible] . . . , no state interests could outweigh the rights of an individual in Nancy Cruzan's position. Whatever a state's possible interest in mandating [requiring] life-support treatment under other circumstances, there is no good to be obtained here by Missouri's insistence that Nancy Cruzan remain on life-support systems if it is indeed her wish not to do so.**

Further Explanation

Justice Sandra Day O'Connor, agreeing with the majority, expanded the meaning of the ruling. She pointed out that the Court considered both the advanced medical technology and simple food and water as the same. A person could refuse not only the complex treatment but the simple sustaining efforts. She wrote of the "difficult and sensitive" nature of right-to-die issues emphasizing that in this ruling the Court had only ruled that one state's, Missouri's, law did not violate the Constitution. However, O'Connor suggested the best place to develop "appropriate procedures for safeguarding incompetent's liberty interests is entrusted to the 'laboratory' of the states."

OREGON – LABORATORY FOR THE STATES

In the 1990s the hottest topic involving death and dying was physician-assisted suicide. U.S. Supreme Court decisions of the 1980s and 1990s showed an inclination to give states broad decision-making power to develop laws to aid a person to die with dignity. Oregon became the first state in the United States to approve an assisted-suicide law. Oregon's Death With Dignity Act legalized physician-assisted suicide took effect October 27, 1997.

The law, carefully developed with many safeguards such as psychological evaluation and a fifteen-day waiting period, allowed terminally-ill state residents to receive from a doctor a prescription for lethal drugs which the patient would use to end his life. Opponents feared that terminally-ill patients, guilt-ridden over expensive medical care, would rush to use the option. After the first year, only twenty-three patients had received prescriptions for lethal drugs. Fifteen of those actually used the drugs and died. None of the fifteen had expressed concern about medical financial problems. Instead, patients were most concerned about loss of personal autonomy (self-control) and control over the manner in which they died.

Ironically, the law has prompted improvements in health care. Hoping to avoid requests for assisted suicide, Oregon doctors showed increasing interest in relieving patient's suffering by offering seminars on improving care for the terminally ill. Also, although Oregon was already a leader in hospice care (care for the terminally ill), this type of care further expanded.

Impact

Although the Court's ruling went against the Cruzans' wishes because of Nancy's incompetency, it nevertheless did much to support patient's rights to influence medical decisions in their natural dying process. First, the Court affirmed as a constitutional right that a competent person may

**THE RIGHT
TO DIE AND
ASSISTED SUICIDE**

reject life-preserving medical treatment. Secondly, the Court ruled that a person could reject not only complex medical treatments but also food and water. Thirdly, the Court made it clear that the states are the most appropriate government bodies to best develop ways of protecting liberty interests of incompetent persons. The states could use either the "substituted judgement" of family or other means, such as clear evidence laws like Missouri.

Suggestions for further reading

Baird, Robert M., and Stuart E. Rosenbaum, eds. *Euthanasia: The Moral Issues*. Buffalo, NY: Prometheus Books, 1989.

Humphrey, Derek, and Mary Clement. *Freedom to Die: People, Politics, and the Right-to-Die Movement*. New York: St. Martin's Press, 1998.

McKhanna, Charles F. *A Time to Die: The Place for Physician Assistance*. New Haven: Yale University Press, 1999.

Vacco v. Quill
1997

Petitioners: Dennis C. Vacco, Attorney General of New York

Respondents: Timothy E. Quill, Samuel C. Klagsbrun, Howard A. Grossman

Petitioners' Claim: That New York's ban on physician-assisted suicide did not violate the Equal Protection Clause.

Chief Lawyers for Petitioners: Barbara Gott Billet, Daniel Smirlock, Michael S. Popkin

Chief Lawyers for Respondents: Laurence H. Tribe, David J. Burman, Carla A. Kerr, Peter J. Rubin, Kari Anne Smith, Kathryn L. Tucker

Justices for the Court: Stephen Breyer, Ruth Bader Ginsburg, Anthony M. Kennedy, Sandra Day O'Connor, Chief Justice William H. Rehnquist, Antonio Scalia, David H. Souter, John Paul Stevens, Clarence Thomas

Justices Dissenting: None

Date of Decision: June 26, 1997

Decision: Ruling in favor of New York state, the Court decided laws banning physician-assisted suicide do not violate the constitutional equal protection guarantees.

Significance: The ruling provided constitutional support to state laws banning physician-assisted suicide. The Court recognized a legal difference between ending life-prolonging treatment to terminally ill patients and assisted suicide.

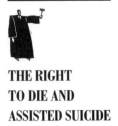

**THE RIGHT
TO DIE AND
ASSISTED SUICIDE**

Advances in medical science had greatly extended human life expectancy by the dawn of the twenty-first century. Although generally viewed as a desirable development, prolonging the lives of terminally ill (not expected to recover) patients can lead to great suffering. Desiring a quick and dignified death, terminal patients sometimes turned to others, especially physicians to help end their life. Many individuals sympathized with this need including a number of doctors (physicians) in the medical profession. Physician-assisted suicide, or simply assisted suicide, means that one individual, most often a doctor, helps another to take his own life. Generally, a physician does this by prescribing a lethal (deadly) dose of a drug which the patient may then use to commit suicide. The issue of physician-assisted suicide is hotly debated among the general public and in legislative activities.

"Right to Die," or "Death With Dignity"

The debate reached the U.S. Supreme Court in 1990 in *Cruzan v. Director, Missouri Department of Health.* In *Cruzan* the Court recognized the right of a competent (able to make decisions) adult to refuse unwanted medical treatment even if exercising that right would most likely result in death. The Court defined this right as a constitutional liberty protected under the Fourteenth Amendment. The Fourteenth Amendment provides that no state shall "deprive any person of life, *liberty,* or property, without due process of law [fair legal procedures]." To be ruled a constitutionally protected liberty, an activity must be supported by a long tradition. The Court's decision that refusing medical treatment is a protected liberty was based on an ancient common law (common practices of individuals carried on for centuries) tradition of protecting patients from unwanted medical treatment. In historical times this protective tradition was known as freedom from "unwanted touching."

In 1997 the Court tackled physician-assisted suicide in two cases, *Washington et al. v. Glucksberg* and *Vacco v. Quill,* both involving the Fourteenth Amendment. In *Washington et al.,* the Court found that physician-assisted suicide, unlike the right to refusing medical treatment, was not a constitutionally protected liberty and, therefore, not protected by Due Process Clause of the Fourteenth Amendment. The Court found that physician-assisted suicide was not rooted either in common law practices or in U.S. history. Rather, it has generally been considered a crime and prohibited in almost every state.

The Court took the opportunity in *Vacco v. Quill* (1997) to explain further the difference between refusing life sustaining support and assisted-suicide.

Dying in the State of New York

In 1965 New York passed laws prohibiting assisted suicide. By the early 1990s, New York laws allowed physicians to withhold life-prolonging treatment to terminally ill patients who did not wish to receive it. This did not mean the state endorsed physician-assisted suicide, however. New York carefully drew a line between "killing" and "letting die."

Three New York state physicians, Timothy E. Quill, Samuel C. Klagsbrun, and Howard A. Grossman, were sympathetic to patients wishing to end their lives. They were willing to prescribe lethal medication for competent, terminally-ill patients but could not because of the state's ban on assisted suicide. To challenge the ban, the three physicians and three terminally-ill patients sued the New York's attorney general, Dennis C. Vacco. The three physicians claimed New York's law violated the Equal Protection Clause of the Fourteenth Amendment. The physicians argued that terminally-ill patients receiving life-prolonging treatment could choose to die by ending the treatment, but those not receiving life-prolonging treatment could not choose to end their lives with medical assistance. They claimed refusing the treatment was essentially the same as physician-assisted suicide. Therefore, the New York law did not treat all terminally-ill competent persons wishing to end their life the same. It treated those on life support one way and those not on life support another way and, therefore, violated "equal protection under the laws."

The Equal Protection Clause commands that no state shall "deny to any person within its jurisdiction (geographical area over which it has control) the equal protection of the laws." Equal protection of the laws means individuals in like situations must be treated the same.

Upholding the state law, the District Court disagreed with the physicians but the Court of Appeals for the Second Circuit reversed (changing an earlier decision by a lower court) the district court's decision. The court of appeals viewed removal of life support and assisted suicide as like actions. Allowing those on life support to "hasten their deaths" by removing their support but not allowing those who happened not to be on life support to hasten death with prescribed drugs was unequal treatment or unequal protection under the New York law. New York appealed to the U.S. Supreme Court and the Court agreed to hear the case.

**THE RIGHT
TO DIE AND
ASSISTED SUICIDE**

The Same or Different?

Determining whether refusing life supporting medical care and physician assisted suicide are the same or different activities was the key point on which the case turned. Agreeing with the earlier district court decision, the Supreme Court ruled that New York's assisted suicide ban did not violate the Equal Protection Clause of the Fourteenth Amendment. Chief Justice William H. Rehnquist wrote the opinion for the unanimous, 9-0, Court. Rehnquist rejected the Court of Appeals' conclusion that removal of life support and assisted suicide were the same:

> **When a patient refuses life-sustaining medical treatment, he dies from an underlying fatal disease . . . but if a patient ingests lethal medication prescribed by a physician he is killed by that medication.**

Rehnquist wrote that this distinction "has been widely recognized and endorsed in the medical profession, the state courts, and the overwhelming majority of state legislatures." Since the two actions are different, they can be dealt with differently without conflicting with equal protection. According to the Rehnquist, the Equal Protection Clause "embodies [contains] a general rule that States must treat like cases alike but may treat unlike cases accordingly [differently]." Rehnquist pointed out the Constitution does not require things that are different in fact or opinion to be treated by law as though they were the same.

Chief Justice Rehnquist listed New York's many important reasons for forbidding assisted suicide:

> **prohibiting intentional killing and preserving life; preventing suicide; maintaining physicians' role as their patients' healers; protecting vulnerable people . . . pressure to end their lives; and avoiding a possible slide toward euthanasia [assisted suicide].**

A Perplexing Issue

The Court announced its decision in *Vacco* on the same day it announced its decision in *Washington et al. v. Glucksberg. Vacco* and *Washington et al.* each ruled specifically on two state laws banning assisted suicide, New York's and Washington's. The rulings confirmed states could enact

JACK KEVORKIAN

Jack Kevorkian, known as "Dr. Death" or "the suicide doctor," was born in Pontiac, Michigan in 1928. Jack's parents were Armenian refugees who had many relatives murdered in what is referred to as the Armenian holocaust during World War I. Kevorkian graduated from the University of Michigan School of Medicine in 1952 and served in the medical profession as a pathologist, a doctor who performs autopsies. One of his experiences during medical school involved dealing with a terminally-ill cancer patient who seemed to be pleading for a quick death. At this time Kevorkian decided that assisted suicide was ethical, regardless of public opinion.

Beginning in the late 1950s and continuing until the late 1980s, Kevorkian engaged in controversial research and writing concerning such topics as the appearance of the eyes of dying patients and legalizing medical experiments on death-row inmates. Kevorkian was banished from the medical establishment and did not hold a hospital staff position after 1982. By 1989 he developed a suicide machine that would allow people to kill themselves by touching a button. During the 1990s Kevorkian admittedly assisted in 130 suicides. He was charged with murder several times but always acquitted until 1999 when he was found guilty of murdering Thomas York who suffered from Lou Gehrig's disease.

Kevorkian, assisted suicide's most visible advocate, became Inmate No. 284797 in a Michigan prison. However, supporters of assisted suicide as well as opponents say he sparked their debate and brought the issue to the forefront of American society.

such laws without violating either the Due Process Clause or the Equal Protection Clause of the Fourteenth Amendment. However, several justices wrote concurring opinions (agreeing but for different reasons) that applied to both cases and expanded discussions on how to treat "death with dignity" issues.

**THE RIGHT
TO DIE AND
ASSISTED SUICIDE**

Justice Sandra Day O'Connor, joined by Justice Ruth Bader Ginsburg, stressed that finding a proper balance between the interests of terminally ill patients and the interests of society is best left to the states. Both Justice John Paul Stevens and Justice Stephen Breyer remained open to the possibility that death with dignity might include a competent patient's right to control the manner of death and degree of physician intervention. In certain situations the patient's interest in hastening death might outweigh a state's interest in preserving life.

In the year 2000 only Oregon allowed assisted suicide and no cases challenging the law had yet reached the courts. Americans continued their earnest debate about the legality and morality of physician-assisted suicide.

Suggestions for further reading

Humphrey, Derek, and Mary Clement. *Freedom to Die: People, Politics, and the Right-to-Die Movement.* New York: St. Martin's Press, 1998.

McKhanna, Charles F. *A Time to Die: The Place for Physician Assistance.* New Haven: Yale University Press, 1999.

Woodman, Sue. *Last Rights: The Struggle Over the Right to Die.* New York: Plenum Press, 1998.

Washington v. Glucksberg
1997

Petitioner: State of Washington

Respondent: Harold Glucksberg

Petitioner's Claim: That Washington's ban on assisting or aiding a suicide does not violate the Due Process Clause of the Fourteenth Amendment.

Chief Lawyer for Petitioner: William L. Williams

Chief Lawyer for Respondent: Kathryn L. Tucker

Justices for the Court: Stephen Breyer, Ruth Bader Ginsburg, Anthony M. Kennedy, Sandra Day O'Connor, Chief Justice William H. Rehnquist, Antonin Scalia, David H. Souter, John Paul Stevens, Clarence Thomas

Justices Dissenting: None

Date of Decision: June 26, 1997

Decision: Ruled that Washington's ban on assisted suicide is constitutional.

Significance: The Court ruled that assisted suicide is not a fundamental liberty protected by the Constitution. State laws prohibiting assisted suicide are, therefore, constitutional.

B y the beginning of the twenty-first century the process of dying had become complicated, involving more choices and actions. Choices about artificial life support in determining how and when an individual dies were common. Historically, assisted suicide had not been one of those choices. Assisted suicide, frequently referred to as physician-assisted suicide, means that one individual, generally a doctor, helps another person take his own life. A physician does this by prescribing a lethal (deadly) dose of a drug that the doctor knows will be used by the patient to commit suicide. The patient dies by human action, not by natural causes.

Felony in Washington

Throughout U.S. history most states prohibited assisted suicide. For example, it has always been a felony (serious) crime to assist a suicide in the state of Washington. Washington's first Territorial Legislature in 1854 outlawed "assisting another in the commission of self murder."

*Dr. Jack Kevorkian
has been a very
vocal supporter and
participant in the
assisted suicide
cause.*
Reproduced by
permission of Archive
Photos, Inc.

In 1994 four medical physicians from the state of Washington, three gravely ill patients, and Compassion in Dying, a non-profit organization that counsels people considering physician-assisted suicide, decided to challenge the modern-day Washington state law prohibiting physician assisted suicide. The physicians, who occasionally treated terminally ill patients, had said they would assist these patients in ending their lives if

not for Washington's assisted suicide ban. The Washington law provides: "A person is guilty of promoting a suicide attempt when he knowingly causes or aids another person to attempt suicide." The plaintiffs (group bringing the suit) claimed there is "a liberty interest protected by the Fourteenth Amendment which extends to a personal choice by a mentally competent terminally ill adult to commit physician assisted suicide." The Fourteenth Amendment to the Constitution provides that a state may not deprive a person of life, *liberty,* or property without the *due process of law.* Due process means all legal proceedings will be fair. The Washington law, charged the plaintiffs, is unconstitutional (does not follow the intent of the U.S. Constitution) because it bans the liberty of assisted suicide which they claim is protected by the Fourteenth Amendment's Due Process Clause. Both the liberty in question and the due process which protects it are of a special legal nature.

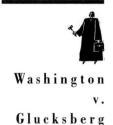

Special Liberties and Due Process

The words "physician-assisted suicide" are certainly never mentioned in the Constitution or Bill of Rights. The type of liberty the plaintiffs referred to is an "unenumerated" liberty or right. Unenumerated liberties are not written into the text of the Constitution or Bill of Rights but come from common law (common practices of individuals carried on for centuries) and philosophy, and are deeply rooted in the U.S. legal system. Such liberties are fundamental (essential) freedoms in which a person may participate relatively free from government interference. A few examples of such liberties are a person's right to marry, have children, raise children, direct their child's education, marital privacy, and the right to refuse life saving medical treatment. These abstract fundamental liberty interests have been recognized by the U.S. Supreme Court in various cases and are considered protected by the Due Process Clause of the Fourteenth Amendment. This special type of due process protection is known as substantive due process. Substantive due process protects those unenumerated liberties which are generally beyond the reach of governmental interference. The government may not regulate these liberties even by the use of fair procedures.

Is assisted suicide an unenumerated fundamental liberty? If it is, it is protected as the plaintiffs claim. If it is not, it is not protected and the state of Washington may ban it without violating the Fourteenth Amendment.

**THE RIGHT
TO DIE AND
ASSISTED SUICIDE**

Let the Courts Decide

The U.S. District Court for the Western District of Washington ruled assisted suicide a liberty protected by substantive due process and, ruling in favor of the plaintiffs, found the Washington law unconstitutional. The U.S. Court of Appeals for the Ninth Circuit agreed with the district court. The state of Washington next appealed to the U.S. Supreme Court who agreed to hear the case.

The U.S. Supreme Court, reversing the appeals court decision, ruled assisted suicide is not a fundamental liberty interest, therefore not protected by substantive due process. Chief Justice William H. Rehnquist wrote for the unanimous (9–0) court.

Determining a Liberty Interest

The Court applied a two-part test to determine what truly is a fundamental liberty interest. First, the fundamental liberty interest must be "deeply rooted in this Nation's history and tradition." On this first point Chief Justice Rehnquist wrote:

> **An examination of our Nation's history, legal traditions, and practices demonstrates that Anglo American common law has punished or otherwise disapproved of assisting suicide for over 700 years.**

Rehnquist continued that assisted suicide was certainly not rooted in U.S. history because it is considered a crime and prohibited in almost every state. The laws make no exception for those persons near death. Further, "the prohibitions have in recent years been reexamined and, for the most part reaffirmed in a number of States." In the year 2000 assisted suicide was legal only in Oregon. Thus, assisted suicide fails the first part of the test.

Second, the fundamental liberty interest must be carefully defined and described. Chief Justice Rehnquist lists the Ninth Circuit Court's various descriptions of the liberty interest as "right to die," "right to control one's final days," and "the liberty to shape death." The Court found that the Ninth Circuit Court did not properly describe the liberty interest. Redefining the liberty in dispute, Rehnquist wrote,

> **Since the Washington statute prohibits 'aid[ing], another person to attempt suicide,' the question**

before the Court is more properly characterized as whether the 'liberty' specially protected by the [Due Process] Clause includes a right to commit suicide which itself includes a right to assistance in doing so.

Therefore, it also failed the second part of the test. The Court concluded, " . . . the respondents [plaintiffs] asserted [claimed] 'right' to assistance in committing suicide is not a fundamental liberty interest protected by the Due Process Clause."

Furthermore, the Court found that Washington's assisted suicide ban was rationally (reasonably) connected to many governmental interests. Some of "these interests include prohibiting intentional killing and preserving human life; preventing the serious public health problem of suicide, . . . maintaining physicians' role as their patients' healers," and protecting vulnerable (aged, mentally retarded, and seriously ill) groups from pressure to end their life.

Washington
v.
Glucksberg

Refusal of Treatment Versus Assisted Suicide

The Court made it clear that assisted suicide is far different from a competent person's right to refuse unwanted medical treatment, even if it means such refusal would hasten their death. Assisted suicide results in a death caused by another person. When a person dies because they have refused medical treatment, they have essentially died a natural death. Historically, a person has had the right to refuse medical treatment. In *Cruzan v. Director, Missouri Department of Health* (1990) the Court affirmed as a constitutional liberty the right to reject not only life preserving medical treatment but also life sustaining food and water.

An Earnest Debate

The justices did not entirely agree on the reasoning, but all nine agreed that no fundamental right exists to assisted suicide. The Washington law banning assisted suicide was upheld. The decision left it to each individual state to decide how to most appropriately deal with the assisted suicide issue. As the Court concluded,

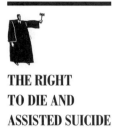

HEMLOCK SOCIETY

By the beginning of the twenty-first century many organizations, both supporting and opposing assisted suicide, promoted their beliefs through the Internet, books, and various publications. Founded in 1980 by Derek Humphrey, The Hemlock Society is the oldest and largest pro-assisted suicide organization with more than 27,000 members in the United States. As do most pro-assisted suicide groups, The Hemlock Society refers to itself as a "right-to-die organization" involved in the "right-to-die movement." The society takes its name from a poisonous herb, hemlock. The Greek philosopher, Socrates, died by drinking a hemlock brew.

Hemlock believes "that people who wish to retain their dignity and choice at the end of life should have the option of a peaceful, gentle, certain and swift death in the company of their loved ones. The means to accomplish this with . . . medication . . . prescribed by the doctor and self-administered." Hemlock educates both citizens and physicians, advocates, legislates (helps change and design the laws), and litigates (takes court action). Hemlock strongly opposes suicide for reasons other than ending the suffering of dying.

The Patients' Rights Organization (PRO-USA) is Hemlock's legislative arm. Its funds go directly into legislative efforts to change laws through lobbying and to promote state ballot measures. It has supported legislation for physician-aided dying in more than twenty states.

Throughout the Nation, Americans are engaged in an earnest and profound debate about the morality, legality, and practicality of physician-assisted suicide. Our holding permits this debate to continue, as it should in a democratic society.

Assisted suicide was legalized in Oregon in 1997. However, no case challenging the law had reached the courts in its the first few years.

Suggestions for further reading

**Washington
v.
Glucksberg**

Longwood College of Virginia Library (A comprehensive guide to doctor assisted suicide websites and literature). [Online] Website: http://web.lwc.edu/administrative/library/suic.htm.

Ontario Consultants on Religious Tolerance (all viewpoints including religious). [Online] Website: http://www.religioustolerance.org/euthanas.htm (Accessed on July 31, 2000).

The Hemlock Society. [Online] Website: http://www.hemlock.org (Accessed on July 31, 2000).

Webb, Marilyn, et al. *The Good Death: The New American Search to Reshape the End of Life.* New York: Bantam Books, 1997.

Woodman, Sue. *Last Rights: The Struggle Over the Right to Die.* New York: Plenum Press, 1998.

CIVIL RIGHTS AND EQUAL PROTECTION

An American belief in fairness is basic to present-day U.S. society. Consequently, the use of personal traits such as race, gender (sex of the person), or nationality to legally set apart one group of people from others raises serious concerns over human equality. However, this notion of equality in the United States at the beginning of the twenty-first century is not the same as when America was very young. Although the 1776 Declaration of Independence proclaimed that "all Men are created equal" with certain basic rights including "Life, Liberty, and the Pursuit of Happiness," the goal of liberty from England was stronger than striving for equality among the colonists. As a result, some classes of people enjoyed more rights than others. For example, in the first years of the nation only white male adult citizens who owned property could vote. Excluded were women, people of color, and the poor who held no property to speak of. Slavery was recognized as an important part of the nation's economy. In fact, nowhere did the term equality appear in the U.S. Constitution adopted in 1789 or the Bill of Rights of 1791.

Following the American Civil War (1861–65), Congress passed three new amendments to the Constitution, the Thirteenth, Fourteenth, and Fifteenth amendments. Collectively known as the Civil Rights

Amendments, their main purpose was to abolish slavery, provide citizenship to the newly-freed slaves, and to guarantee their civil rights. Civil rights refers to the idea of participating free from discrimination (giving privileges to one group but not another) in public activities such as voting, staying in an inn, attending a theater performance, or seeking employment. The idea of equality under the law first appeared in the Constitution with the passage of the Fourteenth Amendment ratified (approval) in 1868. The amendment contained wording that people refer to as the Equal Protection Clause. The Equal Protection Clause declares that state governments can not "deprive any person of life, liberty, or property, without due process of the law (all legal proceedings must be fair); nor deny to any person within its jurisdiction (geographical area over which authority extends) the equal protection of the laws." Equal protection of the laws means no person or persons will be denied the same protection of the laws that is enjoyed by other persons or groups.

The Long Struggle Toward Equality

Equal treatment of America's diverse population, however, did not immediately follow. When cases involving equality issues were first brought before the federal courts including the U.S. Supreme Court, the courts consistently interpreted the Fourteenth Amendment narrowly (very limited in meaning). The first major interpretation came in the *Slaughterhouse Cases* (1873). The Supreme Court held that basic civil rights of individuals were primarily protected by state law. Federal government protection was limited to a narrow set of rights such as protection on the high seas and the right to travel to and from the nation's capital. A second example of narrow interpretation came in 1883 in the ***Civil Rights Cases*** involving the Civil Rights Act of 1875 passed by Congress to enforce the Civil War Amendments. This act sought to assure equal access to public transportation and public places such as inns and theaters. The Supreme Court ruled that the Fourteenth Amendment only applied to discrimination by state governments, not to discrimination by private persons such as owners of railroads, theaters or inns. The Court ruling largely overturned (negated) the 1875 act leaving the federal government virtually powerless to control discrimination against blacks by private persons. Taking advantage of this powerlessness, the governments of many Southern states created segregation (separation of groups by race) laws in the 1880s known as Jim Crow laws. Black supporters of racial justice, such as Frederick Douglass and Ida B. Wells-Barnett (see sidebar), crusaded against the often violent treatment of African Americans.

The next major setback to those seeking true equality in access to public facilities (places) was the **Plessy v. Ferguson** (1896) decision in which the Court established the "separate but equal" rule. The rule meant that violation of the Equal Protection Clause would not occur as long as African Americans had access to the same kind of facilities as whites, even if they were separate from those used by whites. This ruling led to African Americans and whites having separate water fountains, separate public restrooms, and separate schools. The ruling basically promoted racial segregation, and rarely were the separate facilities of equal quality.

Ironically, aliens (citizens from foreign countries) initially received more favorable treatment from the courts concerning equality than African Americans. In **Yick Wo v. Hopkins** (1886) the Supreme Court ruled in favor of a Chinese laundry owner. The owner claimed a San Francisco city ordinance (law) concerning business licenses, although containing no discriminatory wording, was intended to shut down Chinese laundry businesses in the city. *Yick Wo* was the only successful equal protection challenge among the first cases brought to the Supreme Court in the decades following the ratification of the Fourteenth Amendment. In fact, the Fourteenth Amendment's guarantee of equal protection seemed useless for seventy years after it became a part of the Constitution. During those decades the Court tended to view equality in terms of protection of property rights or business interests, not individual civil rights.

A Shift to Individual Civil Rights

The historically important shift in applying equal protection to individual civil rights began to occur in the late 1930s through efforts of the National Association for the Advancement of Colored People (NAACP) and other groups. The courts responded with favorable decisions for racial minorities suffering injustices. For example, in *Missouri ex rel. Gaines v. Canada* (1938) the Supreme Court ruled in favor of an individual denied entrance into a state law school. The Court found that a requirement based solely on race violated the Equal Protection Clause.

The Modern Civil Rights Era

Two major 1954 Court decisions introduced the modern civil rights era. In the epic case of **Brown v. Board of Education,** the Supreme Court struck down the "separate but equal" rule by finding that public school segregation was unconstitutional (not following the intent of the U.S.

Constitution). A civil rights revolution was begun. That same year in *Bolling v. Sharpe* the Court held that the Due Process Clause in the Fifth Amendment prohibited racial discrimination by the federal government just as the Equal Protection Clause of the Fourteenth Amendment prohibits discrimination by state governments. The door was opened to much broader protection of individuals' civil rights.

Still, progress in society recognizing individual civil rights following decades of discrimination was slow. Numerous protests followed often involving highly publicized acts of civil disobedience (peacefully disobeying laws considered unjust) under the leadership of Dr. Martin Luther King, Jr. and others. Eventually widespread violence erupted in the nation's cities.

The Federal government began responding to the growing social unrest in the mid-1960s with a series of laws designed to further recognize civil rights and equality under the law. The 1963 Equal Pay Act required that men and women receive similar pay for performing similar work. The landmark 1964 Civil Rights Act prohibited discrimination based on race, color, national origin, or religion at most privately-owned businesses that serve the public. The 1964 act also established equal opportunity in employment on the basis of race, religion, and sex. An important Court decision occurred in 1964 as well. In **Reynolds v. Sims** the Court extended equal protection to voters rights. The "one person, one vote" rule resulting from the decision was put into law by Congress the following year in the 1965 Voting Rights Act. Prohibited were state residency requirements, poll taxes (pay a tax before voting), and candidate filing fees that traditionally were used to discriminate against poorer minority voters. In 1967 the Court in **Loving v. Virginia** ruled that state law could not prohibit interracial marriages thus recognizing the right of individuals to select their own marriage partners. A fourth important law followed in 1968 with the Fair Housing Act prohibiting discrimination in housing.

The successes of the civil rights movement of the 1950s and 1960s, focused primarily on racial discrimination, began to influence concerns over other forms of inequality. In 1971, the Court in **Reed v. Reed** overturned a state law arbitrarily discriminating against women. This decision extended the Equal Protection Clause to apply to gender discrimination. Courts also found some laws discriminatory against illegitimate children (parents not married) and unwed fathers. In *Weber v. Aetna Casualty & Surety Co.* (1972) the Court ruled that illegitimate children should have the same rights as other children. They should not be penalized through life for their parents' actions over which they had no control. Through the 1980s and 1990s equal protection issues tackled new topics such as sexual harassment, gay rights, affirmative (vigorous encouragement of increased representation of women and minorities) action, and assisted suicide (right to choose when to die).

Standards of Scrutiny

The Equal Protection Clause does not require that all people be treated equally at all times. Discrimination is sometimes legally permitted, such as not allowing people under eighteen years of age to vote in elections. The key decision often before the courts is to determine when discrimination is justified.

Through the nineteenth and twentieth centuries the Supreme Court increasingly recognized that throughout America's history some groups tended to be inappropriately discriminated against more than other groups. For example, people of color and women are two groups who have been traditionally discriminated against more than white men. Over the last 150 years of Supreme Court debates and decisions, the Court determined that to properly defend these groups' civil rights, the cases involving them would have to be looked at very closely. At the beginning of the twenty-first century the Court used three different standards or levels of examination or inquiry, called scrutiny, to test a case for equal protection violations. A case receives the highest level of scrutiny or "strict scrutiny" if it involves racial issues, aliens, or issues of nationality. At the intermediate level of scrutiny are cases involving women or "illegitimate persons" (individuals whose parents were not married). All other cases involving equal protection considerations fall into what is called "rational basis" scrutiny.

Changing Government Roles

The role of government regarding civil rights and equal protection changed dramatically through the twentieth century. Originally, the government primarily sought to resolve conflicts between individuals or other parties and to protect a private individual's behavior from government restrictions unless the behavior was extreme or endangering others. By the end of the century the government had become more of a promoter of community general welfare. It became acceptable to limit the behavior or actions of some people in order to protect the rights of others. An example is a requirement that owners of restaurants, whether they want to or not, must serve all members of the public unless questions of safety or health arise. Many saw this change as a shift from emphasis on political liberty from government rules during the eighteenth century colonial period to ensuring equality for all in the later years of the twentieth century. The Equal Protection Clause has become the primary constitutional shield for protecting the civil rights of the many groups of people in the United States.

Suggestions for further reading

Barker, Lucius J., Mack H. Jones, and Katherine Tate. *African Americans and the American Political System.* Fourth Edition. Upper Saddle River, NJ: Prentice-Hall, 1999.

Clayton, Ed. *Martin Luther King: The Peaceful Warrior.* Englewood Cliffs: Prentice-Hall, 1996.

Duster, Alfreda M. *Crusade for Justice: The Autobiography of Ida B. Wells.* Chicago: University of Chicago Press, 1970.

Weber, Michael. *Causes and Consequences of the African American Civil Rights Movement.* Austin, TX: Raintree Steck-Vaughn Publishers, 1998.

United States v. Cinque
1841

Appellant: United States

Appellees: Joseph Cinque and forty-eight other African captives

Appellant's Claim: That the slaves aboard the *Amistad* were guilty of murder and piracy for taking over the ship on which they were being transported.

Chief Lawyer for Appellant: Harry D. Gilpin, U.S. Attorney General

Chief Lawyer for Appellees: John Quincy Adams, Roger S. Baldwin

Justices for the Court: Philip P. Barbour, John Catron, John McKinley, John McLean, Joseph Story, Smith Thompson, Chief Justice Roger B. Taney, James M. Wayne

Justices Dissenting: Henry Baldwin

Date of Decision: January 1841

Decision: Found Cinque and the other captive Africans not guilty of mutiny since they were held captive in violation of international slave trade laws.

Significance: Abolitionists seeking to end slavery in the United States hailed as a victory the decision not to convict slaves from the schooner *Amistad* for killing two of their captors in order to gain freedom. Though the ruling did not directly apply to slavery, it served to fuel increasing tensions in the United States over the slavery issue ultimately leading to the American Civil War.

The verdict poster from the United States v. Cinque *case.*
Courtesy of the Library of Congress.

JOSEPH CINQUEZ.

The brave Congolese Chief, who prefers death to Slavery, and who now lies in Jail in Irons at New Haven Conn. awaiting his trial for daring for freedom.

SPEECH TO HIS COMRADE SLAVES AFTER MURDERING THE CAPTAIN &C. AND GETTING POSSESSION OF THE VESSEL AND CARGO

"*Brothers, we have done that which we purposed, our hands are now clean for we have Striven to regain the precious heritage we received from our fathers. We have only to persevere. Where the Sun rises there is our home, our brethren, our fathers. Do not seek to defeat my orders, if so I shall sacrifice any one who would endanger the rest, when at home we will kill the Old Man, the young one shall be saved he is kind and gave you bread, we must not kill those who give us water.*
Brothers, I am resolved that it is better to die than be a while mans slave, and I will not complain if by dying I save you. Let us be careful what we eat, that we may not be sick. The deed is done and I need say no more."

An extensive slave trade involving the shipping of captured Africans to the New World colonies grew in the seventeenth and eighteenth centuries. By the Revolutionary War (1776–83) over a half million black slaves lived in the American colonies. Given their importance to the economy of the Southern colonies, the U.S. Constitution did not address slavery. In fact, protection was provided to the Southern states, including a prohibition against Congress from passing legislation outlawing slavery until at least after 1808. In addition, fugitive slaves who escaped from Southern states to the North had to be returned when caught.

In 1808 Congress did begin to take action against slavery by banning the importation of new slaves into the country. With the growth throughout Europe and the United States of the abolitionist movement intent on abolishing (ending) slavery, most European nations had also outlawed the shipping of slaves to the New World by the 1830s. Among those was Spain which, under pressure from Great Britain, finally passed its own laws in 1835.

With its international power in decline, Spain was unable to enforce its restrictions. Wealthy landowners who dominated the Spanish colonies, including Cuba, needed a steady supply of slaves to work their large estates. They could not afford to obey the new Spanish law and wait for children of their existing slaves to grow up to meet their growing demand. Consequently, an illegal slave trade mushroomed despite international efforts to stop it. Slavers would capture healthy young black women and men in western Africa and ship them to Cuba for sale. Spanish colonial governmental authorities did nothing to stop this trade.

Joseph Cinque's Journey to America

In April of 1839, slavers brought yet another shipment of slaves to Havana, Cuba from what is now Sierra Leone on the West African coast. Among them was a black man known to the Spaniards as Joseph Cinque. In June, two Spaniards, Jose Ruiz and Pedro Montes, who owned estates in the Cuban town of Puerto Principe purchased fifty-three captured Africans, including Cinque. The slaves were loaded on the schooner *Amistad* under command of shipmaster Ramon Ferrer to sail along the Cuban coast from Havana to their estates.

Having left Havana on June 28 for Puerto Principe, the desperate Africans quickly saw their chance for freedom. On the night of July 1, the captives led by Cinque rebelled, killing Ferrer and a crew member, and gained control of the ship. Four of the Africans died. They spared the lives of Ruiz and Montes so they could steer the ship back home to Africa across the Atlantic Ocean.

By day the *Amistad* journeyed east and by night the two Spaniards secretly reversed their course back west. Finally, after meandering for almost two months, the winds and currents drove the schooner northward drifting along the coast of the United States. On August 26th the U.S.S. Washington spotted the *Amistad* anchored a half mile off the coast of Long Island, New York. The Americans seized the ship and crew, and

*This diagram of a
slave ship shows one
example of how
Africans were
imprisoned in very
tight quarters while
being smuggled from
their homelands.*
Courtesy of the Library
of Congress.

brought them to New London, Connecticut. U.S. authorities placed the surviving forty-nine Africans in prison.

Upon arrival in New London, Ruiz and Montes pressed their claim for the ship and its cargo including the slaves. The minister to the United States from Spain also filed a claim requesting the release of the ship and its cargo to the two Spaniards in keeping with a 1795 international treaty between the United States and Spain. Spain requested return of the slaves unless U.S. authorities determined the Africans had been illegally captured and hence not Spanish property. Wishing to avoid diplomatic headaches with Spain, U.S. President Martin Van Buren, directed U.S. District Attorney William S. Holabird to charge Cinque and the other captives with murder and piracy aboard the *Amistad.* The United States sought their return to Spanish authorities in Cuba to face punishment.

The plight of the forty-nine Africans quickly became the subject of impassioned debate in the United States between pro-slavery and anti-slavery proponents for the next two years. Seizing the case as a major opportunity to combat slavery, abolitionist Lewis Tappan led an extensive campaign arousing public sympathy for the Africans.

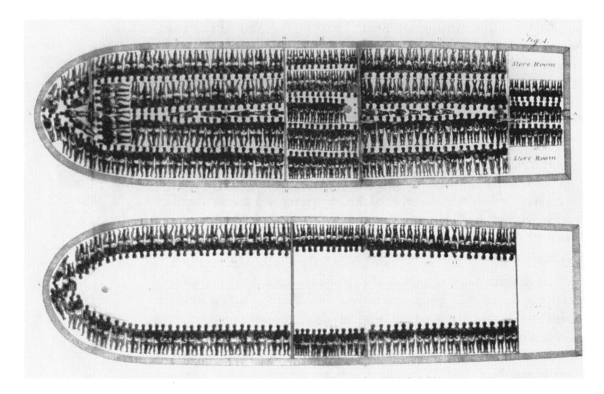

The Captives Are Not Slaves

The Africans' case went to trial in September of 1839 in the U.S. District for Connecticut in Hartford. The district court judge Andrew T. Judson. Judson had a history of rulings against blacks. Representing Cinque and the other captives were defense lawyers recruited by abolitionists. Among them was future Senator Roger S. Baldwin and former U.S. President John Quincy Adams. The defense argued that Cinque and the others had been captured in violation of Spanish law, hence they were not legal slaves and not "property" of Ruiz and Montes. Consequently, they had a right to free themselves due to the horrible conditions they had been held under. In addition, they would meet almost certain death at the hands of the Spanish colonial authorities once returned to Cuba for their actions on the *Amistad*.

United States v. Cinque

Key to the African's defense was a British official stationed in Havana, Dr. Richard R. Madden, who related his observations while traveling about Cuba. Describing the condition of Cuban slaves, Madden stated, " . . . so terrible were these atrocities [horrible treatment], so murderous the system of slavery, so transcendent [unspeakable] the evils I witnessed, over all I have ever heard or seen of the rigour [hardship] of slavery elsewhere, that at first I could hardly believe the evidence of my senses." Madden testified about the European laws banning slave trade and that the Africans had been illegally smuggled into Cuba. Consequently, they were not legal slave property.

On January 23, 1840, Judge Judson to the surprise of many including Van Buren ruled in favor of Cinque and the other Africans. Because they were attempting to free themselves from illegal capture, they were found not guilty of murder and piracy. The *Amistad* and its cargo not including the African captives would be returned to Ruiz and Montes. The United States appealed the decision to the U.S. Supreme Court.

Knowing the Supreme Court included five justices, including Chief Justice Roger B. Taney, from the South who had owned slaves, the defense for Cinque relied on the prestige of John Quincy Adams to present their case. Arguments were made on February 22, 1840. Less than a month later on March 9th, Justice Joseph Story presented the Court's decision. They voted 8-1 to uphold the lower court's decision in favor of Cinque. Cinque and the others were finally free, but no money was provided for their return to Africa. With donated private funds, the Africans finally were able to return home with two African American missionaries.

JOSEPH CINQUE

Despite having captured the imagination of the American public for three years, little is actually known about the life of the leader of the *Amistad* rebellion except for what court testimony revealed. A member of the Mende of Western Africa, his African name as translated in English was Sengbe Pieh, translated to Cinque by his Spanish captors. Cinque was from the town of Mani, about ten days walk from the African coast. Born around 1811, he was a rice farmer in his late twenties when captured in January of 1839 while walking on a trail near his home, as he recalled. He described his father as a Mende chief. He was married with three children.

Those who met Cinque during his brief stay in the United States described him as a very charismatic (influential) leader. He posed an aggressive intensity, even while in chains in an American prison. During the period between trials, Cinque traveled with abolitionist leaders giving anti-slavery speeches.

Upon returning to Africa, Cinque found that his family had been wiped out in slaving wars. Working with the American Mende Mission, Cinque traded goods along the coast and little was known of his later life. There were many rumors about his later life, including becoming a slaver himself, but no information has ever been found.

A Key Step

Though claimed a major victory by abolitionists, the decision of the Court was actually not so broadsweeping as to abolish slavery. It primarily held that Africans who were not considered slaves could not be considered property. However, the ruling was considered a major step on the road for total elimination of slavery which came over twenty years later. The story of Cinque and the *Amistad* became the subject of a major motion picture in 1997, *Amistad,* by famed director Steven Spielberg.

Suggestions for further reading

Cable, Mary. *Black Odyssey: The Case of the Slave Ship* Amistad. New York: Penguin Books, 1977.

Jones, Howard. *Mutiny on the* Amistad: *The Saga of a Slave Revolt and Its Impact on American Abolition, Law, and Diplomacy.* New York: Oxford University Press, 1987.

Martin, Christopher. *The* Amistad *Affair.* New York: Abelard-Schuman, 1970.

Owens, William A. *Black Mutiny: The Revolt on the Schooner* Amistad. Baltimore: Black Classic Press, 1997.

Prigg v. Pennsylvania
1842

Appellant: Edward Prigg

Appellee: Commonwealth of Pennsylvania

Appellant's Claim: That the Pennsylvania law under which he was convicted for returning a runaway slave to her master was unconstitutional.

Chief Lawyers for Appellant: Messrs. Meredith and Nelson

Chief Lawyer for Appellee: Mr. Johnson, Attorney General of Pennsylvania

Justices for the Court: Henry Baldwin, John Catron, Peter Vivian Daniel, John McKinley, Joseph Story, Roger Brooke Taney, Smith Thompson, James Moore Wayne

Justices Dissenting: John McLean

Date of Decision: March 1, 1942

Decision: The Supreme Court struck down Pennsylvania's law and reversed Prigg's conviction.

Significance: On one level, *Prigg* strengthened the federal government's power and weakened state power. On another level, the decision was a victory for slavery, which would divide the country in a civil war nineteen years later.

Margaret Morgan was an African American slave in Maryland in 1832. That year, Morgan escaped from her owner, Margaret Ashmore, and fled to Pennsylvania, which had abolished slavery. Morgan spent the next couple years in Pennsylvania raising her children, one of whom was born a free person in Pennsylvania.

When the United States wrote the Constitution in 1787, the states that allowed slavery wanted to make sure slaves could not escape to the free states. In Article IV of the Constitution, the framers said escaped slaves must be returned to their owners on demand. Six years later, Congress passed the first Fugitive Slave Act. The law said a slave owner could demand return of an escaped slave by getting a warrant from a federal or state judge or magistrate. The owner needed no evidence except his own word to prove that he owned an escaped slave.

In February 1837, Margaret Ashmore appointed attorney Edward Prigg as her agent to return Margaret Morgan. That month, Prigg went to see Thomas Henderson, a justice of the peace in York county, Pennsylvania, where Morgan was living. Prigg asked Henderson to arrest Morgan for delivery back to Ashmore. Henderson had the constable arrest Morgan and her children but then declined to take any more action.

Kidnapped

Prigg was determined to return Morgan to Ashmore. Using force and violence with help from three other men, Prigg captured Morgan on April 1, 1837 and took her to Maryland. There Morgan was forced back into slavery.

In March 1826, Pennsylvania had passed its own law about returning escaped slaves. The law made it a felony to kidnap a person and take her to captivity without following the proper procedures to prove she was a slave. To prove ownership, a slave owner had to present testimony from a neutral person. The purpose of the law was to make sure free people were not captured and taken to slavery in a Southern state on the strength of just the owner's word.

Pennsylvania arrested Prigg and charged him with violating the law by kidnapping Margaret Morgan. The trial court convicted Prigg and the Supreme Court of Pennsylvania affirmed. Prigg appealed to the U.S. Supreme Court.

At the time of Prigg's case, turmoil over slavery was just beginning to simmer in the United States. Northern states wanted the federal government to outlaw slavery in all new territories and states. Southern states did not think the federal government had such power. They believed each state should be free to decide for itself whether or not to allow slavery.

When Prigg appealed his case to the Supreme Court, he based his argument on the issue of federal versus state power. Prigg said the U.S. Consti-tution required Penn-sylvania to return escaped slaves to their owners by following federal law. Pennsylvania was not

Associate Justice Joseph Story.
Reproduced by permission of Archive Photos, Inc.

free to enact its own law with its own procedures for returning escaped slaves. That made Pennsylvania's law unconstitutional. Because Pennsylvania convicted Prigg under an unconstitutional law, Prigg said his conviction must be overturned.

Federal Government Reigns Supreme

With an 8–1 decision, the Supreme Court ruled in favor of Prigg. Justice Joseph Story wrote the Court's opinion. Justice Story said the Constitution clearly said states must return escaped slaves to their owners on demand. Congress, then, necessarily had the power to enact legislation to enforce that part of the Constitution. Under the Constitution, fed-

JUSTICE JOSEPH STORY

Joseph Story was born in Marblehead, Massachusetts, on September 18, 1779. He was a child of the American Revolution whose father participated in the Boston Tea Party in 1773. In 1798, Story graduated second in his class from Harvard University and went to study law in Marblehead and then Salem, Massachusetts. Story was admitted to the bar in 1801 and practiced law in Salem for the next few years.

Story served in the Massachusetts legislature from 1805 to 1808, when he was elected to the U.S. House of Representatives. A member of Jefferson's Republican-Democratic party, Story fell into disfavor with the party and ended up back in the Massachusetts legislature as speaker of the house in 1811. Later that year, President James Madison appointed Story to the U.S. Supreme Court.

As an associate justice for thirty-four years, Story supported a strong national government. During his service on the Court he also taught law at Harvard University. While at Harvard, Story wrote a famous series of treatises on American law. Story died on September 10, 1845, after a sudden illness.

eral law is the "supreme Law of the land." States cannot interfere with federal law.

The ultimate question, then, was whether Congress and the states both could enact legislation on the subject. Story said only Congress could enact appropriate legislation. Otherwise different states might enact conflicting laws. That would make the process for returning escaped slaves different from state to state. It would allow some states to make it more difficult than others made it to return escaped slaves. The Court said that would be unworkable and unfair to the Southern states.

Pennsylvania, then, had no power to enact the 1826 law under which it convicted Prigg. The Court overturned Prigg's conviction and set him free. Margaret Morgan remained in captivity in Maryland.

Impact

Prigg was a victory for the states that allowed slavery. It forced the free states to follow the federal procedure for returning escaped slaves. *Prigg* also was a victory for the federal government. It gave the federal government power to prevent the states from passing legislation in areas that the Constitution reserved for the federal government. Nineteen years later, the issues of federal power, state power, and slavery would divide the United States in the American Civil War.

Suggestions for further reading

Adams, Judith. *The Tenth Amendment.* Englewood Cliffs: Silver Burdett Press, 1991.

Batchelor, John E. *States' Rights.* New York: Franklin Watts, 1986.

Bourgoin, Suzanne Michele, and Paula Kay Byers, eds. *Encyclopedia of World Biography.* Detroit: Gale Research, 1998.

Goode, Stephen. *The New Federalism: States' Rights in American History.* New York: Watts, 1983.

Witt, Elder, ed. *Congressional Quarterly's Guide to the U.S. Supreme Court.* District of Columbia: Congressional Quarterly Inc., 1990.

Ableman v. Booth
1859

Appellants: Stephen V.R. Ableman and the United States

Appellee: Sherman M. Booth

Appellant's Claim: That Booth, who had been freed from jail by the Supreme Court of Wisconsin, should serve the sentence imposed by a federal court for helping a slave escape.

Chief Lawyer for Appellants: Jeremiah S. Black, U.S. Attorney General

Chief Lawyer for Appellee: None

Justices for the Court: John Archibald Campbell, John Catron, Nathan Clifford, Peter Vivian Daniel, Robert Cooper Grier, John McLean, Samuel Nelson, Roger Brooke Taney, James Moore Wayne

Justices Dissenting: None

Date of Decision: March 7, 1859

Decision: A state court cannot free a prisoner from confinement by the United States government.

Significance: On one level, *Ableman* strengthened the federal government's power and weakened state power by declaring federal law supreme. On another level, the decision was a victory for slavery, which would divide the country in a civil war just two years later.

The *Ableman* cases were part of the turmoil that split the United States apart in the American Civil War. Just like the war, the cases concerned the issues of slavery, the supreme power of the federal government, and states' rights.

Joshua Glover was a slave on a farm in St. Louis, Missouri. In 1852, Glover escaped from his owner, Bennami S. Garland, and fled to the free state of Wisconsin. There Glover found work at a sawmill near Racine.

Article IV of the U.S. Constitution said escaped slaves must be returned to their owners. Under the Fugitive Slave Act of 1850, Congress set up a procedure to accomplish this. The law allowed slave owners to get a warrant from a federal commissioner to return an escaped slave to captivity. The commissioners were allowed to recruit people to help the slave owner capture the escaped slave.

On March 10, 1854, Glover was playing cards with two African American friends in a cabin on the outskirts of Racine. Garland appeared at the cabin with two U.S. deputy marshals and four other men to capture Glover. Garland and his men injured Glover during a struggle, handcuffed him, and took him to a jail in Milwaukee. At the time, the federal government used state and local jails because it did not have many of its own.

Escape

Abolitionists in Milwaukee soon learned of Glover's arrest. Abolitionists were people who wanted to get rid of, or abolish, slavery. Sherman M. Booth, one of their leaders, was the fiery editor of an abolitionist newspaper. Booth rode throughout the streets of Milwaukee shouting, "Freemen! To the rescue! Slave catchers are in our midst! Be at the courthouse at two o'clock!"

On the evening of March 11, a large crowd gathered outside the Milwaukee courthouse where Glover was imprisoned. Booth gave a passionate speech attacking the return of fugitive slaves. The crowd then broke down the courthouse door, took Glover out, and put him on a ship going to Canada.

On March 15, U.S. Marshal Stephen V.R. Ableman arrested Booth under a warrant issued by a commissioner under the Fugitive Slave Act of 1850. The commissioner charged Booth with violating the Fugitive Slave Act by helping Glover escape. The commissioner ordered Booth to be held in jail for trial in the U.S. District Court in Wisconsin.

Wisconsin Challenges the Federal Government

On May 27, Booth asked Associate Justice Abram D. Smith of the Supreme Court of Wisconsin for a writ of habeas corpus. A writ of habeas corpus is an order to free someone who is being jailed in violation of the U.S. Constitution. Booth said the Fugitive Slave Act, under which he was being held for trial, was unconstitutional because it did not give escaped slaves a fair trial.

Chief Justice Roger Brooke Taney.
Courtesy of the Library of Congress.

Justice Smith agreed with Booth and ordered Ableman to set Booth free. Ableman did so but also asked the entire Supreme Court of Wisconsin to review the case. The court reviewed the case and affirmed Justice Smith's decision, so Ableman appealed to the U.S. Supreme Court.

In January 1855, before the Supreme Court had decided the case, Booth was arrested again under a new warrant from the U.S. District Court in Wisconsin. The new warrant charged Booth with the same violation as the commissioner had charged. This time, however, Booth faced a full trial and was convicted and sentenced to one month in jail and a $1,000 fine.

Once again, Booth asked the Supreme Court of Wisconsin for a writ of habeas corpus. On February 3, the court freed Booth a second time, ruling that the United States was holding him in prison under an

Often escaped slaves would set up group homes to support and aid one another in finding their way North and finding new homes.
Courtesy of the Library of Congress.

unconstitutional law. The court said the state of Wisconsin had the power to protect its citizens from wrongful federal laws. The United States appealed this decision to the U.S. Supreme Court, which said it would decide both cases together.

Federal Courts Reign Supreme

With a unanimous decision, the Supreme Court ruled in favor of Ableman and the federal government. Writing for the Court, Chief Justice Roger Brooke Taney used the Supremacy Clause of the Constitution. That Clause says the Constitution and federal laws "shall be the supreme Law of the Land, and the judges in every State shall be bound thereby." Under this clause, states cannot interfere with federal law because federal law is supreme.

By setting Booth free, the Supreme Court of Wisconsin had disregarded federal law. It made federal law inferior instead of superior. Chief Justice Taney said if states were allowed to do that, the federal government could not survive. Each state would interpret federal law differently,

FUGITIVE SLAVE ACT

In 1793, Congress passed the first Fugitive Slave Act. The law allowed slave owners to capture escaped slaves in free states and return them to slavery by getting a warrant from a federal or state judge or magistrate. The law gave slave owners the burden of capturing escaped slaves. It also made it difficult to get a warrant because there were few federal judges with that power in each state.

Southern states with slavery pressured Congress to enact a stricter law, which it did in 1850. The Fugitive Slave Act of 1850 allowed federal judges to appoint commissioners to hear slave cases. These commissioners also had power to recruit citizens to capture escaped slaves. If the commissioner decided in favor of the slave owner, he got a $10 fee. If he decided in favor of the accused slave, he only got a $5 fee. The new law obviously favored slave owners and slavery over humanity and the free states.

Northern states rebelled against the Fugitive Slave Act of 1850. Some called for repeal of the law. Many African Americans in the north left the United States for Canada. Lawyers challenged the new law in court. When those challenges failed, Northerners took to forcible resistance, fighting against slave catchers and hiding escaped slaves. Some states passed personal liberty laws to frustrate the Fugitive Slave Act.

Ableman v. Booth was one of the final victories for slave owners in the federal government. After Abraham Lincoln became president in 1860, the country split apart in a civil war over the issues of slavery and states' rights.

leading to conflict and confusion. The only solution was to require states governments and their courts to obey federal law and treat it as supreme.

Taney warned Wisconsin that it had no reason to be jealous of the federal government's power. Each state voluntarily joined the United States by agreeing to obey the U.S. Constitution. In return, the states

received protection by the federal government from other states and for-eign nations. The price of admittance, however, was to make state governments inferior to the federal government.

Because it decided that Wisconsin had no power to disregard federal law, the Supreme Court said it did not have to decide whether the Fugitive Slave Act was constitutional. Without explanation, however, the Court said the law was constitutional and the decisions by the Supreme Court of Wisconsin would have to be reversed.

Aftermath

The Supreme Court of Wisconsin ignored Chief Justice Taney's decision. The federal government, however, arrested Booth in March 1860 and put him in prison in the federal customs house in Milwaukee. A state court issued another writ of habeas corpus to release Booth, but the federal marshal ignored it. Because he would not pay his fine, Booth remained in prison until early 1861.

Suggestions for further reading

Adams, Judith. *The Tenth Amendment.* Englewood Cliffs: Silver Burdett Press, 1991.

Batchelor, John E. *States' Rights.* New York: Franklin Watts, 1986.

Brown, Thomas J., ed. *American Eras: 1850–1877.* Detroit: Gale Research, 1997.

Goode, Stephen. *The New Federalism: States' Rights in American History.* New York: Watts, 1983.

Civil Rights Cases
1883

Appellants: United States in four cases,
Mr. and Mrs. Richard A. Robinson in one case

Appellees: Stanley, Ryan, Nichols, Singleton,
Memphis & Charleston Railroad

Appellant's Claim: That their right of equal access to
various publicly used facilities was violated.

Chief Lawyers for Appellants: U.S. Solicitor General
Samuel F. Phillips; William M. Randolph for the Robinsons

Chief Lawyers for Appellees: William Y. C. Humes
and David Postern

Justices for the Court: Samuel Blatchford, Joseph P. Bradley,
Stephen Johnson Field, Horace Gray, Stanley Matthews,
Samuel Freeman Miller, Chief Justice Morrison R. Waite,
and William B. Woods.

Justices Dissenting: John Marshall Harlan I

Date of Decision: October 15, 1883

Decision: Found in favor of the appellees because the 1875
Civil Rights Act was unconstitutional.

Significance: The Court ruled 8–1 that Congress did not have the constitutional power to enforce civil rights requirements on private individuals or businesses. The decision greatly undermined the laws passed by Congress during the Reconstruction which were designed to grant equal rights to the newly freed African American slaves.

CIVIL RIGHTS AND EQUAL PROTECTION

"They raise their voices in song and dance in the streets. I wish you could see these people as they step from slavery into freedom. Families, a long time broken up, are reunited and oh! such happiness. I am glad I am here." An unknown Union officer wrote these words to his wife in 1865 at the conclusion of the American Civil War (1861–65) as slaves throughout the South took their first cautious steps as freed people. Yet, the celebration would be short-lived. The joy of freedom gave way to a struggle for black American's civil rights (personal rights belonging to an individual as a resident of a particular country).

The civil right's struggle of black Americans included not only such sweeping issues as voting rights but also seemingly simple everyday activities like freely choosing what inn or hotel to stay at, admission to a theater, or where to sit in a railroad car. Even early Supreme Court rulings, rather than furthering the civil rights of the former slaves, would actually delay the freedom process for at least four decades following the Civil War.

An Uncertain Freedom

The economic effects of the Civil War on the South were devastating with small farms as well as plantations destroyed. African Americans, although finally freed, were uneducated, poor, and still largely remained at the mercy of the white population.

The United States government began to rebuild the South with a process known as Reconstruction lasting from 1865 to 1877. The South was put under military occupation which provided a temporary measure of protection for the ex-slaves. Realizing the former slaves' liberty was insecure, Congress approved and the states ratified (approved) three amendments between 1865 and 1870, known as the Civil Rights or Reconstruction Amendments. The Thirteenth, Fourteenth, and Fifteenth Amendments together were meant to guarantee blacks liberties outlined in the Bill of Rights and ensure equal protection of the laws. Equal protection means that no person or persons will be denied the same protection of the laws that is enjoyed by other persons or groups.

Civil Rights Amendments

The Thirteenth Amendment, ratified in 1865 just eight months after the end of the Civil War, prohibited slavery. Ratified in 1868, the Fourteenth Amendment made black persons citizens and stated:

> No State shall make or enforce any law which shall abridge [take away] the privileges . . . of citizens of the United States; nor shall any State deprive [take from] any person of life, liberty or property, without due process of law [fair legal hearings]; nor deny to any person within its jurisdiction [geographic area] the equal protection of the laws.

The Fifteenth Amendment, ratified in 1870, was designed to protect the voting rights of blacks. All three ended with a section stating that Congress could enforce the amendments by passing appropriate laws.

Public Accommodations and the Fourteenth Amendment

Opposition to ending slavery remained strong in Southern states and many whites refused to treat freed slaves equally. For example, former slaves were routinely denied the use of "public accommodations" including inns, theaters, restaurants, railroad cars, and other facilities whose services are available to the general population. These denials took away black Americans' privileges as citizens of the United States in defiance of the Fourteenth Amendment. Therefore, Congress found it necessary to pass laws ensuring the enforcement of the Civil Rights Amendments. One such law, based on both the Thirteenth and Fourteenth amendments, was the Civil Rights Act of 1875. The first section of the act addressed the accommodations problem by prohibiting discrimination (giving privileges to one group but not another) in public facilities.

Whites Only

Following passage of the 1875 Civil Rights Act, many cases came to courts claiming discrimination. Five reached the Supreme Court. All five were based upon the failure of blacks to be treated the same as whites. In four of the cases, the United States, representing the black Americans, was the party bringing suit against the offenders. Two cases, against individuals named Stanley and Nichols, resulted from the denial of inn or hotel accommodations to black persons. The other two cases, filed against people named Ryan and Singleton, involved denial of theater admission. Ryan, refused to seat a black person in a certain section of Maguire's theater in San Francisco. Singleton denied a black person a seat in the Grand

CIVIL RIGHTS AND EQUAL PROTECTION

Opera House in New York. In the fifth case, Mr. and Mrs. Richard A. Robinson brought action against the Memphis and Charleston Railroad Company in Tennessee. A conductor on the line refused to allow Mrs. Robinson access to the ladies' car because she was of African descent. The Supreme Court combined the cases which became known as the *Civil Rights Cases*. All the cases, relying on the Civil Rights Act of 1875, claimed discrimination against African Americans by private individuals who denied the black persons access to public accommodations and that these denials were yet another form of slavery.

Questioning Constitutionality

Immediately, the Court identified the primary question in the *Civil Rights Cases* as whether or not the 1875 act was a constitutional law. To be constitutional a law must reflect what the U.S. Constitution and its amendment intended. If the Court found the law to be unconstitutional then none of the suits could stand. On October 15, 1883, the Court decided by an eight to one vote that neither the Thirteenth nor Fourteenth Amendment gave the United States government power to sue private persons for discrimination against black persons. Since no other basis but the Thirteenth and Fourteenth amendments were used to justify the law, the Court ruled the first and second sections of the Civil Rights Act of 1875 unconstitutional and void (no longer valid). The black Americans lost in all five cases.

Badge of Slavery

Writing the majority opinion, Justice Joseph Bradley commented the Fourteenth Amendment prohibited discriminatory actions by a state but not discrimination by private individuals. Therefore, if private business owners refused to serve or accommodate African Americans, Congress could not force them to do so. Bradley wrote, "Individual invasion of individual rights is not the subject-matter of the amendment." The Court also observed, "It [the Fourteenth Amendment] does not authorize Congress to create a code of municipal [local] law for the regulation of private rights."

Bradley also rejected the law based on the Thirteenth Amendment. Bradley stated the Thirteenth Amendment clearly allowed Congress "to enact all necessary and proper laws for the . . . prevention of slavery," but he refused to view racial discrimination as a "badge of slavery." Agreeing with the defense he observed,

JIM CROW LAWS

Following a series of Supreme Court decisions restricting Congress' power to enforce the Civil War Amendments, the Southern states in the 1880s began passing laws to keep white and black people separate in public and private places. These laws came to be known as Jim Crow laws. Named after a minstrel show character who sang a funny song which ended in the words "But everytime I turn around I jump Jim Crow." These laws made life very hard for black Americans. It seemed every time they turned around there was a strict new law.

By the early twentieth century the word segregation was used to describe the system of separating people on the basis of race. Racial segregation existed in hotels, transportation systems, parks, schools, and hospitals throughout the South for many decades.

Such an act of refusal has nothing to do with slavery or involuntary servitude. . . It would be running the slavery argument into the ground to make it apply to every act of discrimination which a person may see to make as to the guests he will entertain, or as to the people he will take into his coach or cab or car, or admit to his concert or theater.

The Lone Dissenter

Justice John Marshall Harlan I, a former slave owner, was the only justice to disagree with the majority. In a famous dissent, he argued that the spirit of the Thirteenth and Fourteenth Amendments was to guarantee equal rights to African Americans. The Civil Rights Act of 1875 had been passed with that intent in mind. Harlan pointed out that inns, theaters, and transportation vehicles, even though privately owned, are generally available to the public. Discrimination against African Americans in these accommodations was indeed a "badge of slavery." The amendments gave Congress the authority to outlaw all "badges and incidents" of slavery be they state or private actions.

**CIVIL RIGHTS
AND EQUAL
PROTECTION**

Aftermath

Over the next eighty years the *Civil Rights Cases'* decision severely limited the federal government's power to guarantee the civil rights of black Americans. Following the decision, several northern and western states enacted their own bans on discriminatory practices in public places but other states, especially Southern states, did the opposite. They began writing racial discrimination and segregation (separation of groups by race) policies into laws that became known as Jim Crow laws. The laws segregated blacks from whites in hotels, theaters, and public transportation and persisted for many decades. Not until 1964 did Congress, referring to Justice Harlan's dissent, pass the landmark Civil Rights Act of the modern era. One of its sections prohibited discrimination in public accommodations. The 1964 act's constitutionality was quickly upheld by the Supreme Court's decision in **Heart of Atlanta Motel, Inc. v. United States** thus reversing the earlier ruling in *Civil Rights Cases.*

Suggestions for further reading

Hoobler, Dorothy, and Thomas Hoobler. *The African American Family Album.* New York: Oxford University Press, 1994.

Hughes, Langston, and Milton Meltzer. *A Pictorial History of the Negro in America.* Third Revised Edition. New York: Crown Publishers, Inc., 1968.

Liston, Robert. *Slavery in America: The Heritage of Slavery.* New York: McGraw-Hill Book Company, 1972.

Medearis, Angela Shelf. *Come This Far to Freedom: A History of African Americans.* New York: Atheneum, 1993.

Meltzer, Milton, ed. *In Their Own Words: A History of the American Negro, 1865–1916.* New York: Thomas Y. Crowell Company, 1965.

Meltzer, Milton, ed. *The Black Americans: A History in Their Own Words, 1619–1983.* New York: Thomas Y. Crowell, 1984.

Myers, Walter D. *Now is Your Time! The African-American Struggle for Freedom.* New York: HarperTrophy, 1991.

Time-Life Books. *African Americans Voices of Triumph: Perseverance.* Alexandria, VA: Time-Life Books, 1993.

Yick Wo v. Hopkins
1886

Petitioner: Yick Wo

Respondent: Peter Hopkins, San Francisco Sheriff

Petitioner's Claim: That San Francisco was enforcing an ordinance (city law) in a discriminatory manner against Chinese persons.

Chief Lawyers for Petitioner: Hall McAllister, D.L. Smoot, L.H. Van Schaick

Chief Lawyers for Respondent: Alfred Clarke, H.G. Sieberst

Justices for the Court: Samuel Blatchford, Joseph P. Bradley, Stephen Johnson Field, Horace Gray, John Marshall Harlan I, Stanley Matthews, Samuel Freeman Miller, Chief Justice Morrison R. Waite, and William B. Woods

Justices Dissenting: None

Date of Decision: May 10, 1886

Decision: The earlier conviction of Yick Wo for violating the ordinance was unconstitutional.

Significance: The Court ruled that even if a law is written in a non-discriminatory way, enforcing the law in a discriminatory manner is still unconstitutional. The Court also ruled that the Equal Protection Clause of the Fourteenth Amendment applies to non-U.S. citizens as well as citizens in the country. Importantly, the case represented an early step by the Court to protect individual's civil rights.

CIVIL RIGHTS AND EQUAL PROTECTION

For Chinese men and boys who had never been more than a few miles from home, starting out on a 7,000 mile journey across the Pacific could be terrifying. Yet with hope and courage, beginning in 1849 they crowded in the holds of ships, then suffered eight long weeks of ocean voyage to arrive in America, the land they called *Gum Sahn* or Gold Mountain. The first immigrants came to work in the mines during the California gold rush of 1849. Thousands more arrived in the 1860s to help build the Central Pacific Railroad, part of the first transcontinental railroad system in the United States.

Between 1850 and 1880 the Chinese immigrant population in the United States grew from 7,000 to more than 100,000. Approximately 75,000 settled in California, which amounted to ten percent of that state's population. Half of those 75,000 lived in San Francisco. During the 1870s the hardworking Chinese became essential to the important industries of cigar making, shoemaking, woolen mills, and laundering.

Anti-Chinese Feelings

Chinese immigrants in America often faced prejudice (hateful attitudes against a group) and lived in segregated (separated by race) neighborhoods, called "Chinatowns." Not only were their customs and language very different from those of Americans, but they were willing to work for low wages. Whites feared losing their jobs to the Chinese. California experienced an economic depression (decrease in business activity with fewer jobs) in the 1870s suffering widespread unemployment and bank failures. Many unemployed workers blamed their troubles on Chinese laborers. Anti-Chinese riots took place in San Francisco in 1877. Through the 1870s the city of San Francisco passed several ordinances (city laws) to discourage Chinese settlement.

The Laundry Ordinance

By 1880 Chinese owned most laundries in San Francisco, commonly operated in wooden buildings. On May 26, 1880, during the height of white Californians' concern over the Chinese, San Francisco passed an ordinance requiring all laundries to be in brick or stone buildings. To stay in business, owners of laundries in wooden buildings had to obtain a laundry operating license issued by the city's Board of Supervisors. Failure to obtain a license while continuing to operate a laundry in a

Yick Wo v.
Hopkins

Many immigrants
found themselves
working long hours
in tough conditions.
Reproduced by
permission of the
Corbis Corporation.

wooden building could lead to a misdemeanor (less serious crime) conviction, a thousand dollar fine, and jail term of up to six months. The city had a compelling interest (important need) to pass the ordinance, to minimize fire danger. As written, the ordinance made no distinction (did not mention any difference) between laundries run by Chinese immigrants and those run by whites. Therefore, the ordinance seemed to not concern itself with the race of the laundries' operators.

However, since almost all Chinese laundries were located in wooden buildings the ordinance seemed to take aim at Chinese businesses. Additionally, the Board of Supervisors routinely approved all white applications to run laundries in wooden buildings. Yet, in 1885 the Board denied all but one of 200 Chinese applications even though their laundries had previously passed city inspections. The only Chinese owner given a license had probably not been identified as Chinese by the Board.

Yick Wo

Yick Wo, a Chinese resident of San Francisco, had lived in California since 1861 and operated a laundry for twenty-two years. In 1884 his laundry which was located in a wooden structure passed an inspection by local fire and health authorities. However, in 1885 the Board of Supervisors denied his application for a license to continue running his laundry. Wo discovered that all the owners of wooden Chinese laundries with one exception were also denied licenses.

Highly suspicious of discriminatory (giving privileges to one group but not another) practices, Wo decided to legally challenge the ordinance. He continued to operate his laundry and was arrested, convicted in police court, and ordered to pay a fine of $10. Refusing to pay the fine, he was ordered to jail for ten days. When the California Supreme Court refused to hear his case, Wo appealed to the U.S. Supreme Court which did agree to hear the case. Wo named San Francisco Sheriff Peter Hopkins, who locally enforced the ordinance, in the suit.

Homework Done, Argument Ready

Wo's lawyers argued before the U.S. Supreme Court that the ordinance was being unfairly enforced in an obviously discriminatory manner. Having done his homework, Wo supported his charge by producing statistics showing that eighty laundries located in wooden structures were legally operating under the Board of Supervisor's licensing requirements. Of those, seventy-nine were owned by non-Chinese and only one by a Chinese. Reminding the Court nearly two hundred Chinese laundries located in similar structures had been denied licenses by the San Francisco Board of Supervisors, Wo proceeded to charge the Board with seeking to wipe out the city's Chinese laundry business. Wo continued that he and the other Chinese business owners were being denied equal protection under the law, a right guaranteed to them by the Fourteenth Amendment. The amendment reads, "No State shall . . . deny to any person within its jurisdiction [geographic area over which a government has authority] the equal protection of the laws." That is, no person or persons shall be denied the same protection of the laws that is enjoyed by other persons or groups.

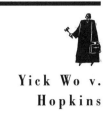

Y i c k W o v.
H o p k i n s

The city of San Francisco argued that the Fourteenth Amendment could not interfere with police powers granted by the U.S. Constitution to cities and states to enforce local laws concerning use of property.

Pledge of Equal Protection

Supreme Court Justice Stanley Matthews observed the laundry ordinance seemed to be written without intending to discriminate against anyone, legally described as "neutral on its face," and for a compelling reason, fire safety. However the ordinance was enforced in such a way to show flagrant (extreme) discrimination to one class, the Chinese. Matthews, writing for the unanimous (all members in agreement) court, penned:

"Though the law itself be fair on its face [as written] and impartial [fair] in appearance, yet, if it is applied and administered by public authority [enforced by supervisors and police] with an evil eye and an unequal hand, so as to make unjust and illegal discriminations between persons. . . "

Pointing out the clearly unjust manner with which enforcement was carried out, Matthews continued:

"While this consent [licenses granted] of the supervisors is withheld from them [the Chinese] and from two hundred others who also petitioned [applied], all of whom happen to be Chinese subjects, eighty others, not Chinese subjects, are permitted to carry on the same business under similar conditions. The fact of this discrimination is admitted. . . No reason for it exists except hostility to the race and nationality to which the petitioners belong, and which in the eye of the law is not justified."

CHINATOWNS

Upon arriving in America, Chinese banded together to live in distinct communities. The first Chinatown grew up in San Francisco in the early 1850s. With not enough timber available to supply the building needs, entire structures were often shipped from China and put back together in San Francisco. The people dressed in native costumes and kept stores as they would in China. Most Chinatown businesses were small with their street front open, vegetables and groceries overflowing on the sidewalks. Cigar stands, shoe cobblers, pharmacies with herbal medicines, fortune tellers, and gambling and opium dens shared spaces up and down a system of streets, alleys, and passages. A stranger easily could become hopelessly lost in the maze.

As anti-Chinese feelings increased, some sought new homes eastward. By 1920 thousands of Chinese lived in communities in Boston, New York, and Chicago. Only in Chinatowns did Chinese live a freer, more humane life among family and friends, creating the illusion that Chinatown was really China.

Matthews agreed with Wo that equal protection under the law granted by the Fourteenth Amendment was denied to Wo and the other Chinese businessmen.

"The discrimination is therefore, illegal, and the public administration which enforces it is a denial of the equal protection of the laws and a violation of the Fourteenth Amendment of the Constitution."

Justice Matthews also addressed the fact that Wo was an alien, a citizen of a foreign country living in the United States. He wrote the equal protection of the Fourteenth Amendment applies "to all persons within the territorial jurisdiction [geographical area of a government's authority], without regard to any differences of race, of color, or of nationality, and the equal protection of the laws is a pledge of the protection of equal laws."

With that, the Supreme Court found in favor of Yick Wo, ordered him discharged, and struck down the ordinance.

Yick Wo v. Hopkins pioneered three key ideas. First, the Fourteenth Amendment protected all persons living in the United States, not just citizens. Second, if a law has a discriminatory purpose or is enforced unfairly, even though it is neutral on its face, the courts will apply the equal protection pledge of the Fourteenth Amendment and strike down the law. Third, the case began a process of more carefully looking at laws affecting groups of people which through American history had been persistently discriminated against. However, building on the ideas proved to be a slow process. Eventually, the *Yick Wo* case became a central part of the civil rights law but not until the mid-twentieth century.

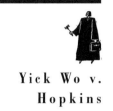

Yick Wo v. Hopkins

Suggestions for further reading

Chen, Jack. *The Chinese of America.* San Francisco: Harper & Row, 1980.

Chin, Frank. *Donald Duk.* Minneapolis, MN: Coffee House Press, 1991.

Hoobler, Dorothy, and Thomas Hoobler. *The Chinese American Family Album.* New York: Oxford University Press, 1994.

Jones, Claire. *The Chinese in America.* Minneapolis, MN: Lerner Publications Company, 1972.

McCunn, Ruthanne L. *Chinese American Portraits: Personal Histories, 1828–1988.* San Francisco: Chronicle Books, 1988.

See, Lisa. *On Gold Mountain.* New York: St. Martin's Press, 1995.

Wilson, John. *Chinese Americans.* Vero Beach, FL: Rourke Corporation, Inc., 1991.

Wu, Dana Ying-Hui, and Jeffrey Dao-Sheng Tung. *Coming to America: The Chinese American Experience.* Brookfield, CT: The Millbrook Press, 1993.

Korematsu v. United States
1944

Petitioner: Toyosaburo Korematsu

Respondent: United States

Petitioner's Claim: That convicting him for refusing to leave the West coast during World War II violated the U.S. Constitution.

Chief Lawyers for Petitioner: Wayne M. Collins and Charles A. Horsky

Chief Lawyer for Respondent: Charles Fahy, U.S. Solicitor General

Justices for the Court: Hugo Lafayette Black, William O. Douglas, Felix Frankfurter, Stanley Forman Reed, Wiley Blount Rutledge, Harlan Fiske Stone

Justices Dissenting: Robert H. Jackson, Frank Murphy, Owen Josephus Roberts

Date of Decision: December 18, 1944

Decision: The Supreme Court said Korematsu's conviction was constitutional.

Significance: In *Korematsu,* the Supreme Court tacitly approved laws and military orders that sent Japanese Americans into confinement during World War II.

On December 7, 1941, Japan brought the United States into World War II by attacking the American Pacific fleet at Pearl Harbor, Hawaii. Japan killed 2,043 Americans during the surprise attack and destroyed American warships and aircraft. The next day, Congress declared war on Japan.

After being surprised at Pearl Harbor, the United States feared Japan would attack or invade along the Pacific coast. In February 1942, President Franklin D. Roosevelt issued Executive Order 9066. President Roosevelt said wartime success depended on protecting the United States from espionage and sabotage. In his executive order, the president gave the military authority to define and take control over vulnerable areas of the country.

Lieutenant General DeWitt was in charge of the U.S. military in the westernmost part of the nation. On 27 March 1942, General Dewitt issued an order preventing persons of Japanese descent from leaving the West coast region. On May 3, 1942, General DeWitt issued another order forcing Japanese Americans to leave the West coast region through a Civil Control Station. The combined effect of both orders was to allow the United States to round up Japanese Americans for confinement in internment camps during the war. The purpose of confinement was to prevent Japanese Americans from helping the Japanese Empire in its war against the United States. The United States made no effort to distinguish between loyal and disloyal Japanese Americans.

Civil Disobedience

Toyosaburo Korematsu, who went by the name of Fred, was an American citizen of Japanese descent. Korematsu lived in San Leandro, California, near San Francisco. Korematsu was rejected for military service for health reasons but had a good job in the defense industry. Korematsu was a loyal, law-abiding American citizen in every way.

Korematsu did not think it was right for the United States to force Japanese Americans into internment camps. Instead of obeying the military orders, he fled from the San Francisco Bay area. Determined to escape confinement, Korematsu had some minor facial surgery, changed his name, and pretended to be a Mexican American. Eventually, however, he was arrested and charged with disobeying the military order to leave the West coast.

Korematsu pleaded not guilty and fought the government's case. He said the United States had no power to send an entire race of Americans into confinement when they had done nothing wrong. The court, however, convicted Korematsu and put him on probation for five years. The military then seized Korematsu, sent him to an Assembly Center, and eventually confined him in an internment camp in Topaz, Utah. Meanwhile, Korematsu took his case to the U.S. Supreme Court.

Military Orders Reign Supreme

With a 6–3 decision, the Supreme Court ruled in favor of the United States. Justice Hugo Lafayette Black wrote the Court's opinion. Justice Black said the government needs an extremely good reason for any law that limits the civil rights of an entire racial group. Sadly, the Court found a good reason in the federal government's military powers.

This young girl is waiting for her family to be checked into a internment camp. Courtesy of the Library of Congress.

The U.S. Constitution gives the president and Congress certain war powers. Congress has the power to declare war and to provide for the defense of the United States. The president is the commander-in-chief of

the military forces. Under their constitutional powers, the president and the military may do anything that is reasonable to conduct a war.

Justice Black said it was reasonable for the military to order all Japanese Americans to leave the West coast. Although not all Japanese Americans were disloyal, some were. During investigations after the relocation, five thousand Japanese Americans refused to swear unqualified allegiance to the United States or to renounce allegiance to the Japanese Emperor. Several thousand even asked to be sent back to Japan.

Justice Black said that under the war emergency that existed after Japan bombed Pearl Harbor, the government did not have time to separate the loyal from the disloyal. It was reasonable, then, to order all Japanese Americans to leave the vulnerable area of the West coast. By refusing to obey that order, Korematsu had violated federal law and his conviction was constitutional.

To the dismay of many, the Court refused to decide whether it was legal to confine Japanese Americans in internment camps. Korematsu had only been convicted for refusing to leave San Leandro to report to a Civil Control Station. He was not convicted for refusing to report to an

**Korematsu
v. United
States**

Many Japanese Americans were held at the Manzanar Internment Camp in Independence, California. Reproduced by permission of the Corbis Corporation.

JAPANESE AMERICAN RELOCATION DURING WORLD WAR II

During World War II, the United States of America, the land of the free, forced 112,000 people of Japanese ancestry to leave their homes in the West coast region. Around 70,000 of those people were American citizens. Many of them spent time in ten internment camps located in California, Arizona, Wyoming, Colorado, Utah, and Arkansas. Some who were certified as "loyal" were allowed to go free to settle in the Midwest or the East.

As they left the West coast, Japanese Americans were allowed to take only what they could carry. This forced them to sell their homes and belongings, often at unfairly low prices. A 1983 study estimated that Japanese Americans lost as much as $2 billion in property during this time to arson, theft, and vandalism. Once in the internment camps, Japanese Americans lived like prisoners. They received the barest essentials needed for survival and could not leave the camps on their own.

On December 18, 1944, the United States announced that it would close the internment camps by the end of 1945. It was not until 1988, however, that Congress apologized to Japanese Americans for their confinement. That year it passed a law giving $20,000 to each confinee who was still alive.

internment camp. Nonetheless, the Court's decision was a tacit approval of the internment of Japanese Americans during the war.

Concentration Camps

Justices Robert H. Jackson, Frank Murphy, and Owen Josephus Roberts dissented, which means they disagreed with the Court's decision. These justices thought it was unfair for the Court to avoid the question of whether internment was legal. After all, the only reason for requiring Korematsu to report to a Civil Control Station was to send him to an Assembly Center for delivery to an internment camp.

The internment of Japanese Americans deeply disturbed the dissenting justices. Justice Roberts called it a "case of convicting a citizen as a punishment for not submitting to imprisonment in a concentration camp, based on his ancestry, and solely because of his ancestry." Justice Murphy called the relocation racial discrimination that deprived Americans of their right to live, work, and move about freely. Justice Jackson warned that the Court's decision would be a "loaded weapon ready for the hand of any authority" that decided to imprison an entire race of Americans in the future.

Korematsu v. United States

Suggestions for further reading

Alonso, Karen. *Korematsu v. United States: Japanese-American Internment Camps.* Enslow Publishers, Inc., 1998.

Bondi, Victor, ed. *American Decades: 1940–1949.* Detroit: Gale Research Inc., 1995.

Chin, Steven A. *When Justice Failed: The Fred Korematsu Story.* Raintree/Steck-Vaughn, 1995.

Davis, Daniel S. *Behind Barbed Wire: The Imprisonment of Japanese Americans during World War II.* New York: Dutton, 1982.

Dictionary of American History. Vol. III. New York: Charles Scribner's Sons, 1976.

Fremon, David K. *Japanese-American Internment in American History.* Enslow Publishers, Inc., 1996.

Sinnott, Susan. *Our Burden of Shame: The Japanese-American Internment during World War II.* New York: Franklin Watts, Inc., 1995.

Stanley, Jerry. *I Am an American: A True Story of Japanese Internment.* New York: Crown Publishers, 1994.

Tunnell, Michael O., and George W. Chilcoat. *The Children of Topaz: The Story of a Japanese-American Internment Camp Based on a Classroom Diary.* Holiday House, 1996.

Boynton v. Virginia
1960

Petitioner: Bruce Boynton

Respondent: Commonwealth of Virginia

Petitioner's Claim: That arresting a black interstate bus passenger for refusing to leave a whites-only section of a bus station restaurant violated the Interstate Commerce Act and the Equal Protection Clause of the U.S. Constitution.

Chief Lawyer for Petitioner: Thurgood Marshall

Chief Lawyer for Respondent: Walter E. Rogers

Justices for the Court: William J. Brennan, Jr., Tom C. Clark, William O. Douglas, Felix Frankfurter, John Marshall Harlan II, Potter Stewart, Chief Justice Earl Warren

Justices Dissenting: Hugo L. Black, Charles E. Whittaker

Date of Decision: December 5, 1960

Decision: Ruled in favor of Boynton by finding that restaurant facilities in bus terminals that primarily exist to serve interstate bus passengers can not discriminate based on race according to the Interstate Commerce Act.

Significance: The decision supporting federal government actions in desegregating certain public facilities paved the way for further civil rights activism. Resistance to the ruling by many Southerners led to the Freedom Rides on interstate buses by young activists the following summer. The Rides in addition to other protest activities the next two years led to the 1964 Civil Rights Act banning racial discrimination in all public facilities.

Businesses known as "common carriers" are transportation companies that advertise to the public to carry passengers for a fee. States regulate carriers that operate solely within their borders, but the federal government through authority in the Commerce Clause of the U.S. Constitution regulate carriers involved in interstate (traveling from one state to another) or foreign travel.

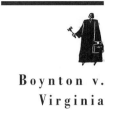

To regulate various aspects of business between states Congress passed the landmark Interstate Commerce Act in 1887 and amended it through later years. As stated in Section 203, the act applied to "all vehicles . . . together with all facilities and property operated or controlled by any such carrier or carriers, and used in the transportation of passengers or property in interstate or foreign commerce." Further, Section 216(d) of Part II of the act states,

> **It shall be unlawful for any common carrier [using a] motor vehicle engaged in interstate . . . commerce to make, give, or cause any undue or unreasonable preference [favorite choice] or advantage to any particular person . . . in any respect whatsoever; or to subject any particular person . . . to any unjust discrimination [treating individuals in similar situations differently] or any unjust or unreasonable prejudice [bias] or disadvantage in any respect whatsoever. . .**

Based on the act, the U.S. Supreme Court ruled in *Mitchell v. United States* (1941) that if a railroad provides dining cars, then passengers must be treated equally by the dining car service. Later in *Henderson v. United States* (1950) the Court further affirmed that service to passengers in railroad dining cars could not be separated according to race (racial segregation) by curtains or even signs.

Bruce Boynton

In 1958 Bruce Boynton, a black student at Howard University Law School in Washington, D.C., boarded a Trailways bus in Washington bound for his home in Montgomery, Alabama. Leaving Washington at 8:00 PM, the bus stopped at about 10:40 PM at the Trailways Bus Terminal in Richmond, Virginia. Given a forty minute stopover, Boynton got off the bus to eat a bite at the Bus Terminal Restaurant located in the terminal building. The restaurant was racially segregated (keeping racial groups from mixing), divided into sections for whites and blacks. Boynton proceeded to sit down on a stool in the white section and ordered a sandwich and tea. After refusing to move to the colored section at the request of the waitress, the assistant manager appeared and ordered Boynton to move to the other section. He insisted he was an interstate bus passenger protected by federal desegregation laws (prohibiting the practice of separating races) and did not have to move. As a result, a local police officer arrested Boynton charging him with misdemeanor trespassing. The Police Justice's Court of Richmond found Boynton guilty of violating Virginia state trespass law and fined him ten dollars.

Boynton appealed his conviction to the Hustings Court of Richmond asserting that "he had a federal right . . . to be served without discrimination by this restaurant used by the bus carrier for the accommodation of its interstate passengers." He was on the property with "authority of law." He argued that since the restaurant "was an integral part of the bus service for interstate passengers" the use of the Virginia trespass law violated the Interstate Commerce Act as well as various parts of the U.S. Constitution including the Fourteenth Amendment. The amendment reads, "nor shall any State . . . deny any person within its

Freedom Riders, following the Boynton *decision, were protected at every bus stop.* Reproduced by permission of Magnum Photos.

jurisdiction the equal protection of the laws." Nevertheless, Hustings Court confirmed his conviction.

Appeal to the Virginia Supreme Court led to the same results. With the assistance of lawyers from the National Association for the Advancement of Colored People (NAACP), Boynton next took his constitutional arguments to the U.S. Supreme Court which agreed to hear his case.

A Part of Bus Service

Presenting arguments for Boynton in October of 1960 was the future first black Supreme Court justice Thurgood Marshall. Marshall had played a key role in the earlier landmark victory in **Brown v. Board of Education** (1954) involving discrimination in public schools. Marshall pressed the issue of constitutional violations including the Fourteenth Amendment's Equal Protection Clause. The U.S. Justice Department also joined the case on behalf of Boynton raising the issue that Boynton faced "unjust discrimination" in violation of the Interstate Commerce Act. In an unusual move, the Supreme Court decided to not hear the case based on Boynton's charges of constitutional violations, but instead chose to rule on the conflict between the Interstate Commerce Act and the Virginia state law in this case.

The state of Virginia argued that the Bus Terminal Restaurant of Richmond, Inc., was neither owned nor operated by the bus company. In fact, the restaurant served the general public as well as bus passengers. Being a private company, it was not subject to the same federal law restrictions as the interstate carrier, they argued.

Justice Hugo L. Black wrote the decision of the Court. Justice Black recalled the earlier *Mitchell* and *Henderson* decisions asserting that those decisions readily applied to all transportation services in terminals and terminal restaurants provided for passengers by interstate carriers. In fact, Black stated that the facilities did not even have to be owned or operated by the carrier, but simply "an integral [important] part of transportation" that they provide. Black commented, "Interstate passengers have to eat, and they have a right to expect that this essential . . . food service . . . would be rendered [provided] without discrimination prohibited by the Interstate Commerce Act."

To address in more detail the restaurant's arguments, Black explored the relationship between Trailways bus line and the restaurant.

**CIVIL RIGHTS
AND EQUAL
PROTECTION**

He claimed the contract between the two clearly showed that, though the restaurant was open to the general public, clearly its primary purpose was to serve bus passengers. The bus line owned the building in which it leased space to the restaurant company and the restaurant paid $30,000 annually to the bus line plus a percentage of profits. Black concluded it had "a single purpose . . . to serve passengers of one or more bus companies. . . " Trailways used the restaurant facilities regularly as if it owned it thus providing "continuous cooperative transportation services between the terminal, the restaurant and buses like Trailways."

Black wrote,

> **. . . if the bus carrier has volunteered to make terminal and restaurant facilities and services available to its interstate passengers as a regular part of their transportation, and the terminal and restaurant have acquiesced [agreed] and cooperated in this undertaking, the terminal and restaurant must perform these services without discriminations prohibited by the Act.**

Ella Josephine Baker was one of the founding forces behind the Freedom Rides. Reproduced by permission of AP/Wide World Photos.

ELLA JOSEPHINE BAKER AND SNICK

The *Boynton* ruling was among many events fueling the civil rights movement of the 1950s and 1960s. One key black organizer during this period was Ella Josephine Baker. Born in Norfolk, Virginia, Baker quickly became involved in political activities concerning social justice and equality by the later 1920s. In the 1930s Baker joined the National Association for the Advancement of Colored People (NAACP) as an assistant field secretary working to increase its Southern membership. In 1957 she was a founding member of the Southern Christian Leadership Conference (SCLC) as was Dr. Martin Luther King, Jr.

To better organize the rising tide of nonviolent protests by black Americans in the 1950s, Baker founded the Student Nonviolent Coordinating Committee (SNCC), popularly known as Snick. Under Ella's direction, Snick quickly developed an aggressive approach to protests. Following the *Boynton* decision banning segregation of interstate bus facilities, Snick along with other organizations promoted the Freedom Rides of 1961. The Rides challenged segregationist policies along bus routes from Washington, D.C. to Jackson, Mississippi. After the Freedom Rides, Baker pursued voter registration efforts in the South in 1963. Later, Baker led Snick in protests against the Viet Nam War and pursued civil rights for blacks in Africa and Latin America. Ella Baker died in New York City at the age of eighty-three.

Therefore, Boynton "had a federal right to remain in the white portion of the restaurant. He was there under 'authority of law'—the Interstate Commerce Act. . . "

Black added that this decision did not mean that all independent roadside restaurants that a bus might stop at would need to comply with the anti-discrimination measures in the act, only those restaurants that "operate as an integral part of the . . . bus carrier's transportation service for interstate passengers." The Court, voting 7-2, reversed the trespass conviction and sent the case back to Virginia.

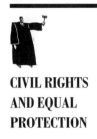

Freedom Riders

Angered by the *Boynton* decision many whites in the South ignored the ruling and continued segregationist policies for public facilities. In reaction to the Southern resistance, the "Freedom Rides" occurred in 1961. The Rides consisted of seven black and six white students riding two buses from Washington, D.C. destined for New Orleans, Louisiana. The students purposefully violated segregation policies on buses, public restrooms, terminal waiting areas, and restaurants along the way. Faced with violent reactions along the route, including one bus being fire-bombed, they ended their rides early at Jackson, Mississippi under guard of U.S. Marshalls. The Rides caught the attention of the public and Congress leading to passage of the 1964 Civil Rights Act banning racial segregation in all public facilities including restaurants and hotels.

Suggestions for further reading

Cashman, Sean D. *African Americans and the Quest for Civil Rights, 1900-1990.* New York: New York University Press, 1991.

Levine, Michael L. *African Americans and Civil Rights: From 1619 to the Present.* Phoenix, AZ: Oryx Press, 1996.

Steinhorn, Leonard, and Barbara Diggs-Brown. *By the Color of Our Skin: The Illusion of Integration and the Reality of Race.* New York: E.P. Dutton, 1999.

Thermstrom, Stephan, and Abigail Thermstrom. *America in Black and White: One Nation, Indivisible.* New York: Simon & Schuster, 1999.

Monroe v. Pape
1961

Petitioners: Mr. Monroe and his family members

Respondents: Detective Pape, the City of Chicago, and twelve other city police officers

Petitioners' Claim: That a warrantless search of a private residence conducted in a humiliating manner by police violated the families' civil rights under the 1871 Civil Rights Act.

Chief Lawyer for Petitioners: Donald P. Moore

Chief Lawyer for Respondents: Sydney R. Drebin

Justices for the Court: Hugo L. Black, William J. Brennan, Jr., Tom C. Clark, John Marshall Harlan II, William O. Douglas, Felix Frankfurter, Potter Stewart, Chief Justice Earl Warren, Charles E. Whittaker

Justices Dissenting: None

Date of Decision: February 20, 1961

Decision: Ruled in favor of Monroe by finding that Monroe could sue individual policeman, but not the city of Chicago.

Significance: The decision upheld the rights of individuals to seek compensation (payment) for abuses of their civil rights by state or local government authorities. Though excluding cities from liability (responsibility) in this case, the Court later extended liability to city and state governments in a 1978 ruling.

**CIVIL RIGHTS
AND EQUAL
PROTECTION**

Immediately after the American Civil War (1861–65), the U.S. government began rebuilding the South's society and devastated economy through a program known as Reconstruction. The program included placing the South under military occupation to provide some protection for ex-slaves. Knowing well how insecure liberty was for the former slaves, three U.S. constitutional amendments were adopted between 1865 and 1870, known as the Civil Rights Amendments. Together, the Thirteenth, Fourteenth, and Fifteenth amendments guaranteed blacks individual rights provided for in the Bill of Rights in addition to other rights. For example, the Fourteenth Amendment reads,

> **No State shall make or enforce any law which shall abridge [take away] the privileges . . . of citizens of the United States; nor shall any State deprive [take from] any person of life, liberty or property, without due process of law [fair legal hearings]; nor deny to any person within its jurisdiction [geographic area] the equal protection of the laws.**

Despite these national efforts, conditions for the former slaves improved little as many whites refused to treat freed slaves equally. A Southern white backlash rose. White supremacist (those believing one race is superior than all others) organizations, including the Ku Klux Klan established in 1866, increasingly turned to terrorist activities directed against blacks involving murder, bombings, and lynching. Often these activities were conducted with the approval if not active support of local officials and law enforcement. In other situations, local white police, juries, and judges were pressured to not protect black Americans or enforce laws. Consequently, local and state courts were often not effective in prosecuting the Klansmen.

The Ku Klux Klan Act

As violence against blacks continued to escalate, President Ulysses S. Grant urged Congress to take action. In a 1871 note to Congress, Grant wrote that in some states life and property were no longer safe and that "the power to correct these evils is beyond the control of State authorities I do not doubt." In response, Congress passed the Civil Rights Act of 1871 to enforce the Fourteenth Amendment's equal protection and due process of the laws. The act was also known as the Ku Klux Klan Act since its purpose was to protect blacks from Klan intimidation (threats of violence) and from government authorities either sympathetic to Klan goals or intimidated by Klan threats as well.

The Klan Act declared that any state or local government official, such as a police officer enforcing the law, treating a citizen in a way that denies them their constitutional rights could be held responsible to pay the wronged person for damages. The act opened the door for individuals who experienced improper police behavior, such as unreasonable searches or seizures prohibited by the U.S. Constitution's Fourth Amendment, to sue those officers for their actions. Police "search and seizure" is the inspection of a place or person for evidence related to an investigation and taking the evidence, if found, to court. To avoid Klan-influenced state or local courts, the act also gave victims the choice of going directly to federal courts concerning their charges where they might receive a fairer trial.

However, for ninety years following the law's passage courts applied it in very few instances. Courts still relied on early English legal traditions in which a person's right to sue governmental officials was very limited, a concept known as "official immunity [safe from lawsuit]." Consequently, black Americans received little protection under the 1871 act until the 1960s.

The Monroe Household Ransacked

Early in the morning of October 29, 1958 at 5:45 AM while investigating a murder case, twelve Chicago police officers led by Deputy Chief of Detectives Pape broke through two doors into the Monroe family home to conduct a search. They had obtained no search warrants beforehand. At gunpoint, the police forced all members of the family out of bed, including six children and both parents. They were forcefully led to the middle of their living room where they stood together naked. According to the Monroes' complaint, Pape struck Mr. Monroe several times with a flashlight while calling him "nigger" and "black boy." Mrs. Monroe and several of the children were pushed and kicked. The police aggressively searched the house dumping out the contents of drawers and closets on the floors and ripping mattresses open. After finding no evidence, Pape took Mr. Monroe to the police station and held him for ten hours. Pape neither brought specific charges against him nor did he bring Mr. Monroe before a judge when first arriving at the police station as legally required. Monroe was not allowed to contact an attorney as well.

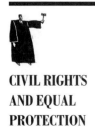
Not wanting to let matters die after their ordeal, the Monroes filed a lawsuit against the city of Chicago and the thirteen police officers in the local district court charging them in violation of the Ku Klux Klan Act. Claiming they were merely performing their duties in a potentially hazardous situation, the city and police sought a dismissal of charges and received it. The Monroes appealed but the court of appeals upheld the district court's actions. Not receiving satisfactory results locally, the Monroes decided to take their case directly to the U.S. Supreme Court. The Court agreed to hear it.

The Court Overrules

Before the Court in November of 1961, the city of Chicago and the police officers argued that federal courts had no jurisdiction (proper authority to hear the case) in such disputes between local authorities and citizens. Local courts and state laws were quite sufficient to resolve such complaints. The Monroes argued that they were denied due process under the Fourteenth Amendment because of the illegal search and seizure. In response, the Court ruled unanimously in favor of the Monroes. They could legally sue the individual police officers for damages. However, the Court upheld the lower court decisions regarding the city of Chicago. City governments were not open to lawsuit under the 1871 act.

Justice William O. Douglas, writing the Court's opinion, first asserted that the federal courts did have jurisdiction in this case. The Fourth Amendment of the Constitution prohibits unreasonable search and seizures and these prohibitions apply to states through the Due Process Clause of the Fourteenth Amendment. Regarding the Monroes' charges, Douglas affirmed that the 1871 act requires states to enforce their laws fairly for all their citizens.

Douglas wrote, "Congress has the power to enforce provisions of the Fourteenth Amendment against those who carry a badge of authority of a State and represent it in some capacity, whether they act in accordance with their authority or misuse it."

The Right to Sue Cities, Too

The *Monroe* decision brought the long neglected Ku Klux Klan Act into full effect as Congress had originally intended. The ruling allowed citizens to sue state or local authorities for damages when the authorities

THE KU KLUX KLAN

Following the American Civil War (1861–65), resentment among white Southerners quickly grew as the U.S. government introduced policies designed to restructure Southern society to include newly freed black slaves. Seeking to reestablish political control by Southern whites, a group of former Confederate soldiers in Tennessee founded the Ku Klux Klan in 1866. A secret fraternal organization opposed to the granting of civil rights to black Americans, it was not specifically created for terrorism. However, the Klan quickly became involved in violent activities, including the lynching of blacks, murders, rapes, and bombings. The goal was to scare blacks into continued social oppression. The Klan's trademark was the wearing of white robes and hoods, reportedly representing the ghosts of Confederate dead but also useful for concealing individual identities and enhancing their menacing behavior.

Membership quickly grew to several hundred thousand by 1870. As Southern whites began to regain political power in the later 1870s, the Klan's membership and influence sharply declined. However, its peak years came later in the 1920s as anitracial sentiment flared in the cities. Klan numbers grew to three or four million and its substantial political influence extended to states outside the South. The Klan helped elect to state and national positions many candidates who agreed with their cause. Faced with a public backlash by 1930, the Klan's popularity once again declined. Another smaller rise in Klan activity occurred in the 1960s in reaction to the Civil Rights Movement as the Klan became associated with several highly publicized violent acts against civil rights activists. By the 1990s Klan membership fell below 10,000 as white supremacists splintered into several organizations, including the Aryan Nations. Besides opposing civil rights for blacks, through its history the Klan has also fought against the rights of Jews, Catholics, foreign immigrants, and unions.

CIVIL RIGHTS AND EQUAL PROTECTION

behaved improperly while carrying out their official duties. However, the Court's decision that a city could not be sued still restricted the ability of victims to seek damages when city authorities had violated their civil rights. The Court later recognized the individual's right to sue cities in *Monell v. Department of Social Services* (1978). Importantly, the *Monroe* decision also affirmed that for cases involving federal civil rights violations, citizens did not have to go to possibly unsympathetic state or local courts before taking their complaints to federal courts.

Suggestions for further reading

Collins, Allyson. *Shielded From Justice: Police Brutality and Accountability in the United States.* Washington, DC: Human Rights Watch, 1998.

Horowitz, David A. *Inside the Klavern: The Secret History of a Ku Klux Klan of the 1920s.* Carbondale, IL: Southern Illinois University Press, 1999.

Jackson, Kenneth T. *The Ku Klux Klan in the City, 1915-1930.* Chicago: I. R. Dee, 1992.

Washington, Linn. *The Beating Goes On: Police Brutality in America.* Belfast, ME: Common Courage Press, 2000.

Heart of Atlanta Motel v. United States 1964

Appellant: Heart of Atlanta Motel, Inc.

Appellee: United States

Appellant's Claim: That Title II of the Civil Rights Act of 1964, requiring hotel and motel owners to provide accommodations to black Americans, cannot be enforced against privately owned establishments.

Chief Lawyer for Appellant: Moreton Rolleston, Jr.

Chief Lawyer for Appellee: Archibald Cox, U.S. Solicitor General

Justices for the Court: Hugo L. Black, William J. Brennan, Jr., Tom C. Clark, William O. Douglas, Arthur Goldberg, John Marshall Harlan II, Potter Steward, Chief Justice Earl Warren, Byron R. White

Justices Dissenting: None

Date of Decision: December 14, 1964

Decision: Ruled in favor of the United States by upholding Title II of the Civil Rights Act of 1964.

Significance: In the first major test of the landmark Civil Rights Act of 1964, the Court unanimously upheld the act. The decision greatly aided black Americans in their civil rights struggle. The Commerce Clause of the U.S. Constitution proved to be a powerful tool in the battle to end racial discrimination.

**CIVIL RIGHTS
AND EQUAL
PROTECTION**

*President Lyndon B.
Johnson signing the
Civil Rights Act
of 1964.*
Courtesy of the Library
of Congress.

More often than not, black Americans in the early 1960s had to rely on rented rooms in private homes or the hospitality of friends if they were to travel far from their home. Hotels and motels dotted along highways and in towns provided comfortable accommodations for white Americans but black Americans had no access to these establishments.

Discrimination in Accommodations

The accommodation problem was recognized as early as the 1870s when Congress passed the Civil Rights Act of 1875. The act prohibited discrimination (giving privileges to one group, but not to another similar group) in facilities such as inns and theaters which were privately owned but commonly open to the public. Yet, in *Civil Rights Cases* (1883) the U.S. Supreme Court struck down the act. Saying that discrimination prohibitions applied only to government actions, the Court ruled the act could not apply to the discriminatory actions of private persons. The government remained powerless to stop discrimination by private persons for the next eighty years.

Decades of discrimination led to the civil rights movement of the 1950s and 1960s. Civil rights are a person's individual rights set by law. Black Americans, denied their civil rights, protested in the streets. Congress responded to the social unrest by passing comprehensive civil rights legislation, the Civil Rights Act of 1964. Title II of this act prohibited discrimination based on race, color religion, or national origin in public accommodations that were in any way involved in interstate commerce. Examples of public accommodations are privately owned inns, hotels, motels, and restaurants which are open to the general public. Interstate commerce means any business or trade carried on between different states. Inns, hotels, and motels do business with guests traveling between states by providing them lodging. Therefore, they are part of interstate commerce.

Article I, Section 8 of the Constitution, known as the Commerce Clause, grants Congress the power to regulate all interstate commerce. Does Congress have the power to regulate discriminatory practices by private individuals such as owners of motels that affect interstate commerce? It had tried to do just that with passage of Title II of the Civil Rights Act of 1964. The first case challenging the constitutionality of the landmark act reached the Supreme Court within the year.

Heart of Atlanta Motel v. United States

The Heart of Atlanta Motel

The Heart of Atlanta Motel, located near interstate and state highways, had 216 rooms available to guests. The motel advertised extensively outside the state of Georgia through national media and magazines with national circulation. It also accepted convention trade from outside Georgia. Approximately 75 percent of its registered guests were from out of state. Before passage of the Civil Rights Act of 1964 the motel followed the common practice of refusing to rent rooms to black Americans. They fully intended to continue the practice. The motel's owner filed a lawsuit contending that Congress had exceeded its power under the Commerce Clause by passing Title II of the act to regulate local private businesses such as his hotel. Second, the owner claimed that the act violated "the Fifth Amendment because appellant [the owner] is deprived of the right to choose its customers and operate its business as it wishes, resulting in a taking of its liberty and property without due process of law." The Fifth Amendment says that no person shall be "deprived of life, liberty, or property, without due process of law."

**CIVIL RIGHTS
AND EQUAL
PROTECTION**

The U.S. government countered by claiming the "unavailability to Negroes of adequate accommodations interferes significantly with interstate travel" hence interferes with interstate commerce. Therefore, under the Commerce Clause Congress had not exceeded its power and could regulate "such obstructions" to interstate commerce. Furthermore, the Fifth Amendment allows "reasonable regulation" and neither the appellant's liberty nor due process was violated.

The District Court upheld Title II of the act and ordered the motel owner to stop "refusing to accept Negroes as guests in the motel by reason of their race or color." The hotel operators appealed to the U.S. Supreme Court which agreed to hear the case.

The Civil Rights Act of 1964 Upheld

Writing for a unanimous (9-0) Court which found against Heart of Atlanta Motel, Justice Tom C. Clark delivered the decision upholding Title II of the Civil Rights Act of 1964. Justice Clark wrote that in researching Congress' debate over the Civil Rights Act of 1964 the evidence was clear the difficulties black Americans encountered in their attempts to find accommodations "had the effect of discouraging travel on the part of a substantial [large] portion of the Negro community." The evidence was "overwhelming . . . that discrimination by hotels and motels impedes [interferes with] interstate travel" and, therefore, obstructs interstate commerce. Justice Clark quoting from *Caminetti v. United States* (1917) wrote "the transportation of passengers in interstate commerce, it has long been settled, is within the regulatory powers of Congress, under the commerce clause of the constitution and the authority of Congress to keep the channels of interstate commerce free . . . is no longer open to question."

Next, Justice Clark wrote that not only did the Commerce Clause authorize Congress to regulate interstate commerce but allowed it to regulate activities within a state that had a "harmful effect" on interstate commerce. Because of its harmful effect on interstate commerce, "racial discrimination by motels serving travelers, however 'local' their operations may appear" could be regulated by Congress. Although the Heart of Atlanta Motel claimed its operation was local, the Court decided that the effects of its policies and practices reached far beyond Atlanta and the state border. Congress' regulation of racial discrimination in accommodations through Title II of the Civil Rights Act of 1964 was a constitutional approach which also contributed to correcting a "moral and social wrong."

COMMERCE CLAUSE

Article I, Section 8, Clause 3 of the U.S. Constitution gives solely to Congress the power to regulate commerce between states and with foreign countries and Indian tribes. As used by the Constitution, the term commerce means all business or trade in any form between citizens. Interstate commerce is business between citizens across state lines. Sale and transportation of a product by persons in Florida to persons in Texas would be interstate commerce. In contrast, intrastate commerce is business conducted within one state only and subject to state control only.

The Commerce Clause empowers Congress to pass laws to regulate the flow of interstate commerce in order to keep interstate transactions free from local restrictions imposed by the states. If Congress finds that intrastate activities influence business between different states, it may regulate that area of intrastate commerce. For example, access to lodgings and restaurants located in each state allow persons to travel and do business from state to state. Therefore, they fall under interstate commerce regulation.

Other examples of federally regulated interstate commerce are transportation of goods between states and transmission of information across state lines by telephone, radio, television, or mail.

Turning to the issue of whether or not the Fifth Amendment rights of the owner of Heart of Atlanta Motel had been violated by Title II, the Court rejected the charge. Justice Clark found "a long line of cases" where the Court had denied the claim that "prohibition of racial discrimination in public accommodations interferes with personal liberty."

The Commerce Clause—A Powerful Tool

Heart of Atlanta Motel was the first legal challenge to the Civil Rights Act of 1964. The U.S. Supreme Court promptly and unanimously upheld

the act. This outcome was far different than the decision in the *Civil Rights Cases* (1883) which left the Civil Rights Act of 1875 useless. The Commerce Clause became a powerful tool for combating racial discrimination. It gave Congress the constitutional backing to pass legislation promoting equal rights for black Americans. In a case decided the same day, *Katzenbach v. McClung* (1964), the Court reasoned in a similar manner as in *Heart of Atlanta Motel. Katzenbach* involved a small restaurant which did not serve blacks. Its customers were mostly local, but the restaurant did purchase some supplies which originally came from out of state. Because of the purchases of these supplies, the restaurant's activities were part of interstate commerce. Therefore, the government could regulate the restaurant and require it to serve blacks. Taken together, *Heart of Atlanta Motel* and *Katzenbach* demonstrated that Congress had found an effective constitutional pathway for combating racism in America.

Suggestions for further reading

Chideya, Farai. *The Color of Our Future: Our Multiracial Future.* New York: William Morrow & Co., 1999.

Griffin, John H. *Black Like Me.* New York: Signet, 1996.

Steinhorn, Leonard, and Barbara Diggs-Brown. *By the Color of Our Skin.* New York: E.P. Dutton, 1999.

Loving v. Virginia
1967

Appellants: Mildred Jeter Loving, Richard Perry Loving

Appellee: Commonwealth of Virginia

Appellant's Claim: That Virginia state laws prohibiting interracial marriages violate the Fourteenth Amendment's equal protection and due process clauses.

Chief Lawyer for Appellants: Bernard S. Cohen

Chief Lawyer for Appellee: R.D. McIlwaine III

Justices for the Court: Hugo L. Black, William J. Brennan, Jr., William O. Douglas, Abe Fortas, John Marshall Harlan II, Potter Stewart, Chief Justice Earl Warren, Byron R. White

Justices Dissenting: None (Justice Thurgood Marshall did not participate)

Date of Decision: June 12, 1967

Decision: Ruled in favor of the Lovings by finding Virginia's laws banning interracial marriage unconstitutional.

Significance: The Court emphasized that all racial classifications are suspect and subject to strict scrutiny by the courts. Protecting an individual's freedom to choose a marriage partner, the ruling outlawed all state laws prohibiting interracial marriage.

In the United States at the beginning of the twenty-first century, Americans considered the freedom to choose a marriage partner a fundamental right. The idea that government could interfere with that choice was unthinkable. Yet, as late as 1967 laws prohibiting "miscegenation" were on the books in sixteen states. Miscegenation refers to marriage between a Caucasian (white) and a member of any other race. It was not until June of 1967 that the U.S. Supreme Court finally declared such laws unconstitutional in *Loving v. Virginia.*

Richard and Mildred Loving fought all the way to the Supreme Court for their right to be married in any state. Reproduced by permission of AP/Wide World Photos.

Interracial Marriage in Virginia

Virginia was one of the sixteen states with miscegenation laws in 1967. Three laws applied: (1) Provision 20-57 of the Virginia Code automatically voided all marriages between "a white person and a colored person" without any legal hearings; (2) 20-58 made it a crime for any white person and colored person to leave Virginia to be married and then return to live in Virginia; and, (3) 20-59 provided punishment by declaring interracial marriages a felony leading to a prison sentence of not less than one nor more than five years for each individual involved. Although

penalties for miscegenation had been common in Virginia since slavery times, Virginia's codes were based on the Racial Integrity Act of 1924. This act absolutely prohibited a white person from marrying anyone other than another white person. Virginia passed the act following World War I in a time of distrust for anyone not Caucasian. The miscegenation codes were still actively enforced into the 1960s.

Mildred Jeter and Richard Loving

In June of 1958, two Virginia residents, Mildred Jeter, a black American woman, and Richard Loving, a white man, married in the District of Columbia according to its laws. Shortly after their marriage, the Lovings returned to Caroline County, Virginia where they established their home. In October of 1958 a grand jury for the Circuit Court of Caroline County issued an indictment (charge) against the Lovings for violating Virginia's codes banning interracial (between different races) marriage. The Lovings pleaded guilty to the charge and were sentenced to one year in jail. The trial judge suspended the sentence on the condition the Lovings leave Virginia and not return together for twenty-five years. In his opinion, the trial judge stated,

> **Almighty God created the races white, black, yellow, . . . and red, and he placed them on separate continents. And, but for the interference with his arrangement, there would be no cause for such marriage. The fact that he separated the races shows that he did not intend for the races to mix.**

After their convictions, the Lovings moved to the District of Columbia. They requested a state trial court to vacate (to set aside or make void) the judgement against them on the ground that the Virginia miscegenation laws violated the Fourteenth Amendment. The Fourteenth Amendment declares that no state shall "deprive any person of life, liberty, or property, without due process of law [Due Process Clause]; nor deny to any person within its jurisdiction [geographical area over which a government has authority] the equal protection of the laws [Equal Protection Clause]." Due process of law means fair legal hearings must take place. Equal protection of the laws means persons or groups of persons in similar situations must be treated equally by the laws. The Lovings' request was denied in January of 1965 but their case moved onto the Virginia Supreme Court of Appeals the following month.

The appeals court upheld the constitutionality of the miscegenation laws and affirmed the Lovings' convictions. The court referred to its 1955 decision in *Naim v. Naim* where it concluded that Virginia had legitimate (honest) purposes for the miscegenation laws. Those purposes were "to preserve the racial integrity of its citizens," and to prevent "the corruption of blood," and "a mongrel breed of citizens." Furthermore, the appeals court asserted that for a law "containing" racial classifications (groupings of people based on some selected factor) all the Equal Protection Clause required was that both the white and black participants be punished equally thus avoiding discrimination (treating individuals in similar situations differently) claims. This equal punishment idea was known as "equal application." If both were punished equally, as was the case with the Lovings, then no violation of the Equal Protection Clause existed and, likewise, no "invidious [objectionable, intent to harm] discrimination against race." The state found support for "equal application" theory in the U.S. Supreme Court case of *Pace v. Alabama* (1883).

The Lovings next appealed to the U.S. Supreme Court which agreed to hear the case.

To the U.S. Supreme Court

In a 8–0 decision, the Court disagreed with the lower courts' decisions and reversed the Lovings' convictions. Justice Thurgood Marshall did not participate. Delivering the Court's opinion, Chief Justice Earl Warren wrote,

> **This case presents a constitutional question never addressed by this Court: whether a statutory [law] . . . to prevent marriages between persons solely on the basis of racial classifications violates the Equal Protection and Due Process Clauses of the Fourteenth Amendment.**

The Court answered the question in a two-part decision.

Race Classification Is Always Suspicious

First, the Court rejected the Virginia Supreme Court of Appeals' finding that because of "equal application," or equal punishment, there was no racial discrimination. The Court pointed out that the *Pace v. Alabama* (1883) decision had not survived later decisions by the Court. The "equal application" concept was no longer valid.

Chief Justice Warren wrote, "The clear and central purpose of the Fourteenth Amendment was to eliminate all official state sources of invidious racial discrimination." Warren continued that the Equal Protection Clause of the Fourteenth Amendment "demands" that any law based on racial classification is "suspect" (suspicious) and must be examined with rigid scrutiny (strict, intense examination). In other words, the Court automatically viewed racial classification as suspicious and would assume that it probably violated the Equal Protection Clause. A law with suspect classification would normally be judged unconstitutional unless the government could justify it with a compelling (extremely important) reason for its need. A law that's purpose is racial discrimination or antagonism can never be found constitutional.

Chief Justice Warren stated that "there can be no question" Virginia's miscegenation laws were clearly based solely on classification of people according to race. The Court, applying strict scrutiny, found no compelling (overwhelming need for) reason for Virginia's action. Therefore, Warren wrote, "There can be no doubt that restricting the freedom to marry solely because of racial classifications violates the central meaning of the Equal Protection Clause."

The Fundamental Freedom to Marry

Secondly, the Court identified marriage as one of the "basic civil rights of man."

Restricting the freedom to marry was in direct violation of the Due Process Clause of the Fourteenth Amendment. Chief Justice Warren eloquently explained,

> **to deny this fundamental freedom on so unsupportable a basis as the racial classifications [in the Virginia law], . . . classifications so directly subversive of the principle of equality at the heart of the Fourteenth Amendment is sure to deprive all the State's citizens liberty without due process of law. The Fourteenth Amendment requires that the freedom of choice to marry not be restricted by invidious racial discrimination. Under our Constitution, the freedom to marry, or not marry, a person of another race resides with the individual and cannot be infringed [restricted] by the State.**

**CIVIL RIGHTS
AND EQUAL
PROTECTION**

INTERRACIAL MARRIAGES

By 1990 there were four times as many interracial marriages as in 1960 but the overall number remained small. Considering only black-white marriages, in 1991 just 0.4 percent of total marriages were black-white couples.

With a further decline in social prejudices in the 1990s, surveys indicated young Americans were more open to the idea of interracial union. Experts predicted an increase of cross-cultural marriages involving not only black and white Americans but many other races. Between 1980 and 1996 the number of total married couples in the United States increased 10 percent to 54,664,000, but the number of interracial marriages had almost doubled to 1,260,000.

Interestingly, however, by the late 1990s many black women began to oppose the idea of interracial marriage. Instead, they preferred black to black marriages for racial strength and stabilization of the black family.

In *Loving* the Court held that all racial classifications are suspect classifications subject to strict scrutiny. It struck down all laws prohibiting interracial marriage.

Suggestions for further reading

Funderburg, Lise. *Black, White, Other: Biracial Americans Talk About Race and Identity.* New York: W. Morrow and Co., 1994.

Higginbotham, A. Leon. *Shades of Freedom: Racial Politics and Presumptions of the American Legal Press.* New York: Oxford University Press, 1996.

Kaeser, Gigi. *Of Many Colors: Portraits of Multiracial Families.* Amherst: University of Massachusetts Press, 1997.

McDonald, Laughlin, and John A. Powell. *The Rights of Racial Minorities* (ACLU Handbooks for Young Americans). New York:

Reed v. Reed
1971

Appellant: Sally Reed

Appellee: Cecil Reed

Appellant's Claim: That a Idaho law favoring the appointment of a man, merely because he was male, over a woman to be administrator of a deceased person's estate violates the Equal Protection Clause of the Fourteenth Amendment.

Chief Lawyers for Appellant: Allen R. Derr, Ruth Bader Ginsburg

Chief Lawyers for Appellee: Charles S. Stout, Myron E. Anderson

Justices for the Court: Hugo L. Black, Harry A. Blackmun, William J. Brennan, Jr., Chief Justice Warren E. Burger, William O. Douglas, John Marshall Harlan II, Thurgood Marshall, Potter Stewart, Byron R. White

Justices Dissenting: None

Date of Decision: November 22, 1971

Decision: Ruled in favor of Sally Reed by finding that Idaho's probate law discriminated against women.

Significance: This decision was the first time in the Fourteenth Amendment's 103-year history that the Supreme Court ruled that its Equal Protection Clause protected women's rights. The ruling formed the basis for protecting women's and men's rights in gender discrimination claims in many situations over the next thirty years.

The Fourteenth Amendment of the U.S. Constitution reads, "No State shall make or enforce any law which shall abridge [lessen] the privileges . . . of citizens of the United States . . . nor deny to any person within its jurisdiction [geographical area over which a government has control] the equal protection of the laws." Equal protection of the laws means persons or groups of persons in similar situations must be treated equally by the laws. Although the Fourteenth Amendment was adopted in 1868, it was 103 years before the U.S. Supreme Court applied this constitutional guarantee of equal protection to women. The Court did so with *Reed v. Reed* in 1971. Lawyer in the case and future Supreme Court Justice Ruth Bader Ginsburg labeled Reed a "turning point case." The Court for the first time held a state law invalid because it discriminated (unfairly giving privileges to one group but not to another similar group) against women.

*Associate Justice
Ruth Bader
Ginsburg.*
Courtesy of the
Supreme Court of
the United States.

The Reeds of Idaho

The case had its beginning on March 29, 1967 in Ada County, Idaho when nineteen-year-old Richard Lynn Reed, using his father's rifle, committed suicide. Richard's adoptive parents, Sally and Cecil Reed, had

separated sometime prior to his death. Richard's early childhood was spent in the custody (the legal right to make key decisions for another) of Sally, but once he reached his teenage years custody was transferred to his father. Ginsburg recalled that Sally had opposed the custody change and later believed part of the responsibility for her son's death rested with Cecil.

Probate Court

Richard died without a will, so Sally filed a petition in the Probate Court of Ada County to be administrator (director) of Richard's estate (all that a person owns), valued at less than one thousand dollars. Probate courts oversee the administration of deceased persons' estates. Cecil Reed filed a competing petition seeking to have himself appointed as the administrator of his son's estate.

Following a hearing on the two petitions, the Probate Court appointed Cecil the administrator. In deciding who would be administrator, the court did not consider the capabilities of each parent but went strictly by Idaho's mandatory (required) probate code. Section 15-312 of the code reads:

> **Administrator of the estate of a person dying intestate [to die without a valid will] must be granted to some one . . . in the following order: (1) the surviving husband or wife or . . . ; (2) the children; (3) the father or mother. . .**

Under this section "father" and "mother" were equal in being entitled (authorized) to administer the will. However, Section 15-314 provided, "Of several persons claiming and equally entitled to administer, males must be preferred to females and relatives of whole to those of the half blood."

Apparently, the probate judge considered himself bound by Section 15-314 to choose the male, Cecil, over the female, Sally, since the two were otherwise "equally entitled."

Mixed Signals

Sally appealed the Probate Court's decision to the District Court of the Fourth Judicial District. Sally's lawyer, Allen R. Derr, argued that Idaho's law violated Sally's constitutional rights of equal protection of the laws

guaranteed in the Fourteenth Amendment. The District Court agreed, held the challenged section of the law unconstitutional, and ordered the case back to the Probate Court to determine which parent was better qualified, regardless of sex, to be administrator. However, the order was not carried out since Cecil immediately appealed to the Idaho Supreme Court.

The Idaho Supreme Court rejected the District Court's ruling and reestablished Cecil, since he was male, as administrator of his son's estate. In reaching their decision, the Idaho Supreme Court looked at why the Idaho legislature had passed Section 15-314 in the first place. They found that Idaho's legislature "evidently concluded that in general men are better qualified to act as an administrator than women." Also, they found that the workload of the Probate Court would be lessened if it was not required to have a hearing every time two or more relatives petitioned to be administrator. Therefore, the Idaho Supreme Court found it neither unreasonable nor arbitrary (dictatorial, not open to other opinions) but an easy convenience for the courts to decide simply on the basis of being male or female. Sally appealed to the U.S. Supreme Court which agreed to hear the case.

Equal Protection for Women, Too

Ginsburg along with others associated with the Women's Rights Project of the American Civil Liberties Union (ACLU) joined Derr to represent Sally before the U.S. Supreme Court. Derr's team argued, as women's rights advocates had since the 1870s, that women's rights were protected under the Fourteenth Amendment's Equal Protection Clause. Cecil's lawyers argued that the Idaho law provided a reasonable way of cutting Probate Court's heavy workload.

The Court, in a unanimous (9–0) decision, ruled that the Idaho probate law violated the Fourteenth Amendment. Chief Justice Warren E. Burger, in delivering the opinion of the Court, wrote:

> **Having examined the record and considered the briefs [summaries written by the lawyers] and oral arguments of the parties, we have concluded that the arbitrary preference established in favor of males by 15-314 of the Idaho Code cannot stand in the face of the Fourteenth Amendment's command that no State deny the equal protection of the laws to any person within its jurisdiction.**

RUTH BADER GINSBURG

Born in Brooklyn, New York in 1933, Ruth Bader Ginsburg graduated Phi Beta Kappa (with high honors) in 1954 from Cornell University. She married, gave birth to her first child, then entered Harvard University Law School by 1956. As editor of the highly respected *Harvard Law Review,* she gained the nickname "Ruthless Ruthie." When her husband began work with a New York law firm, she transferred to Columbia Law School where she received her law degree in 1959, tied for first in her class.

Although an accomplished scholar, when Ginsburg sought employment she ran into the traditional stereotyping (fixed impression) of female lawyers which limited opportunities in a male-dominated profession. In addition to being female, she was also Jewish and a mother. Ginsburg persevered, eventually becoming a law professor at Rutgers University School of Law from 1963 to 1972. She then taught at Columbia Law School from 1972 to 1980, becoming the first female faculty member to earn tenure (permanent staff position).

During her time at Columbia, she was also an attorney for the American Civil Liberties Union where she founded the Women's Rights Project. Championing the rights of women, she argued six cases before the U.S. Supreme Court between 1973 and 1976 and won five of them. Ginsburg demanded equal protection be applied to gender issues and the end of discrimination along gender lines. President Jimmy Carter appointed Ginsburg in 1980 to the U.S. Court of Appeals for the District of Columbia Circuit where she served until 1993 when President Bill Clinton nominated her for Associate Justice on the U.S. Supreme Court. The Senate confirmed Ginsburg by a vote of 96-3. As a justice, Ginsburg became a tireless supporter of equal rights and equal treatment for all.

Although the Court pointed out that at times the Fourteenth Amendment allows persons or a group of persons to be put into classifications (groupings of people based on some selected factor) and treated

differently, those classifications "must be reasonable, not arbitrary" and must honestly relate to a state objective (goal). The Idaho Supreme Court had found Section 15-314's objective was to reduce workload; however, the U.S. Supreme Court found:

> **The crucial question . . . is whether 15-314 advances that objective in a manner consistent with the command of the Equal Protection Clause. We hold that it does not. To give a mandatory preference to members of either sex over members of the other, merely to accomplish the elimination of hearings . . . is to make the very kind of arbitrary legislative choice forbidden by the Equal Protection Clause of the Fourteenth Amendment; and . . . the choice . . . may not lawfully be mandated solely on the basis of sex.**

Sally Reed and her lawyers had won what women had sought in the courts for a century—Fourteenth Amendment protection of women's equal rights under the laws.

A Cornerstone for Future Cases

Reed v. Reed was the first ruling by the U.S. Supreme Court that concluded laws arbitrarily requiring gender (based on the sex of the person) discrimination were violations of the Equal Protection Clause of the Fourteenth Amendment. During the following decades, the Court used this decision as a basis to strike down many laws discriminating against women. Men also benefitted from the ruling since it prevents courts from basing opinions on generalizations about either gender.

Suggestions for further reading

American Civil Liberties Union. [Online] Website: http://www.aclu.org (Accessed on July 31, 2000).

Cullen-DuPont, Kathryn. *The Encyclopedia of Women's History in America.* New York: Facts on File, 2000.

Davis, Flora. *Moving the Mountain: The Women's Movement in America Since 1960.* Chicago: University of Illinois Press, 1999.

Ross, Susan D., Lisabelle K. Pingler, Deborah A. Ellis, and Kary L. Moss. *The Rights of Women: The Basic ACLU Guide to Women's Rights.* 3rd Edition. Carbondale: Southern Illinois University Press, 1993.

GENDER DISCRIMINATION AND SEXUAL HARASSMENT

Gender discrimination, or sex discrimination, may be described as the unfair treatment of a person because of that person's sex. Historically, females have been discriminated against in the United States based solely on their gender. The Supreme Court did not consider women under the Fourteenth Amendment's guarantee of "equal protection of the laws" until the 1970s. By the late twentieth century, civil rights laws prohibiting sex discrimination were being applied to the protection of males as well.

Fatherly Protection

Paternalism is defined as the protective behavior of a father toward his child. Like the general public's view toward women at the time, the Supreme Court's attitude toward women and their role in American society in the nineteenth century was one of paternalism. Women, they believed, belonged at home to care for their families and were much too delicate to have occupations or deal with issues outside of the home. This philosophy was used repeatedly from the 1870s until the 1960s to justify ignoring the Fourteenth Amendment's "equal protection of the laws" when issues concerning unfair treatment of women arose. Equal protection was intended to be a constitutional guarantee that no person or persons would be denied protection of the laws that is enjoyed by other persons or groups.

An early example of this disregard for the Fourteenth Amendment came in *Bradwell v. Illinois* (1873). Based completely on gender, a state refused to issue a woman a license to practice law, an apparent clear violation of "equal protection of the laws." However, the Court agreed with the state and justified their decision with a paternalistic explanation. Justice Joseph P. Bradley wrote that women's "natural . . . delicacy" made them unfit "for many of the occupations of civil life [such as being a lawyer]." Continuing, he observed that "divine ordinance [God's laws]" and the very "nature of things" indicated that a woman must remain within her home circle.

Likewise, the Court ruled in **Minor v. Happersett** (1875), that the Fourteenth Amendment did not require state governments to allow women to vote. The *Minor* decision was not erased until 1920, when the Nineteenth Amendment to the U.S. Constitution giving women the right to vote was adopted. Concerning jury duty, the Court in **Strauder v. West Virginia** (1880) decided that state governments could prohibit women from serving on juries. Concerned about women's health and morals, the Court in *Cronin v. Adams* (1904) upheld a Denver law barring the sale of liquor to women and prohibiting them to work in bars or stores where liquor was sold. The Court with the same fatherly attitude also addressed and upheld state laws setting maximum working hours for women in **Muller v. Oregon** (1908). However, for men, setting similar limitations on working hours was considered a violation of their right to work. This protective attitude was still alive in 1961 with the ruling in *Hoyt v. Florida*. In that case, the Court again upheld an exemption (free of a duty) for women from jury duty commenting, "Woman is still regarded as the center of home and family life."

Civil Rights Era of the 1950s and 1960s

Despite paternalistic views, the mid-twentieth century found many women working outside the home to support themselves and their families. Because women had traditionally been expected to remain at home with limited access to colleges, they were less educated, and thus, left with only low paying, low skill jobs. Women frequently received less pay than a man for the same job. This was based on the idea that women's earnings were less important than a man's when looking at support of families.

The civil rights movement of the 1950s and 1960s made more people aware of all types of discrimination, including gender discrimination. The fact that women were suffering from discrimination that was traditionally rooted in the nation's paternalistic attitudes became apparent to many, including members of Congress. Congress began passing legislation with the intention of fixing this unjust situation. They passed the Equal Pay Act in 1963, followed by the monumental Civil Rights Act of 1964.

Title VII of the Civil Rights Act of 1964 makes it "an unlawful employment practice for an employer . . . to discriminate against any individual with respect to his compensation [pay], terms, conditions, or privileges of employment, because of such individual's race, color, religion, sex, or national origin." Interestingly, Title VII was originally drafted to prohibit discrimination on the basis of "race, color, religion, or national origin," not sex. In a move to defeat the proposed bill, Southern conservatives added sex to the Title VII wording. The conservatives believed this addition was so outrageous that the entire bill would fail. The strategy, however, back-fired and the bill passed. President Lyndon Johnson signed the bill into law without raising any issue with the new wording prohibiting discrimination based on sex. The act also established the Equal Employment Opportunity Commission (EEOC), whose job was to create regulations to enforce the law.

Success in the 1970s

Beginning in the 1970s, women successfully challenged discrimination based on sex in the courts. With the passage of the Civil Rights Act of 1964, women finally had a law under which they could seek equal protection. The Supreme Court's first ruling that struck down a state law that unfairly discriminated against women was in *Reed v. Reed* (1971). In that case, an Idaho law gave men automatic preference over women to administer (to have charge over) the estate (all possessions) of someone who died without a will. In 1975 in **Taylor v. Louisiana,** the Court overturned the 1880 *Strauder* decision by ruling that states could not exclude women from jury duty based on sex alone. During this period, Congress continued to pass laws barring gender-based discrimination. For example, the Education Amendments of 1972 prohibited sex discrimination in all educational programs receiving federal aid. In 1973 Congress approved a bill prohibiting the denial of financial credit based on sex.

Men also sought equal protection from gender discrimination. In *Frontiero v. Richardson* (1973) the Court ruled on a military regulation that required husbands, in order to receive certain benefits, to prove they were dependents or relied on their military wife for support. A wife of a military man never had to prove dependency. Therefore, the law was based purely on gender and was struck down. Likewise, the Court struck down in *Craig v. Boren* (1976) an Oklahoma law permitting the sale of low-alcohol beer to women at the age of eighteen, but to men at the age of twenty-one.

Gender discrimination in educational programs

Title IX of the Education Amendments of 1972 prohibits gender discrimination in federally funded education programs, including athletic activities. Title IX has prompted legal action by female athletes, who claim they are not provided the same benefits, treatments, services, and opportunities as their male peers.

In 1982 the Court in **Mississippi University for Women v. Hogan** struck down a women-only admissions policy at a state university school of nursing. In yet another strike against the paternalistic view toward women, the Supreme Court in **United States v. Virginia** (1996) found a male-only admission policy practiced by Virginia Military Institute (VMI) unconstitutional (does not follow the intent of the Constitution).

Sexual harassment defined

Although great strides in fighting gender discrimination were taken in the 1970s, largely due to the Civil Rights Act of 1964, abuses falling within the category of sexual harassment generally were not addressed. Finally, in 1980 due to pressure from women's groups, the EEOC wrote and released guidelines (instructions) which defined sexual harassment. They described it as one form of sex discrimination prohibited by the 1964 act. EEOC guidelines define sexual harassment in the following way:

> **Unwelcome sexual advances, requests for sexual favors, and other verbal or physical conducts of a sexual nature constitute (are) sexual harassment when: (1) submission to (agree to) . . . or rejection of such conduct by an individual is used as the basis for employment decisions affecting such indi-**

viduals, or (2) such conduct has the purpose or effect of unreasonably interfering with an individual's work performance or creating an intimidating, hostile (threatening), or offensive working environment.

The first key word in the definition is "unwelcome." Unwelcome or uninvited sexual communication or conduct is prohibited. A court will review the whole circumstance of a reported situation to determine if the conduct was unwelcome. The next key words in the definition are sexual advances or favors. Verbal advances or favors might include oral or written requests for dates or sex, comments about the victim's body, jokes, or whistles. Physical advances or favors might include hugging, kissing, grabbing, staring, or standing very close. Cartoons or pictures of a sexual nature may also be considered advances.

Next, the EEOC guidelines distinguish between two types of sexual harassment. The first type is referred to as "quid pro quo," giving one valuable thing to receive another valuable thing. In familiar terms, this is called a "sex for jobs" situation. An example of sexual harassment that would be considered "quid pro quo" is when a supervisor seeks sex from an employee in exchange for a pay raise, a promotion, or even continuation of the employee's job. The second type of sexual harassment is referred to as "hostile working environment." An example of "hostile working environment" sexual harassment is when the repeated sexual conduct or communication of a supervisor or co-worker creates a threatening work environment for an employee. The employee's salary or job security may not be involved. However, the offensive actions have poisoned the work environment making it difficult or unpleasant for an employee to do his or her job.

Supreme Court begins to speak

The Supreme Court did not address the issue of sexual harassment until the 1986 case of **Meritor Savings Bank v. Vinson** The ruling in *Meritor* became a turning point for sexual harassment cases. The Court used the EEOC's guidelines to unanimously (all justices in agreement) decide that sexual harassment in the workplace is illegal and protected under Title VII of the Civil Rights Act of 1964. After 1986, both state courts and the Supreme Court continued to clarify (make clearer) what constituted sexual harassment.

Damages or monetary awards for victims

In 1991, the U.S. Senate held confirmation hearings on Clarence Thomas' appointment to a justice position on the Supreme Court. During the hearings Anita Hill testified that she had been sexually harassed by Thomas. Although Justice Thomas' appointment was not blocked, the hearings did bring sexual harassment to the attention of the entire nation. Partly due to this increased visibility, Congress passed the 1991 Civil Rights Act allowing for monetary payments (damages) to be paid to victims of sexual harassment.

Supreme Court adds further insights

In *Harris v. Forklift* (1993) the Court ruled that a victim has to suffer psychological damage in order to prove a hostile work environment. The Court ruled in *Burlington Industries, Inc. v. Ellerth* (1997) that a quid pro quo case could come from a single incident, but a hostile work environment generally develops over time and the victim must show "severe or pervasive (persistent over time)" conduct. Also in *Burlington Industries,* the Court outlined important steps employers could take to help them avoid liability (employer held responsible for an employees conduct), such as putting policies in place to prevent and correct sexually harassing behavior. *Faragher v. Boca Raton* (1998) provided yet another wake-up call to large employers. The Court asserted that companies must establish policies against sexual harassment by describing ways to investigate and correct wrongdoings. They must also clearly communicate these policies to their employees. Failing to communicate with employees could result in employer liability for the offensive behavior of its supervisors.

In ***Oncale v. Sundowner Offshore Services Incorporated et al.*** (1998), the Court dealt with "same sex" offenses. The Court ruled that an employee can seek damages from his employer even when the victim is sexually harassed by another employee of the same sex.

Sexual harassment in schools

Sexual harassment is prohibited in all federally funded schools under Title IX of the Education Amendments of 1972. Schools must have a policy prohibiting sexual discrimination including sexual harassment, and must inform students, employees, and parents of the policy. Similar categories of quid pro quo and hostile work environment exist under

Title IX. For example, a situation in which a teacher or coach makes sex a requirement for a passing grade would be considered quid pro quo harassment. Hostile environment, on the other hand, applies when a student is subjected to "unwelcome" and "pervasive" actions. In the academic setting, the party claiming harassment must report the incident to authorities who have the power to correct the situation within the system. In *Gebser et al. v. Lago Vista Independent School District* (1998), the Court held that a student could not recover damages for sexual harassment because school officials were never notified of the alleged harassment. Therefore, the school had no opportunity to resolve the situation.

Sexual harassment in the U.S. Military

Sexual harassment is prohibited in all branches of the military. In 1994, Secretary of Defense, William Perry, created the military's version of the EEOC, the Defense Equal Opportunity Council Task Force on Discrimination and Sexual Harassment (DEOC). The DEOC was created to investigate the procedures used by the military to register complaints and to suggest means of improving the procedures. Sexual harassment in the military can be particularly harmful to a victim's life. Victims and offenders may often live close together, and a superior in the military has great power to influence a subordinate's (soldier) future life path. Despite attempts to prevent sexual harassment in the military, top officials admitted that sexual harassment persisted within all ranks, genders, and racial groups at the end of the twentieth century.

Prevention of sexual harassment

The Supreme Court and state courts have clearly shown that they will apply EEOC guidelines in sexual harassment cases. EEOC guidelines include directions for employers on how to prevent, recognize, investigate, and resolve sexual harassment within businesses. As a result, many organizations established steps to follow with complaints. Complaints may be filed within the business or directly with the EEOC or state or local agencies responsible for fair employment practices. In severe or unresolved cases, lawsuits may be filed seeking damages (monetary payments). The ongoing battle of eliminating sexual harassment depends on constant vigilance (watchfulness) in the workplace, educational system, and the military.

Suggestions for Further Reading

Chaiet, Donna. *Staying Safe at School*. New York: Rosen Publishing Group, 1995.

O'Shea, Tracy, and Jane LaLonde. *Sexual Harassment: A Practical Guide to the Law, Your Rights, and Your Options for Taking Action*. New York: St. Martin's Griffin, 1998.

Petrocelli, William, and Barbara Kate Repa. *Sexual Harassment on the Job*. Berkeley, CA: Nolo Press, 1994.

Segrave, Kerry. *The Sexual Harassment of Women in the Workplace, 1600 to 1993*. Jefferson, NC: McFarland & Company, Inc., 1994.

Minor v. Happersett
1875

Appellant: Virginia Minor

Appellee: Reese Happersett

Appellant's Claim: That Missouri violated the U.S. Constitution by refusing to let women vote.

Chief Lawyer for Appellant: Francis Minor

Chief Lawyer for Appellee: None

Justices for the Court: Joseph P. Bradley, Nathan Clifford, David Davis, Stephen Johnson Field, Ward Hunt, Samuel Freeman Miller, William Strong, Noah Haynes Swayne, Morrison Remick Waite

Justices Dissenting: None

Date of Decision: March 29, 1875

Decision: The Supreme Court said Missouri did not violate the Constitution.

Significance: With *Minor*, the Supreme Court said voting is not a privilege of citizenship. Women did not get the right to vote nationwide until the United States adopted the Nineteenth Amendment in 1920.

**GENDER
DISCRIMINATION
AND SEXUAL
HARASSMENT**

*The fight for
women's suffrage
generated many
interesting and
witty posters.*
Courtesy of the
Library of Congress.

Many Americans consider the right to vote to be a privilege of citizenship. When the United States was born in 1776, however, voting was reserved almost exclusively for white men. Women and black men had to fight for the right to vote, which is called suffrage.

When the American Civil War ended in 1865, the United States ended slavery with the Thirteenth Amendment. Three years later in 1868, it adopted the Fourteenth Amendment to prevent states from giving black Americans fewer rights than white Americans received. The Fourteenth

Amendment says, "No State shall make or enforce any law which shall abridge [limit] the privileges and immunities of citizens of the United States." In 1870, African American men received the right to vote under the Fifteenth Amendment.

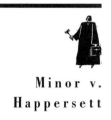

Women's Suffrage

When the United States adopted the Fourteenth Amendment, Virginia Minor was president of the Woman Suffrage Association of Missouri. At the time, Missouri's constitution said only men could vote. Minor decided to challenge the law. On October 15, 1872, Minor went to register to vote in the November 1872 presidential election. Reese Happersett, the registrar of voters, refused to register Minor because she was a woman.

With help from her husband, attorney Francis Minor, Virginia Minor filed a lawsuit against Happersett in the Circuit Court of St. Louis. Minor said Happersett violated the U.S. Constitution by refusing to register her to vote. Minor's main argument was that voting was a right of citizenship. She said the Fourteenth Amendment made it illegal for Missouri to take the right to vote away from any citizens, including women. She also said Missouri's constitution violated many other parts of the U.S. Constitution, such as the guarantee of a republican form of government.

All or Nothing at All

The Circuit Court of St. Louis and the Supreme Court of Missouri ruled in favor of Happersett. Determined to succeed, Minor appealed to the U.S. Supreme Court. She told the nation's highest court, "There can be no half-way citizenship. Woman, as a citizen of the United States, is entitled to all the benefits of that position, and liable to all its obligations, or to none."

With a unanimous decision, however, the Supreme Court ruled in favor of Happersett. Writing for the Court, Chief Justice Morrison Remick Waite said, "There is no doubt that women may be citizens." In fact, he said, women had been citizens of the United States from the very beginning, well before adoption of the Fourteenth Amendment. The question was whether all citizens are entitled to be voters.

**GENDER
DISCRIMINATION
AND SEXUAL
HARASSMENT**

*Women marched,
petitioned and
picketed for their
right to vote.*
Reproduced by
permission of Archive
Photos, Inc.

It took many dedicated and devoted volunteers to win the vote for women. Reproduced by permission of Culver Photos.

The Constitution does not define the "privileges and immunities" of citizens. To decide if the right to vote was a privilege of citizenship, Waite looked to the American colonies. When the original thirteen colonies adopted the U.S. Constitution, women could not vote anywhere except in New Jersey. Since ratification of the Constitution in 1790, no state that had been admitted to the Union allowed women to vote. Chief Justice Waite said that meant the right to vote was not a privilege of citizenship. Since suffrage was not a

THE NINETEENTH AMENDMENT

When the United States declared independence in 1776, New Jersey was the only colony that allowed women to vote. It took 144 years for the United States to give women the right to vote nationwide with the Nineteenth Amendment in 1920.

The Nineteenth Amendment was the achievement of the women's suffrage movement that began at the Seneca Falls Convention of 1848. Elizabeth Cady Stanton started the movement there by writing the Seneca Falls Declaration of Rights and Sentiments. Over the next seven decades, women fought for suffrage through groups such as the National Woman Suffrage Association, the American Woman Suffrage Association, the National American Woman Suffrage Association, and the Congressional Union for Woman Suffrage.

In 1866, Democratic Representative James Brooks of New York offered the first women's suffrage amendment in Congress. Congressmen offered similar amendments on a regular basis beginning in 1880, only to be defeated time after time. In May 1919, President Woodrow Wilson called a special session of Congress to consider the Nineteenth Amendment. The Senate finally passed it that month and the United States ratified, or approved, it in August 1920.

privilege of citizenship, the Fourteenth Amendment did not prevent states from denying the right to women.

Impact

At the end of his opinion, Chief Justice Waite said, "Our province is to decide what the law is, not to declare what it should be. ... If the law is wrong, it ought to be changed; but the power for that is not with us." The power, of course, was with the people of the United States through their representatives in Congress and state government. It was not until 1920, forty-five years after *Minor v. Happersett,* that the United States gave the right to vote to women and men alike.

Suggestions for further reading

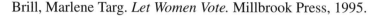

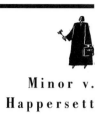

Baughman, Judith S., ed. *American Decades: 1920–1929.* Detroit: Gale Research Inc., 1996.

Brill, Marlene Targ. *Let Women Vote.* Millbrook Press, 1995.

Frost, Elizabeth, and Kathryn Cullen-DuPont. *Women's Suffrage in America: An Eyewitness History.* New York: Facts on File, 1992.

Grote, Joann A. *Women Win the Vote.* Barbour & Co., 1998.

Harvey, Miles. *Women's Voting Rights.* Children's Press, 1998.

Meyers, Madeleine. *Forward into the Light: The Struggle for Women's Suffrage.* Lowell: Discovery Enterprises, 1994.

Nash, Carol Rust. *The Fight for Women's Right to Vote in American History.* Enslow Publishers, Inc., 1998.

Pascoe, Elaine. *The Right to Vote.* Millbrook Press, 2000.

Vile, John R., ed. *Encyclopedia of Constitutional Amendments, Proposed Amendments, and Amending Issues.* Santa Barbara: ABC-CLIO, Inc., 1996.

Michael M. v. Superior Court of Sonoma County
1981

Petitioner: Michael M.

Respondent: Superior Court of Sonoma County

Petitioner's Claim: That the California "statutory rape" statute unlawfully discriminated on the basis of gender.

Chief Lawyer for Petitioner: Gregory F. Jilka

Chief Lawyer for Respondent: Sandy R. Kriegler

Justices for the Court: Harry A. Blackmun, Chief Justice Warren E. Burger, Lewis F. Powell, Jr., William H. Rehnquist, Potter Stewart

Justices Dissenting: William J. Brennan, Jr., Thurgood Marshall, John Paul Stevens, Byron R. White

Date of Decision: March 23, 1981

Decision: Ruled in favor of the state of California, upholding its statutory rape law.

Significance: Using intermediate scrutiny, the Court upheld a gender-based distinction in criminal law because it addressed an important state goal.

On the summer evening of June 3, 1978, three males including a seventeen-year-old male named Michael M. approached a sixteen-year-old female, Sharon, and her sister. Michael and Sharon, although they had not known each other previously, left the group. Sharon recalled what happened next in a preliminary hearing.

> **We were drinking at the railroad tracks and we walked over to this bush and he started kissing me and stuff, and I was kissing him back, too, at first. Then I was telling him to stop . . . and I was telling him to slow down and stop. He said, 'Okay, okay.' But then he just kept doing it . . . he asked me if I wanted to walk him over to the park; so we walked over to the park and we sat down on a bench and then he started kissing me again and we were laying on the bench. And he told me to take my pants off . . . I said, 'No,' and I was trying to get up and he hit me back down on the bench and then I just said to myself, 'Forget it,' and I let him do what he wanted to do. . .**

Sharon then had sexual intercourse with Michael.

Statutory Rape

A criminal charge was filed in the Municipal Court of Sonoma County, California, claiming that Michael M. had unlawful sexual intercourse with a woman under the age of eighteen. This action violated California's "statutory rape" law. Statutory rape is the crime of having sexual intercourse with a female under an age set by statute (law passed by a legislature), regardless of whether or not she consents (agrees) to the act. Under California's statutory rape law, when two people between the ages of fourteen and seventeen had sexual intercourse and they were not married, the male was guilty of statutory rape but the female was not.

In his defense, Michael M. challenged the constitutionality of California's statutory rape law on the basis of "equal protection of the laws," a civil rights guarantee of the Fourteenth Amendment. To be constitutional, a law must follow the intent of the Constitution. Michael M. claimed the law discriminated (giving privileges to one group but not to another similar group) on the basis of gender (the sex of the person) since males alone could be charged under the law. He charged this was unequal protection of the laws and, therefore, unconstitutional. The California Supreme Court ruled against Michael, and upheld (gave support to) the law. Appeal was taken to the U.S. Supreme Court.

U.S. Supreme Court Decides

The U.S. Supreme Court in a 5-4 vote, upheld California's statutory rape law. The Court stated that the law did not violate the Equal Protection Clause of the Fourteenth Amendment. A majority of justices agreed on the result but could not agree on the reasons for so ruling. Therefore, the Court's opinion, delivered by Justice William H. Rehnquist, is called a plurality opinion. Justice Rehnquist's opinion explained the various arguments in favor of the law.

Preventing Underage Pregnancy

First, the Court recognized that the California law discriminated against a certain group of persons, males, based on gender alone. Under scrutiny (close examination) standards set by the Court, increased scrutiny must be given to cases involving discrimination based on gender. The scrutiny level used in gender cases is intermediate scrutiny as was established in *Mississippi University for Women v. Hogan.* Under intermediate scrutiny, the law in question must address an "important" interest of the state and if written so that it is "substantially [strongly] related" to that state interest. In other words, the state must have a very important reason to write the law in the first place and the law must be written so that it strongly and directly addresses the issue. The Court ruled that the state's important reason was to prevent underage pregnancy. Rehnquist commented,

> **We are satisfied not only that the prevention of illegitimate [teenage] pregnancy is at least one of the 'purposes' of the statute, but that the State has a strong interest in preventing such pregnancy.**

Consequences Fall to the Female

Equal protection of the laws historically has not been interpreted by the courts to mean that all persons in a state must be equally affected by each law all the time. For instance, persons in state prisons will not have the same equal protection of the laws granted persons who are not in prison. Groups of persons must be in similar circumstances or situations to receive equal protection. The courts call this "similarly situated."

The Court reasoned that males and females are not "similarly situated" with regard to the burdens of pregnancy. For example, pregnancy poses a health risk to young women, but does not pose such a risk to men. As long as the law being applied to one gender and not the other is based on realistic sex differences, it can be seen as constitutional. Rehnquist wrote,

> **Because virtually all of the significant harmful . . . consequences of teenage pregnancy fall on the young female, a legislature acts well within its authority when it elects to punish only the participant [the male] who, by nature, suffers few of the consequences of his conduct. . . Moreover, the risk of pregnancy itself constitutes a substantial [strong] deterrence [prevent from acting] to young females. [A] criminal sanction [control] imposed solely on males thus serves to roughly 'equalize' the deterrents on the sexes.**

Thus, the Court saw the law as equalizing consequences and deterrence for males and females.

Would a Gender-Neutral Law Be Better?

Michael M.'s defense argued that a gender-neutral law would serve California just as well in preventing teenage pregnancies. A gender-neutral law would hold both male and female equally criminally responsible. However, the plurality of justices were convinced by California's argument that a gender-neutral statute rape law would be harder to enforce. The state argued it would reduce the likelihood of a woman reporting a violation if she herself might be subject to prosecution.

Dissenting Justices

The dissenting justices also used the intermediate-scrutiny test but found the California law failed to pass the test. They argued that there was not enough evidence to prove that the law as written strongly addressed the problem of teenage pregnancy. They said that California had not proved that the gender-based discriminatory law prevents underage women from having sexual intercourse or that there are fewer teenage pregnancies under the law than their would be under a gender-neutral law. They pointed out that thirty-seven states have gender-neutral statutory rape laws. These laws, they believed, are potentially greater preventatives for underage sexual activity since two persons instead of one could be punished.

DATE RAPE

According to the National Victim Center, one out of every eight adult women has been raped and eighty-four percent of rape victims are under the age of twenty-four. The typical rapist is not a stranger. A troubling statistic is four out of five rape victims knew their attackers, according to the FBI. Date rape or acquaintance rape most often is carried out not only by people a victim knows but, much worse, a person they trust. The typical rapist shames, threatens, or intimidates the female into having sex with him. Some victims of date rape become overwhelmed with guilt, especially if they made a bad judgement call about becoming physically involved with the male in the first place. It is common for victims of date rape to feel like they somehow "asked for it." Studies estimate as many as eighty-five percent of rapes go unreported.

Impact

The decision showed that a state can apply laws to males and females differently and be considered constitutionally correct by the courts when the state can show an important reason for doing so. The decision, however, raised unanswered questions for the future about determining when males and females are or are not legally similarly situated when issues arise.

Suggestions for further reading

Miklowitz, Gloria D. *Past Forgiving.* New York: Simon & Schuster Books for Young Readers, 1995.

Parrot, Andrea. *Coping with Date Rape and Acquaintance Rape.* New York: Rosen Publishing Group, 1999.

Warshaw, Robin. *I Never Called It Rape: The Ms. Report on Recognizing, Fighting, and Surviving Date and Acquaintance Rape.* New York: Harper Perennial, 1994.

Williams, Mary E., ed. *Date Rape.* San Diego, CA: Greenhaven Press, 1998.

Mississippi University for Women v. Hogan 1982

Petitioner: Mississippi University for Women

Respondent: Joe Hogan

Petitioner's Claim: That the state supported school's nursing program did not violate gender discrimination laws because its single-sex admission policy was a form of affirmative action.

Chief Lawyer for Petitioner: Hunter M. Gholson

Chief Lawyer for Respondent: Wilbur O. Colom

Justices for the Court: William J. Brennan, Jr., Thurgood Marshall, Sandra Day O'Connor, John Paul Stevens, Byron R. White

Justices Dissenting: Harry A. Blackmun, Chief Justice Warren E. Burger, Lewis F. Powell, Jr., William H. Rehnquist

Date of Decision: July 1, 1982

Decision: That the Mississippi University for Women had violated Hogan's constitutional right to equal protection of the law guaranteed by the Fourteenth Amendment by barring his admission to its nursing school.

Significance: The Court found that men as well as women are constitutionally protected against gender discrimination. A new level of scrutiny, intermediate scrutiny, is applied in gender discrimination cases. The case lead to the end of publicly funded single-sex schools.

*The Mississippi
University for
Women had a long
history of quality,
single-sex
education.*
Reproduced by
permission of the
Mississippi University
for Women.

In 1979 Joe Hogan was a surgical nurse and nursing supervisor in a medical center in Columbia, Mississippi. Through various two- and three-year programs, it was possible to have a nursing career without obtaining a four-year university degree. However, as in the case of many careers, a four-year degree meant a higher skill level which also meant a higher salary. Desiring to complete his four-year degree, Hogan applied to a university in his hometown of Columbus. The problem he ran into was reflected in the name of the school, Mississippi University for Women.

The Fourteenth Amendment to the U.S. Constitution, approved in 1868, guaranteed "equal protection of the laws" to "any person" within a state. However, it would take the passage of the 1964 Civil Rights Act almost a century later to begin correcting gender (sex) discrimination. Gender discrimination is the unfair treatment of a person or group because of their sex. Traditionally, in the thoughts of most Americans and in reality, gender discrimination meant discrimination against women. However, "any person" in the Fourteenth Amendment certainly referred to both women and men. Increasingly in the 1970s cases involving discrimination against men began to reach the U.S. Supreme Court.

Mississippi University for Women v. Hogan

Males Need Not Apply

Although men were allowed to audit (to attend without receiving formal credit) courses, the Mississippi University for Women was a single-sex school and its nursing program was only open to women. Founded in 1884 as the Mississippi Industrial Institute and College for the Education of White Girls of the State of Mississippi, it was one of the country's first public state-supported, single-sex universities for women. Many single-sex private colleges also existed. The nursing school was founded in 1971 and had been offering a four-year degree in nursing since 1974. Since the nearest co-educational (for both men and women) nursing program was 147 miles away, Hogan applied to Mississippi University for Women and was rejected only on the basis of his gender. The school suggested he audit courses but he decided to turn to the courts for help.

Hogan filed a lawsuit in U.S. District Court claiming the school policy violated his constitutional freedom of equal protection of the laws under the Fourteenth Amendment. Hogan, determined to make a change in his community, requested that the university's women-only admissions policy be changed. Eventually, Hogan's suit made not only a change in his community but changed the way equal protection cases are examined when it appears a person has been discriminated against because of gender.

Standards of Examination in Equal Protection Cases

The U.S. Supreme Court, to be certain it looks at cases fairly, develops standards to follow. These standards are applied in the same manner to cases asking similar questions. In equal protection cases courts look

especially in depth when it appears an individual or a group of people is being discriminated against simply because they belong to a certain race or nationality. This in-depth look is called strict scrutiny (examination). For example an equal protection case involving a black American or an Irish American would be looked at with strict scrutiny to be sure the person was not unfairly singled out by the policy or law because of race or nationality. If it is determined by the court that an individual or group is being unfairly treated due to race, nationality, or alienage (a person living in the United States but a citizen of another country), then the court will next apply a test called "compelling" state interest. A state would be required to prove that no other way existed to accomplish the goal of the law and that the law was essential to the interest or operation of the state. Few laws survive the strict scrutiny examination. Most are struck down.

Until the 1970s if the equal protection case did not involve race, nationality, or alienage, then a low-level scrutiny was applied. Gender cases were included in the low-level scrutiny. This low-level scrutiny was called "rational basis." The state only had to prove the law in question was based on a "legitimate" (honest) interest of the state. For example, a state discriminates against persons under sixteen years of age by having a law which prevents them from driving a car. The court recognizes that this law applies to all persons under sixteen, not just persons of a certain race, so strict scrutiny is not applied. Instead, rational-basis scrutiny is applied. Therefore, the state must simply prove it has a legitimate interest to allow this law. The legitimate interest is safety of the public roads. The court agrees this is an honest interest of the state and the law stands.

In Joe Hogan's case the U.S. Supreme Court confirmed a new midway standard between strict scrutiny and low-level rational basis, called intermediate scrutiny, to use in gender cases. This mid-way standard was first introduced by Justice William J. Brennan, Jr., in *Craig v. Boren* (1976) but became much better defined with Justice Sandra Day O'Connor's opinion in *Mississippi University for Women v. Hogan.*

You Take the Low Road, I'll Take the High Road

Earlier in Hogan's case, the U.S. District Court for the Northern District of Mississippi took the low-level rational basis road by applying only "minimal" scrutiny. Deciding against Hogan, the court ruled that the state had a legitimate interest in providing a female-only nursing program.

The appeals court, rejecting the district court decision, said the low-level "minimal" scrutiny was not enough examination and needed a higher level of scrutiny. The appeals court noted that gender discrimination had long been a problem and found no differences between men and women to rationalize separate educational facilities for nursing. The court ruled that the admissions policies of Mississippi University for Women as a whole were discriminatory and, indeed, unconstitutional. The appeals court declared Hogan should be admitted. To resolve the two conflicting lower court opinions, the U.S. Supreme Court agreed to hear the case.

Mississippi
University
for Women
v. Hogan

Affirmative Action Meets Equal Protection

Arguing its case before the Supreme Court, Mississippi University claimed that its single-sex nursing school was a form of "affirmative action." Affirmative action programs, begun in the 1960s, were widespread in government agencies and educational institutions by the 1970s. The programs sought to correct past discrimination by providing preferential treatment to women and blacks. In defending its rejection of Mr. Hogan, the university argued that (1) having a school for women only made up for past gender discrimination, and (2) the presence of men would hurt female students' performance.

In a 5-4 decision, the Court upheld the appeals court ruling in favor of Hogan. Justice Sandra Day O'Connor, writing her first opinion for the Court, begun by deciding which level of scrutiny to use. Obviously, a gender problem does not fall in strict scrutiny reserved for race, nationality, or alienage. However, low-level rational basis scrutiny did not give enough examination to the historic gender discrimination problem. O'Connor chose an intermediate-level scrutiny for gender cases. She wrote that the state must show "important governmental objectives [goals]" for the law or policy.

Using intermediate scrutiny, O'Connor concluded Mississippi University for Women's goal of correcting past discrimination against women with their women-only policy was unimportant. Noting that 98.6 percent of all nursing degrees in the United States are earned by women, she reasoned there was no discrimination against women in their pursuit of a nursing degree. In fact, restricting the program to women tended to further the stereotype (fixed mental picture) of nursing as "woman's work."

GENDER AND REVERSE DISCRIMINATION

Women have long fought for equal rights in areas of compensation that range from pay to benefits; but cases such as *Mississippi University for Women v. Hogan* signify a countertrend, that of reverse-discrimination lawsuits. The most famous of these was *University of California v. Bakke* (1978), which challenged reverse discrimination on the basis of race; but challenges on the basis of gender have been viewed differently by the Supreme Court. This is perhaps because gender, unlike race, was not a factor in the drafting or the passage of the Fourteenth Amendment.

Part of what makes questions about reverse discrimination difficult is the fact that they can be approached on many different levels. There is, for instance, the political or legal level, based on the Constitution, statutes, and general beliefs about fairness. But there are also viewpoints based on tradition or on actual practices. Thus for instance, alimony laws, which have tended to favor women, are written that way because past experience—at least, prior to the 1970s—showed that women were more likely than men to be financially hurt in a divorce settlement.

In answer to the university's second argument, O'Connor observed that men already sit in on classes with no negative effect on the female students' performance.

Therefore, the O'Connor agreed with the court of appeals' ruling. The Court found the gender-discrimination policies of Mississippi University for Women unconstitutional in violation of the Fourteenth Amendment's "equal protection of the laws."

The End of Public Single-Sex Schools

Dissenting (not agreeing with majority opinion) justices argued that single-sex educational facilities were historically an important part of the American educational scene. The dissenters feared this decision would lead to the elimination of publicly supported colleges exclusively for women, which is what happened.

Despite later public pressure to raise the standard to strict scrutiny for gender issues, the intermediate-scrutiny level as used in the *Mississippi University for Women* case continued to be applied by courts in the late 1990s. In **United States v. Virginia** (1996), the Court used intermediate scrutiny in striking down Virginia Military Institute's policy excluding women as students. By the end of the twentieth century, the only single-sex universities still operating were private institutions.

Suggestions for further reading

Beckwith, Francis J., and Todd E. Jones, eds. *Affirmative Action: Social Justice or Reverse Discrimination?* Amherst, NY: Prometheus Books, 1997.

Nerad, Maresi. *The Academic Kitchen: A Social History of Gender Stratification at the University of California, Berkeley.* Albany: State University of New York Press, 1999.

Streitmatter, Janice L. *For Girls Only: Making a Case for Single-Sex Schooling.* Albany: State University of New York Press, 1999.

Meritor Savings Bank v. Vinson
1986

Petitioner: Meritor Savings Bank

Respondent: Mechelle Vinson

Petitioner's Claim: That under the Civil Rights Act of 1964 businesses are responsible for sexual discrimination in the workplace only when resulting in economic loss to the victim.

Chief Lawyer for Petitioner: F. Robert Troll, Jr.

Chief Lawyer for Respondent: Patricia J. Barry

Justices for the Court: Harry A. Blackmun, William J. Brennan, Jr., Chief Justice Warren E. Burger, Thurgood Marshall, Sandra Day O'Connor, Lewis F. Powell, Jr., William H. Rehnquist, John Paul Stevens, Byron R. White

Justices Dissenting: None

Date of Decision: June 19, 1986

Decision: Ruled in favor of Mechelle Vinson

Significance: This case became the cornerstone for answering sexual harassment questions raised under Title VII of the Civil Rights Act of 1964. The Court, using Equal Employment Opportunities Commission guidelines, established that hostile environment is a form of sexual harassment even when the victim suffers no economic losses.

Testifying at the 1991 Senate hearings on the confirmation of Clarence Thomas to the U.S. Supreme Court, Ellen Wells talked about a form of gender or sex discrimination (unequal treatment of a person because of that person's sex) known as sexual harassment:

> **You blame yourself. Perhaps its the perfume I have on. . . And so you try to change your behavior because you think it must be me. . . And then I think you perhaps start to get angry and frustrated. But there's always that sense of powerlessness. And you're also ashamed. . . What did you do? And so you keep it in. You don't say anything. And if someone says to you: You should go forward, you have to think: How am I going to pay the phone bill if I do that? . . . So you're quiet. And you're ashamed. And you sit there and you take it.**

Although Wells said this in the 1990s, history indicates that sexual harassment is not new. For example, the following quote from *A History of Women in America,* by C. Hymowitz and M. Weissman (1978), describes the plight of women factory workers in the early twentieth century.

> **Wherever they worked, women were sexually harassed by male workers, foremen and bosses. Learning to 'put up' with this abuse was one of the first lessons on the job. . . It was common practice at the factories for male employers to demand sexual favors from women workers in exchange for a job, a raise, or better position.**

The Fourteenth Amendment, approved in 1868, guaranteed "equal protection of the laws" to all persons living in America. That is, no person or persons shall be denied the same protection of the laws that is enjoyed by other persons or groups. However, equal protection rights were not extended to women until almost a century later.

Congress Takes Action

By the 1950s and 1960s various forms of discrimination including racial and gender discrimination, had become a focus of the nation. To help remedy (correct) various forms of discrimination, Congress passed the

GENDER DISCRIMINATION AND SEXUAL HARASSMENT

Civil Rights Act of 1964. Title VII of the act prohibited discrimination on the basis of race, color, religion, sex, or national origin in employment matters. The act also created the Equal Employment Opportunities Commission (EEOC) to enforce Title VII. However, not until 1980 did the EEOC define sexual harassment as a form of sex discrimination prohibited by the 1964 act.

The EEOC developed guidelines which women could use to finally gain equal protection rights in sexual harassment matters. The guidelines defined sexual harassment as unwelcome sexual advances of either a verbal or physical nature. Examples of verbal or physical advances could include

Associate Justice Clarence Thomas was questioned about accusations of sexual harassment at his nomination hearings.
Reproduced by permission of AP/Wide World Photos.

requests for dates or sex, comments about a person's body, whistles, hugging, kissing, or grabbing. For unwelcome sexual advances to be considered harassment they must be associated with at least one of the two following situations. First, the "agreement to" or "reflection of" the advances is tied to the targeted person's job. "Agreement to" could mean promise of promotions, raises or simply keeping the job. "Rejection of" could have the opposite effects. This type of sexual harassment is referred to as "quid pro quo," Latin for "you have to do 'this' to get 'that.'" In familiar terms this is called sex-for-jobs. The second type of harassment, referred to as hostile environment, occurs when the advances make a workplace so unpleasant or difficult that targeted persons have trouble doing their jobs.

The Story of Mechelle Vinson

Mr. Sidney Taylor, vice president and branch manager of Meritor Savings Bank, hired Ms. Mechelle Vinson as a teller trainee in September of 1974. She steadily rose from teller to head teller to assistant branch manager on merit (her abilities). After four years working at the same branch, Vinson informed Taylor in September of 1978 that she was taking sick leave for an unknown period of time. After two months the bank fired her for using too much leave.

Vinson sued both Taylor and the bank under Title VII. She claimed that Taylor had constantly subjected her to sexual harassment during her four years at the bank. Vinson alleged (claimed) Taylor improperly touched her, exposed himself to her, and had sex with her. Fearing the loss of her job, Vinson never told the bank of Taylor's behavior nor had she submitted a complaint to the EEOC. Taylor, contending Vinson's charges resulted from a work dispute, denied all charges. Meritor Savings pointed out Vinson had suffered no economic loss, therefore no quid pro quo harassment existed, and also the bank claimed no liability (responsibility) since it was never notified of the behavior.

Conflicting Lower Court Decisions

At the first trial, a district court concluded Vinson was not the victim of sexual harassment because the sexual relationship with Taylor was "voluntary" and had no impact on her continued employment. No quid pro quo harassment existed. Also, the court agreed with the bank that it had no liability for its supervisor's actions since Vinson had never formally complained through its grievance (complaint) procedures.

Vinson appealed the court's decision. The court of appeals disagreed with the district court and reversed (changed) the decision. The appeals court ruled that it did not matter that Vinson's employment was not affected. What did matter was that a hostile environment "existed for years and that environment was a type of sexual harassment prohibited under Title VII." The court also questioned the "voluntary" nature of the Vinson-Taylor relationship. Considering the liability issue the appeals court ruled that businesses are always responsible for sexual harassment committed by their supervisors. Meritor Savings then appealed to the U.S. Supreme Court.

At Last, a Sexual Harassment Case Reaches Supreme Court

Agreeing to hear the case, the Supreme Court considered three questions most important: (1) is a hostile working environment created by unwelcome sexual behavior a form of employment discrimination prohibited under Title VII when no economic loss or quid pro quo harassment exists; (2) does a Title VII violation exist when the relationship is "voluntary"; and, (3) is a business liable for a hostile working environment if it is not aware of the misconduct?

Supreme Court's Opinion

Justice William H. Rehnquist, writing for the unanimous court (all justices in agreement) and following the EEOC guidelines, answered the three questions.

(1) The Court rejected the bank's argument that Title VII prohibits only quid pro quo harassment. EEOC guidelines state that hostile environ-

Women's organizations found Anita Hill to be a strong spokesperson for the issue of sexual harassment in the workplace. Reproduced by permission of AP/Wide World Photos.

CLARENCE THOMAS—
ANITA HILL HEARINGS

The issue of sexual harassment exploded into the living rooms of Americans the weekend of October 11 to October 13, 1991, preempting everything network television had to offer. Black conservative Clarence Thomas, a Supreme Court nominee, seemed on his way to a Senate confirmation. Then on October 6, a story broke through the news media that Anita Hill, a black law professor, had revealed to the Senate Judiciary Committee investigating Thomas' nomination that she had been sexually harassed by Thomas in the early 1980s as they worked together. Thomas' confirmation was thrown in doubt.

Amid public pressure, the Senate Judiciary Committee held a fully televised hearing to air Hill's complaint and Thomas' defense. Some of the most extraordinary public testimony ever given to a congressional committee began. Both Hill and Thomas spoke convincingly and with great emotion. Hill spent seven hours describing Thomas' sexual advances. Thomas denied all charges describing the hearing as a "high-tech lynching." In the end the Senate voted to confirm Thomas, but the controversy continued. Some critics accused Hill of being part of a liberal political or feminist move to defeat Thomas. Hill supporters, outraged at the committee's treatment of her, flooded women's organizations with calls and letters. The nature of sexual harassment in the workplace had come to the forefront of American discussion.

ment is a type of sexual discrimination prohibited in the workplace. The Court found Vinson's charges sufficient to claim hostile environment sexual harassment. The Court did write that hostile environment harassment must be severe or pervasive (happened again and again) to support a claim.

(2) The Court also asserted that whether a sexual relationship was "voluntary" is not important, the key is whether or not the advances were unwelcome. A person, out of fear of losing a job, might well voluntarily

**GENDER
DISCRIMINATION
AND SEXUAL
HARASSMENT**

cooperate even if the conduct was unwelcome. Therefore, to determine if the conduct was unwelcome the Court must look at all aspects of the case.

(3) The Court did not specifically define employer liability, but did disagree with both the district and appeals court decisions. The Court stated that the "absence of notice to an employer does not necessarily insulate (protect) that employer from liability." At the same time, employers are not always automatically liable for sexual harassment by their supervisors. The Court went along with EEOC suggestions which said liability issues require careful examination of the role of the supervisor in the company and whether or not an appropriate complaint procedure which employees knew about was in place.

Building on Meritor

After 1986, both state courts and the Supreme Court continued to clarify (make clearer) what constituted sexual harassment. For example, (1) damages (money payments) paid to the victim may be allowed, (2) psychological damage does not need to occur to claim a hostile work environment, (3) companies must have sexual harassment policies, and (4) harassment can occur even if the offender and victim are of the same sex.

Suggestions for further reading

Eskenazi, Martin, and David Gallen. *Sexual Harassment: Know Your Rights!* New York: Carroll & Graf Publishers, Inc., 1992.

Nash, Carol R. *Sexual Harassment: What Teens Should Know.* Springfield, NJ: Enslow Publishers, 1996.

Petrocelli, William, and Barbara Kate Repa. *Sexual Harassment on the Job.* Berkeley, CA: Nolo Press, 1994.

Swisher, Karin L. *Sexual Harassment.* San Diego, CA: Greenhaven Press, Inc., 1992.

Automobile Workers v. Johnson Controls 1991

Petitioners: International Union, United Automobile, Aerospace, and Agricultural Implement Workers of America, and others

Respondent: Johnson Controls, Inc.

Petitioner's Claim: That Johnson Controls' fetal protection policy discriminates against women in violation of Title VII of the 1964 Civil Rights Act as amended by the Pregnancy Discrimination Act (PDA).

Chief Lawyer for Petitioners: Marsha S. Berzon

Chief Lawyer for Respondent: Stanley S. Jaspan

Justices for the Court: Harry A. Blackmun, Anthony Kennedy, Thurgood Marshall, Sandra Day O'Connor, Chief Justice William H. Rehnquist, Antonin Scalia, David H. Souter, John Paul Stevens, Byron R. White

Justices Dissenting: None

Date of Decision: March 20, 1991

Decision: Ruled against Johnson Controls, Inc. by finding that their fetal protection policy violated Title VII of the Civil Rights Act of 1964 as amended by the PDA

Significance: The ruling prohibited any discrimination based on a worker's ability to have children. The Court recognized a woman's right to make her own decisions about pregnancy, during potentially harmful work, and the economic needs of her family.

GENDER DISCRIMINATION AND SEXUAL HARASSMENT

Sex (gender) discrimination, the unfair treatment of a person or group of persons because of their sex, was common in the American workplace until passage of the Civil Rights Act of 1964. Title VII (Equal Employment Opportunity), Section 703, parts (a)(2) of the act read,

> **It shall be an unlawful employment practice for an employer . . . to limit, segregate [separate out] or classify his employees in any way which would deprive [take away] or tend to deprive any individual of employment opportunities . . . because of such individual's race, color, religion, sex, or national origin.**

Although the act clearly prohibited discrimination based on sex in the workplace, nowhere did it address the issue of pregnant workers. Fetal (referring to the unborn child) protection policies barring fertile women (capable of bearing children) from certain jobs out of fear that those jobs could cause harm to a fetus (unborn child) carried by the women became widespread in the 1970s. Given the fact that only women can become pregnant, these policies quickly became controversial. Women's rights advocates believed the policies violated Title VII of the Civil Rights Act of 1964 by depriving women workers certain employment opportunities. In response, Congress amended (changed or add to make clearer) Title VII with the Pregnancy Discrimination Act (PDA) in 1978. The part of the PDA which amended Title VII stated that unless pregnant employees differ from others "in their ability or inability to work" they must be "treated the same" as other employees "for all employment-related purposes." In other words, a woman could not be discriminated against merely for her potential to become pregnant or for her actual pregnancy unless it affected her ability to do the job. Nevertheless, fetal protection policies continued in many companies into the 1980s. Not until this case did the U.S. Supreme Court rule in this area.

Johnson Controls, Inc. – Battery Manufacturer

Johnson Controls manufactured batteries. The battery manufacturing process used lead as a main ingredient. Lead exposure (come in contact with) in both men and women may cause health problems such as fertility problems and possibly birth defects in children born to workers.

*The Court decided
that companies
could not
discriminate
against a worker
based on their
ability to have
children.*
Reproduced by
permission of
Robert J. Huffman.

   Originally Johnson Controls only hired males but after passage of
the 1964 Civil Rights Act the business began hiring women. As women
began working in its plants, Johnson Controls developed and issued an
official policy concerning employment of women in lead-exposure work
which read,

> **Since not all women who can become mothers wish
> to become mothers, (or will become mothers), it
> would appear to be illegal discrimination to treat**

**all who are capable of pregnancy as though they
will become pregnant.**

By adopting this policy, Johnson Controls hoped to avoid discrimination problems since it stopped short of excluding all women capable of becoming pregnant from lead exposure jobs. The company required any woman wishing to work where lead exposure existed to sign a statement stating that she had been advised of the risk of having a child while being exposed to lead. Over the next five years, eight women employees with high lead blood levels became pregnant. Although none of the babies suffered defects, Johnson Controls developed a new fetal protection policy banning all "women . . . capable of bearing children" from lead exposed jobs. "Capable of bearing children" was defined as "all women except those whose inability to bear children is medically documented."

Class-action Lawsuit

A class-action lawsuit is one which is brought by a large number of people as a group. These people all have a common interest. Various labor unions brought a class-action lawsuit in Wisconsin against Johnson Controls, claiming its fetal protection policy was sex discrimination prohibited by Title VII of the Civil Rights Act as amended by the PDA. Two individuals included in the suit were Mary Craig and Elsie Nason. Mary Craig had chosen to be sterilized rather than lose her job. Elsie Nason, a fifty-year-old divorcee, had suffered a loss of pay when she was transferred out of a job where she was exposed to lead.

A Business Necessity

The local district court decided in favor of Johnson Controls. The court stressed the likelihood that exposure to lead put a fetus, as well as the reproductive abilities of would-be parents, at risk. Neither the union nor employees had previously offered an acceptable alternative way to protect the fetus. The court found the company's policy to be a "business necessity." The suing groups appealed.

The Court of Appeals next also ruled in favor of Johnson Controls. Not only did the Court of Appeals decide Johnson's policy was a business necessity but decided that such policies could exclude women without being called discrimination under "a bona fide occupational qualification" (BFOQ) clause found in Title VII, section 703, part (e)(1) of the

Civil Rights Act. No other court of appeals had applied BFOQ in similar cases. Use of the BFOQ caught the U.S. Supreme Court's attention and the Court decided to hear the case.

Outright Sex Discrimination

Justice Harry A. Blackmun delivered the opinion of the Court in a close 5-4 decision. After noting that "we are concerned with an employer's gender-based fetal-protection policy" he asked,"May an employer exclude a fertile female employee from certain jobs because of its concern for the health of the fetus the woman might conceive [become pregnant]?"

Ruling against Johnson Controls, the opinion of the Court was that Johnson clearly had discriminated against women. Blackmun wrote,

> **The bias (prejudiced view) in Johnson Controls policy is obvious. Fertile men, but not fertile women are given a choice as to whether they wish to risk their reproductive health for a particular job. Section 703(a) of the Civil Rights Act of 1964 . . . as amended [by PDA] . . . prohibits sex-based classification in terms and conditions of employment. . .**

The Court also held that Johnson's policy was outright sex discrimination. The lower courts discussion of business necessity, they asserted, was a mistake and not at all appropriate. Using BFOQ consideration was a better way to approach the issue.

Don't Let the Plane Crash

BFOQ consideration permits an employer to discriminate only when it is necessary to the normal operation of that particular business or as interpreted by the courts, when a severe safety problem would be created. For example, in *Western Airlines, Inc. v. Criswell* (1985), one type of discrimination was allowed, age discrimination. It was determined that a flight engineer over the age of sixty might not perform all tasks assigned causing a "safety emergency." For the safety of the passengers, planes must not crash. This fact was "indispensable" to the operation of the airline business and age discrimination was allowed. In the case of Johnson Controls, sex or pregnancy did not actually interfere with the employees ability to perform the job.

Blackmun wrote,

> **We have no difficulty concluding that Johnson Controls cannot establish a BFOQ. Fertile women as far as appears in the record, participate in the manufacture of batteries as efficiently as anyone else.**

Strictly a Family Affair

Blackmun further commented that "danger to a woman herself does not justify discrimination." It is her business to decide if she will take the risk. Likewise, the risks a pregnant woman assumes for her fetus are not her employer's concern. Such decisions, Blackmun wrote,

> **Must be left to the parents . . . rather than the employers. . . Title VII and the PDA simply do not allow a woman's dismissal because of her failure to submit to sterilization [or because she may become pregnant].**

Company Liability (Responsibility)

Blackmun commented that although forty states permitted lawsuits to recover money for injuries to a fetus, the cases were always based on negligence (carelessness). If the company complies with basic national safety standards and fully informs the woman of the risk, as Johnson Controls did, then the employer has not been negligent and will not be liable for injury.

Fearful of a Mixed Reaction

Anticipating a mixed reaction from the general public to the Court's finding, Blackmun, giving powerful reasons for the ruling, wrote,

> **Our holding today . . . is neither remarkable nor unprecedented [a new idea or occurrence]. Concern for a woman's existing or potential offspring historically has been the excuse for denying women equal employment opportunities. . . It is no more appropriate for the courts than it is for individual employers to decide whether a woman's reproductive role is more important to herself and**

her family than her economic role. Congress has
left this choice to the woman as hers to make.

Suggestions for further reading

Blank, Robert H. *Fetal Protection in the Workplace: Women's Rights,
Business Interests, and the Unborn.* New York: Columbia
University Press, 1993.

Daniels, Cynthia R. *At Women's Expense: State Power and the Politics of
Fetal Rights.* Cambridge, MA: Harvard University Press, 1993.

Morgan, Lynn M., and Meredith W. Michaels, eds. *Fetal Subjects,
Feminist Positions.* Philadelphia: University of Pennsylvania Press,
1999.

Samuels, Suzanne Uttaro. *Fetal Rights, Women's Rights: Gender
Equality in the Workplace.* Madison, WI: University of Wisconsin
Press, 1995.

Automobile
Workers v.
Johnson
Controls

United States v. Virginia
1996

Petitioner: United States

Respondents: Commonwealth of Virginia, Governor Lawrence
Douglas Wilder, Virginia Military Institute, et al.

Petitioner's Claim: That the Virginia Military Institute's refusal to
admit female students violated the Fourteenth Amendment

Chief Lawyer for Petitioner: Paul Bender,
U.S. Deputy Solicitor General

Chief Lawyer for Respondent: Theodore B. Olsen

Justices for the Court: Stephen Breyer, Ruth Bader Ginsburg,
Anthony M. Kennedy, Sandra Day O'Connor, William H.
Rehnquist, David H. Souter, John Paul Stevens

Justices Dissenting: Antonin Scalia
(Clarence Thomas did not participate)

Date of Decision: June 26, 1996

Decision: Excluding women from state-funded schools
violates the Fourteenth Amendment.

Significance: America's last two state-funded all-male colleges
were forced to admit women or give up state funding.

The Equal Protection Clause of the Fourteenth Amendment of the U.S. Constitution protects citizens from discrimination by state governments. (Discrimination is unequal treatment of people in the same situation.) States and organizations that receive state funding must obey the Equal Protection Clause. Governments use the Equal Protection Clause to end discrimination based on race, religion, and sex or gender. In 1996 the U.S. Supreme Court used it to force an all-male, state-funded military college in Virginia to accept female students.

The Virginia Military Institute (VMI) is a state-funded military college that opened in Lexington, Virginia, in 1839. Around 1990 a female high school student complained to the U.S. Department of Justice that VMI would not accept female students. (The U.S. Department of Justice is the branch of the federal government that enforces federal law by prosecuting people who violate the law.) In 1990 the Justice Department filed a case accusing Virginia and VMI of violating the Equal Protection Clause by refusing to accept women at VMI. In the two years before the lawsuit, VMI ignored requests from more than 300 women about attending college there.

When the case went to trial in a federal court, VMI said that its long tradition of excluding women was important to its goal of producing citizen-soldiers. According to VMI, citizen-soldiers are men who can be military leaders during war and leaders in society during peacetime. Students at VMI receive a military-style education that includes tough physical training and cramped living quarters. VMI said admitting women would prevent it from providing this education to men.

After a six-day trial, Judge Jackson L. Kiser ruled that VMI could continue to exclude women. Kiser agreed that the all-male school served Virginia's substantial interest in giving men a military-style education.

The U.S. Department of Justice appealed to the U.S. Court of Appeals for the Fourth Circuit. Writing for the court on October 5, 1992, Judge Paul V. Niemeyer agreed that Virginia had a substantial interest in providing a military education to its citizens. But Judge Niemeyer also said that providing that education to men only violated the Equal Protection Clause. Judge Niemeyer ruled that Virginia must either admit women to VMI, open a separate military school for women, or stop giving money to VMI. (A school that does not get money from the state or federal government does not have to obey the Equal Protection Clause.) Niemeyer ordered Virginia to choose an option and to ask Judge Kiser to approve the plan.

Separate but equal?

Virginia and VMI responded by creating Virginia Women's Institute for Leadership (VWIL), an all-female program at Mary Baldwin College in Virginia. VWIL shared VMI's goal of producing citizen-soldiers, but it did not have the same military-style features. VWIL cadets lived separately instead of together and had more classroom instruction than physical training. VWIL also had fewer academic programs, received less state funding, and had fewer Ph.D. professors than VMI. Finally, VWIL could not offer the reputation VMI had earned over 150 years of providing education.

After reviewing VWIL's program, Judge Kiser ruled that it satisfied the Equal Protection Clause. When the Justice Department appealed this time, the Fourth Circuit Court of Appeals approved Judge Kiser's decision. It said that although VMI and VWIL were not identical, they were close enough to provide both men and women with a military-style education in Virginia.

Reversing discrimination

The Justice Department appealed to the U.S. Supreme Court. On June 26, 1996, the Supreme Court voted 7–1 that VMI must either give up state funding or admit women. Justice Ruth Bader Ginsburg, the second woman to serve on the Supreme Court, wrote the opinion for the Court. (Justice Clarence Thomas did not participate in the decision because his son was attending VMI.)

In her opinion, Justice Ginsburg said that under the Equal Protection Clause, sex discrimination is allowed only if it serves a substantial state interest. A substantial state interest is one that is important enough to make sex discrimination acceptable, such as creating jobs for women. According to Ginsburg, the state interest being served may not rely on old ideas that women are less talented than men. It also may not "create or perpetuate [continue] the legal, social, and economic inferiority of women."

Ginsburg decided that VMI's all-male program did not serve a substantial state interest in Virginia. She said the goal of producing citizen-soldiers with a military education does not require excluding women, and that women are able to succeed at VMI and would not ruin the quality of its program. Ginsburg said, "Women's successful entry into the Federal military academies, and their participation in the nation's military forces, indicate that Virginia's fear for the future of VMI may not be solidly grounded."

FIRST WOMAN AT THE CITADEL

It took a legal battle for Shannon R. Faulkner to become the first female cadet at the Citadel, a previously all-male military college in Charleston, South Carolina. The Citadel accepted Faulkner's application in 1993 only because she failed to say she was female. The Citadel refused to admit Faulkner when it learned her gender. Faulkner filed a lawsuit, and on July 22, 1994, a federal trial court ruled that the Citadel violated the Equal Protection Clause. The Fourth Circuit Court of Appeals agreed, ruling in April 1995 that South Carolina either had to admit women to the Citadel or create a military school for women.

Faulkner joined the Citadel's Corps of Cadets on August 14, 1995. On her first day of training, she suffered heat exhaustion and received treatment at the school's medical facility, where four male cadets also were treated. Faulkner returned to classes four days later, but then left the Citadel. Observers said that it was difficult for Faulkner to be the only woman at a school that did not want to accept her. Thirty-four male cadets from her group, however, also quit during the first week. Faulkner's failure to complete the Citadel's program did not harm the example she set for women.

Ginsburg also addressed the idea that VWIL provided a separate but equal education for women. After looking at the two programs, Ginsburg decided that VWIL was a "pale shadow" of VMI's famous program. "Women seeking and fit for a VMI quality education cannot be offered anything less under the State's obligation to afford the genuinely equal protection," she wrote.

Justice Antonin Scalia wrote a dissenting opinion, disagreeing with the Supreme Court's decision. Justice Scalia believed that single-gender education was an important option for students, and that the Court's decision would destroy that option. Scalia wrote, "I do not think any of us, women included, will be better off for its destruction."

A few good women

The Supreme Court's decision opened the doors for women at both VMI and the Citadel in South Carolina, the United States's last two state-funded, all-male military colleges. Although officials at both colleges were disappointed by the decision, they promised to obey it with honor. On May 15, 1999, Melissa K. Graham and Chih-Yuan Ho became the first women to graduate from VMI.

Suggestions for further reading

Hanmer, Trudy J. *Sexism and Sex Discrimination.* New York, NY: Franklin Watts, 1990.

The World Book Encyclopedia, 1997 ed., entries on "Education," "Coeducation." Chicago, IL: World Book, 1997.

Oncale v. Sundowner Offshore Services Incorporated et al. 1998

Petitioner: Joseph Oncale

Respondent: Sundowner Onshore Services Incorporated, John Lyons, Danny Pippen, and Brandon Johnson

Petitioner's Claim: That on-the-job sexual harassment by coworkers of the same sex is still sexual discrimination.

Chief Lawyers for Petitioner: Nicholas Canaday III

Chief Lawyers for Respondent: Harry M. Reasoner

Justices for the Court: Stephen Breyer, Ruth Bader Ginsburg, Anthony M. Kennedy, Sandra Day O'Connor, Chief Justice William H. Rehnquist, Antonin Scalia, David H. Souter, John Paul Stevens, Clarence Thomas

Justices Dissenting: None

Date of Decision: March 4, 1998

Decision: Ruled in favor of Oncale by finding that one person harassing another person of the same sex is sex discrimination prohibited by federal law.

Significance: The ruling recognized the right of individuals to claim sexual harassment even when the threatening individual and the victim are of the same sex. The Court found that Title VII applies to all sexual harassment situations which affect a person's employment.

GENDER DISCRIMINATION AND SEXUAL HARASSMENT

Sex discrimination involves the selection of one person over another for a job or for promotion purely on the basis of their gender (sex). Discrimination against women in the workplace had a long history in the United States. Women were routinely paid less than male workers doing the same work, not considered for management positions, and barred from certain professions, such as lawyers and even serving on juries. To correct this longstanding bias against women, Congress passed Section VII of the Civil Rights Act of 1964 that prohibited sex discrimination in employment. Title VII made it "an unlawful employment practice for an employer . . . to discriminate against any individual with respect to his compensation [pay], terms, conditions, or privileges of employment, because of such individual's race, color, religion, sex, or national origin." Discrimination against men by women was hardly considered an issue, not to mention sex discrimination between two women or two men. In fact, not until 1973 in *Frontiero v. Richardson* did the Court even recognize that men could be victims of sex discrimination.

A new kind of gender issue grew in the 1980s called sexual harassment. Sexual harassment usually meant that a person at work was demanding sex from another person in an harassing way. Often a supervisor would be demanding sexual favors in exchange for some favorable employment action, such as a promotion or even keeping a job. Less clearly sexual harassment could occur simply through constant workplace threats, insults, or ridicule, creating what is known as a "hostile work environment." In **Meritor Savings Bank v. Vinson** (1986) the Supreme Court ruled for the first time that these types of sexual harassment were a form of legally prohibited sex discrimination. Sexual harassment was a federal offense covered by the Civil Rights Act.

Before long cases of alleged sexual harassment between individuals of the same sex began to make it to the courts. The resulting court rulings were very inconsistent. Often the courts stated that same-sex sexual harassment would have to include some form of demands for sex, such as between a homosexual employer and an employee of the same sex. A district court decision in *Garcia v. Elf Atochem* (1994) ruled that there could be no same-sex sexual harassment. Another district court in *Baskerville v. Culligan International Co.* (1995) disagreed, ruling that same-sex claims could be covered by Title VII. And a third in 1996 ruled that same-sex harassment could not be responsible for a hostile work environment. The Supreme Court had yet to be clearly heard on the subject.

The Plight of Joseph Oncale

In August of 1991 twenty-one-year-old Joseph Oncale was hired by Sundowner Offshore Services in Houma, Louisiana to be a roustabout. Roustabouts are unskilled laborers working in an oilfield. Oncale was part of an eight-man crew working on a Chevron USA oil platform in the Gulf of Mexico. The crew included John Lyons, Danny Pippen, and Brandon Johnson. Pippen and Lyons were supervisors over Oncale. After a few weeks of work, Oncale began to be the target of a series of threatening and humiliating actions by Lyons, Pippen, and Johnson, often in front of co-workers. In one instance, while on a small boat going from one oil plat-form to another, the three men physically assailed him in a sexual manner. The assaults continued with threats of rape over the next several weeks.

Desperate, Oncale complained to company officials. However, when the officials approached the workers about the complaints they denied Oncale's charges. The company, claiming only horseplay had taken place, took no action, not even an investigation. Oncale, fearing what would eventually happen to him, quit in November, only four months after being hired.

Oncale Goes to Court

After leaving, Oncale filed a sex discrimination lawsuit with the Fifth Circuit Court of Appeals in New Orleans, Louisiana. The suit sought pay-ment for damages from Sundowner and the three men who had threatened and accosted him. He had lost his job because of the embarrassing behav-ior of the co-workers and lack of response by the company to his pleas.

Based on the recent *Garcia* decision, the district court dismissed the case claiming that no federal laws recognized same-sex sexual discrimi-nation. Oncale appealed the decision, but the appeals court promptly agreed with the first opinion. Upon the appeals court decision, the U.S. Department of Justice decided to help Oncale take his case to the Supreme Court, which agreed to hear it.

The Supreme Court

Before the Supreme Court, Oncale's and the government's lawyers argued that Title VII of the Civil Rights Act was written simply in sex-neutral terms. It did not mention harassment only in terms of men harass-ing women. Sex discrimination is prohibited regardless of the gender of

Oncale v. Sundowner Offshore Services Incorporated et al.

the people involved. On the other hand, Sundowner argued that same-sex harassment was not even in the minds of legislators when the act was passed. According to Sundowner, the law was clearly intended to protect females. Applying it to a case like Oncale's, they argued, would be a great misuse of the law, making it more of a code for decent behavior rather than a discrimination law. Rowdy behavior would be confused with sexual harassment.

In an unanimous (all nine justices agreeing) decision, the Court ruled in favor of Oncale thus reversing the two lower court decisions. Justice Antonin Scalia, writing for the Court, presented a forceful response. Though he noted that no doubt same-sex harassment was not the primary problem Congress had in mind when writing the law, he emphasized that the harm from same-sex harassment was no less serious than if the two people were of different sexes. Therefore, any form of sexual harassment in the workplace directly affecting a person's employment clearly violated Title VII of the Civil Rights Act. As Scalia noted, the law was intended "to strike at the entire spectrum [variation] of disparate [unequal] treatment of men and women in employment." The law is violated when "discriminatory intimidation, ridicule, and insult" becomes so overwhelming that an abusive work environment is created.

Scalia further noted that "harassing conduct need not be motivated by sexual desire to support an inference [idea] of discrimination on the basis of sex." In conclusion, Scalia wrote that routine interaction between employees should not be affected by the Court's ruling. Only behavior "so . . . offensive as to alter 'conditions' of the victim's employment" would be prohibited. Determining when sexual harassment had indeed occurred would be tricky. The situation in which the actions occur is all-important in deciding if harassment in fact occurred. As Scalia noted, a pat on the rear of a football player by his coach on the field is quite different than the same action toward the coach's secretary in the office. The "surrounding circumstances, expectations, and relationships" would have to be closely examined for each case using common sense.

By the time of the Supreme Court decision, Oncale was twenty-seven years old, married, and had two children. The Court returned his case to the district court so that he might have a trial to try to prove that the actions by his co-workers constituted sexual harassment in the workplace.

The *Oncale* decision finally made clear the legal status of same-sex sexual harassment. Two other Supreme Court decisions in 1998 further broadened employers' legal responsibilities for protecting their workers

RESOLVING SEXUAL HARASSMENT DISPUTES

In a series of rulings in the 1990s including *Oncale,* the Supreme Court clarified and broadened employer responsibilities. Faced with potentially expensive lawsuits and costly damage payments to victims of on-the-job sexual harassment by the employers, both public agencies and private businesses began educating their employees on how to avoid sexual harassment situations. It also became apparent that quick resolution of disputes was needed. Training materials described what sexual harassment is, what rights employees have to correct an unwanted situation, and penalties employees faced for violating the rules.

The bigger organizations also adopted in-house procedures for resolving sexual harassment claims before they could reach the courts. The usual goal is to resolve the dispute as quickly and informally as possible to save money, time, and workplace disruptions. These procedures commonly involve the harassed employee contacting a counselor designated by the company, a person to whom an employee could file a complaint, different from the employee's supervisor, within a certain time period after the incident, often within 45 days. The counselor normally (1) advises the employee of their rights, (2) helps define the dispute, (3) offers a solution, usually within a required time span such as 30 days, and (4) takes the dispute resolution to managers for acceptance. The counselors also keep company managers aware of troublesome patterns related to discrimination or harassment so as to avoid disputes. If this informal process fails, the employee can then proceed with a formal complaint possibly leading to more formal investigations by the company or outside parties. Courts have normally recognized these kinds of informal resolution processes and will not accept cases if the alleged victim has not followed company policies in making complaints.

**GENDER
DISCRIMINATION
AND SEXUAL
HARASSMENT**

from on-the-job sexual harassment. For instance, hostile actions based on the sex of the victim could justify sexual harassment claims, even without involvement of sexual desire. If sex or gender was not a key factor in the incidents, then the hostile actions would not be considered sexual harassment and would not necessarily violate federal law. The actions would be considered assault under state laws. Employers in the late 1990s began more diligently developing company policies and guidelines for their employees, giving training, providing handbooks to each employee, and informing employees of their rights.

Suggestions for further reading

Baridon, Andrea P., and David R. Eyler. *Working Together: New Rules and Realities for Managing Men and Women at Work.* New York: McGraw-Hill, 1994.

Eskenazi, Martin, and David Gallen. *Sexual Harassment: Know Your Rights.* New York: Carroll & Graf Publishers, Inc., 1992.

Petrocelli, William, and Barbara Kate Repa. *Sexual Harassment on the Job.* Berkeley, CA: Nolo Press, 1994.

REPRODUCTIVE
RIGHTS

The right of a woman to determine when and how she will give birth, commonly known as reproductive rights, was not legally recognized until the last half of the twentieth century. Reproductive rights includes not only the highly controversial issue of abortion, but also a wide range of other related topics including contraception (preventing pregnancy), sex education, surrogate (substitute) motherhood, in-vitro fertilization ("test tube babies"), condom availability, and sterilization (making incapable of reproduction). Public acceptance of birth control and other measures associated with reproductive choices have changed dramatically through the years in the United States.

Changing Attitudes in the Nineteenth Century

In the early nineteenth century, the average white American woman gave birth to seven children. As the nineteenth century progressed, the American economy changed from a predominately agricultural society with families living and working together on farms to growth of industrial centers involving factory work for husbands. The economic need for large families declined. As a result, scientific information on birth control began to be distributed by social reformers. In addition, few criminal laws existed banning abortion (ending a pregnancy before childbirth by removing the unborn child) and abortion was legal under common law (following common practices rather than laws passed by legislatures). Abortions were commonly associated with disposing of fetuses (unborn child) resulting from rape or conception out of wedlock. They normally were performed in the first four or five months of pregnancy. Abortions, however, were very dangerous to the woman with many left unable to bear children later, or actually dying from the procedure.

As the number of abortions began to significantly increase in the mid-nineteenth century, particularly among white middle-class women, conservatives rallied in opposition to birth control and abortion. They lobbied Congress for laws banning such activities. As a result, Congress passed the Comstock Law in 1873. The law prohibited the distribution of information that promoted methods of preventing pregnancy or that supported abortion. States also began passing laws prohibiting the use of contraceptives. Established in 1847, the American Medical Association (AMA) was interested in driving out of business unlicensed people performing abortions. Joined by religious leaders, they successfully led a campaign outlawing abortion. By the 1880s all states had passed laws banning abortion based on their police powers to regulate public health and safety. All had criminal penalties for persons performing abortions and some even adopted penalties for the women who had the abortions. Abortions were only legal when needed to save the mother's life. These restrictions changed little until the 1960s.

The Long Struggle for Reproductive Rights

Those supportive of birth control options for women began an active campaign in the early twentieth century to end the many prohibitions (forbidden by law) established in the late nineteenth century. Guided by reformer Margaret Sanger, a national movement developed leading eventually to establishment of Planned Parenthood Federation of America in 1942. By the 1960s birth control was legalized in almost all states though the actual distribution of birth control information was still commonly illegal. Many states also loosened their abortion laws to allow abortions when pregnancies resulted from rape or when the fetus likely had a serious birth defect.

The first major U.S. Supreme Court case recognizing reproductive rights came in 1965 in **Griswold v. Connecticut.** The Court, in recognizing a basic constitutional right to privacy, struck down a Connecticut state law prohibiting married couples from using contraceptives. Seven years later in 1972 the Court extended the right to use contraceptives to unmarried people as well in **Eisenstadt v. Baird.** Later in 1977 the Court in *Carey v. Population Services International* extended the right to contraceptive use to minors. The decisions opened the door for providing information to school students in sex education programs and even providing contraceptives.

The landmark Supreme Court ruling in reproductive rights however came in 1973. In the famous **Roe v. Wade** decision, the Court extended the right to privacy to include the right to abortions as well. A Texas law had prohibited abortions during the first trimester (first three months) of pregnancy except in situations where the mother's life was threatened. The Court ruled this prohibition violated the Equal Protection Clause of the Fourteenth Amendment. In a major determination, the Court wrote that a fetus was not a viable human being (capable of meaningful life after birth) until the third trimester (last three months of pregnancy). Therefore, prohibitions on abortions were not legally appropriate until after that time in a pregnancy. Even at that late point in the pregnancy the state must still make allowance for abortions when necessary to save the mother's life or protect her health.

By recognizing reproductive rights of women, many believed the Court had helped women gain some social and economic equality with men through their ability to control their reproductive processes. Women could pursue professions, like men, largely free of unexpected or unwanted disruptions of child birth or tending to children.

The Abortion Battle Continues in the Courts

The next major ruling in reproductive rights came in **Planned Parenthood of Central Missouri v. Danforth** in 1976. State law had required minors to obtain written permission from at least one parent and required a wife to obtain permission from a husband before having an abortion. The Court ruled these requirements unconstitutional (not following the intent of the constitution).

After suffering these major defeats in the courts, opponents to abortion adopted a new strategy to combat abortions. Also, many organizations were created opposing such sweeping reproduction rights. Pressing for legislation banning the use of public funds to pay for abortions, they succeeded in having Congress pass a law in 1976 prohibiting the use of federal monies for almost all abortions. The new law was immediately challenged, but the Supreme Court in a series of 1977 rulings held the law as constitutional. Public funds could only be used in situations of clear medical need. In a much bolder move, a constitutional amendment banning abortions was attempted but fell just short of adoption in 1983.

The debate over parental involvement in abortions for minors also continued in the courts. In 1979 in *Bellotti v. Baird II* the Court further strengthened the 1976 *Danforth* ruling that had prohibited parental consent requirements in state laws. However, anti-abortion advocates made some gains in 1990 in *Hodgson v. Minnesota* and *Ohio v. Akron Center for Reproductive Health.* In these cases the Supreme Court upheld state laws requiring some forms of parental notification prior to obtaining an abortion, but not requiring parental approval. Most states soon passed laws adopting the parental notification requirements.

Since the *Roe v. Wade* decision, the debate over abortion rights has continued, even involving several U.S. Presidents encouraging the Supreme Court to reverse its 1973 ruling. In 1989 in *Webster v. Reproductive Health Services* the Court expanded the right of states to regulate abortions. The ruling upheld a Missouri law prohibiting use of publically funded facilities or personnel to perform abortions and created certain other requirements of the attending doctors. In 1992 the Court accepted another reproductive rights case which many anticipated would lead to a reversal of the *Roe* decision. However, much to the surprise of many, the Court did not overturn *Roe,* but did give states more flexibility to regulate abortions. In **Planned Parenthood of Southeastern Pennsylvania v. Casey** the Court ruled that states could regulate abortions prior to fetus viability, but they must not place "undue burdens" on the mother seeking an abortion. A new, weaker standard was created to judge the appropriateness of restrictions on abortions. In sum, since the *Roe* decision in 1973 the Court has steadily increased restrictions on reproductive rights regarding abortions.

War in the Streets

Violence against abortion clinics escalated in the 1990s involving blockades, arson, bombings, vandalism, and shootings. The anti-abortion organization, Operation Rescue, organized mass demonstrations outside abortion clinics, blocking their entrances and harassing women seeking abortions. Court injunctions (orders) against such activities led to a Supreme Court decision. In *Schenck v. Pro-Choice Network of Western New York* (1997) the justices identified the types of restrictions lower court judges could apply to anti-abortion protesters. The Court was attempting to balance free speech rights of the protesters with public safety, property rights, and reproductive rights of those seeking and giving abortions.

In reaction to the violent disruption of legal abortions, Congress passed the Freedom of Access to Clinic Entrances Act in 1994 prohibiting physical threats, blockades, and property damage. Congress also addressed other aspects of abortions. In 1997 it passed the Partial Birth Abortion Ban to prohibit certain types of abortions. But the bill was vetoed by President Bill Clinton over concerns that it did not adequately take into account the mother's safety and health. Abortion rights continued to be a hot topic in Congress.

Artificial Insemination, In Vitro Fertilization, and Surrogacy

Advances in medical technology late in the twentieth century brought new ways of creating pregnancy and with it new legal issues regarding reproductive rights. Artificial insemination involves the sperm of a donor father being medically placed in a woman. This technique not only extended reproductive rights to a woman whose husband may be sterile and cannot produce sufficient sperm, but also to lesbian couples. In vitro fertilization came to the public's attention in 1978 with the birth of the first "test tube child" conceived through the technique. This procedure involves fertilization of a human egg outside the womb and then medically placing the resulting embryo in a woman.

These new forms of conception brought the use of surrogate (substitute) motherhood. The surrogate mother could either be artificially inseminated with sperm from a donor father, or with the fertilized egg cell inserted in her. The surrogate mother then would give custody of the child to the intended parents upon birth. Though initially surrogate mothers were close friends or relatives of the intended parents, by the 1980s contracts with previous strangers became more common.

The first case addressing disputes involving surrogacy came to the courts in 1986 in *In re Baby M.* William and Dr. Elizabeth Stern had arranged for Mary Beth Whitehead to be a surrogate mother. Whitehead was medically inseminated with Stern's sperm and agreed to give the resulting child to the Sterns after birth. She was to be paid $10,000 in addition to medical expenses. However, upon birth of the baby, Whitehead refused to turn custody of the baby to the Sterns. The New Jersey Supreme Court ruled that such contracts were inappropriate and against the public good. Reproductive rights did not include the right to establish such contracts. Surrogacy by contract, the court asserted, was another form of illegal child selling. However, in the best interest of the child in this instance, the court awarded custody to Mr. Sterns and gave Whitehead visitation rights.

The 1990s brought other complex legal disputes over surrogacy. Determining the true legal parents is one complex issue resulting from the expanded reproductive rights. The California Supreme Court in *Johnson v. Calvert* (1993) affirmed the California Uniform Parentage Act in which both the intended mother and the surrogate mother could be identified as the legal mother. Also, the intended father could be a legal father. Implications of such rights came up in California a short time later. John and Luanne Buzzanca had anonymous (unknown contributor) egg and sperm implanted in the mother's womb. However, the Buzzanca's divorced shortly before birth of the child and Luanne sued John for child support. John Buzzanca resisted, claiming the child was not a biological product of their marriage. In 1999 in *In re Marriage of Buzzanca* a California appellate court ruled that Luanne and John were indeed both the legal parents and John was responsible to provide financial child support. Because of the numerous complexities that can result from all different types of parent relationships, the courts have sought to resolve disputes on a case by case basis rather than broad sweeping rulings.

As the twenty-first century began, other complex family law issues faced the courts. Issues involving rights to frozen sperm and eggs, often associated with divorce cases and death of donors, began to occur. Family law appeared to still have plenty of potential for great expansion as reproductive technologies continued to evolve.

Suggestions for further reading

Butler, Douglas J., ed. *Abortion and Reproductive Rights.* CD-ROM, J. Douglas Butler, Inc., 1997.

Currie, Stephen. *Abortion.* San Diego: Greenhaven Press, 2000.

Ginsburg, Faye D. *Contested Lives: The Abortion Debate in an American Community.* Berkeley, CA: University of California Press, 1988.

National Abortion & Reproductive Rights Action League. [Online] Website: http://www.naral.org (Accessed on July 31, 2000).

Olasky, Marvin. *Abortion Rites: A Social History of Abortion in America.* Washington, DC: Regnery Publishing, Inc., 1995.

Stevens, Leonard A. *The Case of Roe v. Wade.* New York: Putnam and Sons, 1996.

Buck v. Bell
1927

Appellant: Carrie Buck

Appellee: Dr. J. H. Bell

Appellant's Claim: That Virginia's eugenic sterilization law violated Carrie Buck's right to equal protection of the laws and due process provided by the U.S. Constitution's Fourteenth Amendment.

Chief Lawyers for Appellant: Irving Whitehead

Chief Lawyers for Appellee: Aubrey E. Strode

Justices for the Court: Louis D. Brandeis, Oliver Wendell Holmes, James Clark McReynolds, Edward T. Sanford, Harlan F. Stone, George Sutherland, William H. Taft, Willis Van Devanter

Justices Dissenting: Pierce Butler

Date of Decision: May 2, 1927

Decision: Upheld as constitutional Virginia's compulsory sterilization of young women considered "unfit [to] continue their kind."

Significance: Virginia's law served as a model for similar laws in thirty states, under which 50,000 U.S. citizens were sterilized without their consent. During the Nuremberg war trials following World War II (1939–45) , German lawyers cited the decision as a precedent for the sterilization of two million people in its "Rassenhygiene" (race hygiene) program. U.S. sterilization programs continued into the 1970s.

Sterilization of "Mental Defectives"

In a 1927 letter written shortly after the *Buck v. Bell* decision, Supreme Court justice Oliver Wendell Holmes said, "One decision . . . gave me pleasure, establishing the constitutionality of a law permitting the sterilization [to make incapable of producing children] of imbeciles." "Imbeciles," "feebleminded," and "mental defectives" were harsh terms frequently used during the nineteenth and early twentieth centuries when referring to persons with mental retardation (MR). A fear of allowing persons with MR to have children grew from the eugenics movement in the late nineteenth century. Based on newly developing scientific theories concerning heredity, the movement sought to control mating and reproduction to improve both physical and mental qualities of the general human population. By the 1910s a scientific foundation for eugenics had accumulated data based on studies of generations of "mental defectives." Experts called for sterilization of the "feebleminded" as the best way to stop future generations of "mental defectives."

Consequently, personal decisions of the mentally retarded about becoming parents and raising children became increasingly subjected to government regulation. State laws were passed directing others to make these choices for them. Several state asylums (institutions housing persons with MR and other mental problems) began sterilizing their patients. By 1917 twelve states passed sterilization laws.

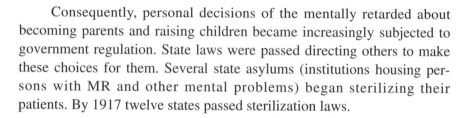

Dr. Albert Priddy

Central to the drive for population improvement through the eugenics movement and sterilization was Dr. Albert Priddy, superintendent of the State Colony for Epileptics and Feeble-Minded at Lynchburg, Virginia. During the 1910s, with encouragement of the colony's board of directors, Priddy sterilized some seventy-five to one hundred young women without their consent. However, the Virginia legislature had not clearly endorsed sterilization and Priddy discontinued the operations in 1918. Priddy, his friend Aubrey Strode who was a state legislator and chief administrator of the colony, and the eugenical community pressured the legislature for a clear sterilization law. With the state experiencing budget problems, Priddy's group proposed a law that provided for release after sterilization of individuals who otherwise might require permanent costly stays at the Colony.

In 1924 the Virginia Assembly enacted a law permitting forced sterilization of "feebleminded" or "socially inadequate person[s]." The law outlined the process to be followed including appointing a guardian, hearings, and court appeals. Three generations of the Buck family living in Virginia soon became entangled in this legal web.

The Bucks

Emma Buck, the widowed mother of three small children, supported her children through prostitution and charity until they were finally taken from her. Three year-old Carrie Buck, Emma's daughter, went to live with J. T. and Alice Dobbs. Carrie progressed normally through five years of school before being taken out so she could assume more household duties. The Dobbs were completely satisfied with Carrie until at age seventeen she claimed she had been raped by the Dobbs' son and became pregnant. A Binet-Simon I. Q. test revealed Carrie's mental age as nine. As soon as Carrie's baby, Vivian, was born the Dobbs had Carrie committed to the Colony for the Epileptic and

Carrie Buck Eagle and her husband, William Eagle.
Courtesy of the Library of Congress.

Feebleminded in 1924. Only four years earlier, Carrie's mother had been found to have a mental age of eight and was confined at the same institution.

Concluding Carrie had inherited her feeblemindedness from her mother and that baby Vivian had no doubt inherited the same condition, Dr. Priddy saw Carrie as a perfect test case for Virginia's new sterilization law. He recommended she be sterilized because she was feebleminded and a "moral delinquent."

The Perfect Test Case

Dr. Priddy's recommendation met with the Colony board's approval. They hired Aubrey Strode to represent the Colony and Irving Whitehead, former Colony board member and friend of Strode, to represent Carrie.

In November of 1924, *Buck v. Priddy* was argued before the Circuit Court of Amherst. Strode called eight witnesses and presented one expert's written testimony. Carrie was characterized as having inherited her feeblemindedness from her mother. Although Carries's baby, Vivian, was only eight months old, she was likewise described as "not quite a normal baby." Carrie, already having one illegitimate child, was described as the "potential parent of [more] socially inadequate offspring." Dr. Priddy testified that Carrie, "would cease to be a charge on society if sterilized. It would remove one potential source" of more feebleminded offspring.

Whitehead made no defense for Carrie neglecting to point out her church attendance and normal school record. Although he would be required to argue for Carrie in the higher courts, Whitehead really sought the same result as Priddy and Strode. They intended to appeal the case through all the courts hoping to receive total support for the sterilization law.

The Circuit Court upheld the law and ordered the sterilization of Carrie Buck. Whitehead appealed in 1925 to the Supreme Court of Appeals of the State of Virginia which upheld the Circuit Court decision. The case was now *Buck v. Bell* because Dr. Priddy had died and Dr. J. H. Bell had taken his place at the Colony. Whitehead next appealed the case to the U.S. Supreme Court.

"Three generations of imbeciles are enough."

In the brief (a summary outlining the essential information) he submitted to the Supreme Court, Whitehead claimed that the Virginia law was void (should no longer be law) because it denied Carrie due process of law and equal protection of the laws, rights guaranteed by the Fourteenth Amendment. The Fourteenth Amendment states that no state shall "deprive any person of life, liberty or property without due process of law; nor deny to any person . . . equal protection of the laws." Due process means a person must have fair legal proceedings. Equal protection means persons or groups of persons in similar situations must be treated equally by the laws.

Strode's brief countered that Carrie had been given a great deal of due process and that the state could make sterilization decisions for people like Carrie without violating equal protection. Justice Oliver Wendell Holmes delivered the 8-1 opinion upholding the Virginia sterilization law.

After reviewing the long process the law requires a superintendent of a hospital or colony to follow before carrying out sterilization, Holmes concluded due process was not violated. Holmes wrote,

> There can be no doubt that so far as procedure is concerned the rights of the patient are most carefully considered, and . . . every step in this case was taken in scrupulous compliance with the statute [followed exactly the procedures outlined by the law].

Holmes similarly rejected the claim of equal protection violation saying the law treated all persons in similar situations as Carrie.

Agreeing with the philosophy of eugenics, Justice Holmes proclaimed that society must be protected from "being swamped with incompetence." He wrote, "It is better for all the world, if instead of waiting to execute offspring for crime, or to let them starve for their imbecility, society can prevent those who are manifestly unfit from continuing their kind . . . three generations of imbeciles are enough [referring to the three Bucks]."

What Became of Carrie Buck?

Dr. Bell sterilized Carrie Buck in October of 1927 and then released her from the Colony. She married William Davis Eagle in 1932 and, after his

EUGENICS

Eugenics is a science theory developed in the late nineteenth century concerned with improving hereditary qualities of the human population by encouraging persons who are considered above average mentally and physically to have more children and discouraging offspring from parents of lesser mental and physical abilities. Francis Galton began using the term in 1883 which is Greek meaning good birth. Charles Darwin's theory of natural selection introduced in 1859 provided the basic concepts behind eugenics. Galton reasoned that society's sympathy and caring for the weak stopped proper natural selection in mankind. This allowed "inferior" humans to live and reproduce when they otherwise would have been selected against and eliminated. Therefore, eugenics is a replacement of natural selection with conscious, controlled selection of desirable characteristics and the elimination of undesirable ones.

By 1931 eugenicists had convinced American states to pass sterilization laws barring "flawed" individuals from reproducing. Worldwide, by the mid-1930s Norway, Sweden, Denmark, Switzerland, and Germany followed suit. In 1933 Germany had passed the Hereditary Health Law. In the name of eugenics, Germany's Adolf Hitler sterilized and murdered millions in the 1930s and 1940s.

While sterilizations were no longer practiced, eugenic organizations still exist in the United States at the beginning of the twenty-first century. New forms of selecting hereditary traits appeared such as the widely accepted practice of aborting a fetus (unborn child) if found to have a disability and through sperm selection from sperm donor banks for methods of artificial conception.

death, married Charlie Detamore. Later recollections of her minister, neighbors, friends, and health care providers plus letters she wrote to the Virginia colony seeking custody of her mother all suggest Carrie was truly not "feebleminded."

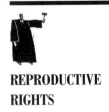
At least twenty-seven other states and several countries passed laws similar to Virginia's resulting in forced sterilization of thousands of people. By the mid-twentieth century Americans had become more sensitive to and educated about the needs of persons with MR. By the 1960s people with MR began to mainstream into a more normal everyday life in schools and with their families. Sterilization of persons with MR still continued in the United States until the mid-1970s. However, by the close of the twentieth century the *Buck v. Bell* decision had not yet been overturned.

Suggestions for further reading

Brantlinger, Ellen A. *Sterilization of People with Mental Disabilities.* Westport, CT: Auburn House Publications, 1995.

Eugenics Watch. [Online] Website: http://www.africa2000.com/ENDX/endx.htm (Accessed on July 31, 2000).

Field, Martha A., and Valerie A. Sanchez. *Equal Treatment for People with Mental Retardation: Having and Raising Children.* Boston: Harvard University Press, 2000.

Future Generations. [Online] Website: http://www.eugenics.net (Accessed on July 31, 2000).

Smith, J. David, and K. Ray Nelson. *The Sterilization of Carrie Buck.* Far Hills, NJ: New Horizon Press, 1989.

Eisenstadt v. Baird
1972

Appellant: Thomas Eisenstadt, Sheriff of Suffolk County, Massachusetts

Appellee: William R. Baird, Jr.

Appellant's Claim: That the Massachusetts Supreme Judicial Court erred in overturning Baird's conviction on charges of distributing contraceptives without a proper liscense.

Chief Lawyers for Appellant: Joseph R. Nolan

Chief Lawyers for Appellee: Joseph D. Tydings

Justices for the Court: Harry A. Blackmun, William J. Brennan, Jr., William O. Douglas, Thurgood Marshall, Potter Stewart, Byron R. White

Justices Dissenting: Chief Justice Warren E. Burger (Lewis F. Powell, Jr., and William H. Rehnquist did not participate)

Date of Decision: March 22, 1972

Decision: Ruling in favor of Baird, the Court upheld the Massachusetts Supreme Judicial Court decision that the state law was unconstitutional because it denied unmarried and married persons equal protection in violation the Fourteenth Amendment.

Significance: The decision expanded the right of privacy to unmarried people and made contraceptives legally available to them throughout the United States. Importantly, the decision broadened the constitutional right of privacy in a way that foreshadowed the Court's landmark finding the following year that the right to privacy protects a woman's right to have an abortion.

REPRODUCTIVE RIGHTS

In 1873 U.S. Congress passed of a federal law, commonly known as the Comstock Act, prohibiting the distribution of birth control devices as well as information about birth control methods. Most states also had laws banning the sale, distribution, and advertising of contraceptives (birth control devices). One state law, Connecticut's, completely banned the use of contraceptives for anyone anywhere. In spite of the laws, the need for birth control resulted in the growth of birth control advocacy (support, in favor of) groups. In 1916 Margaret Sanger opened a birth control clinic in New York City and, continuing her role of reforming attitudes toward birth control, founded the organization Planned Parenthood in 1942.

Opened in 1961, the Planned Parenthood League of Connecticut, directed by Estelle Griswold, provided information to married people about the use of birth control methods to prevent pregnancy. Soon, Griswold faced charges of violating Connecticut's 1879 law banning the use of contraceptives. The U.S. Supreme Court struck down the law in *Griswold v. Connecticut* (1964) as an unconstitutional invasion of an

TYPES OF CONTRACEPTIVES		
Effectiveness	**Predicted (%)**	**Actual (%)**
Birth control pills	99.9	97
Condoms	98	88
Depo Provera	99.7	99.7
Diaphragm	94	82
IUDs	99.2	97
Norplant	99.7	99.7
Tubal sterilization	99.8	99.6
Spermicides	97	79
Vasectomy	99.9	99.9

Source: Adapted from Trousel et al, *Obstetrics and Gynecology*, 76 1990: 558.

The effectiveness of different kinds of contraception. Reproduced by permission of Stanley Publishing.

individual's right to privacy in relationships between married adults. The Court ruled that contraceptives could not be banned for married adults. However, furnishing contraceptives to unmarried people remained illegal in many states. In Massachusetts a birth control law made it a felony (serious crime),

> **for anyone to give away a drug, medicine, instrument or article for the prevention of conception [pregnancy] except in the case of (1) a registered [licensed] physician administering or prescribing it for a married person or (2) an active registered pharmacist furnishing it to a married person presenting a registered physician's prescription.**

William R. Baird, Jr., Arrested for Lecture

In 1967, birth control activist William R. Baird, Jr. came to the campus of Boston University to give a lecture to students on birth control methods and to distribute birth control devices to interested coeds. Pointing out that over ten thousand women had died from illegal abortions in 1966, he condemned laws making contraceptives available only to married women under a doctor's care. He intended to "test this law in Massachusetts. . . No group, no law, no individual can dictate to a woman what goes on in her own body." Baird was neither a licensed physician nor licensed pharmacist. Between 1500 to 2000 people attended his lecture on contraception and at the end he gave a woman a package of contraceptive foam directly violating the law. Baird was immediately arrested.

Baird Convicted

Baird was not arrested for distributing the contraceptive foam to an unmarried person. No proof was actually ever offered that the woman was unmarried. Instead, Baird was charged under the law with having no license and, therefore, no authority to distribute to anyone. The Massachusetts Superior Court found Baird guilty of violating the law as did the Massachusetts Supreme Judicial Court. The Supreme Judicial Court saw the law as a health measure designed to prevent "dangerous physical consequences" by allowing only a licensed physician or pharmacist to legally distribute contraceptives. Baird was neither a licensed physician nor pharmacist, therefore not authorized to distribute the contraceptive. Hence, he violated the law.

**REPRODUCTIVE
RIGHTS**

*Contraceptives come
in many different
forms.*
Reproduced by
permission of the Gamma
Liaison Network.

Almost three years after his first conviction, the First Circuit Court of Appeals ruled in July of 1970 that the Massachusetts birth control law was unconstitutional and reversed Baird's conviction. The appeals court interpreted the law as actually a prohibition on contraception which the *Griswold* decision outlawed when it struck down Connecticut's prohibition against the use of contraceptives by married couples. Sheriff Thomas Eisenstadt of Suffolk County, Massachusetts appealed to the U.S. Supreme Court. The Supreme Court agreed to hear the case.

Equal Protection Violation

Baird's chief argument for the Court was simple, the law was unconstitutional because it treated two similar groups (married and unmarried persons) unequally and the state did not have a compelling (very important) reason or purpose to do so. Justice William J. Brennan, Jr., delivered the opinion of the Court, a 6–1 vote as two justices did not take part.

After accepting that Baird could indeed speak for unmarried persons who had been denied access to contraceptives, the Court examined

the Massachusetts law to see if it violated the Equal Protection Clause of the Fourteenth Amendment. The Equal Protection Clause says that a state shall not deny equal protection of the laws to any person. The Massachusetts law, obviously, treated unmarried persons and married persons unequally in their access to contraceptive. If it did violate equal protection, the Court would then have to find a compelling purpose for the state to need the law or it could not stand. The Court considered three points before coming to their conclusion.

First, the Court inspected the law to see if the state's purpose could legitimately be to discourage premarital sexual intercourse, called "fornication" in legal matters. Brennan wrote, "the statute [law] is riddled with exceptions making contraceptives freely available for use in premarital sexual relations [under various circumstances]." Because of the many exceptions or holes in the law, Brennan noted deterring fornication could not reasonably be considered as the key purpose of the ban on distribution of contraceptives to unmarried persons.

Secondly, the Court, continuing to look for a compelling state aim, explored the Massachusetts Supreme Judicial Court's decision. The purpose of the law was, according to that court, to protect "the health needs of the community by regulating the distribution of potentially harmful articles [some types of contraceptives]." The Court found that when the law was first written by the Massachusetts legislature, its purpose had nothing to do with health, but was directed at preserving morals. Besides, this law would still be "discriminatory against the unmarried, and was overbroad [reach too far]." There were other laws to prohibit distribution of harmful drugs. Justice Brennan rejected health as the law's purpose.

Thirdly, Justice Brennan asked, "If the Massachusetts statute cannot be upheld as a deterrent to fornication or as a health measure, may it, nevertheless, be sustained simply as a prohibition on contraception?" Agreeing with the First Circuit Court of Appeals, Brennan wrote,

> **whatever the rights of the individual to access . . .
> contraceptives may be, the rights must be the same
> for the unmarried and married alike. If under
> *Griswold* the distribution of contraceptives to married persons cannot be prohibited, a ban on distribution to unmarried persons would be equally
> impermissible [not permitted].**

Next came Justice Brennan's famous and memorable reasoning,

REPRODUCTIVE RIGHTS

Many schools and community centers have started handing out contraceptives and health information as a way of keeping teens safe and informed.
Reproduced by permission of AP/Wide World Photos.

It is true that in *Griswold* the right of privacy in question inhered [exists in] in the marital relationship. Yet the marital couple is not an independent entity [body] with a mind and heart of its own, but an association of two individuals each with a separate intellectual and emotional makeup. If the right of privacy means anything, it is the right of the individual, married or single, to be free from unwarranted governmental intrusion into matters so fundamentally affecting a person as the decision whether to bear or beget [create] a child.

With that the Court held the Massachusetts laws clearly violated the Equal Protection Clause by treating married and unmarried persons unequally. It further found that Massachusetts had no compelling reason to have the law. The Court affirmed the First Circuit Court of Appeals ruling that the law was unconstitutional and overturned Baird's conviction.

PLANNED PARENTHOOD FEDERATION/WESTERN HEMISPHERE REGION (IPPF/WHR)

IPPF/WHR was founded in New York City in 1954 and is one of six regions that make up the International Planned Parenthood Federation. The IPPF/WHR region covers forty-six countries throughout Latin America, the Caribbean, the United States, and Canada. The IPPF/WHR serves more than eight million people each year through over 40,000 service clinics. Their mission is to "Promote and defend the right of women and men, including young people, to decide freely the number and spacing of their children, and the right to the highest possible level of sexual and reproductive health."

IPPF/WHR focuses especially on advancing the family planning movement in traditionally underserved areas and emphasizes mother and child health. Through information, support, and providing access to family planning services, IPPF/WHR works to eliminate unsafe abortions.

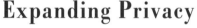

Expanding Privacy

The Supreme Court established a broader view of privacy in *Eisenstadt,* stating that all individuals married or single, enjoy the liberty to make certain personal decisions free from government interference. This clearly included the decision whether or not to have a baby. This reasoning would foreshadow the Court's 1973 finding in **Roe v. Wade** that the right to privacy protected a woman's right to have an abortion. Four years later the Supreme Court also cited *Eisenstadt* in ruling in *Carey v. Population Services International* (1977) that states could not prohibit the distribution of contraceptives to minors.

Suggestions for further reading

Benson, Michael D. *Coping with Birth Control.* New York: Rosen
   Publishing Group, 1998.

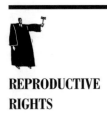

**REPRODUCTIVE
RIGHTS**

International Planned Parenthood Federation, Western Hemisphere Region, Inc. [Online] Website: http://www.ippfwhr.org (Accessed July 31, 2000).

Jacobs, Thomas A. *What Are My Rights?: 95 Questions and Answers About Teens and the Law.* Minneapolis, MN: Free Spirit Publishing, Inc., 1997.

Roe v. Wade
1973

Plaintiff: Norma McCorvey (known as Jane Roe)

Defendant: Henry B. Wade, Texas District Attorney

Plaintiff's Claim: That a 1859 Texas abortion law violated women's constitutional right to have an abortion.

Chief Lawyers for Plaintiff: Sarah Weddington and Linda Coffee

Chief Lawyers for Defendant: Jay Floyd and Robert Flowers

Justices for the Court: Harry A. Blackmun, William J. Brennan, Jr., Chief Justice Warren E. Burger, William O. Douglas, Thurgood Marshall, Lewis F. Powell, Potter Stewart

Justices Dissenting: William H. Rehnquist, Byron R. White

Date of Decision: January 22, 1973

Decision: Ruled in favor of Roe and struck down the Texas abortion law as unconstitutional.

Significance: The decision legalized abortion. The ruling included three key ideas. First, the ruling recognized the right of women to choose to have an abortion during the stage of pregnancy (one to six months) when the fetus has little chance of survival outside the womb and to obtain the abortion without unreasonable interference from the state. Secondly, the ruling confirmed a state's power to restrict abortions, except to protect a woman's life or health, at the stage (seven to nine months) when a fetus could live outside the womb. Third, the ruling confirmed the principle that the state has interests in both the health of the woman and the life of the fetus.

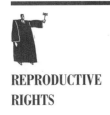

"**M**y name is Norma McCorvey, but you know me as 'Jane Roe.' Twenty-one years ago, when I was poor and alone and pregnant, I was the plaintiff in *Roe v. Wade,* the Supreme Court decision that gave American women the right to choose abortion, to control their . . . own bodies, lives, and destinies" (from *I Am Roe* [1994], an autobiography by Norma McCorvey).

For years after the *Roe v. Wade* decision McCorvey remained anonymous. But in the early 1990s she began to emerge as a public figure. She worked as a telephone counselor in an abortion clinic and later as a cleaning woman, but when time allowed she would travel to various parts of the country to speak at colleges and to women's groups. People reacted to McCorvey in different ways. Some saw her as a famous woman whose name appears in many publications. Others think of her as a "heavy-duty feminist theorist or even a politician," characterizations she laughed at in her autobiography. Those opposed to abortion often called her a "demon" or "baby-killer." But in her own words, "Actually, Norma McCorvey is none of these women. I'm just a regular woman who like so many other regular women, got pregnant and didn't know what to do. . . "

Perhaps more than any other U.S. Supreme Court decision in history, the *Roe v. Wade* ruling, legalizing abortion, aroused passion and controversy. The 1973 decision touched off a battle between supporters of the Pro-Life movement seeking to overturn the ruling and the Pro-Choice supporters working to prevent the decision from being reversed or weakened. The Pro-Life group viewed abortion as murder. The Pro-Choice group was completely convinced that denying a woman the "right to choose" whether or not to have an abortion was an unacceptable government invasion of her freedom and privacy.

A look back at the history of abortion legislation in the United States reveals the stage that was set for *Roe v. Wade.*

Abortion Legal History

No abortion laws existed in the United States until the nineteenth century. The American Medical Association (AMA), established in 1847, became interested in driving out of business unlicensed persons performing abortions. Joined by religious leaders, the AMA successfully lead campaigns to outlaw abortions. By the 1880s all states had laws banning abortions except those performed to save the mother's life. In the 1960s two incidents influenced a re-examination of abortion laws: (1) the discovery that thalidomide, a drug commonly prescribed for the nausea of early pregnancy, caused birth defects and (2) the 1962 to 1965 German measles epidemic. Both resulted in thousands of children born with often severe defects. Pregnant women affected by the incidents could not seek abortions due to the strict laws.

Influenced by the 1960s civil rights movement seeking equality for black Americans, women's rights organizations began to see abortion reform as an important step in the quest for equality of the sexes. Women, they reasoned, needed control of their bodies if they were to

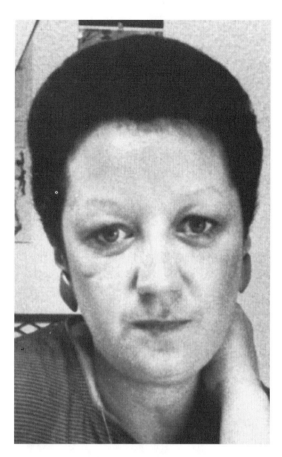

Norma McCorvey decided she was going to support the anti-abortion cause in the 1990s.
Reproduced by permission of the Corbis Corporation.

have control of their lives. Under the banner of reproductive freedom, they demanded outright repeal (cancellation) of state abortion laws. Soon, courts began to attack the most strict state laws. At the same time, the U.S. Supreme Court was developing a concept of the right to privacy in a person's sexual matters. Into this setting entered three women, Norma McCorvey, Sarah Weddington, and Linda Coffee.

Three Women From Texas

Twenty-one year old Norma McCorvey's marriage had ended, and her five year old daughter was being raised by her mother. In 1969 McCorvey, working as a traveling carnival ticket seller, became pregnant again. McCorvey first sought an illegal abortion but became terrified by what she discovered and decided against it. Although illegal abortions were fairly common, many women were permanently injured or died because of the unsanitary conditions under which the abortions were performed. The Texas anti-abortion law, adopted in 1859, prohibited abortions except when considered necessary to save the mother's life. Women who could afford it traveled to other states where abortion laws were less strict or where they could find a doctor who would certify that their abortion was necessary to protect their health. However, McCorvey was poor and, more often than not, poor women got the bad abortions.

Sarah Weddington and Linda Coffee were two of five women in the freshman law school class of 1965 at the University of Texas. Like many women of their generation, both of them became involved in the women's civil rights movement. With the doors to traditional law practices still largely closed to women at the time of their graduation, Weddington and Coffee decided to test the Texas abortion law. They began actively looking for a suitable case. Soon, Coffee learned of Norma McCorvey's plight. Although McCorvey's pregnancy would come to a conclusion before any lawsuit could successfully work its way through the courts,

The abortion struggle has shown little evidence of changing over the years.
Reproduced by permission of the Corbis Corporation.

she agreed to be the plaintiff (the party that sues) in Coffee's and Weddington's test case. McCorvey would be known as "Jane Roe" to protect her real identity. Later, Coffee and Weddington both admitted they were too young and inexperienced to fully understand what they were taking on but both knew the case would be an important one.

A Jammed Dallas Courtroom

The case was first argued before three judges of the Fifth Circuit Court in Dallas on May 23, 1970. Coffee and Weddington had restructured their case to a class-action suit (a lawsuit representing a large number of people with a common interest) so that McCorvey would represent not just herself but all pregnant women.

Coffee and Weddington wanted a decision on whether or not a pregnant woman had the right to decide for herself if an abortion was necessary. They based their arguments on the Ninth and Fourteenth amendments to the U.S. Constitution. The Ninth Amendment stated that even though certain rights were not specifically named in the Constitution, they could still be held by the people. The Fourteenth Amendment prohibited states from denying citizens life, liberty, or property without due process of law (fair legal hearings). In 1965 the U.S. Supreme Court case *Griswold v. Connecticut* had clearly established a constitutional right to privacy found in and protected by the Ninth and Fourteenth amendments. In their case, Coffee and Weddington believed the right or liberty denied Roe by the Texas law was this right to privacy. The Texas law was, they stated, unconstitutional, violating privacy protections the Court found in both amendments. They reasoned this right to privacy should certainly protect the right of a woman to decide whether or not to become a mother.

District Attorney Henry Wade chose John Tolles to defend the enforcement of the Texas abortion law. The Texas Attorney General chose Jay Floyd to defend the law itself. The state prepared its case primarily on the basis that a fetus had legal rights which must be protected by the Constitution.

For the defense, Floyd first claimed that, since Roe's pregnancy had reached a point by that time where an abortion would certainly be unsafe, there was no case. Tolles followed by stating the position "that the right of the child to life is superior to that of a woman's right to privacy."

The three judges disagreed with Floyd and Tolles. They ruled that the Texas law violated Roe's right to privacy found in the Ninth and

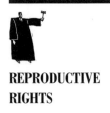
Fourteenth Amendment. A woman did have the right to terminate her pregnancy. The case proceeded to the U.S. Supreme Court.

A Landmark Decision

The case generated intense interest from all over the nation. Forty-two *amici curiae* or "friend of the court" briefs (summary of the beliefs of a certain group about the case) supporting a woman's right to choose an abortion were filed with the Court.

Standing before the Court on December 13, 1971, Coffee, Weddington, Floyd, and Tolles argued the case. However, only seven judges were present and, after hearing the arguments, they decided the case so important that it should be re-argued when the two newly appointed justices, William Rehnquist and Lewis Powell, had joined the Court. The four lawyers did so on October 10, 1972, repeating their arguments.

Justice Harry A. Blackmun wrote the majority opinion for the 7-2 Court which found in favor of Roe. On January 22, 1973, Justice

Sarah Weddington was one of the lawyers arguing Norma McCorvey's case in front of the Supreme Court. Reproduced by permission of the Corbis Corporation.

Blackmun, acknowledging the extreme "sensitive and emotional nature of the abortion controversy," read his majority opinion in the Court chamber filled with reporters.

Rooted in Common Law

The Court first had to decide if the right to choose to terminate pregnancy was indeed a fundamental liberty protected by the Ninth and Fourteenth Amendment. Traditionally, the Court refuses to recognize new fundamental liberties unless they had historically been a right in English common law (based on common practices of a people through time) dating back sometimes as far as the twelfth and thirteenth centuries. Blackmun related the findings of the Court's research. Until the mid-nineteenth century, common law basically relied on the concept of "quickening." Quickening is the first recognizable movement of the fetus within the mother's womb, generally in the fourth to sixth months of pregnancy. Before quickening, the fetus (unborn child) was regarded as part of the mother rather than a separate person. Its destruction was allowed and not considered a crime. Even after quickening, early common law generally viewed termination of the pregnancy not as a crime, certainly not murder. Therefore, the termination of pregnancy *was* indeed rooted in common law. Laws strictly prohibiting abortion did not appear until in the mid-nineteenth century apparently to protect women's health from the then dangerous abortion procedure. Justice Blackmun concluded that abortion, allowed throughout common law, could be considered a protected liberty, and since medical advances had made abortion safe when properly carried out, no reason existed to continue the abortion laws.

Right of Privacy

Next, Justice Blackmun established that the right to an abortion fell within the right of privacy. Delivering the crucial point of the decision, Blackmun wrote,

> **The right of privacy, whether it be founded in the Fourteenth Amendment's concept of personal liberty and restrictions on state action . . . or . . . in the Ninth Amendment's reservation of rights to the people is broad enough to encompass [include] a woman's decision to terminate her pregnancy.**

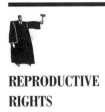

REPRODUCTIVE RIGHTS

Continuing, Justice Blackmun disagreed with Texas' claim that the law protected "prenatal life [before birth]." He explained that "the word 'person' as used in the Fourteenth Amendment, does not include the unborn."

However, Blackmun said that neither the woman's right to privacy in abortion nor the fetus' lack of a right to the state's protection was unlimited. He wrote,

> **The State does have an important and legitimate [honest] interest in preserving and protecting the health of the pregnant woman . . . and . . . it has still another important and legitimate interest in protecting the potentiality of human life [the not yet but soon to be born] . . . as the woman approaches term [ninth month of pregnancy]. . . .**

Roughly following the quickening concept in common law, Justice Blackmun offered the states a formula to balance these competing interests. During the first trimester (first three months of pregnancy) the decision to abort would be the mother's and her physician. During the second trimester (months 4-6; the stage when quickening occurs), a state might regulate the abortion "in ways that are reasonably related to maternal [mother's] health." This meant that the state, recognizing several medical procedures existed to carry out abortion, must encourage the procedures which are safest for the mother's health. The fetus, at this stage, most likely could not live outside the mother's womb, so the mother's health is the primary concern. In the last trimester (months 7-9) until birth, a state might "regulate," even prohibit, abortion except to preserve the life or health of the mother. By this stage of pregnancy the fetus could likely live outside the womb, therefore emphasis should be shifted to protection of the unborn child. Hence, abortion may be prohibited.

The Texas abortion law was found unconstitutional and struck down.

In Dissent

Justices Rehnquist and Byron R. White dissented. Rehnquist disagreed that a medical abortion fell under the right of privacy. White believed the Court had wrongly considered a mother's convenience or whim over the "life or potential life of the fetus."

SARAH WEDDINGTON

Sarah Ragle Weddington was born in Abilene, Texas to a Methodist minister father and a mother who taught school. Excelling in her studies, she graduated from high school early and earned a college degree from McMurray College in 1965. Working at various jobs in the Texas legislature in the state capitol of Austin, Weddington quickly became interested in a law career. She, consequently, earned a law degree from the University of Texas in 1967 and began a law practice in Austin. Soon, she along with Linda Coffee, became the chief lawyers challenging Texas' abortion law in Roe v. Wade. In 1972 at age twenty-seven, Sarah presented legal arguments for the case before the Supreme Court justices. She also served in the Texas House of Representatives from 1972 to 1977.

Following success in the landmark abortion case, Sarah became a national figure. President Jimmy Carter appointed her to several key positions including special presidential assistant on various matters including women's rights. In 1977 Weddington was also appointed as a lawyer for the U.S. Department of Agriculture in Washington, D.C. In 1980 Weddington represented the United States at the World Conference of Women in Copenhagen, Denmark. Sarah later returned to Austin and the University of Texas as instructor and public speaker. In 1992 she published a book, *A Question of Choice,* on abortion rights and other women's issues.

Pro-Life v. Pro-Choice

Following the decision in *Roe v. Wade,* nineteen states needed to rework their abortion laws while thirty-one, including Texas, saw their strict anti-abortion laws entirely struck down. Immediately, *Roe* opponents, "Pro-Life" groups, began their assault on the decision. Several constitutional amendments prohibiting abortions were introduced in Congress. When these failed, *Roe*'s opponents tried to organize the required thirty-

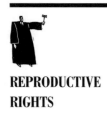

REPRODUCTIVE RIGHTS

four state legislatures to call for a constitutional convention but this also failed by the mid-1980s.

By the early 1980s the Republican Party adopted the Pro-Life position, gaining support of many religious leaders' but losing much support among women. Both Republican presidents, Ronald Reagan and President George Bush, asked the Supreme Court to overturn *Roe.* The Democratic Party, which supported *Roe,* benefitted from the women's vote as Bill Clinton, a supporter of a woman's right to choose, was elected president in 1992 and 1996.

By 1999, Gallup polls showed that 45 percent of Americans fell into the Pro-Choice camp, believing an abortion decision must be left to the woman and her physician. Forty-two percent considered themselves Pro-Life supporters. Pro-Lifers were well-organized, well-funded, and on occasion radical elements turned violent.

Following the *Roe* decision, many of the Supreme Court's more liberal members retired in the 1980s and 1990s. The more conservative Court steadily allowed the states more flexibility in regulating abortion and indicated a willingness to re-examine the *Roe* decision. Many predicted ***Planned Parenthood of Southeastern Pennsylvania v. Casey*** (1992) would overturn *Roe,* but the Court upheld *Roe.* In the year 2000, the basic decision still stood.

Suggestions for further reading

Faux, Marian. *Roe v. Wade: The Untold Story of the Landmark Supreme Court Decision That Made Abortion Legal.* New York: Macmillan Publishing Company, 1988.

McCorvey, Norma. *I Am Roe: My Life, Roe v. Wade, and Freedom of Choice.* New York: HarperCollins Publishers, Inc., 1994.

Stevens, Leonard A. *The Case of Roe v. Wade.* New York: G. P. Putnam's Sons, 1996.

Weddington, Sarah. *A Question of Choice.* New York: Putnam, 1992.

Planned Parenthood of Central Missouri v. Danforth 1976

Appellants: Planned Parenthood of Central Missouri, David Hall, M.D., and Michael Freiman, M.D.

Appellee: John C. Danforth, Attorney General of Missouri

Appellants' Claim: That a Missouri abortion law was too restrictive on many aspects of the abortion process thus violating the patients' constitutional rights.

Chief Lawyers for Appellants: Frank Susman

Chief Lawyers for Appellees: John C. Danforth

Justices of the Court: Harry A. Blackmun, William J. Brennan, Jr., Thurgood Marshall, Lewis F. Powell, Jr.

Justices Dissenting: Chief Justice Warren E. Burger, William H. Rehnquist, John Paul Stevens, Byron R. White

Date of Decision: July 1, 1976

Decision: Ruled in favor of Danforth on some state requirements including provisions defining viability of the fetus, requiring a written consent by the pregnant women before an abortion, and keeping detailed medical records by abortion clinics. On other parts of the law, the Court ruled in favor of Planned Parenthood striking down Missouri's requirement for a husband's consent and, for unmarried minors, parental consent before receiving an abortion, prohibition of the saline amniocentesis abortion procedure, and requirement for physicians to preserve the fetus' life after an abortion.

*P*lanned Parenthood of Central Missouri v. Danforth was just the sort of case the Supreme Court expected on the heels of the landmark *Roe v. Wade* decision legalizing abortion. The case presented many "logical [reasonable]" questions following the earlier ruling.

Decided in 1973 **Roe v. Wade** had been the most important and controversial legal victory for women since achieving the right to vote. *Roe* established a "right to privacy" involving "a woman's decision whether or not to terminate [end] her pregnancy." However, in *Roe* the Supreme Court "emphatically rejected" the idea that "the woman's right is absolute [unlimited] and that she is entitled to terminate her pregnancy at whatever time in whatever way and for whatever reason she alone chooses." Instead, the Court sought to balance a woman's privacy rights against a state's interest in protecting life, in this case the unborn child. The Court provided in *Roe* a balancing formula of acceptable action based on the three stages of pregnancy: (1) during the first three stages of pregnancy the state could not interfere at all in a decision to abort; (2) the next three months of pregnancy (fourth through the sixth month) the state could reasonably regulate the way abortions are done to protect maternal [the mother's] health; and, (3) the last three months of pregnancy (seventh through the ninth month), a stage when the fetus (unborn child) is viable (able to live on its own or with medical help), the state may greatly restrict the mother's decision to have an abortion unless it is necessary "for the life or health of the mother."

Missouri Tackles Abortion Procedures

With the *Roe* decision, strict anti-abortion laws in many states quickly became unconstitutional, including a 1969 Missouri abortion law. However, with the Court recognizing through its balancing formula that states still held an interest in protecting an unborn child, many states began enacting new, revised abortion laws. These new laws, while not directly violating the decisions in Roe, attempted to place some restrictions on abortion. In June of 1974 the Missouri General Assembly passed a new abortion act, House Bill 1211, and the governor signed it into law. The new Missouri law placed a number of requirements on the abortion procedure, and outlawed certain practices.

Within three days of House Bill 1211's passage, Planned Parenthood of Central Missouri and two physicians who regularly performed abortions, David Hall and Michael Freiman, challenged the law in the U.S. Court for the Eastern District of Missouri. The action was

Planned
Parenthood
of Central
Missouri v.
Danforth

Many public figures lend their voices to the pro-choice cause, such as Cybil Shephard, Whoopi Goldberg, and Marlowe Thomas. Reproduced by permission of the Corbis Corporation.

brought on behalf of all licensed physicians involved with abortions and their patients desiring to terminate pregnancy within Missouri. John C. Danforth, Attorney General of Missouri, argued the case for the state of Missouri in support of the new abortion law. Being contested in the suit was the constitutionality of several provisions (parts or sections of the law). The provisions concerned various issues including the definition of viability, required consent before an abortion, use of a procedure called saline amniocentesis, record keeping by clinics, and the professional care given to an aborted fetus.

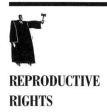

The District Court found in favor of the state of Missouri in all but one of the contested issues. Planned Parenthood and the two doctors then took their case to the U.S. Supreme Court. The Court agreed to hear the case so it could clear up questions concerning abortion procedures.

A Complex Ruling

Justice Harry A. Blackmun, who had written the Court's decision in *Roe v. Wade,* again delivered the Court's opinion, this time in a complex eight-part decision. The Court upheld some parts of the Missouri law but struck down others.

First, the Court dismissed one part that declared if an infant survived the abortion it would be taken from its parents and made a state ward. Blackmun pointed out that neither Planned Parenthood nor the two suing physicians really had anything to do with such a situation and, therefore, could not appropriately challenge that part of the law.

Next, Blackmun turned to the law's definition of viability, "that stage of fetal development when the life of the unborn child may be con-

Supporters on both side of the abortion issue find it to be a very emotional struggle.
Reproduced by permission of the Corbis Corporation.

tinued indefinitely outside the womb by natural or artificial life-support-ive systems." In *Roe* he had loosely defined "viable" as the point where the fetus could possibly live outside the mother's womb, using artificial aid if necessary. While stating that neither legislatures nor the courts should try to define what is essentially a technical medical concept, Blackmun nevertheless concluded Missouri's definition of viability was consistent with Roe and upheld the state's definition.

Three Consent Issues

Blackmun next tackled three separate consent issues in the Missouri law. First, Blackmun found constitutional the requirement that a woman must provide written consent (agreement) to the abortion before undergoing it. Blackmun reasoned abortion was a very stressful operation. Requiring written consent from the woman showed she was in control of the decision.

Secondly, Blackmun ruled that spousal consent (husband must agree to the abortion) was unconstitutional. When it comes to making the final decision about having an abortion, Blackmun concluded that "the woman who physically bears the child" should be the one to decide.

Thirdly, Blackmun found unconstitutional the requirement of parental consent for an unmarried minor's (under eighteen years of age) abortion during the first twelve weeks of pregnancy. Blackmun reasoned that constitutional rights do not "magically" appear when one turns eighteen. Furthermore, Blackmun believed the parent consent requirement "providing the parent with absolute power" would not necessarily "serve to strengthen the family unit" as argued by the state.

Three More Issues

The Missouri law prohibited use of saline amniocentesis, the injection of a saline (salt solution) fluid into the sac surrounding the fetus. The fluid causes the fetus to be almost immediately rejected by the mother's body. Blackmun denied this restriction because the procedure was the most commonly used abortion procedure and provided a high degree of safety for the mother. Blackmun stressed that termination of pregnancy by other available means was "more dangerous to the woman's health than the method outlawed."

Two sections of the law required detailed record keeping of all abortions performed. The law required these records be kept seven years.

HOW THE ABORTION DEBATE HAS CHANGED

At the beginning of the twenty-first century, the 1973 decision of *Roe v. Wade* legalizing abortion in the early stages of pregnancy before the unborn fetus could likely survive outside the womb still stood. Abortion debates remained as passionate as ever but generally concerned a "grab bag" of secondary issues and efforts by states to whittle away at a woman's access to abortion. The various issues at the state level included: requiring waiting periods and counseling for women seeking abortions, requiring parental consent, providing money for contraceptive education and family planning, and setting rules for protestors who attempt to blockade abortion clinics. Possibly the most emotional of all was the banning of "partial-birth abortion" which makes illegal certain abortion procedures performed during the last six months of pregnancy.

Congress likewise passed legislation prohibiting federal funding for abortions for various groups such as poor women enrolled in Medicaid, Native American women covered by Indian Health Services, and women in federal prisons, the military, and the Peace Corps. Meanwhile, technological developments have entered the abortion debates. For example, the new French-developed drug RU-486 with the scientific name of mifepristone, also known as the "morning after pill," induces abortion without surgical procedure. The Feminist Majority Foundation waged a nationwide campaign urging its approval. U.S. clinics began testing the drug by 1998.

Blackmun agreed that these requirements were "reasonably directed to the preservation of maternal [the mother's] health. . . " He, therefore, allowed both.

Lastly, Blackmun declared unconstitutional the law's requirement that physicians provide professional care to the fetus as if it was "intended to be born and not aborted" or face manslaughter charges.

Building on Abortion Law

Looking at many facets of abortion procedures, the Court found constitutional the provisions of the law dealing with the term viability, written consent of the woman having the abortion, and extensive record keeping by clinics. The Court decided four other parts were unconstitutional: (1) requirements for husband consent; (2) requirements for parental consent of an unmarried minor; (3) prohibition of the saline amniocentesis medical procedure; and, (4) requiring professional care of the aborted fetus under the threat of manslaughter against the doctor.

Most important was the decisions concerning consent. The Court's position on parental consent later shifted some. In *Belotti v. Baird* (1979) the Court again struck down a state law requiring consent of both parents or the court. The Court found the law unconstitutional because it took away a minor's ability to choose regardless of her best interests, or ability to make informed decisions. But, in *H.L.V. Matheson* (1981) and *Hodgson v. Minnesota* (1990), the Court upheld laws requiring a physician to notify parents of a minor before performing an abortion. The Court reasoned the laws required only notification rather than consent and were in the best interest of the minor.

In **Planned Parenthood of Southeastern Pennsylvania v. Casey** (1992) the Court placed strong restrictions on minors by requiring that they obtain informed consent from at least one parent or a court before receiving an abortion. In *Casey,* the Court still refused to require husband notification.

Suggestions for further reading

Boyle, Mary. *Re-Thinking Abortion: Psychology, Gender, Power, and the Law.* New York: Routledge, 1997.

Graber, Mark A. *Rethinking Abortion: Equal Choice, the Constitution and Reproductive Politics.* Princeton, NJ: Princeton University Press, 1999.

Rein, Mei Ling, Siegel, Mark A., and Nancy R. Jacobs, eds. *Abortion: An Eternal Social and Moral Issue.* Buffalo, NY: Information Plus, 1998.

Planned
Parenthood
of Central
Missouri v.
Danforth

Planned Parenthood of Southeastern Pennsylvania v. Casey
1992

Petitioner: Planned Parenthood of Southeastern Pennsylvania

Respondent: Robert P. Casey, Governor of Pennsylvania, and others

Petitioner's Claim: That restrictions on abortion in a Pennsylvania abortion law violated the Due Process Clause.

Chief Lawyer for Petitioner: Kathryn Kolbert

Chief Lawyer for Respondent: Ernest D. Preate, Jr., Attorney General of Pennsylvania

Justices for the Court: Harry A. Blackmun, Anthony M. Kennedy, Sandra Day O'Connor, David H. Souter, John Paul Stevens

Justices Dissenting: Chief Justice William H. Rehnquist, Antonin Scalia, Clarence Thomas, Byron R. White

Date of Decision: June 29, 1992

Decision: While reaffirming the earlier *Roe v. Wade* decision, the Court also declared Pennsylvania's Abortion Control Act law largely constitutional with some exceptions.

Significance: The decision resolved a national dispute over abortion by upholding the essentials of *Roe v. Wade* while permitting Pennsylvania to regulate abortions so long as the state did not place an undue burden on women.

Through the 1980s the U.S. Supreme Court, took on a decidedly more conservative viewpoint toward the abortion issue than the 1970s court that had decided *Roe v. Wade* legalizing abortion. President Ronald Reagan had appointed justices Sandra Day O'Connor, Antonin Scalia, and Anthony Kennedy to the Court and promoted William Rehnquist to Chief Justice. The changed Court was willing to allow states more authority to regulate abortion. In 1988 Justice Harry A. Blackmun, the author of the *Roe v. Wade* decision, shocked a University of Arkansas audience by bluntly asking, "Will *Roe v. Wade* go down the drain?" He answered his own question with a prediction. "There's a very distinct possibility that it will. . . You can count votes [of the current justices]."

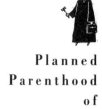
An "Undue Burden"

In 1989, anticipated by Blackmun's words, the Supreme Court in *Webster v. Reproductive Health Services* came within one vote of overturning *Roe v. Wade*. In *Webster* the Court upheld Missouri's right to prohibit using public facilities for abortions, and to require doctors to test for fetal viability (if the unborn child had a possibility of living outside the womb). More importantly four justices, Rehnquist, Kennedy, Scalia, and Byron R. White, voted to completely overturn *Roe v. Wade*. O'Connor was most likely to be the fifth and deciding vote to overturn *Roe*. Yet, she cast her vote to uphold *Roe* suggesting another case would likely come along to more appropriately test *Roe*. However, O'Connor did present a new idea or standard, called "undue burden." She found that Missouri's law was not an "undue burden" (did not create major obstacles) on the right to choose an abortion and was, therefore, constitutionally acceptable.

Testing the Limits

With this new "undue burden" standard left largely undefined and with *Roe v. Wade* having come close to being overturned, *Webster* served as an invitation to state legislators to test just how far the Supreme Court would let them go in regulating abortions. Between 1989 and 1992 more than 700 bills regulating abortion in various ways were introduced across the country. The bills included requirements involving parental consent, husband consent, clinic abortion reporting, and clinic licensing. All were designed to push the limits of the Court's most recent abortion ruling. Some states, such as Louisiana, even attempted to make all abortions illegal, but without success.

REPRODUCTIVE RIGHTS

Pennsylvania became the first in this wave to approve new abortion restrictions when it amended the Abortion Control Act originally enacted in 1982. Governor Robert P. Casey signed the amendment in November of 1989, only four months after the *Webster* decision. Provisions (parts) of the amended Abortion Control Act, which immediately came under fire by Pro-Choice groups (supporting abortion rights), required:

(1) a woman seeking an abortion to give her consent and be provided with state-written information twenty-four hours before the abortion;

(2) a minor to obtain consent from one of her parents or a court;

(3) a married woman to notify her husband of her intended abortion;

(5) reporting requirements for abortion clinics.

To Court

Before any of these provisions took effect, five abortion clinics, a physician representing himself, and a class of physicians who provided abortion services went to court to have the law declared unconstitutional. They contended the law violated a woman's right to choose an abortion

Both sides of the abortion argument express themselves with marches and demonstrations. Reproduced by permission of the Corbis Corporation.

free from state interference. All parties were combined into one case, *Planned Parenthood of Southeastern Pennsylvania v. Casey.*

The District Court ruled that all provisions being challenged were unconstitutional and stopped Pennsylvania from enforcing them. The Court of Appeals for the Third Circuit went almost entirely toward the opposite direction, upholding all the provisions except for the husband notification requirement. The stage was set for the U.S. Supreme Court to hear the case.

To The Heart of Roe v. Wade

Oral arguments began on April 22, 1992 bringing hundreds of thousands of Pro-Choice and Pro-Life (opposing abortions and *Roe v. Wade* decision) women and men to Washington, D.C. As demonstrators rallied outside, lawyers inside took their arguments straight to the heart of *Roe v. Wade.*

Attorneys challenging the Pennsylvania law took the dramatic position that *Roe v. Wade* must be upheld and the law struckdown. Kathryn Holbert, an experienced American Civil Liberties Union (ACLU) lawyer, explained the fundamental issue,

> **[Does] . . . government [have] the power to force a woman to continue or to end pregnancy against her will? Since . . . *Roe v. Wade*, a generation of American women [have been] . . . secure in the knowledge . . . their child-bearing decisions [are protected]. This landmark decision . . . not only protects rights of bodily integrity and autonomy [control over one's own body], but has enabled millions of women to participate fully and equally in society.**

On the other side, attorneys arguing for the Pennsylvania law joined by representatives of President George Bush's administration desired an overthrow of *Roe v. Wade.*

A Surprise Behind Closed Doors

Assuming that a majority of the other justices agreed with him, Chief Justice Rehnquist began to draft the Court's opinion to overturn *Roe.* Rehnquist knew he had Scalia, Clarence Thomas, and White with him. He assumed he also could count on Kennedy and most likely O'Connor.

REPRODUCTIVE RIGHTS

Marches occur all around the country both in support and against abortion. Reproduced by permission of the Corbis Corporation.

However, behind closed doors in a far corner of the Supreme Court building, Justice David H. Souter met with Kennedy and O'Connor. Unexpectedly, Kennedy changed his mind and in a compromise with O'Connor and Souter, the three fashioned an opinion leaving *Roe* intact while upholding the Pennsylvania law. Their private compromise derailed Rehnquist's work. According to *New York Times* reports, Rehnquist and Scalia "were stunned." They failed to gather the five votes needed to overthrow *Roe*. Souter, Kennedy, and O'Connor along with Blackmun and Justice John Paul Stevens voted to uphold the landmark decision.

The Essence of Roe

On Monday morning of June 29, 1992, observers, believing *Roe* would be overturned, were completely unprepared for the decision. The conservative-dominated Court defied all predictions. O'Connor, Kennedy, and Souter delivered the Court's opinion upholding "*Roe*'s essential holding," recognizing a woman's right to choose an abortion. The three thoroughly reviewed the *Roe* decision (see *Roe v. Wade*) and the principles it was based on. The justices affirmed [supported] that the right to have an abortion is indeed a liberty protected by the Due Process Clause of the Fourteenth Amendment. Souter stated, "No state shall 'deprive any person of life, liberty, or property, without due process of law.' The controlling word . . . is 'liberty'."

In a memorable quote, the three justices stated, "It is a promise of the Constitution that there is a realm of personal liberty which the government may not enter."

Planned
Parenthood
o f
Southeastern
Pennsylvania
v. Casey

In Affirming Roe

O'Connor, Kennedy, and Souter used the doctrine of *stare decisis,* meaning courts respect precedents. They are slow to interfere with principles announced in former decisions. Their opinion referred to many former cases which collectively defined liberties not specifically written in the Constitution or Bill of Rights.

The justices rejected "*Roe*'s rigid trimester [based on stages of pregnancy] framework. . . " Instead, the "undue burden standard should be employed. An undue burden exists, and therefore a provision of law is invalid [unlawful], if its purpose or effect is to place substantial obstacles in the path of a woman seeking an abortion before the fetus [unborn child] attains viability."

Since *Roe* recognized a state's interest in the potential life of the fetus, the justices wrote that a state may impose requirements without causing an undue burden on the woman, such as a rquired waiting period during which the woman would receive further information on the process of abortion. With this, the justices upheld all of the provisions of the Pennsylvania Abortion Control Act except requiring the woman to notify her husband of the intended abortion. The Court considered this requirement an undue burden.

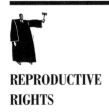

AMERICAN ATTITUDES ON ABORTION

Two questions asked by the Gallup Poll show how Americans's attitudes toward abortion have changed over the years. "With respect to the abortion issue, would you consider yourself to be pro-choice or pro-life?" In September of 1997, 56 percent of Americans regarded themselves as pro-choice and 33 percent pro-life. By Spring of 1999 the gap had closed to 48 percent pro-choice and 42 per cent pro-life.

"Do you think abortions should be legal under any circumstances, legal only under certain circumstances, or illegal in all circumstances?" In April of 1975, 21 percent of Americans answered yes to legal under any circumstance. Fifty-four percent chose legal only under certain circumstances while 22 percent answered illegal in all circumstances. By January of 2000, twenty-seven years after *Roe v. Wade,* the breakdown was 26 percent, 56 percent, and 15 percent. These percentages reflect a small increase in the number of persons supporting abortion under any circumstances.

In all, the Court reaffirmed the essential principles of *Roe* while also allowing states to impose requirements on the abortion process just so long as they do not *cause* an undue burden on the woman.

Reactions

Politically, both sides, Pro-Choice and Pro-Life, declared defeat. Pro-Choice asserted that state regulations such as mandatory waiting periods and parental consent would work together to weaken *Roe.* Furthermore, Pro-Choice groups realized they were only one vote away from seeing *Roe* overturned. On the other side, Pro-Life groups had clearly failed to have abortion made illegal.

For years after the *Casey* decision, the case was widely believed to be the most important abortion decision since *Roe.* It was viewed as a case where justices put respect for earlier Court decisions ahead of political pressures. Because the decision came from a court thought to be conservative, a woman's right to an abortion appeared to rest on somewhat firmer ground.

Suggestions for further reading

The Gallup Poll. [Online] http://www.gallup.com/poll/indicators/ind-abortion.asp (Accessed on July 31, 2000).

The National Abortion and Reproductive Rights Action League Foundation (NARAL). [Online] Website: http://www.naral.org (Accessed on July 31, 2000).

National Right to Life Committee, Inc. [Online] Website: http://www.nrlc.org (Accessed on July 31, 2000).

"Roe v. Wade," A Reader. *Belmont, CA: Wadsworth Publications, 1998.*

Rein, Mei Ling, Siegel, Mark A., and Nancy R. Jacobs, eds. *Abortion: An Eternal Social and Moral Issue.* Buffalo, NY: Information Plus, 1998.

Planned Parenthood of Southeastern Pennsylvania v. Casey

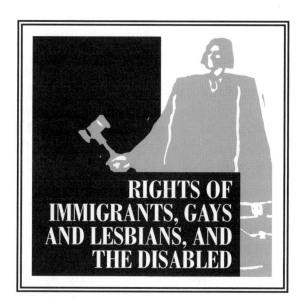

RIGHTS OF IMMIGRANTS, GAYS AND LESBIANS, AND THE DISABLED

The Fourteenth Amendment to the U.S. Constitution has been key to the protection of the civil rights of immigrants, gays and lesbians, and the disabled. The amendment provides that no state shall deny "any person within its jurisdiction [geographical area over which it has authority] the equal protection of the law." This is the Equal Protection Clause. Likewise, the Fourteenth Amendment provides that no state shall deprive any person of life, liberty, or prosperity "without due process of law." Due process means an individual, if charged with a crime, must have fair legal hearings. Many legal actions involving immigrants, gays and lesbians, and the disabled are brought under the Fourteenth Amendment. Resulting court decisions reflect the morals and always changing social standards of a diverse nation.

Immigrant's Rights

"Give us your tired, your poor, your huddled masses yearning to breathe free." Invitation on the Statute of Liberty in New York City.

According to the American Civil Liberties Union (ACLU), some fifty-five million immigrants have come to America from its birth to the end of the twentieth century. Except for Native Americans, all people in the United States have immigrant ancestors, or are present-day immigrants. The United States has been shaped by immigrants and the inscription on the Statute of Liberty testifies to the country's commitment to immigration.

Aliens are foreign born individuals who have not become U.S. citizens through naturalization, the process by which a person becomes a U.S. citizen. Aliens are classified in several ways including non-immigrant and immigrant, and documented (legal alien) and undocumented (illegal alien). Non-immigrants do not intend to settle permanently in the United States. Examples are students, vacationers, and foreign government personnel. Persons granted immigrant status, on the other hand, intend to live and work in the United States and become U.S. citizens.

Immigrants are entitled to many of the same rights as those enjoyed by native-born U.S. citizens. Although they cannot vote or hold federal elective office until they become citizens, the Constitution and Bill of Rights generally apply. The Equal Protection Clause of the Fourteenth Amendments guarantees "equal protection of the laws" to any person living in the United States, citizen or not. States have often passed laws and regulations that violate immigrants' rights and the Equal Protection Clause generally has protected immigrants from these laws.

Even undocumented or illegal aliens (those who have not entered the country legally), once on American soil have some rights under the Constitution. To enter the country illegally is a crime punishable by deportation (forced to leave the country). However, the U.S. Supreme Court, as early as 1903 in *Yamataya v. Fisher* has ruled repeatedly that illegal immigrants may have the right to a hearing that satisfies the Due Process Clause of the Fourteenth Amendment.

Immigration Law

All immigrants are subject to federal immigration law which serves as the nation's gate keeper: who enters, for how long, who may stay, and who may leave. The U.S. Congress has total authority over all immigration law. Although this authority has a long controversial history dating back to the second half of the nineteenth century, the authority was solidified in 1952 with the passage of the Immigration and Nationality Act (INA). INA became the basic source of immigration law. The INA was amended many times as Congress' preferences evolved into a patchwork of regulations reflecting who was wanted and who was not.

Beginning in 1986 Congress passed major new legislation which followed two lines of thought: (1) the need to stop illegal immigration, and (2) the need to make laws more fair for legal immigrants. The Immigration Reform and Control Act (IRCA) of 1986 set up requirements aimed at controlling the entry of illegal immigrants. The Illegal Immigration Reform and Immigrant Responsibility Act of 1996 contained measures to prevent illegal immigration from increasing and to speed up deportation of those illegal immigrants caught. On the other hand the Immigration Act of 1990 dealt with establishing limits on the number of legal immigrants admitted each year and created ways to admit more immigrants from underrepresented countries.

U.S. Supreme Court Cases and Immigrants

Many U.S. Supreme Court cases have protected immigrants from discriminatory state and local laws and enforced the idea that only Congress can enact immigrant law. In *Yick Wo v. Hopkins* (1886), the Court ruled that the Fourteenth Amendment's equal protection of the laws applied to immigrants as well as citizens. The decision rejected a San Francisco law clearly discriminating against Chinese. In 1915 in *Truax v. Raich,* the Court overruled an Arizona law and established the right to earn a living as a basic freedom that could not be denied to immigrants.

The Court's stance changed a bit in the late 1970s and 1980s. The Court upheld New York's restrictive policies denying teacher credentials to alien immigrants in *Ambach v. Norwick* (1979). It then upheld a California law preventing alien immigrants from serving as probation officers in *Cabell v. Chavey-Salido* (1982). On the other hand, the Court ruled in a 1982 Texas case, *Plyler v. Doe,* that children of illegal aliens have the right to attend public schools.

The mid- to late-1990s saw more state attempts to limit immigrants' rights as California voters passed the controversial Proposition 187 in 1994. Proposition 187 restricted public services, such as public school education and non-emergency health care, to illegal aliens, and required immigrant students to learn English. Congress itself passed legislation to cut social benefits such as Medicaid (health insurance) and Supplementary Security Income (additional income payments) in 1996. However, the Court took steps in *League of United Latin American Citizens v. Pete Wilson* (1997) and *Sutich v. Callahan* (1997) to restore such services.

Rights of the Disabled

Roughly forty-three million people in the United States possess one or more physical or mental disabilities. Disability was first defined in Section 504 of the Rehabilitation Act of 1973 as, "any person who has a physical or mental impairment which substantially limits one or more major life activities."

A major life activity is a basic function which the average person can perform with little or no difficulty, such as caring for oneself, walking, seeing, hearing, speaking, learning, and working. Examples of physical impairments are deafness, blindness, speech impairments, and crippling conditions. It also includes such diseases such as cancer, arthritis, and heart disease which have progressed to a point to limit a person's basic functioning. In *Bragdon v. Abbott* (1998) the U.S. Supreme Court ruled that infection with HIV virus (AIDS) constitutes a disability. Mental impairments include mental illness, severe emotional disturbances, traumatic brain injury, and specific learning disabilities, such as the condition commonly known as dyslexia. In every case, the disability must limit an individual's major life activity.

Society has often isolated and restricted persons with disabilities. Disabled individuals have a long history of unequal treatment and occupy an inferior status in society due to characteristics beyond their control. Disabled persons are often politically powerless and unable to pursue legal avenues to counter the discrimination. Rights of disabled persons were established in the second half of the twentieth century though Congressional legislation and in the courts.

Cases and Laws—Laws and Cases

Case decisions and legislative acts (laws) mixed together to develop the rights of disabled persons. Education of the disabled was often a driving force behind cases and laws. In 1971, *Pennsylvania Association for Retarded Citizens (PARC) v. The Commonwealth of Pennsylvania* established the right to a free public education for all children with mental retardation. *Mills v. Board of Education of the District of Columbia* established the right of every child to an education full of equal opportunities. Lack of funds was not an acceptable excuse for lack of educational opportunity. A landmark law extending civil rights to people with disabilities is the Rehabilitation Act of 1973. Section 504 of this law states, "no otherwise qualified handicapped individual shall, solely by reason of his handicap, be excluded from the participation in, be denied the benefits of, or be subjected to discrimination in any program or activity receiving federal financial assistance (monetary funds)." The court orders of the cases decided in 1971 and 1972 are basically contained in Section 504, the name by which the law is commonly referred to. This law, worded almost identically to the Civil Rights Act of 1964 which prohibited discrimination on the basis of race, color, or national origin, expanded opportunities for children and adults with disabilities in education and employment.

Closely following Section 504 was Education for All Handicapped Children Act (EHA) in 1975. This law required a free and appropriate public education for ALL children regardless of their disability. Categories of disability under EHA include specific learning disabilities making up over fifty percent of students identified as having a disability, speech impairments, mental retardation, serious emotional disturbances, and all physical impairments.

Various cases, such as *Board of Education v. Rowley* (1982), heard in the U.S. Supreme Court, further defined an "appropriate" education. Also, persons with mental retardation recorded victories in **O'Connor v. Donaldson** (1975), *Youngberg v. Rome* (1982), and **City of Cleburne v. Cleburne Living Center** (1985). The first two cases established that persons with mental retardation indeed have constitutional rights. In *City of Cleburne* the Court ruled that communities cannot use a discriminatory residential zoning law to prevent establishment of group homes for persons with mental retardation.

Two major pieces of legislation were passed in 1990. The Education of the Handicapped Act Amendments of 1990 changed the name of EHA to Individuals with Disabilities Education Act (IDEA). IDEA was a common term used throughout educational circles at the end of the twentieth century. This act, in addition to expanding services for the disabled, added autism and traumatic brain injury to the list of disabling conditions. In 1999 Attention Deficit Hyperactive Disorder (ADHD) was added as a disabling condition.

The second major piece of 1990 legislation was the sweeping Americans with Disabilities Act (ADA). Congress passed ADA to provide a clear and comprehensive national order for elimination of discrimination against individuals with disabilities. It was built on the foundation of Section 504 and extended coverage into the private employment sector not previously subject to federal law. ADA also extended civil rights protection into to all public services, public accommodations, transportation, and telecommunications.

Major provisions of ADA include: (a) private employers with fifteen or more employees may not refuse to hire or promote a person because of his disability alone; (b) all new vehicles, such as buses purchased by public services, must have handicapped access; (c) public accommodations such as hotels, restaurants, and malls, must be accessible and must not refuse service to persons with disabilities; and, (d) telephone companies must offer services for the deaf.

Gay and Lesbian Rights

Gay and lesbian organizations seek legal and social equality for gay men and lesbians in the United States. The terms gay and lesbian refer to people who are sexually attracted to and sexually prefer people of the same sex. The sexual preference of an individual for one sex or the other is called a person's sexual orientation. "Sexual orientation" is the phrase generally used when crafting legislation or making claims of discrimination concerning gay and lesbian rights. While the term gay can refer to either male or female, gay is generally used to refer to men. Lesbian always refers to women. Homosexual is a term which refers to either gay men or lesbians.

In the United States, through the 1950s gay men and lesbians kept their sexual orientation a secret as homosexual behavior has a long history of being considered a crime. Hiding their sexual orientation was described by the phrase "in the closet." Encouraged by the 1960s Civil Rights Movement involving black Americans and women and spurred in 1969 by a violent incident in New York City known as Stonewall, the homosexual culture began to come out of the closet and openly work for equality. The gay right movement was born.

Sexual Activity as a Crime

Since the eighteenth century colonial period, sodomy (the sexual acts of homosexuals) has been a crime, generally a felony (serious crime). Until 1961 all states outlawed sodomy. The gay rights movement made the repeal (abolishment) of sodomy laws a primary goal.

Handing the movement a setback, in 1986 the U.S. Supreme Court ruled in **Bowers v. Hardwicks** that homosexuals have no right to engage in sodomy even when it is performed in private and between consenting (willing) adults. The Court found state laws prohibiting such activity do not violate constitutional rights to privacy. Although controversial, the ruling would be the Court's only statement on gay and lesbian rights for almost a decade.

Serving in the Military

Gay men and lesbians fought legal battles in the 1980s and 1990s to serve in the nation's armed forces from which they had traditionally been banned. Historically, the disclosure of homosexual orientation led to discharge. Defense Department data from 1980 to 1990 showed that the various service branches discharged approximately 1500 people each year due to sexual orientation. In 1993 the newly elected President Bill Clinton, determined to keep a campaign pledge, attempted to remove the military ban against gays. However, many senior military officials strongly objected to Clinton's proposal. Clinton developed a compromise plan known as "don't ask, don't tell." Congress wrote the policy into law in September of 1993. "Don't ask, don't tell" prohibits the military from asking about the sexual orientation of its military persons without a specific reason. Two 1994 Court cases dealt with the issue of discharging personnel when they made known their sexual orientation, *Meinhold v. United States Department of Defense* and *Cammermeyer v. Aspin.* The first case to test the constitutionality of the "don't ask, don't tell" policy was *McVeigh v. Cohen* (1998). In each case the courts ruled to reinstate the discharged individuals.

Legalizing Gay and Lesbian Relationships

A major concern of many gay men and lesbians is the legal recognition of their relationships. A same-sex marriage is not treated the same legally as a marriage between a man and a woman. Examples of legal benefits which do not extend to same-sex relationship are survivor benefits when one partner dies, health insurance, and custody of children. The AIDS epidemic makes health insurance a vital issue to the gay and lesbian groups.

Recognition of same-sex marriage has been rejected by the courts until 1996 in *Baehr v. Miike.* The First Circuit Court of Hawaii ruled that denial of a marriage contract to same-sex partners violated the Equal Protection Clause of the Hawaii Constitution. The U.S. Congress, believing that same-sex marriages would soon become legal in Hawaii moved quickly to pass the Defense of Marriage Act (DOMA) in 1996. DOMA defines "marriage" and "spouse" to include only partners of the opposite sex and permits states to bar legal recognition of same-sex marriages performed in other states. A major breakthrough came late in 1999 when the Vermont Supreme Court ruled that same-sex couples should have the same state constitutional protections and rights as traditional marriages.

Issues at State and Local Levels

Gay and lesbian organizations have worked for legislation at the state and local level to ban discrimination based on sexual orientation in housing, banking, and employment. In 1998 ten states had such laws. They are California, Connecticut, Hawaii, Massachusetts, Minnesota, New Hampshire, New Jersey, Rhode Island, Vermont, and Wisconsin.

Despite these successes for gay men and lesbians, those opposed to the social and legal equality for homosexuals created a political backlash in various states during the 1990s. Calling homosexuality abnormal and perverse, the Oregon Citizens Alliance placed a voter referendum (proposed law) on the 1992 Oregon ballot. The referendum would have prohibited civil rights protections for gays and lesbians and required local governments and schools to discourage homosexuality. The referendum was defeated with fifty-seven voting against it.

In Colorado, the state legislature took steps to ban what they saw as a growing legal tolerance of homosexuals. They passed an amendment to the state constitution prohibiting the state or any local government from passing laws to protect the civil rights of gays and lesbians. In the first gay rights case to reach the U.S. Supreme Court since *Bowers* in 1986, the Court found in **Romer v. Evans** (1996) the amendment unconstitutional. Writing for the Court, Justice Anthony M. Kennedy commented the only purpose of the Colorado amendment was to make homosexuals "unequal to everyone else. This Colorado cannot do." The decision caused emotional debate predicting future legal battles over gay and lesbian rights.

Future Rights Issues

As time passes, different groups and different issues concerning the groups discussed above will continuously come to the attention of the public, legislatures, and the courts.

Suggestions for further reading

Clendinen, Dudley, and Adam Nagourney. *Out of Good: The Struggle to Build a Gay Rights Movement in America.* New York: Simon & Schuster, 1999.

Cozic, Charles P. *Illegal Immigration: Opposing Viewpoints.* San Diego, CA: Greenhaven Press, Inc., 1997.

Lambda Legal Defense and Educational Fund. [Online] Website: http://www.lambdalegal.org (Accessed on July 31, 2000).

National Gay & Lesbian Task Force. [Online] Website: http://www.ngltf.org (Accessed on July 31, 2000).

The International Dyslexia Association (formerly the Orton Dyslexia Society). [Online] Website: http://www.interdys.org (Accessed on July 31, 2000).

Truax v. Raich
1915

Appellants: William Truax, Sr., Wiley E. Jones, W.G. Gilmore

Appellee: Mike Raich

Appellants' Claim: That an alien had no legal right to sue the state of Arizona or prevent enforcement of Arizona's Anti Alien Act.

Chief Lawyers for Appellants: Wiley E. Jones, Leslie C. Hardy, George W. Harben

Chief Lawyers for Appellee: Alexander Britton, Evans Browne, Francis W. Clements

Justices for the Court: Louis D. Brandeis, William Rufus Day, Oliver Wendell Holmes, Charles E. Hughes, Joseph McKenna, Mahlon Pitney, Willis Van Devanter, Edward D. White

Justices Dissenting: James C. McReynolds

Date of Decision: November 1, 1915

Decision: Ruled in favor of Raich by finding that Arizona's law denied him his Fourteenth Amendment right to equal protection of the laws and was therefore unconstitutional and unenforceable.

Significance: By declaring Arizona's law unconstitutional, the Supreme Court identified the right to earn a living as a basic freedom protected by the Fourteenth Amendment. The decision reaffirmed the Yick Wo decision that the Equal Protection Clause applied to any person, citizen or alien, living within the United States and that only the U.S. Congress could enact immigration law.

Between 1870 and 1920, twenty-six million people arrived at immigration stations in New York City. Ships as far as the eye could see would be lined up for days in New York Harbor until a space to dock opened at the immigrant processing center on Ellis Island. After leaving Ellis Island many headed for New York but others bought tickets for Chicago, Cleveland, St. Louis, and other cities throughout the United States. All were searching for jobs and a new better life in America.

Equal Protection for Immigrants

Only the U.S. Congress has the authority to determine who may enter the United States. Once an immigrant is admitted to the United States, he or she is entitled to equal protection of the law. The Equal Protection Clause is found in the Fourteenth Amendment to the U.S. Constitution and provides that no state shall "deprive any person of life, liberty, or property, without due process of law [fair legal proceedings]; nor deny to any person within its jurisdiction [geographical area over which a government has authority] the equal protection of the laws." Equal protection means that persons or groups of persons in similar situations must be treated equally by the laws.

Extension of equal protection to new immigrants or aliens (citizen or subject of a foreign country living in the United States) was firmly established in the Supreme Court case *Yick Wo v. Hopkins* (1886). The Court ruled that Equal Protection Clause applied "to all persons within the territorial jurisdiction, without regard to any differences of race, of color, or of nationality [referring to country where a person was born]." Beginning with *Yick Wo* the Court generally required states to show a very important reason or need for any law which applied one way to aliens and a different way to citizens. If no important reason was shown, the law would be found unconstitutional.

Also, in *Yick Wo* the Court described a person's right to earn a living as "essential to the enjoyment of life" and protected by the Fourteenth Amendment. Thirty years later the Court again showed support for the *Yick Wo* decision in the 1915 case of *Truax v. Raich.*

Mike Raich and Arizona's Anti-Alien Employment Act

In December of 1914 Mike Raich, an Austrian native living in Arizona, was in danger of losing his job as a restaurant cook. A state-wide vote by

RIGHTS OF IMMIGRANTS, GAYS AND LESBIANS, AND THE DISABLED

Many hopeful immigrants spent weeks on ships to reach the shores of America and the promise of better lives. Courtesy of the Library of Congress.

Arizona citizens had led to the adoption of "an Act to Protect the Citizens of the United States in Their Employment Against Noncitizens of the United States, in Arizona, and to Provide Penalties and Punishment for the Violation Thereof." Shortened to the Anti-Alien Employment Act, the act required all businesses with five or more employees to hire a workforce at least 80 percent native-born American. Penalties subjected violators to not less than a $100 fine and thirty days imprisonment.

Restaurant owner, William Truax, Sr., had nine employees, including Raich. Seven of them were not native-born Americans. Fearing the penalties, Truax informed Raich that he would be fired as soon as the Anti-Alien Act became law. His firing would happen solely because he was an alien.

On December 15, 1914 the act was signed into law. A day later Raich filed a suit in Arizona's U.S. District Court against Arizona Attorney General Wiley E. Jones, Cochise County Attorney W.G. Gilmore, and Truax. Raich charged the act denied his Fourteenth Amendment right to equal protection under the law. The court issued a temporary order preventing Truax from firing Raich.

Gilmore, Jones, and Truax asked for dismissal of Raich's suit against them. But on January 7, 1915 a federal district court in San Francisco ruled Arizona's Anti Alien Act unconstitutional and, therefore, unenforceable. Gilmore, Jones, and Truax appealed to the U.S. Supreme Court which agreed to hear the case.

A Direct Violation

Justice Charles Evans Hughes, writing for the majority in an 8–1 decision, focused on whether or not the act violated the Fourteenth Amendment. Hughes explained that Raich, being a lawful inhabitant of Arizona, was "entitled under the Fourteenth Amendment to the equal protection of its laws." Furthermore, referring to the due process and equal protection clauses of the Fourteenth Amendment and quoting from the *Yick Wo v. Hopkins ruling,* Hughes wrote,

> **The description, 'any person within its jurisdiction,' as it has frequently been held, includes aliens. 'These provisions [clauses] . . . are universal in their application, to all persons within the territorial jurisdiction, without regard to any differences of race, of color, or of nationality; and the equal protection of the laws is a pledge of the protection of equal laws.**

Hughes noted that the Arizona act plainly described its purpose in its lengthy title, "an act to protect the citizens of the United States in their employment against noncitizens [aliens] of the United States, in Arizona." The act clearly separated citizens and aliens into two groups and applied the law differently to each. Raich was forced out of his job "as a cook in a restaurant, simply because he is an alien." The firing directly violated the Fourteenth Amendment's equal protections which extend to aliens.

Clearly, Hughes stated, "It requires no argument to show that the right to work for a living in the common occupations of the community is of the very essence of the personal freedom and opportunity that it was the purpose of the [Fourteenth] Amendment to secure. If this could be refused solely upon the ground of race or nationality, the [Fourteenth Amendment's guarantee of] equal protection of the laws would be a barren form of words [meaningless]."

Hughes continued that a person "cannot live where they cannot work" because work is essential to their livelihood. Therefore, the act was also invalid because it dictated where aliens may or may not live by denying them opportunities to work in the state of Arizona. Only Congress, not states, may regulate where aliens may live and enact immigration law.

A See Saw Court

The *Truax* ruling had a rocky road ahead as suspicions and prejudice against immigrants grew during and after World War I. In 1927 the Court appeared to abandon its 1915 *Truax* decision in the *Clarke v. Deckebach* ruling. While the Court still prohibited "plainly irrational discrimination against aliens," the Court ruled that some instances could occur when a state would have a good reason to deny rights to aliens. In *Clarke,* the Court allowed Cincinnati to prohibit aliens from operating pool halls because the aliens might operate them in an unacceptable manner.

Approximately twenty years later in *Takaahashi v. Fish and Game Commission* (1948) the Court returned to its position that earning a living was a liberty that could not be denied an individual just because he was an alien. Supporting aliens' rights further in 1971, *Graham v. Richardson*

Many immigrants found work in the agricultural industry in the early 1900s. Reproduced by permission of the Corbis Corporation.

DO IMMIGRANTS TAKE JOBS AWAY FROM AMERICANS?

Persons granted legal immigrant status intend to live and work in the United States and become U.S. citizens. A common concern among the U.S. public is that these newly arrived immigrants are taking jobs away from existing U.S. citizens. However, by the end of the twentieth century many studies such as those by the Rand Corporation, the Council of Economic Advisors, the National Research Council, and the Urban Institute concluded that immigrants do not have a negative effect on earnings or the employment opportunities of native-born Americans. In fact, immigrants create more jobs than they fill. The studies show that immigrants are more likely to be self-employed than native Americans and start new businesses. Eighteen percent of new small businesses, which account for 80 percent of new jobs available each year in the United States, are started by immigrants. Immigrants also raise the productivity of already established businesses, invest capital (money) in businesses, and spend dollars on consumer goods. Therefore, there is a strong argument that immigrants are good for the U.S. job market and all Americans benefit from their arrival.

signaled that equal protection cases involving aliens would be subjected to the same thorough review that racial discrimination cases receive.

However, the Court has viewed some occupations as requiring that employees be citizens. In *Ambach v. Norwick* (1979) the Court, in a 5-4 decision, upheld a New York law prohibiting aliens who refused to apply for U.S. citizenship from teaching in public schools. Likewise, in *Cabell v. Chavez* (1982), another 5-4 Court decision upheld a California requirement that all law enforcement personnel be U.S. citizens.

Suggestions for further reading

American Civil Liberties Union. [Online] Website: http://www.aclu.org
    (Accessed July 31, 2000).

**RIGHTS OF
IMMIGRANTS,
GAYS AND
LESBIANS, AND
THE DISABLED**

American Immigration Lawyers Association. [Online] Website: http://www.aila.org (Accessed July 31, 2000).

Fiss, Owen M. *A Community of Equals: The Constitutional Protection of New Americans.* Boston: Beacon Press, 1999.

U.S. Immigration and Naturalization Service. [Online] Website: http://www.ins.usdoj.gov (Accessed July 31, 2000).

O'Connor v. Donaldson
1975

Petitioner: Dr. J. B. O'Connor

Respondent: Kenneth Donaldson

Petitioner's Claim: That O'Connor, representing the Florida State Hospital at Chattahoochee, had violated Donaldson's constitutional rights by keeping him in custody for a supposed mental illness against his will for nearly fifteen years.

Chief Lawyer for Petitioner: Raymond W. Gearney

Chief Lawyer for Respondent: Bruce J. Ennis, Jr.

Justices for the Court: Harry A. Blackmun, William J. Brennan, Jr., Chief Justice Warren E. Burger, William O. Douglas, Thurgood Marshall, Lewis F. Powell, Jr., William H. Rehnquist, Potter Stewart, Byron R. White

Justices Dissenting: None

Date of Decision: June 26, 1975

Decision: Ruled that Donaldson possessed certain constitutional rights which had been violated, and that he could gather damages from those individuals who had violated his rights.

Significance: The decision affirmed that mentally ill persons have constitutional rights which must be protected. This recognition paved the way for people with mental illness to live in their communities rather than institutions.

Society has often isolated and confined persons with mental illness. Likewise, the U.S. mental health system has a long history of unequal treatment of mentally ill individuals. Occupying an inferior status in U.S. culture due to personal characteristics beyond their control, they have commonly been politically powerless, unable to pursue legal paths to establish their own rights. Many persons with mental illness had been subjected to a system which often warehoused them in state mental institutions for years, frequently offering no psychiatric therapy. Non-dangerous persons were likely to be housed with the dangerous in overcrowded conditions. Many were committed (ordered confinement for a mentally ill or incompetent person) to institutions against their will for an indefinite (no specific end) time period and denied basic constitutional civil rights (rights given and defined by laws). An early advocate (one who defends or argues for a cause for another person) for the rights of the mentally ill, Bruce Ennis, Jr., commented in 1973 in "The Legal Rights of the Mentally Handicapped" that mentally-ill individuals were "our country's most profoundly victimized [severely cheated] minorities."

During the 1960s and 1970s many minority groups began to fight for their civil rights. Black Americans, women, and gays and lesbians all worked to halt the discrimination they had faced daily. In response, Congress passed America's most significant law to ban discrimination, the Civil Rights Act of 1964. Within this social activist period, advocates for the mentally ill and those mentally-ill persons who were able began to challenge the mental health system. Just as other minority groups had done, they chose to use the courts to improve the mental health system and to protect their civil rights. Amid a flurry of lawsuits was the case of Kenneth Donaldson, a case that would make it all the way to the U.S. Supreme Court.

The Long Commitment of Kenneth Donaldson

A forty-eight year old man from Philadelphia, Kenneth Donaldson traveled in 1956 to Florida to visit his aging parents. In conversation with his parents, he mentioned that he believed one of his neighbors in Philadelphia might be poisoning his food. Worried that his son suffered from paranoid delusions (a tendency of a person toward excessive suspiciousness or distrustfulness), Donaldson's father asked the court for a sanity hearing. Sanity hearings are held to determine if a person is mentally healthy. Upon evaluation, Donaldson was diagnosed with "paranoid schizophrenia" (disorders in feelings, thoughts, and conduct). The court committed Donaldson, who was not represented by legal council at his commitment hearing, to the Florida mental health facility at Chattahoochee. This commitment was involuntary and of a civil (no criminal action involved) nature.

Even though Donaldson had never been dangerous to himself or others, he was placed with dangerous criminals at the Florida hospital. To make matters worse his ward, with over one thousand males, was severely understaffed. There was only one doctor, who happened to be an obstetrician (delivers babies), one nurse to hand out medications, and no psychiatrists or counselors. Donaldson never received any treatment except what the hospital called "milieu therapy." Milieu therapy in Donaldson's case translated into being kept in a room with sixty criminally committed patients. Donaldson's confinement would last fourteen and a half years.

Bruce Ennis, Jr., represented Kenneth Donaldson in front of the Supreme Court.
Reproduced by permission of AP/Wide World Photos.

Beginning immediately upon confinement, Donaldson, on his own behalf, fought to speak to a lawyer and demand to have his case reheard. Believing he should be freed, Donaldson argued that he did not have a lawyer at his commitment hearing; that he was neither mentally ill nor dangerous; and, that if he was in fact mentally ill, he was not offered any treatment. Later, Donaldson would argue that he had not been released even when two different sources promised to take responsibility for his care.

First, an old college friend had sought to have the state release Donaldson to his care and, later in 1963, a half-way home for the mentally ill in Minnesota had agreed to assume responsibility for him. Apparently for no cause, the hospital rejected both offers. Although the hospital staff had the power to release a patient such as Donaldson, Dr. J. B. O'Connor, the hospital's superintendent during most of this period, refused the release. O'Connor stated that Donaldson would have been unable to make a "successful adjustment outside the institution," although at the eventual trial O'Connor could not recall the basis for that conclusion. It was a few months after O'Connor's retirement that Donaldson finally gained his release.

Released!

Immediately upon his release Donaldson found a responsible job as a hotel clerk. He had no problem keeping his job or living on his own. In February of 1971, almost fifteen years after first being committed, Donaldson brought a lawsuit in the U.S. District Court for the Northern District of Florida against O'Connor and other hospital staff. Donaldson charged "that they had intentionally [on purpose] and maliciously [intent of committing an unlawful act] deprived him of his constitutional right to liberty [freedom]." The Fourteenth Amendment states that no state may "deprive any person of life, liberty, or property, without due process of law [fair legal hearing]." Dr. O'Connor's defense was that he acted in good faith in confining Donaldson since a Florida state law, which had since been repealed, had "authorized indefinite custodial [to protect and maintain confinement] of the 'sick' even if they were not treated and their release would not be harmful. . . " The court found in favor of Donaldson, awarding him monetary damages (money payment for wrongs against an individual). The Court of Appeals for the Fifth Circuit affirmed the ruling. O'Connor appealed to the U.S. Supreme Court which agreed to hear the case. The advocate Bruce Ennis, Jr. represented Donaldson.

Justice At Last

In a unanimous (9-0) decision, the Supreme Court ruled that Donaldson possessed certain rights and that he could be awarded damages from individuals who had taken those rights away. Justice Potter Stewart, writing for the Court, viewed the case as raising a "single, relatively simple, but nonetheless important question concerning every man's constitutional right to liberty" guaranteed by the Fourteenth Amendment.

COMMITMENT

Commitment of mentally ill or incompetent persons against their will (involuntary) has long involved weighing the person's civil rights with the rights of society to be protected from possibly dangerous individuals. Each state has its own laws for involuntary commitment. These laws define the types of mental illnesses and conditions that can lead to institutional commitment and those that can not. Those conditions generally excluded are drug or alcohol addition, mental retardation, and epilepsy.

In most states "dangerousness" to oneself or others is one key factor to consider. But there usually must be other closely related factors as well such as a persistently disabling condition which prevents responsible decisions. Also, hospitalization must not restrain the individual's liberties more than is really needed.

Involuntary commitment of persons convicted of a crime raise many constitutional problems. If a person is acquitted (found not guilty) of a crime by reason of insanity, his length of commitment for treatment is normally determined by the rate of his recovery. Many times this could lead to much longer confinement than if found guilty and sentenced in the first place. Cases of persons convicted of sex-related crimes are especially difficult. Courts have ruled that possibility of future crimes is not a reason to take away a person's freedom. However, under public pressure, state have passed laws allowing commitment of sexually dangerous persons if they seem likely to commit future criminal acts. Challenges are sure to follow.

First, the Court ruled on the authority of the state to hospitalize mentally ill persons. Ruling that diagnosis of mental illness does not alone justify confining individuals against their will for an indefinite period of time, Justice Stewart wrote,

> **A State cannot constitutionally confine . . . a non-dangerous individual who is capable of surviving safely in freedom by himself or with the help of willing and responsible family members or friends.**

**RIGHTS OF
IMMIGRANTS,
GAYS AND
LESBIANS, AND
THE DISABLED**

The ruling applied only to involuntarily civilly committed patients who were not a danger to themselves or others.

Secondly, the Court held that state hospital officials could be held liable (responsible for) for damages if their actions were carried out "maliciously . . . or oppressively [unreasonably severe]" and with the knowledge that their actions violated a person's constitutional rights.

Third and most significantly, the Court decision recognized the necessity of protecting the rights of mentally ill individuals. However, the Court left unsettled the issue of whether a person has a constitutional right to treatment if they are hospitalized for mental illness. Future cases would have to resolve that issue.

The *O'Connor* ruling encouraged others to challenge the mental health system when the civil rights of the mentally ill were abused. The decision also paved the way for many individuals suffering from mental illness to be able to remain within their local communities rather than being institutionalized.

Suggestions for further reading

Melton, Gary B., Philip M. Lyons, and Willis J. Spaulding. *No Place to Go: The Civil Commitment of Minors (Children and Law).* Lincoln, NE: University of Nebraska Press, 1998.

National Alliance for the Mentally Ill. [Online] Website: http://www.nami.org (Accessed on July 31, 2000).

Winick, Bruce, Jr. *The Right to Refuse Mental Health Treatment (Law & Public Policy: Psychology and the Social Sciences).* American Psychological Association, 1997.

Plyler v. Doe
1982

Appellants: J. and R. Doe, certain named and unnamed undocumented alien children

Appellees: James L. Plyler and others

Appellants' Claim: That a Texas law withholding public funds from local school districts for educating children not legally present in the United States and encouraging school districts to deny these children enrollment is constitutionally valid.

Chief Lawyers for Appellants: Peter D. Roos, Peter A. Schey

Chief Lawyers for Appellees: John C. Hardy, Richard L. Arnett

Justices for the Court: Harry A. Blackmun, William J. Brennan, Jr., Thurgood Marshall, Lewis F. Powell, Jr., John Paul Stevens

Justices Dissenting: Chief Justice Warren E. Burger, Sandra Day O'Connor, William Rehnquist, Byron R. White

Date of Decision: June 15, 1982

Decision: Ruled in favor of Doe (the illegal alien children) by finding that the Texas law violated the Fourteenth Amendment's Equal Protection Clause and struck it down.

Significance: With this decision, states could no longer deny public education to children only because they were illegal aliens. The Court's opinion provided an important statement on the importance of education to American society.

**RIGHTS OF
IMMIGRANTS,
GAYS AND
LESBIANS, AND
THE DISABLED**

The school on the Texas-Mexico border is known as a "gate school." Behind the playground is a chain-link fence dividing the United States from Mexico. From the playground children and teachers can see a Border Patrol jeep, its officer continuously peering through binoculars down along the border and school grounds. The officer is waiting and watching for yet another individual or family, desperate for a better way of life, to attempt to illegally (without permission) cross the border into Texas. Of the predominately Hispanic children at the gate school, the principal says it is difficult to tell who is documented (legal) or undocumented (illegal). To the principal it does not matter. She believes that a school should educate all children living within the United States boundaries and she intends to do just that. She is supported by the landmark U.S. Supreme Court ruling of *Plyler v. Doe* (1982) which ended years of controversy by ruling that states have the responsibility to educate children of undocumented aliens.

Equally Protected

Although the United States has restricted entry of foreigners into its borders since the late nineteenth century, countless individuals and families have illegally made their way into America. Border states like Texas, New Mexico, Arizona, and California have seen the largest arrival of "illegal aliens." Illegal aliens are citizens of a foreign country living in America without permission. Illegal entry into the United States is a crime and persons who unlawfully enter are subject to deportation (sending an alien back to the country from which he came). However, once in the United States illegal aliens share some of the same rights as any legal alien or U.S. citizen. One of these rights is equal protection of the laws provided in the Fourteenth Amendment's Equal Protection Clause. The Equal Protection Clause provides that no state shall "deny to any person within its jurisdiction [geographical area over which a government has authority] the equal protection of the laws." Equal protection means that persons or groups of persons in similar situations must be treated equally by the laws. The Court first recognized in *Yick Wo v. Hopkins* (1886) that these rights extended to all persons, not just citizens, living within U.S. boundaries.

Tyler School District

With growing numbers of illegal aliens in the state, the Texas legislature in May of 1975 decided to change its education laws. The new law would withhold from local school districts any state funds used to educate children of illegal aliens. The 1975 change also authorized local school districts to deny enrollment in their public school to children of illegal aliens. Though the Tyler Independent School District continued to allow children of doubtful legal status to attend their schools, in July of 1977 they announced these children must begin paying a "tuition fee" in order to enroll.

In reaction, a class action lawsuit (lawsuit brought on behalf of a large group with a common interest) was filed in the U.S. District Court for the Eastern District of Texas. The lawsuit was on behalf of all school-age children of Mexican origin living in Smith County, Texas, who could not prove they had legally entered the United States. The suit charged that this group of children was being unfairly denied a free public education. The suit named as defendants the Superintendent and members of the Board of Trustees of Tyler Independent School District.

After conducting a thorough hearing, in December of 1977 the district court found that barring undocumented children from the schools might eventually save public money but the quality of education would "not necessarily" improve. Furthermore, these children might become the legal citizens of the future but, without an education, they would be locked into a "subclass" at the lowest economic level. Therefore, the district court found the Texas laws violated the Fourteenth Amendment's Equal Protection Clause which protects illegal aliens from unequal treatment by the laws.

The Court of Appeals for the Fifth Circuit affirmed all the essential points of the district court's analysis and ruling. The case then moved to the U.S. Supreme Court.

Public Education in America

The Supreme Court decision in the *Plyler* case was a 5-4 split in favor of illegal alien children. The debate over the issues ran deep among the justices. Even the justices of the majority who agreed on the final decision had different reasons. Together, the concurring (agreeing with the decision) and dissenting (disagreeing with the decision) opinions provided a powerful look into the justices' beliefs about the importance of public education in American society.

Justice William J. Brennan, Jr., writing for the majority, identified that "the question presented . . . is whether, consistent [carrying out the intention of] with the Equal Protection Clause of the Fourteenth Amendment, Texas may deny to undocumented school-age children the free public education that it provides to children who are citizens of the United States or legally admitted aliens."

The school board argued that equal protection did not apply to those who entered the country illegally. The Court rejected their argument by emphasizing the decision of *Yick Wo* which declared all persons "within its [a government's] jurisdiction" came under Fourteenth Amendment protection. Deciding that illegal aliens came under the Equal Protection Clause was easy. The more difficult question was if Texas law violated equal protection.

A "Pivotal Role"

In arriving at their decision, the justices addressed the relationship between public education, the U.S. Constitution, and the importance of public education in American social order. Justice Brennan affirmed that education was not a right granted by the Constitution but added that education was more than "merely some government 'benefit' indistinguishable [cannot tell the difference] from other forms of social welfare legislation." Education was different because it plays a "fundamental" or "pivotal role" in maintaining our society. He added, "we cannot ignore the significant social costs borne by our Nation when select groups are denied the means to absorb the values and skills upon which our social order rests." Denial of a free public education to the children of illegal aliens places a lifetime hardship on them, for "illiteracy (inability to read) will mark them for the rest of their lives." Brennan found no reason for a state to cause such hardship on any individual. For these reasons the Court concluded the Equal Protection Clause required the Texas law be struck down.

In a concurring opinion, Justice Harry Blackmun stated that to provide an education to some but deny it to others "immediately and inevitably [always] creates class distinctions [differences]" inconsistent with the purposes of the Equal Protection Clause. Blackmun observed "an uneducated child is denied even the opportunity to achieve." Likewise, Justice Thurgood Marshall concurred that denying public education based on class is "utterly incompatible" with the Equal Protection Clause. Justice Lewis Powell pointed out that the Texas law "assigned a legal status [to the children] due to a violation of law by their parents." These children "should not be left on the streets uneducated" as a consequence of their parents' actions over which they had no control.

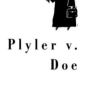

RIGHT TO A PUBLIC EDUCATION

"American people have always regarded education and [the] acquisition of knowledge as matters of supreme importance." *Meyer v. Nebraska* (1923).

" . . . public schools [are] most vital . . . for the preservation of a democratic system of government." *Abington School District v. Schempp* (1963).

These quotes from earlier Supreme Court decisions were used again in the *Plyler v. Doe* (1982) case. Yet, the Constitution makes no mention of education and the Court has never acknowledged it as a fundamental right. According to the Tenth Amendment, powers not given to the federal government are reserved to the states. Educating children in the United States has long been a responsibility of individual states which assign to local school systems. However, since the ***Brown v. Board of Education*** (1954) decision the Court has insisted that public education be equally available to all children. Through a combination of various laws and Supreme Court interpretations of the Fourteenth Amendments' Equal Protection Clause, schools have ever increasing responsibilities to provide equal opportunities to groups or classes previously barred from equal access. These opportunities extend to children of all races, to the physically and mentally disabled, to non-English speaking children, and to children of illegal aliens.

A State Matter

The dissenting opinion, written by Chief Justice Warren Burger, pointed out that the majority opinion, while denying education was a constitutionally protected right nevertheless did not make it clear just where education fell. Though Burger did not deny education's importance, the fact of its importance "does not elevate it to the status of a 'fundamental right.'" Burger observed that the solution of the issue should have been left to the state legislature even as disagreeable "as that may be to some."

The Role of Schools

The Court, in striking down the Texas law, addressed the role of schools in a democratic society and decided it was central to the American culture. The *Plyler* decision added a new responsibility for public schools. Public schools are obliged (required) to provide tuition-free education not only to American citizens and lawful alien children but also to children of illegal aliens.

Public resistance persisted, however. In 1994 California voters passed Proposition 187 restricting public school education for children of illegal aliens. In September of 1999 a U.S. District Court judge ruled that no child in California would be denied an education because of their place of birth.

Suggestions for further reading

Atkin, S. Beth. *Voices From the Field: Children of Migrant Farmworkers Tell Their Stories.* Boston: Joy Street Books, 1993.

Chavez, Leo R. *Shadowed Lives: Undocumented Immigrants in American Society.* Fort Worth, TX: Harcourt Brace College Publications, 1998.

Conover, Ted. *Coyotes: A Journey Through the Secret World of America's Illegal Aliens.* New York: Vintage Books, 1987.

Kellough, Patrick H., and Jean L. Kellough. *Public Education and the Children of Illegal Aliens.* Monticello, IL: Vance Bibliographie, 1985.

Cleburne v. Cleburne Living Center 1985

Petitioner: City of Cleburne, Texas

Respondent: Cleburne Living Center

Petitioner's Claim: That the decision to deny the Cleburne Living Center a special use zoning permit served a legitimate government need and the zoning ordinance was constitutional.

Chief Lawyer for Petitioner: Earl Luna, Robert T. Miller, Jr., Mary Milford

Chief Lawyer for Respondent: Renea Hicks, Diane Shisk, Caryl Oberman

Justices for the Court: Harry A. Blackmun, Chief Justice Warren E. Burger, Sandra Day O'Connor, Lewis F. Powell, Jr., William H. Rehnquist, Byron R. White

Justices Dissenting: William J. Brennan, Jr., Thurgood Marshall, John Paul Stevens

Date of Decision: July 1, 1985

Decision: Ruled in favor of Cleburne Living Center by finding that the denial of a permit was based on prejudice against persons with mental retardation. The zoning ordinance was declared unconstitutional.

Significance: No more groups were added to the intermediate scrutiny list. The ruling helped eliminate housing discrimination against the disabled and encouraged group homes.

Society has often isolated and restricted persons with mental retardation (MR) within institutions and hospitals. The American Association on Mental Retardation defines mental retardation as significantly below average intellectual functioning combined with problems in carrying out everyday life activities. However, people with MR range from those with disabilities hardly noticeable to others needing constant care.

By the 1960s group homes became a desirable living arrangement option. The homes allowed persons with MR to lead normal lives as much as possible by residing in a regular community setting. Twenty-four hour supervision and support was provided. However, controversy grew between organizations trying to establish group homes and existing neighbors. Neighbors' arguments against the homes varied widely from safety fears to potential economic effects on their property values. This scene played out in Cleburne, Texas.

The Feathersone Group Home

Cleburne Living Center (CLC) sought to lease a house at 201 Featherstone Street to establish a group home for the mentally retarded. The home would house thirteen men and women with MR. They would be under constant supervision of the CLC staff. The city of Cleburne identified the group home as a "hospital for the feeble-minded" requiring a special use permit. The zoning ordinance (assigns particular uses to certain areas of a city) for the area required special use permits for construction of "hospitals for the insane or feeble-minded, or alcoholic [sic] or drug addicts or penal or correctional institutions." After a public hearing on CLC's application, the City Council voted three to one to deny CLC a special use permit.

CLC filed suit in Federal District Court charging the city's zoning ordinance was unconstitutional and, therefore, invalid (not legal). It discriminated, they claimed, against persons with MR in violation of the Fourteenth Amendment's Equal Protection Clause in the U.S. Constitution. The Equal Protection Clause states that no state shall "deny to any person within its jurisdiction [geographic area over which a government has authority] the equal protection of the laws." Equal protection means that all people in similar situations must be treated the same under the law.

Was Fear Important?

The District Court found that the Council's decision was based mainly on the fact that the group home's residents would be persons with MR. Nevertheless, the court found the zoning ordinance constitutional. The court applied only the lowest level of scrutiny (examination) required in equal protection cases and found that the city had a legitimate (honest) interest to respect the fears of residents in the immediate neighborhood.

Upon appeal by the CLC, the Court of Appeals for the Fifth Circuit disagreed with the district court and, ruling in favor of CLC, reversed the decision. The Court of Appeals applied an intermediate level of scrutiny to the zoning ordinance. The intermediate level requires that the government, in this case the city of Cleburne, have not just a legitimate reason but an important reason to discriminate against a certain group. Ruling the ordinance unconstitutional and therefore invalid, the Court of Appeal found that the city had no important reason or interest making it necessary to direct discrimination against persons with MR. Cleburne appealed to the U.S. Supreme Court which agreed to hear the case.

In a 6-3 decision, the Supreme Court decided Cleburne's zoning ordinance was unconstitutional and violated the Equal Protection Clause. The Court disagreed with the Court of Appeals on the scrutiny level issue, but, nevertheless, agreed on the end result that invalidated Cleburne's zoning ordinance.

When Is Intermediate Scrutiny Necessary?

Writing for the Court, Justice Byron R. White analyzed the two major points of the case. First, the Court turned its attention to the scrutiny issue. The Court held that the Court of Appeals erred in applying the intermediate level of scrutiny. The Court refused to allow persons with MR to be elevated to a heightened level of scrutiny. White explained that the Court had devised three levels of scrutiny for equal protection cases. The levels assess the constitutionality of different kinds of state and local legislation that affected certain groups or classes of individuals who had been traditionally and purposefully discriminated against through America's history. The highest level of scrutiny applies to laws that classify groups by race, alienage (a person living in the United States but a citizen of a foreign country), or national origin. The next level of scrutiny, intermediate,

Cleburne v. Cleburne Living Center

applies to women and illegitimate children (born out of wedlock). If any of these groups are singled out for particular treatment in a law, the law may be found unconstitutional unless the law serves either a "compelling" (very important) or important interest to the government. If the law does not single out any of these groups, it must only have a rational (reasonable) or legitimate basis for treating groups differently.

As a group persons with MR are neither a certain race, alienage, national origin, all female, or illegitimate. Therefore, they do not automatically fall into the top or intermediate levels of scrutiny. The Court of Appeals was mistaken in trying to elevate them into one of these higher levels. Citing several major pieces of legislation specifically designed to outlaw discrimination against the mentally retarded, White showed that persons with MR have neither been traditionally nor purposefully treated unequally by the laws. White also pointed out that persons with MR have a "reduced ability to cope with and function in the everyday world. . . They are thus different. . . Legislators, guided by qualified professionals . . . " are better able to address their needs than are the courts. A degree of different treatment would indeed be expected to best serve persons with MR. Therefore, the government has a rational basis to enact legislation that treats persons with MR differently. White concluded the lowest level of scrutiny with the rational basis requirement is sufficient protection for persons with MR. The Court reasoned to elevate persons with MR to the intermediate scrutiny level would also require they elevate all persons with disabilities to that level and they were not willing to do so.

Pure Prejudice

Having addressed the scrutiny issue, White next turned to the specific question of whether Cleburne's zoning ordinance requiring special permits for "hospitals" for the "feeble-minded" was constitutional. White stated, "We inquire . . . whether requiring a special use permit for the Featherston home in the circumstances here deprives respondents [CLC] of the equal protection of the laws."

White first wrote,

> **The city does not require a special use permit . . .
> for apartment houses, multiple-dwellings, boarding
> . . . houses . . . nursing homes [etc.]. . . It does,
> however, insist on a special permit for the
> Featherston home, and it does so . . . because it**

ZONING ORDINANCES

Zoning ordinances divide a village, town, city, or county into residential (single family and multi-family), commercial or retail, and industrial (light or heavy manufacturing) districts. Ordinances must be part of a comprehensive plan for the entire area. Ordinances generally require certain building features or architecture, limit density, provide for parking areas, schools, parks, and may establish historical areas or buildings.

Ordinances must promote the common welfare of all people of the community rather than promoting a particular group's desires. The zoning ordinances must be reasonable because by their nature they limit use of property by the owners and they may not be used arbitrarily by governments. With the use of maps, ordinances must be clear and specific in describing districts. Only persons wronged by the regulations may challenge them.

The goals are to maintain the area's characteristics important to the residents, control population density, and create healthful and attractive areas. They must look to the future and strive to bring about orderly growth and development by considering practicalities such as adequate streets, walkways, and drainage sewers.

Municipalities have some flexibility to impose restrictions they otherwise might not be able to require such as requiring special use permits in specific situations. These permits must have reasonable goals before they may be imposed

would be a facility for the mentally retarded. May the city require the permit for this facility when other care and multiple-dwelling facilities are freely permitted?

White looked for a rational basis (all that is required at the lowest scrutiny level) for the city ordinance to treat persons with MR unequally. The City Council argued that the majority of property owners located within 200 feet of the Featherstone facility had negative attitudes toward or fear of the facility. The Court responded, "mere negative attitudes, or fear, . . . are not permissible bases for treating a home for the mentally retarded differently from apartment houses, multiple dwellings, and the like." The Council argued that the facility was across the street from a junior high school and students might harass the Featherstone residents. The Court countered that thirty mentally retarded students attend the junior high suggesting students are already used to persons with MR. The Council put forth several more concerns such as the home's location on a "five hundred year flood plain." The Court reasoned that none of these concerns set the Featherstone home apart. All of the concerns could also apply to any of the other buildings in the area not required to a have a special permit. The Court found no rational basis or reason to treat the mentally retarded differently. White concluded, "The short of it is that requiring the permit in this case appears to us to rest on an irrational prejudice against the mentally retarded." The Court found the ordinance unconstitutional and therefore invalid.

The Cleburne decision closed the door to more groups being added to the heightened scrutiny list. At the same time, it helped eliminate one form of housing discrimination, discrimination against the disabled. The decision opened wider the opportunity for persons with mental retardation to live within "normal" communities.

Suggestions for further reading

American Association on Mental Retardation. [Online] Website: http://www.aamr.org (Accessed on July 31, 2000).

The Arc of the United States (national organization of and for people with mental retardation). [Online] Website: http://www.arc.org (Accessed on July 31, 2000).

Meyer, Donald, ed. *Views From Our Shoes: Growing Up with a Brother or Sister with Special Needs.* Bethesda, MD: Woodbine House, 1997.

Bowers v. Hardwick
1986

Appellant: Michael J. Bowers, Attorney General of Georgia

Appellee: Michael Hardwick

Appellant's Claim: That state laws making sodomy a criminal offense do not violate the constitutionally protected right to privacy.

Chief Lawyer for Appellant: Michael E. Hobs

Chief Lawyer for Appellee: Laurence Tribe

Justices for the Court: Chief Justice Warren E. Burger, Sandra Day O'Connor, Lewis F. Powell, Jr., William H. Rehnquist, Byron R. White

Justices Dissenting: Harry A. Blackmun, William J. Brennan, Jr., Thurgood Marshall, John Paul Stevens

Date of Decision: June 30, 1986

Decision: The ruling upheld the Georgia law by reasoning that no fundamental right has been granted to homosexuals to engage in sodomy and, therefore, the law did not violate the right of privacy guaranteed under due process.

Significance: The decision left existing state sodomy laws intact. The ruling dealt a major setback to the gay and lesbian civil rights movement since their opponents could argue that granting civil rights to persons who regularly commit the criminal act of sodomy could not be justified.

RIGHTS OF IMMIGRANTS, GAYS AND LESBIANS, AND THE DISABLED

In 1986 half a million gay men and lesbians marched in Washington, D. C. protesting the U.S. Supreme Court decision in *Bowers v. Hardwick* (1986), the Court's first ruling on gay rights. The decision upheld a Georgia law forbidding sodomy and was considered a major setback to the gay rights movement. Sodomy is sexual activity common among gays and lesbians. The terms gay and lesbian refer to people sexually attracted to persons of their same sex. The term gay usually refers to men and lesbian always refers to women. Homosexual is a term which refers to either gay men or lesbians.

Sodomy had long been considered a criminal offense in state and local law. Since criminal sodomy laws were aimed at homosexuals, gay men and lesbians kept their sexual orientation (the sexual preference of an individual for one sex or the other) a secret. This secret existence in which homosexuals found themselves was referred to as being "in the closet." Encouraged by successes of black Americans and women during the 1960s' Civil Rights Movement and outraged by an incident, known as Stonewall, at a New York bar in 1969, homosexuals began to "come out." This meant identifying themselves as gay or lesbians and openly working for legal and social equality. The gay rights movement made the repeal (to abolish) of sodomy laws a primary goal.

Michael Hardwick's Private Affairs

Michael Hardwick was a gay bartender living in Atlanta, Georgia. When Hardwick failed to pay a fine for drinking in public, a police officer came to his home to serve a warrant (a written order) against him. The officer gained entrance to the home by another tenant who did not know if Hardwick was home. The officer entered Hardwick's bedroom where he found him having sex with his partner. Hardwick was arrested and charged with committing sodomy with a consenting (willing) male.

Hardwick brought suit in Federal District Court challenging the constitutionality of the Georgia sodomy law. The District Court dismissed the suit without a trial. Hardwick then appealed to the U.S. Court of Appeals for the Eleventh Circuit. The court of appeals found the law violated Hardwick's fundamental right to privacy protected by both the Ninth Amendment and the Due Process Clause of the Fourteenth Amendment. The Ninth Amendment provides that even though certain rights are not specifically named in the U.S. Constitution, they could still be considered fundamental rights held by the people. The Fourteenth Amendment prohibits states from denying citizens "life, liberty or property, without due process of law [fair legal proceedings]." In 1965 the U.S. Supreme Court case, *Griswold v. Connecticut,* dealing with birth control or contraception, had clearly established a constitutional right to privacy as part of the fundamental rights in the Ninth Amendment. The right to privacy was protected by the Due Process Clause of the Fourteenth Amendment. This right in private matters was again stated in *Roe v. Wade* (1973) which dealt with abortion. The court of appeals agreed with Hardwick that the Georgia law violated his fundamental rights because his homosexual actions were in the privacy of his own home and, therefore, beyond the reach of any state interference. In this light, the court of appeals returned the case to the district court, ordering it to try the case.

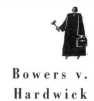

**B o w e r s v.
H a r d w i c k**

Before the trial could begin, Michael Bowers, the Georgia attorney general, appealed to the U.S. Supreme Court for a review of the court of appeals' ruling. The Supreme Court agreed to hear the case.

A Fundamental Right?

Justice Byron R. White, writing the Court's opinion, stated the question before the Court,

> **The issue presented is whether the Federal Constitution confers a fundamental right upon homosexuals to engage in sodomy and hence invalidates the laws of the many States that still make such conduct illegal and have done so for a very long time.**

In a 5-4 decision in favor of Georgia, the Court rejected the thinking of the court of appeals. First, the Court dismissed the idea that its previous rulings on the privacy issues of contraception and abortion had anything to do with this case. In fact, White drew a sharp distinction between the previous cases and homosexual activity:

> **Accepting the decisions in these cases . . . we think it evident [clear] that none of the rights announced in those cases bears any resemblance to the claimed constitutional right of homosexuals to engage in acts of sodomy. . . No connection between family, marriage, or procreation [to have a baby] on the one hand and homosexual activity on the other hand has been demonstrated.**

White next rejected the argument that engaging in homosexual activity was a fundamental right protected by the Due Process Clause. Justice White wrote that fundamental rights or liberties are deeply rooted in U.S. history and tradition. If they did not exist, justice would not exist. He found that sodomy was never rooted in this Nation's history. Quite the opposite, it had long been prohibited by the states. According to White,

> **Sodomy was a criminal offense at common law and was forbidden by the laws of the original 13 States when they ratified the Bill of Rights. In 1868, when the Fourteenth Amendment was ratified, all but 5 of the 37 States in the Union had criminal sodomy laws. In fact, until 1961, all 50 States outlawed sodomy, and today [1986], 24 States and the District of Columbia continue to provide criminal penalties for sodomy performed in private between consenting [willing] adults.**

Likewise, certainly justice and order would still exist even if sodomy did not. White observed, for the Court to declare sodomy a fundamental constitutionally protected right and negate all the state laws would be taking on the role of the legislative branch. Making decisions on how to govern the country is constitutionally a legislative activity in which the Court may not engage.

Don't Go Down That Road

White further addressed the issue that Hardwick's homosexual conduct was carried out in the privacy of his home. White stated that not all acts just because they are done in private are legal. For example, White wrote, " . . . the possession and use of illegal drugs, do not escape the law where they are committed at home." White explained the homosexual conduct could not be allowed "while leaving exposed to prosecution adultery, incest, and other sexual crimes even though they are committed in the home. We are unwilling to start down that road."

A Bitter Dissent

In a bitter dissent, Justice Harry A. Blackmun, the principle author of *Roe v. Wade,* commented the Court's decision "makes for a short opinion, but it does little to make for a persuasive one." He stated that this case was not so much "about a fundamental right to engage in homosexual

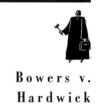
SODOMY LAWS

Sodomy laws generally prohibit certain sexual acts, even between willing adults in the privacy of their homes. Punishment ranges from $200 fines to twenty years imprisonment. Once all fifty states and Puerto Rico had sodomy laws but many have been repealed or struck down in the courts. In 1999 thirteen states and Puerto Rico still had sodomy laws which applied to both same-sex (homosexual) and opposite-sex (heterosexual) activities. Five states, Arkansas, Kansas, Missouri, Oklahoma, and Texas, had sodomy laws targeting only homosexuals.

Sodomy laws have frequently been used to deny gay men and lesbians their civil rights. For example, some courts under the laws have justified removing children from gay or lesbian parents. Occasionally, cities have used the laws to arrest gay individuals for merely discussing sex in conversations, conversations which heterosexuals have daily.

In November of 1998, the Georgia Supreme Court struck down its 182-year-old sodomy law, the same law the U.S. Supreme Court upheld in the 1986 case of *Bowers v. Hardwick*. The Georgia court ruled the law violated the right to privacy protected by the state's constitution. Chief Justice Robert Benham wrote, "We cannot think of any other activity that reasonable persons would rank as more private and more deserving of protection from governmental interference than consensual [willing], private, adult sexual activity."

sodomy" but instead about the most prized right of civilized man, " . . . namely, the right to be let alone." Blackmun eloquently wrote:

> **individuals define themselves in a significant way through their intimate sexual relationships with others suggests, in a Nation as diverse as ours, that there may be many right ways of conducting those relationships, and that much of the richness of a relationship will come from the freedom an indi-**

vidual has to choose the form and nature of these intensely personal bonds.

A Mistake

Justice Lewis F. Powell held the swing vote in the decision. At first Powell had been in favor of striking down the Georgia law as it carried a prison sentence with conviction. This he reasoned would violate the Eighth Amendment as "cruel and unusual punishment." However, because Hardwick had not actually even been tried, "much less convicted and sentenced," Powell could not justify overturning the state law. Powell, therefore, became the fifth justice to vote against striking down the Georgia law. He later publicly confessed that changing his vote in Bowers had probably been a mistake.

Quest For Civil Rights Derailed

Deciding that private homosexual activities did not fall under the right of privacy guaranteed under due process dealt a severe blow to the gay and lesbian rights movement and their quest for civil rights. Gay rights opponents began to charge that it was ridiculous to think about granting civil rights to persons who regularly practiced criminal acts. The Supreme Court would not face gay rights issues again until 1996 in ***Romer v. Evans*** when the decision would be different. In *Romer* the Court granted constitutional protection against government or private discrimination based on sexual orientation. It was hailed as the first key victory in the struggle for gay and lesbian civil rights. The decisions in *Bowers* and then in *Romer* reflected America's changing standards toward the gay and lesbian communities.

Suggestions for further reading

American Civil Liberties Union. [Online] Website: http://www.aclu.org (Accessed on July 31, 2000).

Lambda Legal Defense and Educational Fund. [Online] Website: http://www.lambdalegal.org (Accessed on July 31, 2000).

National Gay and Lesbian Task Force. [Online] Website: http://www.ngltf.org (Accessed on July 31, 2000).

Richards, David A. J. *Women, Gays, and the Constitution: The Grounds for Feminism and Gay Rights in Culture and Law.* Chicago: University of Chicago Press, 1998.

Romer v. Evans
1996

Petitioner: Roy Romer, Governor of Colorado, and others

Respondent: Richard G. Evans and others

Petitioner's Claim: That the Colorado Supreme Court erred in striking down a state constitutional amendment prohibiting any government efforts to protect homosexuals against discrimination.

Chief Lawyers for Petitioner: Timothy M. Tymkovich

Chief Lawyers for Respondent: Jean E. Dubofsky

Justices for the Court: Stephen Breyer, Ruth Bader Ginsburg, Anthony M. Kennedy, Sandra Day O'Connor, David H. Souter, John Paul Stevens

Justices Dissenting: Chief Justice William H. Rehnquist, Antonin Scalia, Clarence Thomas

Date of Decision: May 20, 1996

Decision: Agreeing with the Colorado Supreme Court, ruled in favor of Evans that the state amendment prohibiting protections of gay and lesbian rights was unconstitutional.

Significance: First victory of gay and lesbian civil rights in the U.S. Supreme Court. The Court gave homosexuals constitutional protection against government or private discrimination.

RIGHTS OF IMMIGRANTS, GAYS AND LESBIANS, AND THE DISABLED

The first National March on Washington for Lesbian and Gay Rights occurred in October of 1979. Reproduced by permission of Joan E. Biren.

Gay men and lesbians number in the millions and are found in every sector of American society—doctors, nurses, computer whizzes, musicians, athletes, teachers, construction workers, dads, moms, and teenagers. The terms gay and lesbian refer to people who are sexually attracted to and prefer persons of the same sex. Though the term gay can refer to either men or women, gay usually is used in referring to men and lesbian always refers to women. Homosexual is another term which refers to both gay men and lesbians.

Throughout most of America's history, homosexuals have kept their sexual orientation (the sexual preference of an individual for one sex or the other) a secret or "in the closet." Secrecy was important because homosexuality has been considered a criminal offense in state and local laws, and religious organizations condemned the behavior. However, a fight in a New York bar in 1969 marked the beginning of a nationwide "coming out."

The Coming Out

"Coming out" is the name gay and lesbians give the process of identifying, accepting, and then disclosing their sexual orientation. On June 27,

1969 in New York, police raided the Stonewall Inn, a gay bar located in Greenwich Village. Raiding gay bars was not an uncommon police activity all across America. However, this time the people inside the bar resisted arrest and clashed with the city police. For three nights New York gays rioted, releasing years of suppressed frustration over the discrimination they experienced daily. Especially for younger gay men and women, Stonewall became a symbol of a new attitude of openly "coming out." Resisting negative stereotyping (fixed mental picture or a fixed attitude toward something) and legal and social discrimination suddenly became more common.

Gay Rights Movement is Born

Every year after the Stonewall riots, homosexuals marched in New York City to remember the event. Gay men and lesbians began to seek legal and social equality in America. The federal government had moved to prohibit discrimination on the basis of race, religion, and national origin, but had yet to take a stand on sexual orientation. The movement, which had become known as the gay rights movement, grew during the 1970s and 1980s. Demanding fair legal treatment, between 25,000 and 40,000 gay rights activists marched in San Francisco in November of 1978 and 75,000 strong marched in Washington, D.C. in October of 1979, the first National March on Washington for Lesbian and Gay Rights.

Despite some gains by the movement, in 1986 the U.S. Supreme Court dealt it a major setback. In *Bowers v. Hardwick,* the Court refused to grant a constitutional right of privacy for homosexual acts carried out in private homes. State laws thus continued to criminalize such acts. In response, over half-a-million gay men and lesbians rallied in Washington, D.C. in 1987 in another National March on Washington.

In the 1990s, homosexuals and their lifestyle faced growing opposition from some religious groups and conservatives concerned about the nation's moral values. A decade after *Bowers* the Supreme Court would face gay rights issues again in *Romer v. Evans* (1996). This time the legal battleground was set in the state of Colorado.

Amendment 2—No Civil Rights for Gays

In support of gay rights, several communities in Colorado, including Denver, Aspen, and Boulder, passed local laws banning discrimination in

RIGHTS OF IMMIGRANTS, GAYS AND LESBIANS, AND THE DISABLED

employment, housing, and education on the basis of sexual orientation. By 1992 a group, Colorado for Family Values, concerned that the growing acceptance of homosexual lifestyles would harm American traditions and morals, led an effort against the communities' anti-discrimination laws. They proposed a state constitutional amendment to repeal (cancel) the laws and stop any future efforts to legally protect homosexuals. Following a petition drive, the amendment was placed on the November ballot in 1992.

The ballot measure, known as Amendment 2, passed and became part of the Colorado state constitution. Amendment 2 prohibited all state and local governments and courts to take any action designed to protect persons based on their "homosexual, lesbian, or bisexual [sexually oriented to both males and females] orientation, conduct, practices or relationships." As originally intended, it required the immediate repeal (to abolish) of all existing laws barring discrimination based on sexual preference and allowed discrimination against gay and lesbians in areas such as employment, insurance, housing, and welfare services.

Immediately, eight individuals, including gay municipal worker Richard Evans, and the cities of Denver, Boulder, and Aspen, which had their gay rights laws repealed, challenged Amendment 2 in the state courts. Finally, in 1994 the Colorado Supreme Court ruled that Amendment 2 could not be enforced. It found Amendment 2 prevented one "class" of persons with non-traditional sexual orientations composed of gays, lesbians, and bisexuals from using normal political procedures to protect themselves from discrimination. One normal procedure which all other groups could follow would be to seek passage of a law to correct injustices. Now this named group of persons would have to amend the state constitution before such corrective laws could even be considered, not a normal procedure. The amendment would effectively end any civil rights for gays. Furthermore, the state supreme court could find no compelling (very important) reason demonstrating the government's need for Amendment 2. Colorado, whose governor was Roy Romer, appealed the ruling to the U.S. Supreme Court which agreed to hear the case.

"This Colorado Cannot Do"

Before the U.S. Supreme Court, Colorado argued that Amendment 2 merely took away the "special rights" or a special protection the local laws had granted to homosexuals. The Court in a 6-3 decision strongly disagreed with the state of Colorado. Though following a different line of

Romer v. Evans

Governor Roy Romer worked to deny gays and lesbians special protections under the law.
Reproduced by permission of the Corbis Corporation.

reasoning than the Colorado Supreme Court, the Court upheld the previous decision that Amendment 2 was unconstitutional (does not follow the intent of the U.S. Constitution) and, therefore, unenforceable.

Justice Anthony M. Kennedy wrote the powerfully worded majority opinion. Addressing the so-called "special protections" argument, Kennedy concluded the special protections were not special at all but merely "the safeguards that others enjoy. . . These are protection taken for granted by most people either because they already have them or do not need them. . . " Instead, Kennedy pointed out these safeguards "are protections against exclusion from an almost limitless number of transactions and endeavors [such as employment and housing] that constitute ordinary civic life [life as a citizen] in a free society." In other words, these safeguards are protection against discrimination and to take them away from gay people "imposes a special disability upon those persons alone.

Kennedy identified the real question before the Court. Did Amendment 2 violate the Fourteenth Amendment's Equal Protection Clause that guarantees that no state shall deny to any person the "equal protection of the laws?" The Court found that Amendment 2 did indeed violate the clause. The violation was such a sweeping, across the board denial of gay peoples' rights of protection. The court concluded that it could only have been passed with the goal of harming a politically unpopular group. The Court could identify no "legitimate" (honest) gov-

RIGHTS OF IMMIGRANTS, GAYS AND LESBIANS, AND THE DISABLED

NATIONAL GAY AND LESBIAN ORGANIZATIONS

Lambda Legal Defense and Education Fund, founded in 1972, is dedicated to achieving full recognition of the civil rights of gay men, lesbians, and people with HIV/AIDS. Lambda's legal staff of attorneys together with a network of volunteer Cooperating Attorneys, combat discrimination based on sexual orientation. Working on an average of fifty cases at any one time, issues include a wide variety of topics such as discrimination in employment, housing, the military; HIV/AIDS-related cases, equal marriage rights, parenting, "sodomy" laws, and anti-gay ballot initiatives. Lambda also provides legal services to homosexuals and encourages homosexuals to join the legal profession.

The National Gay and Lesbian Task Force (NGLTF), founded in 1973, supports local communities in organizing advocacy groups for gays and lesbians. The NGLTF strengthens gay and lesbian movements at the state and local levels at the same time connecting these activities to a national scene. At the national level it works to promote legislation to enhance gay and lesbian civil rights. Headquartered in Washington, D.C., it serves as a national resource center.

ernment need or reason for its passage. Amendment 2 is unconstitutional, Kennedy commented, because any law that makes it "more difficult for one group of citizens than all others to seek aid from the government is itself a denial of equal protection of the laws in the most literal [real or concrete] sense."

Kennedy forcefully ended by stating, "We must conclude that Amendment 2 classifies homosexuals not to further a proper legislative end but to make then unequal to everyone else. This Colorado cannot do. A state cannot so deem a class of persons a stranger to its laws."

Homosexual organizations applauded and cheered the decision saying it was the most important victory ever in the struggle for gay men and lesbians' civil rights. Finally, the U.S. Supreme Court had given constitutional protection against government or private discrimination based on sexual orientation. Groups opposed to gay rights, bitterly disappointed with the ruling, said it would greatly heighten tension between those for and against gay rights.

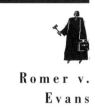

Romer v. Evans

Suggestions for further reading

Cohen, Susan, and Daniel Cohen. *When Someone You Know Is Gay.* New York: Laurel-Leaf Books, 1989.

Lambda Legal Defense and Educational Fund. [Online] Website: http://www.lambdalegal.org (Accessed on July 31, 2000).

National Gay & Lesbian Task Force. [Online] Website: http://www.ngltf.org (Accessed on July 31, 2000).

Nava, Michael, and Robert Dawidoff. *Created Equal: Why Gay Rights Matter to America.* New York: St. Martin's Press, 1994.

Robson, Ruthann. *Gay Men, Lesbians, and the Law.* New York: Chelsea House Publishers, 1997.

SEGREGATION AND DESEGREGATION

Through the early period of American history, races (groups of people normally identified by their skin color) were kept separate by social custom. White business owners simply refused to serve blacks. Slavery of black Americans was recognized as economically crucial to the Southern region. Political and legal liberties were not shared equally. For instance, only white male adults with property could vote in public elections. Boston's segregated (keeping races separate) public school system was affirmed by the Massachusetts Supreme Court in 1850.

First Efforts of Desegregation

The Emancipation Proclamation issued by President Abraham Lincoln in 1863 represented a first step to end these segregationist social customs. Immediately following the end of the American Civil War (1861–65) a series of three constitutional amendments, known as the Civil Rights Amendments were adopted to end such social customs and further racial integration (mixing of the races). The Thirteenth Amendment outlawed slavery. The Fourteenth and Fifteenth Amendments protected the constitutional civil rights of the newly freed slaves. Specifically, the Fourteenth Amendment extended "equal protection of the laws" to all Americans. It also maintained that everyone through the "due process" clause would be subject to the same legal processes. The Fifteenth Amendment extended voting rights to black males.

In spite of the new amendments, efforts to establish desegregation (abolishing segregation) social policies was met with severe resistance, particularly among the Southern states. State laws were passed restricting the freedom of black Americans, such as where blacks could sit on railroad cars and what public schools they could attend. The laws, known as Jim Crow Laws, sought to legally enforce racial segregation. Congress responded with federal laws supporting equal rights among all races. Civil Rights Acts were passed in 1866 and 1870 to enforce the civil rights amendments. With access to public facilities still being denied to many Americans on account of race and skin color, Congress passed another Civil Rights Act in 1875 making public facilities including railroads and hotels accessible to black Americans.

Severely hindering desegregation, Supreme Court decisions involving disputes over these rights commonly sided with the states during this period. The Court greatly limited the federal government's power to enforce the civil rights amendments. For example, in *Civil Rights Cases* (1883), a combination of three separate lower court cases involving similar civil rights disputes, the Supreme Court ruled application of the 1875 Civil Rights Act to private individuals or businesses unconstitutional (not following the intent of the U.S. Constitution and its amendments). The government could not force private businesses, such as hotels, restaurants, and railroad cars to integrate. As a result, by 1890 black Americans had few civil rights, particularly in the South.

"Separate But Equal"

The biggest blow against desegregation of public facilities came in the *Plessy v. Ferguson* (1896) ruling. By upholding a Louisiana law segregating access to railway cars between black and white Americans, a concept known as "separate but equal" was established. The decision maintained that segregation did not violate the equal protection clause of the Fourteenth Amendment if black and white Americans were given access to separate but equal facilities. The decision essentially gave approval to all laws requiring racial segregation.

Following the *Plessy* ruling, Jim Crow laws greatly expanded, particularly in the South where ninety percent of black Americans resided. Racial segregation was introduced into almost every aspect of American life in the fifteen Southern states plus West Virginia and Oklahoma. Other states allowed segregation but did not require it. Many of these laws were designed to keep black Americans from voting, causing segregation in access to political power. Other early laws focused on segregation of trains, both railway car seating and train station waiting rooms. State and local laws soon focused on public drinking fountains and restrooms, schools, hospitals, jails, streetcars, theaters, and amusement parks. There were white drinking fountains and black drinking fountains, white restrooms and black restrooms. Though separate, the facilities were rarely equal. The quality of facilities available to black Americans were normally far inferior to those available to white Americans. In 1915 it was revealed South Carolina was spending twelve times more public funds per student on white schools in comparison to schools for black Americans. Segregation was also enforced in the military where duties were given often on the basis of race. Segregated regiments were used in World War I (1914–18) and again in World War II (1939–45) until 1948 when desegregation was commanded by Presidential order.

With segregation practices more prevalent in the South, between 1900 and 1910 over 300,000 black Americans fled to the North and West seeking a better life. This movement, called the Great Migration, continued through the rest of the twentieth century. However, reception of these new residents in the North was not always friendly. Race riots broke out in 1917. Again in 1919 violence erupted in Chicago where many were killed when four black Americans attempted to enter a beach reserved for white Americans.

The Struggle Again For Desegregation

Organized opposition to segregation laws steadily grew. The National Urban League was formed in 1909 to assist black Americans readjusting from the rural South to the urban North. In 1910 the National Association for the Advancement of Colored People (NAACP) was established. The NAACP focused on lobbying federal and state governments for changes. The organization also began initiating lawsuits challenging segregation policies. Through their actions the Supreme Court ruled in *Buchanan v. Warley* (1917) that segregation of residential areas was unconstitutional. A Louisville, Kentucky city ordinance had prohibited black Americans from living on the same streets as white Americans. The right to serve on juries was upheld in *State v. Young* (1919).

While the NAACP took avenues toward lawsuits and legislation, others seeking desegregation took different approaches. For example, Booker T. Washington, a black educator, believed desegregation would result from becoming more economically equal. He established the Tuskegee Institute to provide industrial job training for black Americans to economically improve themselves.

Despite these efforts racism raged on with violent Ku Klux Klan terrorism peaking in the 1920s. Founded in the late nineteenth century, the Klan was a militant white racist organization with almost five million segregationists were members by 1929.

Limited progress at desegregation was made during the 1930s as the nation, especially black Americans, suffered through the Great Depression (1929–38). Yet, progress was made in some areas. Through continued pressure from the NAACP and others, Philadelphia public schools were desegregated. In 1936, the Supreme Court in *Murray v. Maryland* required desegregation at Maryland law schools.

Separate Is Unequal

The major break finally came in a 1954 Kansas case. A black father, Oliver Brown, refused to send his daughter to a black school which was further from his home than a white school. When the close-by Topeka school refused to enroll his daughter, the NAACP Legal Defense Fund led by future Supreme Court justice Thurgood Marshall took Brown's case to the Supreme Court. In **Brown v. Board of Education** (1954), the Court reversed the earlier *Plessy* decision and struck down the "separate but equal" standard. As the Court asserted, "separate educational facilities are inherently unequal." Racial segregation denied blacks equal protection of the laws under the Fourteenth Amendment, the Court declared. Federal district courts across the nation were given the command to desegregate public schools "with all deliberate speed." In this sweeping and historic decision, the Court reversed decades of legally forced racial segregation.

Rather than actually resolving the issue racial segregation, however, the *Brown* decision led to increased frustrations and violence. Many Southern states and school districts refused to comply with desegregation court orders. Various "freedom of choice" plans were created to preserve segregated schools. These plans allowed families to send their children to the school of their choice. Naturally, white families chose their predominately white neighborhood schools which they had been using while black families stayed in predominately black schools out of fear. Federal troops and law enforcement agents were called to enforce some local court orders. U.S. Marshalls forced integration at a Little Rock, Arkansas high school in 1957. Federal troops were called into action in 1963 at the University of Alabama and University of Mississippi to enforce desegregation and restore peace.

Besides at schools, desegregation was also ordered by the courts in transportation facilities, public housing, voting booths, and other public places like department stores, theaters, beaches, parks, libraries, and restaurants. Continued resistance to desegregation, particularly in the South, led to organized protests by blacks. Often led by Dr. Martin Luther King, Jr., of the Southern Christian Leadership Conference, many non-violent techniques were employed including "sit-ins," picketing, and boycotts. One of the most noted events was the 1955 boycott of the Montgomery, Alabama buses in reaction to the arrest of Rosa Parks, a black woman, for sitting in the white section of a public bus.

The Civil Rights Movement Peaks

By the early 1960s the civil rights movement had become a major national freedom effort. Many white American college students from the North began to get involved in support of black Americans. In 1961 black and white American students conducted Freedom Rides on public buses and stayed at hotels testing desegregation laws along their traveled routes. Violence by Southern white supremacists (those who believe white Americans are superior over black Americans) grew. A leader of the NAACP, Medgar Evers, was shot and killed in 1963 in Mississippi. Four black American young girls were murdered in a Ku Klux Klan church bombing in Birmingham, Alabama. Also in Mississippi, three white students teaching blacks how to register to vote were murdered. Southern law enforcement attacked peaceful black protesters with fire hoses, dogs, and clubs. Dr. King, frequently arrested for various minor charges by Southern authorities in efforts to diffuse the civil rights movement, wrote a famous letter known as "Letter from Birmingham City Jail" in 1963. In it he defended use of civil disobedience (refusing to obey a law to demonstrate against its unfairness) tactics in combating unjust laws. Civil disobedience refers to peacefully not obeying laws considered socially unjust. In an epic civil rights event in 1963, Dr. King led a march of 250,000 people to Washington, D.C. demanding an end to discrimination and segregation.

Congress responded to growing public pressure by passing the landmark Civil Rights Act of 1964, which forbids discrimination on the basis of race, color, religion, and national origin. The act prohibited segregation in all privately owned public facilities associated, however remotely, with interstate commerce. The act also prohibited discrimination in education and employment. The Supreme Court immediately defended the act as constitutional in *Heart of Atlanta Motel v. United States* (1964). Following a 1965 march in Selma, Alabama led by King in protest of voting restrictions on blacks that led to violent police attacks on the protesters, Congress passed the Voting Rights Act of 1965. Soon Congress also passed the Fair Housing Act in 1968 prohibiting discrimination in renting and purchasing homes. Desegregation of neighborhoods was further supported in 1968 in *Jones v. Alfred H. Mayer Co.* when the Court ruled it illegal to refuse to sell or rent to a person because of skin color.

Segregation and discrimination still persisted and frustrations further mounted. Race riots erupted in the Watts section of Los Angeles in 1965. Violence spread through thirty American cities in 1967 causing extensive death, injury, and property damage. In 1968 Dr. King was assassinated, a major blow to the desegregation movement.

The Continued Struggle for Desegregation

Some successes in desegregation continued. Implementing school desegregation orders of the Brown decision continued to be a problem. In *Swann v. Charlotte-Mecklenburg Board of Education* (1971), the Court supported local busing plans. Busing often involved transporting black school children from the inner city largely black schools to the mostly white schools of the suburbs. Busing continued to be a highly controversial desegregation strategy through the end of the twentieth century.

Another face to desegregation efforts came in the form of affirmative action programs in the 1970s. Minorities were given preferences in hiring for employment or admissions to schools in an attempt to further integrate the workforce and student bodies.

Despite major gains in desegregation following the 1950s in education, public places, employment, and transportation, segregation was still a dominant feature of American society. Residential neighborhood patterns and growth of private schools have particularly continued the segregated way of life in America. The workforce and university student bodies saw the most change.

At the end of the twentieth century, old arguments remained alive in American thought. Some continued to oppose governmental desegregation efforts claiming the Fourteenth Amendment only banned discrimination, not segregation. Conversely, others claimed to segregate is to unfairly discriminate.

Suggestions for further reading

Holliday, Laurel. *Children of the Dream: Our Own Stories of Growing Up Black in America.* New York: Pocket Books, 1999.

Lewis, John. *Walking with the Wind: A Memoir of the Movement.* New York: Simon & Schuster, 1998.

Williams, Juan. *Eyes on the Prize: America's Civil Rights Years, 1954–1965.* New York: Viking Penguin, Inc., 1987.

Wolters, Raymond. *The Burden of Brown: Thirty Years of School Desegregation.* Knoxville, TN: The University of Tennessee Press, 1984.

Plessy v. Ferguson
1896

Petitioner: Homer A. Plessy

Respondent: J. H. Ferguson, New Orleans Criminal District Court Judge

Petitioner's Claim: That Louisiana's law requiring blacks and whites to ride in separate railway cars violated Plessy's right to equal protection under the law.

Chief Lawyers for Petitioner: F. D. McKenney, S. F. Phillips

Chief Lawyer for Respondent: M. J. Cunningham, Louisiana Attorney General

Justices for the Court: Henry B. Brown, Stephen J. Field, Melville W. Fuller, Horace Gray, Rufus W. Peckham, George Shiras, Jr., Edward Douglas White

Justices Dissenting: John Marshall Harlan I (David Josiah Brewer did not participate)

Date of Decision: May 18, 1896

Decision: Ruled in favor of Ferguson by finding that Louisiana's law providing for "separate but equal" treatment for blacks and whites was constitutionally valid.

Significance: The decision was a major setback for minorities seeking equality in the United States. The ruling further paved the way for numerous state laws throughout the country making segregation which resulted in discrimination legal in almost all parts of daily life. The "separate but equal" standard lasted until the 1950s when the Supreme Court finally reversed this decision.

In 1900, Theodore Roosevelt was quoted as saying: "As a race . . . the [blacks] are altogether inferior to the whites . . . [and] can never rise to a very high place. . . I do not believe that the average Negro . . . is as yet in any way fit to take care of himself and others. . . If he were . . . there would be no Negro race problems." (from *In Their Own Words: A History of the American Negro* [1965], edited by Milton Meltzer.

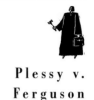
Such were the misguided perceptions of many white Americans in the late nineteenth and early twentieth centuries. Despite efforts by Congress and the federal government in the wake of the American Civil War (1861–65) to abolish slavery and extend the same basic civil rights enjoyed by white Americans to black Americans, prejudice against blacks remained strong. The U.S. Supreme Court consistently delivered decisions greatly limiting how much the government could do to protect the rights of blacks. Southern states increasingly passed laws, known as Jim Crow laws, keeping whites and blacks separated. State-ordered segregation [keeping races from mixing] continued a way of life in the South well established from earlier slavery days.

In 1890, Louisiana passed a law known as the Separate Car Law requiring railroads to provide "equal but separate accommodations for the white and colored races." The law barred anyone from sitting in a railway car not designated for their own race. The law was not only poorly received by Louisiana's black population, but also by the railway companies because of the extra expense needed to provide separate cars.

Homer Adolph Plessy

As soon as the Separate Car Law was passed, black leaders in Louisiana became determined to challenge the law. They formed a Citizen's Committee to develop a strategy to test its constitutionality. Acting on their behalf, Homer A. Plessy, a shoemaker, bought a first class ticket on June 7, 1892 on the East Louisiana Railroad to ride from New Orleans to his home in Covington, Louisiana. Plessy, only one-eighth black, had light colored features and mostly appeared white. Under Louisiana law he was still considered black. When questioned by a railway conductor after finding a seat in the whites-only railroad car, he responded that he was colored. The conductor ordered Plessy to the colored-only car. Refusing to move, Plessy was arrested by Detective Chris Cain, removed from the train, and taken to the New Orleans city jail.

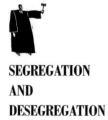

**SEGREGATION
AND
DESEGREGATION**

A Badge of Inferiority

Plessy and the Citizen's Committee immediately filed a lawsuit in the District Court of Orleans Parish claiming the Louisiana law denied him "equal protection of the laws" as guaranteed by the Fourteenth Amendment. The amendment states, "No State shall make or enforce any law which shall abridge [lessen] the privileges . . . of citizens of the United States . . . nor deny to any person within its jurisdiction [geographical area over which a government has authority] the equal protection of the laws." Equal protection of the laws means persons or groups of persons in similar situations must be treated equally by the laws. In addition, Plessy charged the restrictions, in a sense, reintroduced slavery by denying equality. Thus, the law also violated the Thirteenth Amendment's ban on slavery. Plessy argued that the state law "stamps the colored race with a badge of inferiority."

Judge John H. Ferguson, relying on several legal precedents (principles of former decisions), found Plessy guilty and sentenced him to either pay a twenty-five dollar fine or spend twenty days in jail. Plessy appealed to the Louisiana Supreme Court which upheld the conviction. Plessy next appealed to the U.S. Supreme Court for a court order forbidding Ferguson from carrying out the conviction. The Court accepted the case, but due to the large number of cases waiting to be decided by the Court, almost four years passed before it was heard.

Separate But Equal

Finally, on April 13, 1896 Plessy argued his case in Court. The state responded that the Louisiana law merely made a distinction between blacks and whites, but did not actually treat one as inferior to the other. Less than a month later, on May 18, the Court issued its 7-1 decision in accepting the state's arguments. Justice Henry B. Brown, delivering the Court's decision, wrote,

> **A statute [law] which implies [expresses] merely a legal distinction between the white and colored races—a distinction which is found in the color of the two races, and which must always exist so long as white men are distinguished from the other race by color—has no tendency to destroy the legal equality of the two races.**

The Court reaffirmed Plessy's conviction by finding that the Louisiana's law did not violate either the Thirteenth or Fourteenth Amendments. Brown stated that the equal protection clause of the Fourteenth Amendment "could not have been intended to abolish distinctions based upon color, or to enforce social . . . equality." Segregation did not violate equal protection, according to Brown. The state had properly used its police powers in a "reasonable" way to promote the public good by keeping peace between the races. As Brown commented, "If the two races are to meet upon terms of social equality, it must be the result of voluntary consent of the individuals." With that finding, Brown gave Supreme Court approval to the "separate but equal" concept.

Plessy v. Ferguson

A Color-Blind Constitution

In a historically important and emotional dissent, Justice John Marshall Harlan, a native Kentuckian and former slaveholder, boldly wrote,

> **Our Constitution is color-blind, and neither knows nor tolerates classes among citizens. . . In my opinion, the judgement this rendered will, in time, prove to be . . . [harmful]. . . The present decision . . . will not only stimulate aggressions . . . brutal and irritating, on the admitted rights of colored citizens, but will encourage the belief that it is possible, by means of state enactments [laws], to defeat the beneficent [valuable] purposes . . . which the people of the United States had in view when they adopted the recent [Thirteenth and Fourteenth] amendments of the Constitution.**

Agreeing with Plessy's arguments, Harlan charged that segregation created a "badge of servitude" likening it to slavery.

Separate And Unequal

The ruling, that gave constitutional approval to racial segregation, presented a major setback to black Americans and others seeking equality between the races. It would greatly influence social customs in the United States for most of the next six decades. The Court did not address that separate facilities would deny blacks access to the same quality of accommodations as whites. Rarely would separate facilities be as good,

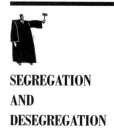

HENRY BILLINGS BROWN

Supreme Court Justice Henry Billings Brown delivered the Court opinion in *Plessy v. Ferguson* (1896) essentially condemning black Americans to extensive racial discrimination for at least the next sixty years. Born in South Lee, Massachusetts in 1836, Brown was the son of a prosperous New England businessman. He was a graduate of Yale University with some limited training in law at Yale and Harvard. After moving to Michigan, Brown married the daughter of a wealthy Detroit lumber trader and, consequently, became independently wealthy. Brown established a successful law practice and taught law. In 1875 he was appointed to the U.S. District Court for the Eastern District of Michigan and in 1890 was appointed by President Benjamin Harrison to the U.S. Supreme Court.

Many considered Brown to be wise and fair during his time and warmly amiable in character. However, Brown largely opposed government regulation of business and recognition of individual civil rights, focusing instead on protecting property rights and free enterprise. Brown was a social elitist [higher social standing than most] who held many of the prejudices prominent during his time toward blacks, women, Jews, and immigrants. He did not believe laws should require changes in social custom when strong public sentiments were against it. Though he was relatively popular at the time, his decision in *Plessy* upholding state-required segregation later greatly affected his reputation. Due to failing eyesight, Brown retired from the Court in 1906 and later died in New York City in 1913 at the age of seventy-seven.

and because of the lengthy history of discrimination in America, blacks held little political power to make sure separate facilities would become equal in quality.

The phrase "separate but equal" became symbolic of forced racial segregation in the nation invading almost every aspect of American society, including restaurants, railroads, streetcars, waiting rooms, parks, cemeteries, churches, hospitals, prisons, elevators, theaters, schools, public restrooms, water fountains, and even public telephones. Not until 1954 in **Brown v. Board of Education** did the Court finally act to overturn the "separate but equal" doctrine, three generations after the fateful *Plessy* decision.

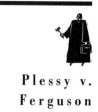

Plessy v.
Ferguson

Suggestions for further reading

Fireside, Harvey. Plessy v. Ferguson: *Separate But Equal?* Enslow Publishers, Inc., 1997.

Howard, John R. *The Shifting Wind: The Supreme Court and Civil Rights from Reconstruction to* Brown. Albany, NY: State University of New York Press, 1999.

Lofgren, Charles A. *The* Plessy *case: a legal-historical interpretation.* New York: Oxford University Press, 1987.

Olsen, Otto H. *The Thin Disguise: Turning Point in Negro History,* Plessy v. Ferguson, *1864–1896.* New York: Humanities Press 1967.

Shelley v. Kraemer
1948

Petitioner: J.D. Shelley

Respondent: Louis Kraemer

Petitioner's Claim: That contracts preventing African Americans from purchasing homes violate the Fourteenth Amendment.

Chief Lawyers for Petitioner: George L. Vaughn and Herman Willer

Chief Lawyer for Respondent: Gerald L. Seegers

Justices for the Court: Hugo Lafayette Black, Harold Burton, William O. Douglas, Felix Frankfurter, Frank Murphy, Frederick Moore Vinson

Justices Dissenting: None (Robert H. Jackson, Stanley Forman Reed, and Wiley Blount Rutledge did not participate)

Date of Decision: May 3, 1948

Decision: The Supreme Court said the Fourteenth Amendment prevents courts from enforcing race discrimination in real estate contracts.

Significance: *Shelley* ended a powerful form of race discrimination in housing.

When the American Civil War ended in 1865, the United States ended slavery with the Thirteenth Amendment. Three years later in 1868, it adopted the Fourteenth Amendment. The Equal Protection Clause of the

Fourteenth Amendment says a state may not "deny to any person within its jurisdiction the equal protection of the laws." The main purpose of the Equal Protection Clause was to prevent states from discriminating against African Americans.

The Fourteenth Amendment only applies to the states. It does not prevent race discrimination by individual people. After 1868, racial prejudice led many people to continue race discrimination on their own.

Whites Only

In 1911 there was a neighborhood in St. Louis, Missouri, where thirty-nine people owned fifty-seven parcels of land. In February of that year, thirty of the owners signed an agreement not to rent or sell their property to African Americans or Asian Americans. Such an agreement is called a restrictive covenant. The owners who signed the restrictive covenant had forty-seven of the fifty-seven parcels in the neighborhood.

In August 1945, J.D. Shelley and his wife, who were African Americans, bought a parcel of land in the neighborhood from someone named Fitzgerald. The Shelleys were unaware of the restrictive covenant. Louis Kraemer and his wife, who owned another parcel in the neighborhood, sued the Shelleys in the Circuit Court of St. Louis. The Kraemers asked the court to take the Shelleys' land away and give it back to Fitzgerald.

The court ruled in favor of the Shelleys because the restrictive covenant did not have the proper signatures. On appeal, however, the Supreme Court of Missouri reversed and ruled in favor of the Kraemers. The court said the restrictive covenant was legal and ordered the Shelleys to leave their land. Determined to stay, the Shelleys took the case to the U.S. Supreme Court.

Race Discrimination Unenforceable

With a 6–0 decision, the Supreme Court reversed again and ruled in favor of the Shelleys. Chief Justice Frederick Moore Vinson wrote the opinion for the Court. Chief Justice Vinson said the right to own property is one of the rights protected by the Fourteenth Amendment. That means a state would not be allowed to create a restrictive covenant that discriminated against people because of their race.

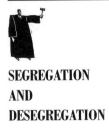

*Real estate
covenants worked to
keep minority
families from buying
houses in nicer
neighborhoods.*
Reproduced by
permission of Ken Estell.

Missouri, of course, did not create the restrictive covenant that applied to the Shelleys' land. Private owners created it in 1911. That meant the restrictive covenant itself did not violate the Fourteenth Amendment. The only way to enforce the covenant, however, was to go to court, as the Kraemers had done.

Chief Justice Vinson said the Fourteenth Amendment made it illegal for state courts to enforce restrictive covenants that discriminate against people because of their race. Vinson said, "freedom from discrimination by the States in the enjoyment of property rights was among

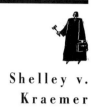

Shelley v.
Kraemer

CHIEF JUSTICE FREDERICK MOORE VINSON

Frederick Moore Vinson was born in Louisa, Kentucky, on January 22, 1890. Vinson worked his way through Centre College in Kentucky, earning an undergraduate degree in 1909 and a law degree in 1911. He then practiced law in his hometown until 1923, serving briefly during that time as city attorney and commonwealth attorney.

In 1923, Vinson was elected to the U.S. House of Representatives. He served there from 1924 to 1929 and again from 1931 to 1938. In between he practiced law in Ashland, Kentucky. In 1938 Vinson became a judge on the U.S. Court of Appeals for the District of Columbia. After working as a judge for five years, Vinson pursued a career in the executive branch of the federal government. He worked for presidents Roosevelt and Truman, serving under Truman as Secretary of the Treasury.

When Chief Justice Harlan Fiske Stone died in 1946, President Truman appointed Vinson to replace Stone. From Vinson's years of loyal service to American presidents, Truman knew Vinson would protect presidential power from the Supreme Court. During his seven years on the Supreme Court, Vinson voted regularly in favor of governmental power over individual rights. *Shelley v. Kraemer* was a rare exception to that tendency. Vinson died from a heart attack on September 8, 1953.

the basic objectives sought ... by the framers of the Fourteenth Amendment. ... The Fourteenth Amendment declares that all persons, whether colored or white, shall stand equal before the laws of the States."

In the end, then, the Kraemers were not allowed to take the Shelleys' land away. The decision was an early victory for African Americans, who were struggling to protect their civil rights. Six years later, the Court would order public schools to stop segregation, the practice of separating blacks and whites in different schools. Such decisions

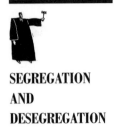

**SEGREGATION
AND
DESEGREGATION**

gave Americans the chance to live and go to school together in the melting pot of the United States.

Suggestions for further reading

Bourgoin, Suzanne Michele, and Paula Kay Byers, eds. *Encyclopedia of World Biography*. Detroit: Gale Research, 1998.

Gillam, Scott. Discrimination: Prejudice in Action. Enslow Publishers, Inc., 1995.

McKissack, Pat. Taking a Stand against Racism and Racial Discrimination. New York: Franklin Watts, 1990.

Phillips, Angela. Discrimination. New Discovery Books, 2000.

Wilson, Anna. African Americans Struggle for Equality. Vero Beach: Rourke, 1992.

Witt, Elder, ed. *Congressional Quarterly's Guide to the U.S. Supreme Court*. District of Columbia: Congressional Quarterly Inc., 1990.

Brown v. Board of Education 1954

Appellants: Oliver Brown and several other parents of black schoolchildren

Appellee: Board of Education of Topeka, Kansas

Appellant's Claim: That racial segregation of public schools denied black schoolchildren equal protection of the law as guaranteed by the Fourteenth Amendment.

Chief Lawyer for Appellants: Robert L. Carter, Thurgood Marshall, Spottswood W. Robinson, Charles S. Scott

Chief Lawyer for Appellee: Harold R. Fatzer, Paul E. Wilson

Justices for the Court: Hugo L. Black, Harold Burton, Tom C. Clark, William O. Douglas, Felix Frankfurter, Robert H. Jackson, Sherman Minton, Stanley Forman Reed, Chief Justice Earl Warren

Justices Dissenting: None

Date of Decision: May 17, 1954

Decision: Ruled in favor of Brown by finding that racial segregation in public schools was unconstitutional.

Significance: The decision was an historic ruling regarding segregation of public places. In ending segregation of public schools, the decision overturned *Plessy*'s "separate but equal" doctrine and paved the way for desegregation of other types of public places in the next two decades.

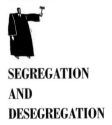

SEGREGATION AND DESEGREGATION

Immediately following the end of the American Civil War (1861–65), the U.S. government took a number of measures to recognize and protect the civil rights of black Americans. Three new constitutional amendments were adopted between 1865 and 1870 banning slavery, extending basic rights to blacks, and granting citizenship. From approximately 1865 to 1877, the U.S. military occupied the former Confederate states to enforce social and political changes in Southern society. In addition, Congress passed civil rights laws to protect black Americans from discrimination in public places. However, resistance by many Southern whites to social change remained strong. Finally, by the mid-1870s government efforts to force social change had weakened and Southern whites began to gain political control of the South again. The Southern states and local governments began to pass laws to keep blacks politically and economically inferior to whites. Many of the laws, known as Jim Crow laws, forced public racial segregation (keeping the races from mixing).

The U.S. Supreme Court handed down rulings which greatly hindered black's drive for social justice. First, in *Civil Rights Cases* (1883) the Court ruled that constitutional protections did not extend to privately owned public places, such as restaurants, inns, and theaters. Therefore, private owners of such establishments could keep blacks from entering. Then, in 1896 the Court ruled in *Plessy v. Ferguson* that keeping races separated was constitutionally valid as long as facilities for blacks were equal to those for whites. This decision establishing the "separate but equal" doctrine added further support to Jim Crow laws. State-required segregation invaded every aspect of public social life in schools, transportation, and housing, particularly in the South.

Greatly disappointed with the Court decisions and not accepting that the Constitution allows racial discrimination, a group of black and white proponents of social justice came together in 1909 to form the National Association for the Advancement of Colored People (NAACP). The NAACP was dedicated to fighting segregation and the Jim Crow laws in the courts. After achieving some courtroom victories, the NAACP began to focus in the 1930s on segregation in public schools. By 1939, future Supreme Court justice Thurgood Marshall assumed leadership of the NAACP's legal department, known as the NAACP Legal Defense Fund.

Following World War II (1939–45), Marshall and the NAACP gained two victories in school segregation. The Court in *Sweatt v. Painter* (1950) ruled that a separate law school for blacks in Texas could not provide the same opportunities as the long established University of Texas Law School. In *McLaurin v. Oklahoma State Regents* (1950) the Court ruled that a separate library and lecture hall seat for a black graduate student were not constitutional. However, the NAACP had not directly addressed the "separate but equal" doctrine or school segregation in general. They began searching for the perfect cases to challenge those social policies.

Oliver Brown's Daughter, Linda

Like many states, Kansas had passed a law giving school districts the choice of segregating their schools. The Topeka school district chose to do just that. By the early 1950s twenty-two public elementary schools existed in town, eighteen for white schoolchildren and four for black schoolchildren.

Born in 1919, Oliver Brown was a railroad welder, a war veteran, and assistant pastor at his church. He had no reputation as a social activist, quietly living in his community. Living close to his work, his neighborhood bordered a railroad switching yard. He and his wife had three daughters. Though they lived only seven blocks from the nearest elementary school, it was for whites only. His children had to walk through the dangerous switching yard to the nearest black school about a mile away. Oliver did not want to have his eight year-old daughter walk through the switchyards to school simply because she was black. Brown learned of the NAACP looking for test cases to challenge school segregation policies and agreed to join the effort in addition to several other parents of black schoolchildren in Topeka. In September of 1950, Oliver took his daughter Linda to the nearby white school to enroll in the third grade. The school's principal refused to admit her.

In March of 1951 Brown aided by NAACP lawyers filed a lawsuit against the Topeka Board of Education in the U.S. District Court for the District of Kansas requesting a court order to prohibit continuation of the segregated school system.

The District Court tried the case in late June. Among witness supporting Brown were experts testifying that segregated schools were automatically unequal despite their quality because the separation gave black children a feeling of inferiority. Such a system could not possibly prepare them for their adult lives. The school board responded that because almost all aspects of public life were racially segregated even restaurants and bathrooms, segregated schools were actually preparing the children

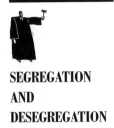
for the realities of adult life. The board did not see segregation as an undesirable way to live. The Board pointed to some famous black Americans as examples that segregation did not keep blacks from success. Brown countered that exceptions always exist, but for most children segregation significantly reduces opportunities later in life. People tend to live up to what is expected of them, and segregation sends a clear message of lower expectations.

In August of 1951 the District Court issued its ruling. Despite agreeing with Brown's arguments concerning the bad effects of school segregation on black schoolchildren, the court stated that because of the Supreme Court ruling in *Plessy* it had no choice but to rule in favor of the Board of Education. No constitutional violations existed.

Oliver Brown Goes to Washington

Brown appealed the court decision to the U.S. Supreme Court. The Court accepted the case and in June of 1952 combined it with four other cases challenging school segregation policies elsewhere in the nation. On December 9, 1952, the two sides presented their arguments before the Court. Brown argued that the school segregation policy violated his family's equal protection of the law under the Fourteenth Amendment. The amendment declares, "No state shall . . . deny to any person within its jurisdiction [geographic area over which the government has authority] the equal protection of the laws." John W. Davis, a presidential candidate earlier in 1924, presented the Board of Education's arguments. He claimed that the Fourteenth Amendment never intended to prevent segregation of schools. Besides, he claimed, "the happiness, the progress and the welfare of these children is best promoted in segregated schools." He further added the courts did not even have constitutional authority to direct how local school districts would be operated.

With only eight members of the Court present instead of the usual nine, a stalemate was reached after hearing arguments. The Court requested the two sides to come back and reargue the case again. The Court further requested that for the second hearing, the two sides should focus on some specific issues, including the Fourteenth Amendment's Equal Protection Clause. The Court wanted to explore more about the amendment's intent toward school segregation at the time of adoption. Though disappointed with the Court's decision to rehear the case, Brown and the NAACP lawyers saw it as an indication the Court was considering overturning *Plessy*.

Mr. Brown Returns to Washington

While the parties were away preparing their new arguments, Chief Justice Fred M. Vinson died and Earl Warren was appointed in his place. Arguments on the points the Court had requested were held almost exactly one year later on December 8, 1953. Research by the parties indicated that school segregation was not really considered when the Fourteenth Amendment was written and adopted. In fact, required school attendance essentially did not exist in the 1860s. Consequently, effects of the amendment on public education was not a major concern at the time.

On May 17, 1954, the Court delivered its unanimous (9-0) ruling with a fairly brief written opinion for such an important case. The Court found in favor of Brown and the NAACP by agreeing segregation is automatically unequal regardless if the black children had the same quality of facilities, teachers, and books. New Chief Justice Earl Warren, writing for the Court, emphasized that education had become a much more important part of American life since the 1890s when the *Plessy* decision had been made. As Warren wrote,

> **Today, education is perhaps the most important function of the state and local governments. . . It is required in the performance of our most basic public responsibilities. . . It is the very foundation of good citizenship. Today it is a principal instrument in awakening the child to cultural values, in preparing him for later professional training, and in helping him to adjust normally to his environment. . . Such an opportunity . . . is a right which must be made available to all on equal terms.**

Building on its 1950 decisions in *Sweatt* and *McLaurin,* Warren wrote,

> **We conclude that in the field of public education the doctrine of 'separate but equal' has no place. Separate educational facilities are inherently [undeniably] unequal. Therefore, we hold that the [Browns] and others similarly situated . . . by reason of the segregation complained of, [are] deprived of the equal protection of the laws guaranteed by the Fourteenth Amendment.**

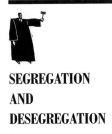

The "separate but equal' doctrine allowing the separation of children by race into different schools violated the Fourteenth Amendment. Relying on the results of seven sociological studies on the harmful effects of racial segregation, he added that segregation gave black schoolchildren "a feeling of inferiority [feeling less worthy than others] as to their status [place] in the community that may affect their hearts and minds in a way unlikely to ever be undone." Not only were their lives harmed, but the general welfare of American society as well.

The Court remanded (returned) Brown's and the other four cases back to the local courts to determine if the local schools were doing enough to move desegregation (outlawing segregation) along.

The Court also requested the NAACP lawyers to come back yet again the following year with suggestions on how school desegregation should be carried out. In 1955 the Court unanimously ruled that all school districts must desegregate "with all deliberate speed." The Court established guidelines giving local school officials the main responsibility for desegregation, but gave the federal district courts responsibility to watch over how the schools were doing. The courts were to consider unique local factors hindering desegregation progress.

Slow Change

The Brown decision introduced fundamental changes in U.S. society. But, just as it took nearly sixty years to reverse legalized discrimination as supported by the *Plessy* decision, another twenty years would pass before school desegregation in America would be accomplished. Resistance to the *Brown* decision contributed to the growth of the civil rights movement in the 1950s. Considerable social unrest and violence followed in the 1960s. Oliver Brown died in 1961, not to see the ultimate results of his efforts to simply have children attend the public school closest to their home. One by one the government took resistant local school districts to court to force desegregation. Finally, by the early 1970s school segregation policies had been largely eliminated.

The *Brown* ruling also set the stage for desegregation in other phases of public life as well, from bus stations to public libraries to restrooms. However, the racial mix in public schools still was an issue by the close of the twentieth century. White flight to the suburbs in the 1960s and growth of private schools still left a largely segregated system with black urban schools and white suburban schools. Still, the *Brown*

THURGOOD MARSHALL

Thurgood Marshall, one of the chief lawyers for Oliver Brown in his case against the Topeka Board of Education, later became the first black American Supreme Court justice. Marshall was born in Baltimore, Maryland on July 2, 1908 and named after his grandfather, a former slave. His father, William, was a railroad dining car waiter and later chief waiter at a private club. His mother, Norma, taught school at a segregated black elementary school. Young Marshall grew up experiencing first hand the widespread racial discrimination of early twentieth century America. He attended Lincoln University in Pennsylvania, the oldest black college in the United States and there displayed strong speaking skills while leading a successful debate team. Unable to attend the University of Maryland Law School because it was white-only, Marshall graduated first in his class in law from Howard University.

Dedicated to combating social injustice, Marshall quickly attracted the attention of the National Association for the Advancement of Colored People (NAACP) which was recruiting lawyers to fight segregation laws. One of his first successful cases was ending the segregation policies of the University of Maryland Law School. At age thirty, Marshall became chief lawyer for the NAACP. He successfully argued twenty-nine cases before the U.S. Supreme Court, becoming known as "Mr. Civil Rights."

In 1961 President John F. Kennedy appointed Marshall to a federal judge position and in 1965 he became Solicitor General of the United States under President Lyndon B. Johnson. In 1967, Johnson nominated him to the Supreme Court where he served until 1991. Thurgood Marshall died of heart failure two years later at age eighty-four. Widely respected for his lifelong fight for individual rights, thousands of mourners waited hours in winter weather to pay their last respects as his body lay in state in the Supreme Court building.

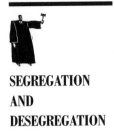

**SEGREGATION
AND
DESEGREGATION**

ruling is regarded as one of the most important Supreme Court decisions in the nation's history.

Suggestions for further reading

Fireside, Harvey, and Sarah B. Fuller. Brown v. Board of Education: *Equal Schooling for All.* Hillside, NJ: Enslow Publishers, Inc., 1994.

Howard, John R. *The Shifting Wind: The Supreme Court and Civil Rights from Reconstruction to* Brown. Albany, NY: State University of New York Press, 1999.

Thomas, Bettye C., and V. P. Franklin. *My Soul Is a Witness: A Chronology of the Civil Rights Era, 1954-1965.* New York: Henry Holt and Company, 1999.

Ware, Leland. *Thurgood Marshall: Freedom's Defender.* Alexandria, VA: Time Life Education, 1999.

Williams, Juan. *Thurgood Marshall: American Revolutionary.* New York: Time Books, 1998.

Swann v. Charlotte-Mecklenburg Board of Education 1971

Appellant: James E. Swann

Appellee: Charlotte-Mecklenburg Board of Education

Appellant's Claim: That the local public school desegregation plan was inadequate to achieve integration and protect the civil rights of its students.

Chief Lawyers for Appellant: Julius LeVonne Chambers, James M. Nabritt III

Chief Lawyers for Appellee: William J. Waggoner, Benjamin S. Horack

Justices for the Court: Hugo L. Black, Harry A. Blackmun, William J. Brennan, Jr., Chief Justice Warren E. Burger, William O. Douglas, John Marshall Harlan II, Thurgood Marshall, Potter Stewart, Byron R. White

Justices Dissenting: None

Date of Decision: April 20, 1971

Decision: Ruled in favor of Swann by upholding the federal district court's ambitious desegregation plan designed to fully integrate the district's public schools.

Significance: The ruling affirmed the role of federal district courts in overseeing operations of local school districts.

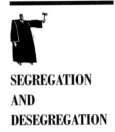

**SEGREGATION
AND
DESEGREGATION**

Following the landmark Supreme Court decision in ***Brown v. Board of Education*** (1954) ending legally enforced racial segregation (keeping races apart) in public schools, progress toward racial integration (mixing of the races) continued to be slow. The tradition of having separate schools for black and white children was well established in American culture.

A Southern Resistance

The Southern states in particular immediately began thinking of ways to avoid obeying the Court's desegregation (ban segregation) directions given in *Brown*. In reaction, the Court in *Brown v. Board of Education II* (1955) directed the lower federal district courts to develop plans to force desegregation. Resistance persisted. One Virginia school board even closed its public schools to avoid integrating them. Tuition monies were granted to students to attend segregated private schools. In reaction, the Supreme Court in *Griffin v. County School Board* (1964) ordered the public schools to open again. "Freedom of choice" plans were also introduced in which children could choose which school to attend, white or black. The Court in *Green v. County School Board* (1968) ruled this approach was not strong enough to truly achieve integration. The Court held that the student bodies of each school should be similar in mix of races as the population in the area in general.

As white Americans fled the trouble-ridden cities to suburbs and predominately white schools, the distinct courts decided the primary way to swiftly integrate schools was through busing. Busing involved carrying students long distances on a daily basis to create more racially-mixed schools.

The Charlotte-Mecklenburg School District

The Charlotte-Mecklenburg School District of North Carolina was large, including both the city of Charlotte as well as the rural region of Mecklenburg County. The district included 101 schools scattered across some 550 square miles. Twenty-nine percent of the 84,000 school-age children in the area were black and most of them lived in one particular section of Charlotte. A desegregation plan was created in 1965 to integrate the public schools. The plan had redrawn school attendance zones and allowed students freedom of choice regarding which school they wished to attend. Almost 30,000 students were bused to distant schools under the plan. However, little integration resulted as over half of the black students remained in all-black schools. The schools remained generally the same as before.

Swann Applies Green

Inspired by the Court's decision in *Green,* James Swann and other residents of the school district finally filed a lawsuit in 1968 claiming the integration plan was not effective. Unlike previous court cases, however, that focused primarily on rural school districts, this case involved urban (city) schools. For example, the school district involved in the Green decision was a small rural school district. Charlotte-Mecklenburg, on the other hand, was what is known as a large "unified" school district including various communities.

Swann won his suit in federal district court. Overseeing a new Charlotte-Mecklenburg plan, the court created a much more ambitious and expensive plan in 1970 involving increased school busing. The plan stated that twenty-nine percent of each public school should consist of

Swann v.
Charlotte-
Mecklenburg
Board of
Education

The police were often forced to monitor the bussing of African American students into white schools for the students' protection. Reproduced by permission of the Corbis Corporation.

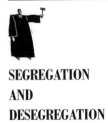
black students, reflecting the percentage of black students in the entire school district. An additional 13,000 students would need to be bused. To begin applying the plan the district had to buy one hundred new buses. The plan would cost a half million dollars a year in addition to one million dollars to get started. Not surprisingly, the new plan met considerable resistance from the school board.

The school board appealed the plan to the Fourth Circuit Court of Appeals. The appeals court, agreeing with the board, reversed part of the plan claiming it placed an unreasonable burden on the board. In response to Swann's defeat in the appeals court, the Legal Defense Fund of the National Association for the Advancement of Colored People (NAACP) appealed the decision to the U.S. Supreme Court which agreed to hear the case.

To the Supreme Court

Challenged in the Supreme Court, the Court in 1971 unanimously ruled in favor of Swann and the NAACP. The more extensive desegregation plan developed by the district court was to be followed. Chief Justice Warren E. Burger, writing for the Court, recognized that busing, though not necessarily a desirable means, may be the only means to begin the school integration process. Freedom of choice in deciding which school a child would like to attend could not adequately solve the segregation issue. As Burger stated,

> **In these circumstances, we find no basis for holding that the local school authorities may not be required to employ bus transportation as one tool of school desegregation. Desegregation plans cannot be limited to the walk-in [close-by] school.**

Chief Justice Burger supplied broad guidelines to district court judges still dealing with segregated school systems. The mathematical ratios imposed on Charlotte-Mecklenburg, in which twenty-nine out of every one hundred students in each school would be black, was one approach meeting the Court's approval. Another tool was redesign of school attendance boundaries to include residential areas of both races.

Courts in Charge of Schools

The Court once again approved supervision of public school districts by federal district court judges. The Court commanded that district courts

SCHOOL BUSING

The Court decision in *Swann v. Charlotte Mecklenburg Board of Education* (1971) firmly established that lower federal district courts could force school districts to adopt school busing plans to achieve racial integration. School busing, itself, was not new to students at the time. Almost forty percent of American school-children in the 1960s rode buses to schools. But the nature of busing changed. Instead of riding to the nearest community school, now children began riding to distant schools in unfamiliar places. For example, in *Evans v. Buchanan* (1977) a massive desegregation busing plan was created in Delaware combining many school districts into one that held forty percent of all the state's school students.

Opposition to such busing was immediately strong from both white and black Americans. Though a number of children received improved educational opportunities in better supported suburban schools, many believed busing placed unnecessary hardships on the schoolchildren. The reasons were many. Often the rides were long, it was more difficult for many parents to participate in their children's education, participating in after-school activities was difficult, bused children lost their sense of community, some children became even more alienated (withdrawn) from school, and limited school funds were being used for busing rather than for education. Often children still tended to socialize with their own race in their new schools. This led to segregation within schools and sometimes actually increasing interracial hostilities and tensions of the community.

Through the 1980s opposition to busing grew steadily. Finally, in 1991 the Court essentially ended the forced-school busing era by ruling in *Board of Education of Oklahoma City Public Schools v. Dowell* that busing was intended only to be a temporary measure. Some school busing programs did continue, largely voluntarily under supervision of local school boards.

Swann v.
Charlotte-
Mecklenburg
Board of
Education

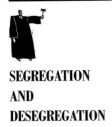

**SEGREGATION
AND
DESEGREGATION**

were to "make every effort to achieve the greatest possible degree of actual desegregation." The severity of the constitutional violation, Burger wrote, should determine the extent of the forced integration measures. In a later ruling the Court added that such fixes could be discontinued when integration was accomplished.

The Court's support of the Charlotte plan led to extensive busing programs in many parts of the United States during the 1970s, including Boston, Los Angeles, Cleveland, and other major cities. Busing became one of the most controversial social issues of the decade. The mood of the Supreme Court toward forced desegregation, particularly through busing, began to change by the 1980s with five new justices appointed. The Court became less supportive of such sweeping district court deseg-regation plans as approved in Charlotte-Mecklenburg. In fact, the 1971 *Swann* decision was the last unanimous ruling (all nine justices agreeing) by the Supreme Court in school desegregation cases, a remarkable trend that had started with the *Brown* decision in 1954.

Busing continued to spark controversy through the end of the century. Busing was highly unpopular among black Americans because of the distances their children were being taken and fears of safety in predomi-nately white schools. Resistance was most pronounced in the North, per-haps less accustomed to long-distance busing than the largely rural South. Such court-ordered desegregation plans as adopted by Charlotte-Mecklenburg led to very mixed results in achieving integration through the years. Despite extensive busing, many schools still remained racially segregated to a large degree. The rise of largely white private schools and the trend of white families moving out of the cities to new school dis-tricts in the suburbs where few minorities lived were key reasons.

Suggestions for further reading

Belknap, Michel R. *Desegregation of Public Education.* New York: Garland Press, 1991.

Leone, Bruno. Racism: *Opposing Viewpoints.* 2nd Edition. St. Paul, MN: Greenhaven Press, 1986.

Schwartz, Bernard. *Swann's Way: The School Busing Case and the Supreme Court.* New York: Oxford University Press, 1986.

Watras, Joseph. *Politics, Race, and Schools: Racial Integration, 1954-1994.* New York: Garland Publications, 1997.

VOTING RIGHTS

$\mathbf{T}$he American governmental system is a representative democracy with a key fundamental element—the right or privilege to vote. The system operates by peaceable argument. People take sides, debate (argue their views), and vote to reach a decision. Just because a decision is reached does not suggest the arguments are over. The decision only means voters will abide by the decision of the majority for a specific amount of time until the next vote is taken. Consequently, in the United States, government by the people never means full consent (everyone agreeing on one way). At any given time many citizens may be opposed to who is in power or may be against what the government is doing.

But even the smallest minorities, by participating actively, may influence a democracy. A democracy undergoes constant change in responding to the needs and concerns of its people. Voting provides the means to change.

Historical Perspective

At the beginning of the twenty-first century most Americans think of the right to vote as one of the most basic rights of U.S. citizenship. However, citizenship and voting have not always been directly related. From the signing of the U.S. Constitution in 1787 until 1971, large numbers of American citizens could not vote.

The Framers of the Constitution feared giving too much political power to the people would encourage mob rule. In 1776 John Adams, a respected advocate for American liberty who would become America's second president, warned that granting the vote to everyone would bring political disaster. In 1787 Alexander Hamilton told the constitutional convention that "the people seldom judge or determine right." The Framers believed voting should be limited to white landowning men. Owning property, they believed, gave men a stake in society and made them more responsible citizens.

As originally adopted, the U.S. Constitution allowed those eligible to vote to only elect members of the House of Representatives. To check the power of the people, the President and senators were elected by state legislators. The Framers also left to the states the power to decide which of their citizens should have the right to vote. As they hoped, most states enacted laws requiring some kind of property or wealth—usually a certain amount of land—before allowing men to vote. The common man who owned no property or lacked a fixed amount of wealth could not vote at all. Congress did reserve for itself in Article I of the Constitution the power to control the time and place of elections.

The property requirements became increasingly unpopular. Beginning in Ohio in 1802, state after state passed laws giving the vote to all white men whether they owned property or not. By the late 1820s only Virginia still had the property requirement. Male citizens also won the right to vote in presidential elections and to choose senators by direct vote when the Seventeenth Amendment was ratified in 1913.

Yet, most adult citizens still could not vote simply because they were female, black, or young. The struggle for the right to vote would continue as a peoples' fight, battling step by step, to turn America into a nation truly "of the people."

Women Gain the Right to Vote

The extraordinary letter by Abigail Adams illustrated that even before the Constitution was penned a few women were not content to be voiceless in the new nation. But the thought of women voting seemed ridiculous to many men and women. Most women accepted the idea of leaving decisions of government, like those of the family, to males. Yet, in July of 1848 five women in the village of Seneca Falls, New York called a meeting that started a fight to secure the woman's right to vote. Lead by Elizabeth Stanton, the group presented a resolution declaring, "we insist that [women] have immediate admission to all rights and privileges which belong to them as citizens of the United States . . . it is the duty of the women of this country to secure to themselves the right of elective franchise [the right to vote]." Suffrage (right to vote) associations concerned with women's rights began to appear around the nation. Victories were small at first but on December 10, 1869 the women of Wyoming became the first to win an unlimited right to vote.

The Supreme Court did not help the suffrage cause. In 1875, in *Minor v. Happersett,* the Court ruled that granting voting rights only to men in a state constitution was legal since the U.S. Constitution left the choice of who was qualified to vote to the states.

At the time, many considered petitions to Congress for a nationwide constitutional amendment granting women the right to vote laughable. However, in 1878 Susan B. Anthony managed a senate committee hearing on an amendment which simply declared, "The right of citizens of the United States to vote shall not be denied or abridged by the United States or any State on account of sex."

By 1890 a more united front emerged with the National American Women's Suffrage Association (NAWSA). By 1910 eleven states had granted women the right to vote. The campaign grew and by 1914 all major women's groups had joined the suffrage campaign with some groups, such as the National Women's Party, becoming militant.

Finally, in 1919 following World War I (1914–18) in which women admirably worked on the home front in support of military efforts, Congress passed a constitutional amendment giving women nationwide the right to vote. By 1920 the Nineteenth Amendment was ratified and became law with wording exactly as Anthony crafted in 1878. Little legal resistance to women's suffrage occurred following adoption of the amendment.

Black Americans Gain the Right to Vote

Ratified in 1870, fifty years before the Nineteenth Amendment, the Fifteenth Amendment stated "The right of citizens of the United States to vote shall not be denied or abridged by the United States or by any State on account of race, color, or previous condition of servitude." Although passed and ratified to assure black Americans the right to vote, blacks would not be able to freely exercise their voting rights until 1965.

Following the end of the American Civil War (1861–65), many people, particularly in the South, were determined to keep newly freed blacks as close to servitude as possible. Yet, by the end of 1867, under federal army rule, about 700,000 Southern black males had become registered voters. Under military protection, they joined in choosing delegates to form new state governments and electing officials to run them.

White Republicans from the North and the new black Republican leaders, primarily controlled the resulting governments. This outraged the Southern population, long a stronghold of the Democratic Party and white supremacy.

Realizing the importance of the right to vote, segregationists (those intent on keeping blacks and whites separate) used any means possible to keep black men from voting. Even with military protection, many black voters had been intimidated (threatened) and cheated of their votes. The intimidation grew violent and that violence became organized with such groups as the Ku Klux Klan. The Klan's hooded midnight riders terrorized their victims by burning their homes, barns, and crops, and whipping, clubbing, and murdering.

Recognizing the Fifteenth Amendment was ineffective, Congress in the 1870s passed laws banning terrorist groups and imposing stiff penalties for interfering with black voters. However, the Supreme Court persisted in a narrow view that only states could define who could vote, consequently taking the teeth out of the laws. Federal enforcement lessened. Furthermore, the Court viewed acts of private individuals denying the voting rights of others as outside the reach of federal government power. By 1900 all eleven former Confederate states had made it virtually impossible for blacks to vote.

Southern states carefully worded their voting requirements to avoid obvious constitutional violations. As long as the states' requirements did not appear to discriminate on the basis of "race, color, or previous condition of servitude" they were not considered in violation of the Fifteenth Amendment. Though written to appear as applying equally to all men, in reality their requirements were directed solely against persons of color. The exclusion strategies included grandfather clauses, literacy tests, white primaries, and the poll tax. These requirements, in their various forms, successfully excluded blacks from political participation until the mid-1960s. Whites completely dominated all levels of government in Southern states.

Grandfather Clauses and Literacy Tests

A "grandfather clause" required all voters to show that their ancestors could vote in 1866, before the post-Civil War Reconstruction era, or pass a literacy (able to read) test. First enacted in Mississippi in 1890, this strategy spread rapidly throughout the Southern states. Most whites were exempted from the literacy test, whether they could read or not, by the grandfather clause because typically most white men had ancestors eligible to vote in 1866. On the other hand, blacks in 1890 had no ancestors who were eligible to vote in 1866. In Mississippi by 1892 black voter registration dropped from approximately 70 percent of black adult males to under 6 percent. When tested in courts, states contended the Fifteenth Amendment was not violated because all voter applicants were required to pass the clause or test. In 1915 the Supreme Court struck down grandfather clauses as unconstitutional in *Guinn v. United States*. However, literacy tests were not suspended.

White Primaries

If a black American somehow managed to get past all the barriers and gain the right to vote, his vote was usually insignificant anyway due to the white-only primaries. Under laws adopted by most Southern states, political parties could set their own rules for membership in their party. While the Republican Party was non-existent, the Democratic Party organized as private clubs in each state excluding all blacks. Only members of the Democratic Party could vote for candidates in its primaries. Since the Democratic Party was overwhelmingly dominate, whoever won the all-white primary would win the general election. The black vote cast in the general election, therefore, was meaningless.

Cases challenging the practice began reaching the Supreme Court. In *Grovey v. Townsend* (1935) the Court unanimously decided the political party was a private club of volunteers, not part of the state government. Therefore, its actions were not restricted by the Constitution. However, in *United States v. Classic* (1941) the Court recognized the primary was becoming a key part of the state election process. Three years later in the landmark case of *Smith v. Allwright* (1944), the Court held that voting in primary elections was "a right secured by the

Constitution." Private all-white primaries were unconstitutional. The decision was later reaffirmed in *Terry v. Adams* (1953) finally ending white-only primaries.

Poll Tax

Another common barrier to black voters and to poor whites was the poll tax. The poll tax was simply a fee charged at the polling (voting) place. When the Constitution was written, the poll tax was considered a legitimate way to raise revenue, but by the 1850s poll taxes had disappeared. They returned in some states in the early twentieth century as a means to exclude blacks from the political process since many could not afford to pay the tax. The Court in *Breedlove v. Suttles* (1937) upheld the poll tax because it was applied to both black and white voters. Public opinion grew against the tax in the 1940s. But, it was not until 1964 that Congress was finally able to pass and the states ratify the Twenty-Fourth Amendment to the Constitution, abolishing the poll tax in federal elections. States still imposed poll taxes for state and local elections until the Court in *Harper v. Virginia State Board of Elections* (1966) finally struck down all poll taxes.

Voting Rights Act of 1965

The Civil Rights Movement of the 1950s and 1960s greatly raised public awareness of racial discrimination in America. Following the historic voting freedom march of 3,200 black protestors and white sympathizers from Selma to Montgomery, Alabama led by Dr. Martin Luther King, the Voting Rights Act of 1965 was signed into law by President Lyndon B. Johnson. Urging the passage of the act, Johnson had spoken to a joint session of Congress in March 1965, "Unless the right to vote be secured and undenied, all other rights are insecure and subject to denial for all citizens. The challenge of this right is a challenge to America itself."

The act prohibited any voting qualification requirements such as literacy tests in federal, state, local, general, and primary elections in any state or county where less than half the voting age residents were registered to vote. It applied to any type of qualification that denied the right of a U.S. citizen to vote because of race, color, or membership in a language minority group. In certain counties, registration would be taken over by federal examiners to ensure fairness in determining voter eligibility. The act also required seven states to obtain federal approval before making any changes to their election systems such as relocating polling sites, changing ballot forms, and altering election districts.

The act was immediately challenged in *South Carolina v. Katzenbach* (1966), but the Supreme Court ruled the act consistent with Congress' power to eliminate racial discrimination in voting. Within only a few years the rise in black voter registration was dramatic. In Mississippi alone black registration rose again to almost 60 percent by 1968. The act was amended in 1970 to suspend literacy tests nationwide. This suspension was upheld by the Court in **Oregon v. Mitchell** (1970).

One More Group—the Young

A still later group of Americans to achieve the right to vote were men and women aged eighteen to twenty. From ancient English common law, the age when a boy became a man was generally considered twenty-one. By the time the Fourteenth Amendment was ratified in 1868, twenty-one had become the standard age adopted by states to first vote. The amendment did not actually say anyone had to be that old to vote, but it did penalize states "when the right to vote . . . is denied to any of the male inhabitants of such State being twenty-one years of age. . . . "

Attempts to lower the voting age to eighteen grew during World War I (1914–18) and World War II (1939–45). If young people were old enough to pay taxes and be sent to war, many believed, they should be able to vote. However, opponents argued that brawn to fight did not mean maturity to vote. By the 1950s opinion polls showed most Americans favored lowering the age, but Congress was unable to pass an amendment until March of 1971. The states took only two months to ratify the Twenty-sixth Amendment. As of 1971, virtually all American citizens age eighteen and older, regardless of race or sex, were eligible to vote.

Redistricting and Representation

A key issue related to voting rights and repeatedly brought before the courts is representation of minorities in the government in proportion to their numbers in the general population. Following passage of the Voting Rights Act, blacks made substantial political gains but were still under represented in proportion to their numbers. In 1975 only fifteen blacks were among the 435 members of the U.S. House of Representatives. By 1989 there were only twenty-five. If blacks were represented proportionately to the number of black Americans in the nation, there should be between forty and fifty members.

A key to fair representation from city to national levels is the way boundaries of political voting districts are drawn. Every ten years after a new national census is taken, state legislatures must redraw district boundaries to reflect population change, a process known as "redistricting" or "reapportionment." The political party in power in the state legislature controls the process. Unfortunately, drawing of boundaries often has more to do with political self-interest than fairness. "Gerrymandering" or the unfair drawing of district lines has frequently been at issue. If Republicans controlled the state legislature they would shape boundaries to create secure Republican districts. Democrats would do the same if they held power. Also, if boundaries split an area of black voters between three or four districts, their chance of electing a black is less. In reaction, black leaders demanded boundaries be drawn in a way to improve chances of electing black legislators.

In *Colegrove v. Green* (1946) the Court expressed reluctance about becoming involved in redistricting issues. Finally in **Baker v. Carr** (1962) the Court ruled federal courts could indeed address problems of unequal distribution of voters in legislative districts. In **Reynolds v. Sims** (1964) the Court applied the "one person, one vote" redistricting rule originally established in *Gray v. Sanders* (1963). The issue leading to the "one person, one vote" decision was the problem of rural district boundaries drawn many years ago. As city populations grew through the 1950s, rural districts with small populations would often have the same legislative representation as city districts containing many more residents. Because the practice violated the Equal Protection Clause of the Fourteenth Amendment, the Court sought to have districts redrawn to better correspond with population size. In *Wesberry v. Sanders* (1964) the Court urged states to make an honest effort to draw congressional districts with as nearly equal populations as possible.

The Road to a Fully Representative Government

By 2000 Americans had been shaping their right to vote for over two hundred years. Expansion of the right to vote came in response to the demands of the people for equality and fairness in the voting process. By consistently enlarging the number of eligible voters, Americans have enlarged their entire base of government through participation of more people. Voting decisions gradually came to represent a diversity of groups having a meaningful voice.

Suggestions for further reading

Severn, Bill. *The Right To Vote.* New York: Ives Washburn, Inc., 1972.

Thernstrom, Stephan, and Abigail Thernstrom. *America in Black and White: One Nation, Indivisible.* New York: Simon & Schuster, 1997.

Baker v. Carr
1962

Appellants: Charles W. Baker and others

Appellees: Joe E. Carr and others

Appellants' Claim: That voting districts drawn in a way that produces unequal political representation violates the Fourteenth Amendment's Equal Protection Clause.

Chief Lawyers for Appellants: Charles S. Rhyme, Z.T. Osborn, Jr.

Chief Lawyer for Appellees: Jack Wilson, Assistant Attorney General of Tennessee

Justices for the Court: Hugo L. Black, William J. Brennan, Jr., Tom C. Clark, William O. Douglas, Potter Stewart, Chief Justice Earl Warren

Justices Dissenting: Felix Frankfurter, John Marshall Harlan II (Charles Evans Whittaker did not participate)

Date of Decision: March 26, 1962

Decision: Ruled in favor of Baker by finding that constitutional challenges to apportionment could be addressed by federal courts.

Significance: This decision opened the door for under represented voters to have their voting districts redrawn under the direction of federal courts. The ruling initiated a decade of lawsuits eventually resulting in a redrawing of the nation's political map. The decision represented a major shift in the Court's position on the relationship of voting districts and constitutional protections.

The purpose of voting in America is to give citizens the opportunity to determine who will be making governmental decisions. Those elected are expected to represent the interests of the people in their district when crafting laws and policies. The way boundaries of voting districts are drawn and the number of voters contained within each district largely determines how fairly people are represented by that process.

For example, electing members to the U.S. House of Representatives is based on population figures. Congress limits the number of House members to a total of 435 nationwide. The number of representatives from each state is subject to change every ten years depending on population changes recorded by the U.S. census, a count of people and where they live. States gaining or losing population between the 1990 census and 2000, must redraw their boundaries of their voting districts to reflect the population change. This process, known as "redistricting," is carried out to distribute, or "apportion," government representatives according to the population. The term "reapportionment" commonly refers to the entire process.

A Political Process

Reapportionment is a very political process. The political party in power in the state legislature controls how district boundaries will be drawn. If Republicans are in power, they will attempt to create or maintain "safe" Republican districts. If Democrats are in power they will do likewise. Another concern in reapportionment involves unfair treatment of minorities such as black Americans and Hispanics. The way districts are drawn will determine how likely they can elect a black or Hispanic legislator.

Reapportionment has long been a difficult process to resolve to everyone's liking. The goal is to have voting districts of relatively equal population and not create districts that discriminate against any particular group of voters. When the drawing of district lines has been considered unfair, the issue has proceeded to the courts. In 1946 in *Colegrove v. Green* the U.S. Supreme Court found that apportionment issues were political questions best left to state legislatures. The Court described apportionment as a "political thicket" into which it was not about to jump. However, in *Baker v. Carr* (1962) the Court "jumped in."

The Tennessee Thicket

In 1900 America was predominately rural with district boundary lines drawn through the farming countryside. However, by the mid-twentieth century a population shift to urban (city) areas occurred, yet states failed to redraw district lines. As a result, a rural district with few people would elect one representative just like a nearby urban district with a large population. Unequal representation resulted with many more representatives elected from rural, less populated districts. City inhabitants cried "foul" to this unfairness.

Such a situation developed in Tennessee. Between 1901 and 1961 Tennessee experienced substantial growth and a redistribution of its population from rural to urban locations. Voting districts had been drawn in 1901 under Tennessee's Apportionment Act. For more than sixty years, all proposals for reapportionment failed to pass in the state assemblies leaving Tennessee city residents under represented. Approximately one-third of the state's population elected two-thirds of the members of the state legislature. One rural representative in the Tennessee House of Representatives was so bold as to say he believed in taxing city populations where the money was so he could spend the revenue on the rural areas.

Charles Baker was mayor of Millington, Tennessee, a rapidly growing Memphis suburb. In attempting to cope with Millington's growing problems, Baker became painfully aware that under representation of urban areas was leading to the neglect of needs and problems of city residents. Baker decided the only way to correct the financial woes of Tennessee cities was to force the Tennessee government to reapportion the legislative districts so that each member of the legislature represented about the same number of people.

Baker and several city dwellers brought suit on behalf of all city residents in the U.S. District Court for the Middle District of Tennessee. Joe C. Carr, Tennessee Secretary of State, was named defendant. They charged that urban voters were denied their equal protection guarantees contained in the Fourteenth Amendment. The amendment reads that no state shall "deny to any person within its jurisdiction [geographic area over which it has authority] the equal protection of the laws." Equal protection means that all persons or groups of persons in similar situations must be treated the same under the laws. Persons living in Tennessee are all in the similar situation of being Tennessee residents. Therefore, they should be treated equally under apportionment law by being equally represented in legislative bodies.

A three judge panel of the district court dismissed Baker's case with the familiar reasoning that Baker's complaint was a political question which the courts had no authority to answer. Such matters, according to the district court, must be dealt with by the state legislature. Baker appealed and the U.S. Supreme Court, jumping into the political thicket of reapportionment, agreed to hear his case.

A Decision of Tremendous Potential

Everyone involved in the case recognized the tremendous impact the ruling could potentially have. The Court heard three hours of oral argument, allowing attorneys to represent their views at far greater length than normal. Following the initial argument on April 19 and 20, 1961, the case was reargued on October 9, 1961. The justices soon released their opinions in 163 pages.

Justice William J. Brennan, Jr., writing for the 6-2 majority, delivered the Court's opinion. Brennan disagreed with the federal district courts decision that it had no power to hear the case. He wrote that Baker's complaint clearly arose from a provision of the U.S. Constitution, namely the Fourteenth Amendment, so it fell within the federal court's power. Brennan continued this federal court power is defined in Article III, Section 2, of the Constitution providing,

> **the judicial Power (the court's power) shall extend to all Cases, in Law and Equity, *arising under this Constitution*, the Laws of the United States, and Treaties made, or which shall be made,. . .**

As a result, federal courts could properly consider questions of reapportionment. It was not a political question out of reach of a court of law. Baker's complaint of being denied equal protection was justified under the Constitution. Brennan observed that failure to apportion legislative districts of a state clearly violated equal protection of the Fourteenth Amendment. The Court, concluding Baker deserved a trial, sent the case back to the federal district court for a trial and resolution.

Extraordinary Impact

The *Baker* decision abruptly abandoned the long held belief that apportionment issues, because of their political nature, could not be argued before the courts. Indeed, it opened the door of federal courts throughout

POLITICAL QUESTIONS AND THE COURTS

Writing for the U.S. Supreme Court in *Marbury v. Madison* (1803), the legendary Chief Justice John Marshall observed that the Court's sole role is to decide on the rights of individuals but, "Questions in their nature political . . . can never be made in this Court." The Court often used this reasoning for not deciding a case. This policy avoided battles with Congress, the president, or the states. Power struggles between political parties, foreign policy and affairs, and questions of legislative procedures have long been considered political questions in which the Court steadfastly refused to intrude. Likewise, the Court viewed challenges to the way states drew legislative districts off limits until *Baker v. Carr* (1962). In *Baker,* the Court concluded the question of unequal distribution of population among districts is a constitutional fairness question rather than a political question. In the 1980s and 1990s the Court also entered into controversies over political gerrymanders, a process of drawing voting district boundaries to give one party or group an advantage over another.

the nation to voters challenging the way states drew voting district boundaries with far reaching results. Justice Brennan's opinion cast doubt on state redistricting systems throughout the nation.

Although opening the federal courts to this issue, the decision did not provide a formula for those courts to follow in determining when apportionment was unfair. But the reapportionment revolution was in motion. By 1964 in *Gray v. Sanders, Wesberry v. Sanders,* and *Reynolds v. Sims,* the Court established and confirmed a policy of equal representation referred to as "one person, one vote." President Jimmy Carter in his book *Turning Point: A Candidate, a State, and a Nation Come of Age,* described how *Baker* transformed state politics, particularly Southern politics, by redrawing districts and opening up new seats. "A landmark [case] in the development of representative government," remarked U.S. Attorney General Robert F. Kennedy. Chief Justice Earl Warren called it "the most vital decision" of his long career on the Court. By the late 1960s, voting districts around the country had been redrawn to obey the Supreme Court's call for equal representation. Following the 1970 census, under representation of urban areas came to an end.

Baker
v. Carr

Suggestions for further reading

Carter, Jimmy. *Turning Point: A Candidate, a State, and a Nation Come of Age.* New York: Times Books, 1994.

Grofman, Bernard. *Voting Rights, Voting Wrongs: The Legacy of* Baker v. Carr. Priority Press Publications, 1990.

Wilson, Anna. Discrimination: African Americans Struggle for Equality. Vero Beach, FL: Rourke Corporation, Inc., 1992.

Reynolds v. Sims
1964

Appellant: R. A. Reynolds

Appellee: M. O. Sims

Appellant's Claim: That the creation of voting districts is the sole responsibility of state legislatures with no appropriate role for federal courts.

Chief Lawyer for Appellant: W. McLean Pitts

Chief Lawyer for Appellee: Charles Morgan, Jr.

Justices for the Court: Hugo L. Black, William J. Brennan, Jr., Tom C. Clark, William O. Douglas, Arthur Goldberg, Potter Stewart, Chief Justice Earl Warren, Byron R. White

Justices Dissenting: John Marshall Harlan II

Date of Decision: June 15, 1964

Decision: Ruled in favor of Sims by finding that the equal protection guarantee of the Fourteenth Amendment requires that legislative voting districts contain approximately the same number of people.

Significance: The decision meant at least one house of most state legislatures was unconstitutional. Within two years of the ruling, the boundaries of legislative districts had been redrawn all across the nation.

The U.S. Supreme Court ruling in *Baker v. Carr* (1962) began a reapportionment revolution. Reapportionment is the redrawing of legislative district voting boundaries to maintain an equal distribution of voters so that each elected representative in a legislative assembly represents approximately the same number of people. In *Baker* the Court found that federal courts could indeed address the problem of unequal numbers of voters in districts or unequal apportionment.

Reynolds
v. Sims

Apportionment problems arose in the early twentieth century with the shift of the American population away from rural areas into urban (city) centers. Most states had drawn their legislative district boundaries around 1900 when the majority of people lived in the country. Most had never redrawn those boundaries. By 1960, with the urban population shift, nearly every state had urban districts populated by many more people than the rural districts. Yet, each district still elected one representative regardless of its population, resulting in under representation of city dwellers.

In keeping with the 1962 *Baker* ruling, one year later, Justice William O. Douglas in *Gray v. Sanders* (1963) coined the phrase "one person, one vote." Douglas wrote,

> **How then can one person be given twice or 10 times the voting power of another person in a statewide election merely because he lives in a rural area [in the country] . . . all who participate in the election are to have an equal vote. . . This is required by the Equal Protection Clause of the Fourteenth Amendment . . . political equality . . . can mean only one thing—one person, one vote.**

Likewise, in *Wesberry v. Sanders* (1964) the Court, invalidating (disapproving) Georgia's unequal congressional districts, applied the "one person, one vote" principle of equal voter representation. Only four months later in the landmark case *Reynolds v. Sims* (1964), eight Supreme Court justices agreed on the requirements under the Fourteenth Amendment for state reapportionment.

Alabama Districts Favor Rural Interests

Reynolds involved the apportionment of Alabama's legislative voting districts. Alabama's history of apportionment had followed the pattern typical of many states. District boundaries had been drawn through

VOTING RIGHTS

rural Alabama in 1901. These remained unchanged for the next sixty years despite Alabama's constitutional requirements for legislative representation based on population and for reapportionment every ten years. Over the sixty years, Alabama's population base had shifted from rural communities to cities and suburbs. In 1960 the inequality was dramatic. For example, Alabama least populated congressional district had 6,700 individuals while its largest had 104,000 people. The 6,700 were represented by one elected legislator just as the 104,000 were represented by one. The 1960 census revealed that counties containing only 27.5 percent of the total population elected a majority of state representatives. Rural interests dominated the legislative agendas. The rural legislators refused to reapportion legislative voting districts because they would likely lose a great deal of power. Many would potentially be voted out of office.

Faced with these markedly lopsided districts and the unwillingness of the Alabama legislature to reapportion, voters in several Alabama counties, including M. O. Sims of urban Jefferson County, brought suit in the U.S. District Court for the Middle District of Alabama challenging the existing apportionment of the Alabama legislature as unconstitutional. These voters claimed that the unequal representation of citizens in Alabama districts violated the equal protection guarantees of the Fourteenth Amendment. The Fourteenth Amendment declares "no state . . . shall deny to any person within its jurisdiction [geographical area over which it has authority] the equal protection of the laws." Equal protection means that persons in similar situations, in this case all voters living in Alabama, must be treated equally under the laws.

At the time, the Alabama Legislature, patterned after the U.S. Congress, consisted of two legislative chambers, a thirty-five member Senate and a House of Representatives with 106 members. The Alabama Senate's representation was based on a system of senate districts and counties, not on population. This was like the U.S. Senate which has two senators for each state, regardless of population.

The three-judge district court panel ordered the legislature to reapportion using a plan based only on population. Alabama immediately challenged the order in the U.S. Supreme Court. The Supreme Court agreed to take the case. Though the case accompanied a number of other reapportionment cases from various states, the Court would announce the reasons for its decisions in *Reynolds v. Sims*.

People, Not Trees or Acres

Alabama argued that states alone should apportion legislative districts. Federal courts should stay out of the issue. Writing for the 8-1 majority, Chief Justice Earl Warren dismissed Alabama's arguments noting that the Alabama legislature had refused to reapportion itself and had left no other avenues open for the urban voters to seek correction of their grievances. The Court had no choice but to intervene (become involved).

Reynolds v. Sims

First, Chief Justice Warren, calling forth the "one person, one vote" principle of equal representation, stated that discrimination in setting legislative voting boundaries could not be tolerated any more than discrimination in voting based on race or economic status. Allowing rural legislative dominance clearly prevented equal representation of Alabama's more urban voters. Penning an often quoted phrase, Warren wrote,

> **Legislators represent people not trees or acres. Legislators are elected by voters, nor farms, or cities or economic interests. As long as ours is a representative form of government, and our legislatures are those instruments of government elected directly by and directly representative of the people, the right to elect legislators in a free and unimpaired fashion is a bedrock of our political system. . .**

Warren continued,

> **. . . the weight of a citizens vote cannot be made to depend on where he lives. . . A citizen, a qualified voter, is no more nor no less so because he lives in the city or on the farm . . . the Equal Protection Clause demands no less than substantially equal state legislative representation for all citizens, of all places as well as all races.**

Secondly, Warren rejected Alabama's argument that it should be allowed to apportion its Senate based on geographical area just as the U.S. Senate in Washington, D.C. Warren noted that state constitutions historically called for legislative assemblies to be based on population. Warren found that the Framers of the U.S. Constitution had no intention of establishing Congress as a model for the state legislative bodies. Warren wrote,

GERRYMANDERING

Gerrymandering is the redrawing, or reapportionment, of legislative voting districts to favor one group over another. This practice generally creates very irregularly shaped districts. The term was coined when Massachusetts voting districts were reapportioned under Governor Elbridge Gerry in 1812. One of the resulting districts was oddly shaped like a salamander. A newspaper editor created a political cartoon by adding wings, claws, and teeth, and named the character Gerrymander.

With state legislatures in charge of reapportionment, a common type of gerrymandering is to draw district lines favoring the political party in power. For example, if the Republican Party is in power, they might divide a district which traditionally votes Democratic. The Democratic district could be split into sections which are then included into voting districts with a Republican majority. The Republican majority would dominate over the Democratic vote. Gerrymandering has also been used to divide up blocks of minority groups such as black Americans or Hispanics. On the other hand, gerrymandering of district lines has also created racial districts to strengthen the chance of an election of racial minority legislators.

The U.S. Supreme Court ruled in *Davis v. Bandemer* (1981) that gerrymandered districts may be challenged constitutionally even when they meet the "one person, one vote" test. Two cases involving racial gerrymandering which reached the Court were *Gomillion v. Lightfoot* (1960) and *Shaw v. Reno* (1993).

> **We hold that as a basic constitutional standard, the Equal Protection Clause requires that the seats in both houses of a bicameral [two assemblies] state legislature must be apportioned on a population basis.**

Third, Warren recognized in practicality that exactly equal mathematical numbers in each district would not be possible but Warren observed,

> **The Equal Protection Clause requires that a State make an honest and good faith effort to construct districts, in both houses of its legislature, as nearly of equal population as is practicable.**

Fourth, Warren directed states to reapportion minimally every ten years.

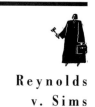

Entire Country Redrawn

With the *Reynolds* ruling, at least one house of most state legislatures was found unconstitutional, making complete redrawing of district boundaries necessary. After the decision, forty-nine state legislatures reapportioned one or both of their assemblies. Only Oregon, in 1961, had completed a fair redrawing of district lines before the Supreme Court cases of the reapportionment revolution.

The decision resulted in a shift away from rural dominated state legislatures. However, the Court had left to the states the actual redrawing of boundaries. Political "gerrymandering," although generally following "one person, one vote" guidelines, manipulated election boundaries to favor certain groups, again threatening fair representation. Gerrymandering cases reached the Supreme Court in the 1980s.

Suggestions for further reading

Clayton, Dewey M. *African Americans and the Politics of Congressional Redistricting*. New York: Garland Publishing, 1999.

Cortner, Richard C. *The Apportionment Cases*. Knoxville: University of Tennessee, 1970.

Rush, Mark E. *Does Redistricting Make a Difference? Partisan Representation and Electoral Behavior*. Baltimore: Johns Hopkins University Press, 1993.

Buckley v. Valeo
1976

Appellant: James L. Buckley

Appellee: Francis R. Valeo, Secretary of the U.S. Senate

Appellant's Claim: That various provisions of the 1974 amendments to the Federal Election Campaign Act of 1971 (FECA) regulating campaign contributions are unconstitutional.

Chief Lawyers for Appellant: Ralph K. Winter, Jr., Joel M. Gora, Brice M. Claggett

Chief Lawyers for Appellee: Daniel M. Friedman, Archibald Cox, Lloyd M. Cutler, Ralph S. Spritzer

Justices for the Court: Harry A. Blackmun, William J. Brennan, Jr., Chief Justice Warren E. Burger, Lewis F. Powell, Jr., William H. Rehnquist, Potter Stewart

Justices Dissenting: Thurgood Marshall, Byron R. White (John Paul Stevens did not participate)

Date of Decision: January 30, 1976

Decision: The Court found some provisions constitutional including limits on contributions, and it found unconstitutional provisions on expenditures and the way Federal Election Commission members are selected.

Significance: The decision greatly changed campaign finance laws. Perhaps, the most significant change was the finding that no restrictions on contributions from individuals and groups could be set so long as the contributions were not directly part of an election campaign.

From 1999 to 2000 a grandmother over eighty years old walked across the United States to draw attention to the need for campaign-finance reform. U.S. Senator John McCain also based his popular but unsuccessful run to become the Republican candidate for president in the 2000 elections on campaign finance reform. What is campaign finance reform and why is it a hot issue? Campaign finance is simply the way political parties and their candidates receive the money they need to carry their message to the public in hopes of being elected to office.

Many believed the campaign finance system at the start of the twenty-first century created distrust and suspicion in the public and weakened concepts of fairness. To many individuals, government seemed increasingly out of reach from their influence, a tool of the rich and powerful special interest groups. Special interest groups gave millions of dollars to congressional campaigns. The laws the interest groups want often get passed, generally leaving consumers to pay the price. For example, U.S. sugar producers in 1995 and 1996 contributed $2.7 million to campaigns. In return they received $1.1 billion in annual sugar price supports. As a result, consumers paid 25 percent higher sugar prices in the grocery stores. U.S. Congressman Dan Miller (R-Florida) in 1997 called the sugar industry "the poster child for why we need campaign reform."

The Supreme Court ruling in *Buckley v. Valeo* (1976) provided an underlying basis for various groups to spend lots of money in support of political candidates. The *Buckley* case involved challenges to a sweeping 1971 campaign finance reform act.

The Federal Election Campaign Act

In an effort to control the spending and influence of special interest groups, Congress passed the Federal Election Campaign Act of 1971 (FECA), and amended (changed) it in 1974. Unhappy with several FECA provisions (parts), a number of federal officer holders and candidates for political office, James L. Buckley among them, and some political organizations brought suit in the U.S. District Court for the District of Columbia. The suit was against various federal officials, including Francis R. Valeo, Secretary of the U.S. Senate, and against the Federal Election Commission (FEC) created by the act. Buckley charged various provisions of the 1974 amendments were unconstitutional. He and the others wished to prevent the amendments from affecting the 1976 election.

The provisions in question were: (1) limiting contributions by individuals, groups, or political committees to candidates and expenditures in support of a "clearly identified candidate" by individuals or groups; (2) requiring detailed record keeping of contributions and expenditures by political committees and disclosing the source of every contribution and expenditure over $100; (3) establishing a public campaign funding system for political parties; and, (4) creating an eight member commission, the FEC, to enforce the act and permitting a majority of those members to be selected by Congress.

For the most part, the district court and the U.S. Court of Appeals for the District of Columbia rejected Buckley's constitutional attacks on FECA. Buckley and the others took their case to the U.S. Supreme Court.

The First Amendment's Broad Protection

The Supreme Court ruling was complex with justices agreeing to and dissenting to various parts. However, they did agree on certain basic issues.

First, the Court found contribution limits to be a proper means to prevent candidates from becoming too reliant on large contributors and their influence. However, in the part of the decision which would have the most far reaching effect, the Court ruled the act's expenditure restrictions on political committees was unconstitutional. If individuals, groups, or political committees operated independently of the candidates or of the candidate's election committees, they had the right to freely spend to support a candidate. For example, an individual or group, acting on their own, could purchase television time to explain their views on why a certain candidate should be elected. The Court found FECA's limits on expenditures a direct violation of First Amendment guarantees of freedom of political expression. The amendment declares, "Congress shall make no law . . . abridging the freedom of speech. . . " The Court observed,

> **The Act's contribution and expenditure limits operate in an area of the most fundamental First Amendment activities. Discussion of public issues and debate on the qualifications of candidates are integral to the operation of the system of government established by our Constitution. The First Amendment affords [gives] the broadest possible protection to such political expression in order to assure unfettered [free] exchange of ideas for the**

bringing about of political and social changes desired by the people.

The Court noted that, "Virtually every means of communicating ideas in today's mass society requires the expenditure of money." Chief Justice William Rehnquist equated free speech with the spending of money to promote political views. He wrote,

> **A restriction on the amount of money a person or group can spend on political communication during a campaign necessarily reduces the quantity of expression by restricting the number of issues discussed, the depth of their exploration, and the size of the audience reached.**

As long as expenditures were not funneled through the candidate or the candidate's campaign, they would be allowed.

Secondly, the Court upheld the record keeping and disclosure provisions of FECA. The Court found the provisions served an important government purpose in informing the public as to who contributes and prevents corruption of the political process.

Thirdly, the Court supported the provision authorizing new measures to promote public funding of presidential campaigns. An example would be checking a box on personal income tax forms indicating the taxpayer will allow a few dollars of their tax bill to go to public campaign funding. The Court saw this provision as furthering First Amendment values by using public monies to encourage political debate.

Fourth, the Court held unconstitutional the provision allowing Congress to select the majority of members of FEC. The Court based this decision on the Appointments Clause of Article II, Section 2, part 2 of the U.S. Constitution. The Clause provides the President shall appoint with the Senate's advice and consent, all "officers of the United States, whose appointments are not . . . otherwise provided for. . . " Therefore, Congress could not assume a responsibility which belongs to the President.

Why the Grandmother Walked

Importantly, *Buckley* legalized unlimited independent expenditures by wealthy individuals and groups. Similarly, the Court in *First National Bank of Boston v. Bellotti* (1978) viewed spending to express political views "is the type of speech indispensable to decision making in a democracy."

CAMPAIGN FINANCE REFORM

Money in politics flows like water, always finding its way to influence policies. According to American University professor James Thurber in the December 8, 1997, issue of *Fortune Magazine*, the problem is bigger than politics. Thurber wrote, "As long as we allow money to be an expression of First Amendment rights, those who have money will have more influence than those who do not."

What can Congress do? Here are six recommendations often voiced by advocates of campaign finance reform gathered by *Money* (magazine) in December of 1997. Limiting PAC contributions and banning "soft money" are considered the easiest ways to stop corporations, unions, and wealthy groups from buying influence in Congress. Cut-rate television times could be offered to candidates who reject PAC money. Tax credits could be given to individuals for small contributions. Require candidates to immediately electronically file their receipts and expenditures with the Federal Election Commission (FEC) to streamline disclosure. Lastly, toughen election laws and enforcement by the FEC.

In 1979 further amendments to FECA lifted spending limits on money given directly to political parties if it was to be used for activities such as volunteer efforts, voter registration, and for campaign materials. This money, known as "soft money," still could not go to specific candidates or to the candidates' election committees but could go, for example, to the Democratic Party as a whole.

An unexpected outcome of the 1970s campaign finance reforms was "political action committees," commonly called PACs. PACs are formed by corporations, labor groups, and other special interest groups to influence elections in hope of special favors. Operating completely independent of candidates or candidate election committees, they collect and pool contributions with their own money to be spent in support of a favorite candidate. Together with the Supreme Court rulings, the "soft money" amendments, and the incredible expense of campaigning, PACs quickly seized the opportunity to independently spend millions in support of candidates they believed would help their causes. For example, by March of 2000 in the 2000 presidential campaign, Common Cause, an organization active in campaign finance reform efforts, reported both the Democratic and Republican parties had received over $50 million in soft money donations. Many feared the voice of the common citizen could hardly be heard anymore. McCain commented, "The founding fathers must be spinning in their graves" given the influence of the special interest groups. Only new dramatic campaign finance reform could alter the situation. This is why in 2000 the grandmother walked to Washington, D.C.

**Buckley
v. Valeo**

Suggestions for further reading

Federal Election Commission. [Online] Website: http://www.fec.gov (Accessed on July 31, 2000).

Gais, Thomas. *Improper Influence: Campaign Finance Law, Political Interest Groups, and the Problem of Equality.* Ann Arbor: University of Michigan Press, 1996

Hrebenar, Ronald J. *Interest Group Politics in America.* Third Edition. New York: M.E. Sharpe, Inc., 1997.

General Bibliography

Aaseng, Nathan. *Great Justices of the Supreme Court*. Minneapolis: Oliver Press, 1992.

Arthur, Joe. *Justice for All: The Story of Thurgood Marshall*. New York: Yearling Books, 1995.

Bains, Rae. *Thurgood Marshall: Fight for Justice*. Mahwah, NJ: Troll Assoc., 1993.

Bernstein, Richard, and Jerome Agel. *Into the Third Century: The Supreme Court*. New York: Walker & Co., 1989.

Cornelius, Kay. *The Supreme Court*. New York: Chelsea House Publishers, 2000.

Coy, Harold. *The Supreme Court*. New York: Franklin Watts, 1981.

Deegan, Paul J. *Anthony Kennedy*. Edina, MN: Abdo & Daughters, 1992.

———. *Antonin Scalia*. Edina, MN: Abdo & Daughters, 1992.

———. *Chief Justice William Rehnquist*. Edina, MN: Abdo & Daughters, 1992.

———. *David Souter*. Edina, MN: Abdo & Daughters, 1992.

———. *Supreme Court Book*. Edina, MN: Abdo & Daughters, 1992.

Deegan, Paul J., and Bob Italia. *John Paul Stevens*. Edina, MN: Abdo & Daughters, 1992.

———. *Sandra Day O'Connor*. Edina, MN: Abdo & Daughters, 1992.

Feinburg, Barbara Silberdick. *Constitutional Amendments*. Twenty First Century Books, 1996.

**General
Bibliography**

Friedman, Leon. *The Supreme Court.* New York: Chelsea House, 1987.

Friedman, Leon, and Fred L. Israel. *The Justices of the United States Supreme Court: Their Lives and Major Opinions.* New York: Chelsea House Publishers, 1995.

Goldish, Meish. *Our Supreme Court.* Brookfield: Millbrook Press, 1994.

Harrison, Michael. *Landmark Decisions of the United States Supreme Court.* San Diego: Excellent Books, 1991.

Health, David. *The Supreme Court of the United States.* New York: Capstone, 1998.

Holland, Gini. *Sandra Day O'Connor.* Austin: Raintree/Steck Vaughn, 1997.

Irons, Peter H. *The Courage of Their Convictions: Sixteen Americans Who Fought Their Way to the Supreme Court.* New York: Penguin, 1990.

Italia, Bob, and Paul Deegan. *Ruth Bader Ginsburg.* Edina, MN: Abdo & Daughters, 1994.

Kallen, Stuart A. *Thurgood Marshall.* Edina, MN: Abdo & Daughters, 1993.

Kent, Deborah. *Thurgood Marshall and the Supreme Court.* Chicago: Children's Press, 1997.

Krull, Kathleen. *A Kids' Guide to America's Bill of Rights: Curfews, Censorship, and the 100-Pound Giant.* New York: Avon Books, 1999.

Macht, Norman L., Christopher E. Henry, and Nathan I. Huggins. *Clarence Thomas: Supreme Court Justice.* New York: Chelsea House Publishers, 1995.

Peterson, Helen Stone. *The Supreme Court in America's Story.* Scarsdale: Garrard Pub. Co., 1976.

Prentzas, G.S. *Thurgood Marshall.* New York: Chelsea House Publishers, 1994.

Prolman, Marilyn. *The Constitution.* Chicago: Children's Press, Inc., 1995.

Reef, Catherine. *The Supreme Court.* New York: Dillon Press, 1994.

Rierden, Anne B. *Reshaping the Supreme Court: New Justices, New Directions.* New York: Franklin Watts, 1988.

Sagarin, Mary. *Equal Justice under Law: Our Court System and How It Works.* New York: Lothrop, Lee & Shephard Co., Inc., 1966.

Stein, R. Conrad. *The Powers of the Supreme Court.* Chicago: Children's Press, Inc., 1995.

——. *The Bill of Rights.* Chicago: Children's Press, Inc., 1992.

White, G. Edward. *Oliver Wendell Holmes: Sage of the Supreme Court.* New York: Oxford University Press Children's Books, 2000.

Justices of the Supreme Court

The Justices are listed by year of appointment and in what way they served the court—as an Associate Justice or Chief Justice.

John Jay (Chief: 1789 - 1795)

John Rutledge (Associate: 1790 - 1791, Chief: 1795 - 1795)

William Cushing (Associate: 1790 - 1810)

James Wilson (Associate: 1789 - 1798)

John Blair (Associate: 1790 - 1795)

James Iredell (Associate: 1790 - 1799)

Thomas Johnson (Associate: 1792 - 1793)

William Paterson (Associate: 1793 - 1806)

Samuel Chase (Associate: 1796 - 1811)

Oliver Ellsworth (Chief: 1796 - 1800)

Bushrod Washington (Associate: 1799 - 1829)

Alfred Moore (Associate: 1800 - 1804)

John Marshall (Chief: 1801 - 1835)

William Johnson (Associate: 1804 - 1834)

Brockholst Livingston (Associate: 1807 - 1823)

Thomas Todd (Associate: 1807 - 1826)

Justices of the Supreme Court

Gabriel Duvall (Associate: 1811 - 1835)

Joseph Story (Associate: 1812 - 1845)

Smith Thompson (Associate: 1823 - 1843)

Robert Trimble (Associate: 1826 - 1828)

John McLean (Associate: 1830 - 1861)

Henry Baldwin (Associate: 1830 - 1844)

James M. Wayne (Associate: 1835 - 1867)

Roger B. Taney (Chief: 1836 - 1864)

Philip P. Barbour (Associate: 1836 - 1841)

John Catron (Associate: 1837 - 1865)

John McKinley (Associate: 1838 - 1852)

Peter V. Daniel (Associate: 1842 - 1860)

Samuel Nelson (Associate: 1845 - 1872)

Levi Woodbury (Associate: 1845 - 1851)

Robert C. Grier (Associate: 1846 - 1870)

Benjamin R. Curtis (Associate: 1851 - 1857)

John A. Campbell (Associate: 1853 - 1861)

Nathan Clifford (Associate: 1858 - 1881)

Noah Swayne (Associate: 1862 - 1881)

Samuel F. Miller (Associate: 1862 - 1890)

David Davis (Associate: 1862 - 1877)

Stephen J. Field (Associate: 1863 - 1897)

Salmon P. Chase (Chief: 1864 - 1873)

William Strong (Associate: 1870 - 1880)

Joseph P. Bradley (Associate: 1870 - 1892)

Ward Hunt (Associate: 1873 - 1882)

Morrison R. Waite (Chief: 1874 - 1888)

John M. Harlan (Associate: 1877 - 1911)

William B. Woods (Associate: 1881 - 1887)

Stanley Matthews (Associate: 1881 - 1889)

Horace Gray (Associate: 1882 - 1902)

Samuel Blatchford (Associate: 1882 - 1893)

Lucius Q.C. Lamar (Associate: 1888 - 1893)

Melville W. Fuller (Chief: 1888 - 1910)

David J. Brewer (Associate: 1890 - 1910)

Henry B. Brown (Associate: 1891 - 1906)

George Shiras, Jr. (Associate: 1892 - 1903)

Howell E. Jackson (Associate: 1893 - 1895)

Edward D. White (Associate: 1894 - 1910, Chief: 1910 - 1921)

Rufus Peckham (Associate: 1896 - 1909)

Joseph McKenna (Associate: 1898 - 1925)

Oliver W. Holmes, Jr. (Associate: 1902 - 1932)

William R. Day (Associate: 1903 - 1922)

William H. Moody (Associate: 1906 - 1910)

Horace H. Lurton (Associate: 1910 - 1914)

Charles E. Hughes (Associate: 1910 - 1916, Chief: 1930 - 1941)

Willis Van Devanter (Associate: 1911 - 1937)

Joseph R. Lamar (Associate: 1911 - 1916)

Mahlon Pitney (Associate: 1912 - 1922)

James C. McReynolds (Associate: 1914 - 1941)

Louis D. Brandeis (Associate: 1916 - 1939)

John H. Clarke (Associate: 1916 - 1922)

William Howard Taft (Chief: 1921 - 1930)

George Sutherland (Associate: 1922 - 1938)

Pierce Butler (Associate: 1923 - 1939)

Edward T. Sanford (Associate: 1923 - 1930)

Harlan Fiske Stone (Associate: 1925 - 1941, Chief: 1941 - 1946)

Owen J. Roberts (Associate: 1930 - 1945)

Benjamin N. Cardozo (Associate: 1932 - 1938)

Hugo L. Black (Associate: 1937 - 1971)

Stanley Reed (Associate: 1938 - 1957)

Felix Frankfurter (Associate: 1939 - 1962)

Justices of the Supreme Court

William O. Douglas (Associate: 1939 - 1975)

Frank Murphy (Associate: 1940 - 1949)

James F. Byrnes (Associate: 1941 - 1942)

Robert H. Jackson (Associate: 1941 - 1954)

Wiley B. Rutledge (Associate: 1943 - 1949)

Harold Burton (Associate: 1945 - 1958)

Fred M. Vinson (Chief: 1946 - 1953)

Tom C. Clark (Associate: 1949 - 1967)

Sherman Minton (Associate: 1949 - 1956)

Earl Warren (Chief: 1953 - 1969)

John M. Harlan (Associate: 1955 - 1971)

William J. Brennan (Associate: 1956 - 1990)

Charles E. Whittaker (Associate: 1957 - 1962)

Potter Stewart (Associate: 1959 - 1981)

Byron R. White (Associate: 1962 - 1993)

Arthur J. Goldberg (Associate: 1962 - 1965)

Abe Fortas (Associate: 1965 - 1969)

Thurgood Marshall (Associate: 1967 - 1991)

Warren E. Burger (Chief: 1969 - 1986)

Harry A. Blackmun (Associate: 1970 - 1994)

Lewis F. Powell, Jr. (Associate: 1972 - 1987)

William H. Rehnquist (Associate: 1972 - 1986, Chief: 1986 -)

John Paul Stevens (Associate: 1975 -)

Sandra Day O'Connor (Associate: 1981 -)

Antonin Scalia (Associate: 1986 -)

Anthony Kennedy (Associate: 1988 -)

David H. Souter (Associate: 1990 -)

Clarence Thomas (Associate: 1991 -)

Ruth Bader Ginsburg (Associate: 1993 -)

Stephen Gerald Breyer (Associate: 1994 -)

The Constitution
of the United States

On February 21, 1787, Congress adopted the resolution that a convention of delegates should meet to revise the Articles of Confederation. The Constitution was signed and submitted to Congress on September 17 of that year. Congress then sent it to the states for ratification; the last state to sign, Rhode Island, did so May 29, 1790.

We The People of the United States, in Order to form a more perfect Union, establish Justice, insure domestic Tranquility, provide for the common defence, promote the general Welfare, and secure the Blessings of Liberty to ourselves and our Posterity, do ordain and establish this Constitution for the United States of America.

Art. I

Sec. 1. All legislative Powers herein granted shall be vested in a Congress of the United States, which shall consist of a Senate and House of Representatives.

Sec. 2. The House of Representatives shall be composed of Members chosen every second Year by the People of the several States, and the Electors in each State shall have the Qualifications requisite for Electors of the most numerous Branch of the State Legislature.

No Person shall be a Representative who shall not have attained to the Age of twenty five Years, and been seven Years a Citizen of the

The Constitution of the United States

United States, and who shall not, when elected, be an Inhabitant of that State in which he shall be chosen.

Representatives and direct Taxes shall be apportioned among the several States which may be included within this Union, according to their respective Numbers, which shall be determined by adding to the whole Number of free Persons, including those bound to Service for a Term of Years, and excluding Indians not taxed, three fifths of all other Persons. The actual Enumeration shall be made within three Years after the first Meeting of the Congress of the United States, and within every subsequent Term of ten Years, in such Manner as they shall by Law direct. The Number of Representatives shall not exceed one for every thirty Thousand, but each State shall have at Least one Representative; and until such enumeration shall be made, the State of New Hampshire shall be entitled to chuse three, Massachusetts eight, Rhode-Island and Providence Plantations one, Connecticut five, New-York six, New Jersey four, Pennsylvania eight, Delaware one, Maryland six, Virginia ten, North Carolina five, South Carolina five, and Georgia three.

When vacancies happen in the Representation from any State, the Executive Authority thereof shall issue Writs of Election to fill such Vacancies.

The House of Representatives shall chuse their Speaker and other Officers; and shall have the sole Power of Impeachment.

Sec. 3. The Senate of the United States shall be composed of two Senators from each State, chosen by the Legislature thereof, for six Years; and each Senator shall have one Vote.

Immediately after they shall be assembled in Consequence of the first Election, they shall be divided as equally as may be into three Classes. The Seats of the Senators of the first Class shall be vacated at the Expiration of the second Year, of the second Class at the Expiration of the fourth Year, and of the third Class at the Expiration of the sixth Year, so that one third may be chosen every second Year; and if Vacancies happen by Resignation, or otherwise, during the Recess of the Legislature of any State, the Executive thereof may make temporary Appointments until the next Meeting of the Legislature, which shall then fill such Vacancies.

No Person shall be a Senator who shall not have attained to the Age of thirty Years, and been nine Years a Citizens of the United States, and who shall not, when elected, be an Inhabitant of that State for which he shall be chosen.

The Vice President of the United States shall be President of the Senate, but shall have no Vote, unless they be equally divided.

The Senate shall chuse their other Officers, and also a President protempore, in the Absence of the Vice President, or when he shall exercise the Office of President of the United States.

The Senate shall have the sole Power to try all Impeachments. When sitting for that Purpose, they shall be on Oath or Affirmation. When the President of the United States is tried, the Chief Justice shall preside: And no Person shall be convicted without the Concurrence of two thirds of the Members present.

Judgment in Cases of Impeachment shall not extend further than to removal from Office, and disqualification to hold and enjoy any Office of honor, Trustor Profit under the United States: but the Party convicted shall nevertheless be liable and subject to Indictment, Trial, Judgment and Punishment, according to Law.

Sec. 4. The Times, Places and Manner of holding Elections for Senators and Representatives, shall be prescribed in each State by the Legislature thereof; but the Congress may at any time by Law make or alter such Regulations, except as to the Places of chusing Senators.

The Congress shall assemble at least once in every Year, and such Meeting shall be on the first Monday in December, unless they shall by Law appoint a different Day.

Sec. 5. Each House shall be the Judge of the Elections, Returns and Qualifications of its own Members, and a Majority of each shall constitute a Quorum to do Business; but a smaller Number may adjourn from day to day, and may be authorized to compel the Attendance of absent Members, in such Manner, and under such Penalties as each House may provide.

Each House may determine the Rules of its Proceedings, punish its Members for disorderly Behaviour, and, with the Concurrence of two thirds, expel a Member.

Each House shall keep a Journal of its Proceedings, and from time to time publish the same, excepting such Parts as may in their Judgment require Secrecy; and the Yeas and Nays of the Members of either House on any question shall, at the Desire of one fifth of those Present, be entered on the Journal.

Neither House, during the Session of Congress, shall, without the Consent of the other, adjourn for more than three days, nor to any other Place than that in which the two Houses shall be sitting.

**The
Constitution
of the
United
States**

Sec. 6. The Senators and Representatives shall receive a Compensation for their Services, to be ascertained by Law, and paid out of the Treasury of the United States. They shall in all Cases, except Treason, Felony and Breach of the Peace, be privileged from Arrest during their Attendance at the Session of their respective Houses, and in going to and returning from the same; and for any Speech or Debate in either House, they shall not be questioned in any other Place.

No Senator or Representative shall, during the Time for which he was elected, be appointed to any civil Office under the Authority of the United States which shall have been created, or the Emoluments whereof shall have been encreased during such time; and no Person holding any Office under the United States, shall be a Member of either House during his Continuance in Office.

Sec. 7. All Bills for raising Revenue shall originate in the House of Representatives; but the Senate may propose or concur with Amendments as another Bills.

Every Bill which shall have passed the House of Representatives and the Senate, shall, before it become a Law, be presented to the President of the United States; If he approve he shall sign it, but if not he shall return it, with his Objections to that House in which it shall have originated, who shall enter the Objections at large on their Journal, and proceed to reconsider it. If after such Reconsideration two thirds of that House shall agree tapes the Bill, it shall be sent, together with the Objections, to the other House, by which it shall likewise be reconsidered, and if approved by two-thirds of that House, it shall become a Law. But in all such Cases the Votes of both Houses shall be determined by yeas and Nays, and the Names of the Persons voting for and against the Bill shall be entered on the Journal of each House respectively. If any Bill shall not be returned by the President within ten Days (Sundays excepted) after it shall have been presented to him, the Same shall be a Law, in like Manner as if he had signed it, unless the Congress by their Adjournment prevent its Return, in which Case it shall note a Law.

Every Order, Resolution, or Vote to which the Concurrence of the Senate and House of Representatives may be necessary (except on a question of Adjournment) shall be presented to the President of the United States; and before the Same shall take Effect, shall be approved by him, or being disapproved by him, shall be repassed by two thirds of the Senate and House of Representatives, according to the Rules and Limitations prescribed in the Case of a Bill.

Sec. 8. The Congress shall have Power To lay and collect Taxes, Duties, Imposts and Excises, to pay the Debts and provide for the common Defence and general Welfare of the United States; but all Duties, Imposts and Excises shall be uniform throughout the United States;

To borrow Money on the credit of the United States;

To regulate Commerce with foreign Nations, and among the several States, and with the Indian Tribes;

To establish an uniform Rule of Naturalization, and uniform Laws on the subject of Bankruptcies throughout the United States;

To coin Money, regulate the Value thereof, and of foreign Coin, and fix the Standard of Weights and Measures;

To provide for the Punishment of counterfeiting the Securities and current Coin of the United States;

To establish Post Offices and post Roads;

To promote the Progress of Science and useful Arts, by securing for limited Times to Authors and Inventors the exclusive Right to their respective Writings and Discoveries;

To constitute Tribunals inferior to the supreme Court;

To define and punish Piracies and Felonies committed on the high Seas, and Offences against the Law of Nations;

To declare War, grant Letters of Marque and Reprisal, and make Rules concerning Captures on Land and Water;

To raise and support Armies, but no Appropriation of Money to that Use shall be for a longer Term than two Years;

To provide and maintain a Navy;

To make Rules for the Government and Regulation of the land and naval forces;

To provide for calling forth the Militia to execute the Laws of the Union, suppress Insurrections and repel Invasions;

To provide for organizing, arming, and disciplining, the Militia, and for governing such Part of them as may be employed in the Service of the United States, reserving to the States respectively, the Appointment of the Officers, and the Authority of training the Militia according to the discipline prescribed by Congress;

The Constitution of the United States

To exercise exclusive Legislation in all Cases whatsoever, over such District (not exceeding ten Miles square) as may, by Cession of particular States, and the Acceptance of Congress, become the Seat of the Government of the United States, and to exercise like Authority over all Places purchased by the Consent of the Legislature of the State in which the Same shall be, for the Erection of Forts, Magazines, Arsenals, dock-Yards, and other needful Buildings;—And

To make all Laws which shall be necessary and proper for carrying into Execution the foregoing Powers, and all other Powers vested by this Constitution in the Government of the United States, or in any Department or Officer thereof.

Sec. 9. The Migration or Importation of such Persons as any of the States now existing shall think proper to admit, shall not be prohibited by the Congress prior to the Year one thousand eight hundred and eight, but a Tax or daytime be imposed on such Importation, not exceeding ten dollars for each Person.

The Privilege of the Writ of Habeas Corpus shall not be suspended, unless when in Cases of Rebellion or Invasion the public Safety may require it.

No Bill of Attainder or ex post facto Law shall be passed.

No Capitation, or other direct, Tax shall be laid, unless in Proportionate the Census or Enumeration herein before directed to be taken.

No Tax or Duty shall be laid on Articles exported from any State.

No Preference shall be given by any Regulation of Commerce or Revenue to the Ports of one State over those of another: nor shall Vessels bound to, or from, one State, be obliged to enter, clear, or pay Duties in another.

No Money shall be drawn from the Treasury, but in Consequence of Appropriations made by Law; and a regular Statement and Account of the Receipts and Expenditures of all public Money shall be published from time to time.

No Title of Nobility shall be granted by the United States: And no Person holding any Office of Profit or Trust under them, shall, without the Consent of the Congress, accept of any present, Emolument, Office, or Title, of any kind whatever, from any King, Prince or foreign State.

Sec. 10. No State shall enter into any Treaty, Alliance, or Confederation; grant Letters of Marque and Reprisal; coin Money; emit

Bills of Credit; make any Thing but gold and silver Coin a Tender in Payment of Debts; pass any Bill of Attainder, ex post facto Law, or Law impairing the Obligation of Contracts, or grant any Title of Nobility.

No State shall, without the Consent of the Congress, lay any Impostor Duties on Imports or Exports, except what may be absolutely necessary for executing it's inspection Laws: and the net Produce of all Duties and Imposts, laid by any State on Imports or Exports, shall be for the Use of the Treasury of the United States; and all such Laws shall be subject to the Revision and Controul of the Congress.

No State shall, without the Consent of Congress, lay any Duty of Tonnage, keep Troops, or Ships of War in time of Peace, enter into any Agreement or Compact with another State, or with a foreign Power, or engage in War, unless actually invaded, or in such imminent Danger as will not admit of delay.

Art. II

Sec. 1. The executive Power shall be vested in a President of the United States of America. He shall hold his Office during the Term of four Years, and, together with the Vice President, chosen for the same Term, be elected, as follows.

Each State shall appoint, in such Manner as the Legislature thereof may direct, a Number of Electors, equal to the whole Number of Senators and Representatives to which the State may be entitled in the Congress: but no Senator or Representative, or Person holding an Office of Trust or Profit under the United States, shall be appointed an Elector.

The Electors shall meet in their respective States, and vote by Ballot for two Persons, of whom one at least shall not be an Inhabitant of the same State with themselves. And they shall make a List of all the Persons voted for, and of the Number of Votes for each; which List they shall sign and certify, and transmit sealed to the Seat of the Government of the United States, directed to the President of the Senate. The President of the Senate shall, in the Presence of the Senate and House of Representatives, open all the Certificates, and the Votes shall then be counted. The Person having the greatest Number of Votes shall be the President, if such Number be a Majority of the whole Number of Electors appointed; and if there be more than one who have such Majority, and have an equal Number of Votes, then the House of Representatives shall immediately chuse by Ballot one of them for

The
Constitution
of the
United
States

President; and if no personae a Majority, then from the five highest on the List the said House shallon like Manner chuse the President. But in chusing the President, the Votes shall be taken by States, the Representation from each State having one Vote; A quorum for this Purpose shall consist of a Member or Members from two thirds of the States, and a Majority of all the States shall be necessary to a Choice. In every Case, after the Choice of the President, the Person having the greatest Number of Votes of the Electors shall be the Vice President. But if there should remain two or more who have equal Votes, the Senate shall chuse frothed by Ballot the Vice President.

The Congress may determine the Time of chusing the Electors, and the day on which they shall give their Votes; which Day shall be the same throughout the United States.

No Person except a natural born Citizen, or a Citizen of the United States, at the time of the Adoption of this Constitution, shall be eligible the Office of President; neither shall any Person be eligible to that Office who shall not have attained to the Age of thirty five Years, and been fourteen Years a Resident within the United States.

In Case of the Removal of the President from Office, or of his Death, Resignation, or Inability to discharge the Powers and Duties of the said Office, the Same shall devolve on the Vice President, and the Congress may by Law provide for the Case of Removal, Death, Resignation or Inability, both of the President and Vice President, declaring what Officer shall then act as President, and such Officer shall act accordingly, until the Disability be removed, or a President shall be elected.

The President shall, at stated Times, receive for his Services, a Compensation, which shall neither be encreased nor diminished during the Period for which he shall have been elected, and he shall not receive within that Period another Emolument from the United States, or any of them.

Before he enter on the Execution of his Office, he shall take the following Oath or Affirmation:—"I do solemnly swear (or affirm) that I will faithfully execute the Office of President of the United States, and will to the bestow my Ability, preserve, protect and defend the Constitution of the United States."

Sec. 2. The President shall be Commander in Chief of the Army and Navy of the United States, and of the Militia of the several States, when called into the actual Service of the United States; he may require the Opinion, in writing, of the principal Officer in each of the executive

Departments, upon any Subject relating to the Duties of their respective Offices, and he shall have Power to grant Reprieves and Pardons for Offences against the United States, except in Cases of Impeachment.

He shall have Power, by and with the Advice and Consent of the Senate, to make Treaties, provided two thirds of the Senators present concur; Andie shall nominate, and by and with the Advice and Consent of the Senate, shall appoint Ambassadors, other public Ministers and Consuls, Judges of the supreme Court, and all other Officers of the United States, whose Appointments are not herein otherwise provided for, and which shall be established by Law: but the Congress may by Law vest the Appointment of such inferior Officers, as they think proper, in the President alone, in the Courts of Law, or in the Heads of Departments.

The President shall have Power to fill up all Vacancies that may happen during the Recess of the Senate, by granting Commissions which shall expire at the End of their next Session.

Sec. 3. He shall from time to time give to the Congress Information of the State of the Union, and recommend to their Consideration such Measures as he shall judge necessary and expedient; he may, on extraordinary Occasions, convene both Houses, or either of them, and in Case of Disagreement between them, with Respect to the Time of Adjournment, he may adjourn them to such Time as he shall think proper; he shall receive Ambassadors and other public Ministers; he shall take Care that the Laws be faithfully executed, and shall Commission all the Officers of the United States.

Sec. 4. The President, Vice President and all civil Officers of the United States, shall be removed from Office on Impeachment for, and Conviction of, Treason, Bribery, or other high Crimes and Misdemeanors.

Art. III

Sec. 1. The judicial Power of the United States, shall be vested none supreme Court, and in such inferior Courts as the Congress may from time to time ordain and establish. The Judges, both of the supreme and inferior Courts, shall hold their Offices during good Behaviour, and shall, at stated Times, receive for their Services, a Compensation, which shall not be diminished during their Continuance in Office.

Sec. 2. The judicial Power shall extend to all Cases, in Law and Equity, arising under this Constitution, the Laws of the United States,

The

Constitution

of the

United

States

and Treaties made, or which shall be made, under their Authority;—to all Cases affecting Ambassadors, other public Ministers and Consuls;—to all Cases of admiralty and maritime Jurisdiction;—to Controversies to which the United States shall be a Party;—to Controversies between two or more States;—between a State and Citizens of another State;—between Citizens of different States,—between Citizens of the same State claiming Lands under Grandson different States, and between a State, or the Citizens thereof, and foreign States, Citizens or Subjects.

In all Cases affecting Ambassadors, other public Ministers and Consuls, and those in which a State shall be Party, the supreme Court shall have original Jurisdiction. In all the other Cases before mentioned, the supreme Court shall have appellate Jurisdiction, both as to Law and Fact, with such Exceptions, and under such Regulations as the Congress shall make.

The Trial of all Crimes, except in Cases of Impeachment, shall be by Jury; and such Trial shall be held in the State where the said Crimes shall have been committed; but when not committed within any State, the Trial shall be at such Place or Places as the Congress may by Law have directed.

Sec. 3. Treason against the United States, shall consist only in levying War against them, or in adhering to their Enemies, giving them Aid and Comfort. No Person shall be convicted of Treason unless on the Testimony of two Witnesses to the same overt Act, or on Confession in open Court.

The Congress shall have Power to declare the Punishment of Treason, but no Attainder of Treason shall work Corruption of Blood, or Forfeiture except during the Life of the Person attainted.

Art. IV

Sec. 1. Full Faith and Credit shall be given in each State to the Public Acts, Records, and judicial Proceedings of every other State. And the Congressman by general Laws prescribe the Manner in which such Acts, Records and Proceedings shall be proved, and the Effect thereof.

Sec. 2. The Citizens of each State shall be entitled to all Privileges and Immunities of Citizens in the several States.

A Person charged in any State with Treason, Felony, or other Crime, who shall flee from Justice, and be found in another State, shall on

Demand of the executive Authority of the State from which he fled, be delivered up, to be removed to the State having Jurisdiction of the Crime.

No Person held to Service or Labour in one State, under the Laws thereof, escaping into another, shall, in Consequence of any Law or Regulation therein, be discharged from such Service or Labour, but shall be delivered up on Claim of the Party to whom such Service or Labour may be due.

Sec. 3. New States may be admitted by the Congress into this Union; but no new States shall be formed or erected within the Jurisdiction of another State; nor any State be formed by the Junction of two or more States, or Parts of States, without the Consent of the Legislatures of the States concerned as well as of the Congress.

The Congress shall have Power to dispose of and make all needful Rules and Regulations respecting the Territory or other Property belonging to the United States; and nothing in this Constitution shall be so construed as to Prejudice any Claims of the United States, or of any particular State.

Sec. 4. The United States shall guarantee to every State in this Union a Republican Form of Government, and shall protect each of them against Invasion; and on Application of the Legislature, or of the Executive (when the Legislature cannot be convened) against domestic Violence.

Art. V

The Congress, whenever two thirds of both Houses shall deem it necessary, shall propose Amendments to this Constitution, or, on the Application of the Legislatures of two thirds of the several States, shall call a Convention for proposing Amendments, which, in either Case, shall be valid to all Intents and Purposes, as Part of this Constitution, when ratified by the Legislatures of three fourths of the several States, or by Conventions in three fourths thereof, as the one or the other Mode of Ratification may be proposed by the Congress; Provided that no Amendment which may be made prior to the Year One thousand eight hundred and eight shall in any Manner affect the first and fourth Clauses in the Ninth Section of the first Article; and that no State, without its Consent, shall be deprived of it's equal Suffrage in the Senate.

Art. VI

All Debts contracted and Engagements entered into, before the Adoption of this Constitution, shall be as valid against the United States under this Constitution, as under the Confederation.

This Constitution, and the Laws of the United States which shall be made in Pursuance thereof; and all Treaties made, or which shall be made, under the Authority of the United States, shall be the supreme Law of the Land; and the Judges in every State shall be bound thereby, any Thing in the Constitution or Laws of any State to the Contrary notwithstanding.

The Senators and Representatives before mentioned, and the Members of the several State Legislatures, and all executive and judicial Officers, both of the United States and of the several States, shall be bound by Oath or Affirmation, to support this Constitution; but no religious Test shall ever be required as a Qualification to any Office or public Trust under the United States.

Art. VII

The Ratification of the Conventions of nine States, shall be sufficient for the Establishment of this Constitution between the States so ratifying the Same.

The Bill of Rights

Articles in addition to, and Amendment of the Constitution of the United States of America, proposed by Congress, and ratified by the Legislatures of the several States, pursuant to the fifth Article of the original Constitution.

[The first ten amendments went into effect November 3, 1791.]

Art. I

Congress shall make no law respecting an establishment of religion, or prohibiting the free exercise thereof; or abridging the freedom of speech, or of the press; or the right of the people peaceably to assemble, and to petition the government for a redress of grievances.

Art. II

A well regulated Militia, being necessary to the security of a free State, the right of the people to keep and bear Arms, shall not be infringed.

Art. III

No Soldier shall, in time of peace be quartered in any house, without the consent of the Owner, nor in time of war, but in a manner to be prescribed by law.

Art. IV

The right of the people to be secure in their persons, houses, papers, and effects, against unreasonable searches and seizures, shall not be violated, and no Warrants shall issue, but upon probable cause, supported by Oath or affirmation, and particularly describing the place to be searched, and the persons or things to be seized.

Art. V

No person shall be held to answer for a capital, or otherwise infamous crime, unless on a presentment or indictment of a Grand Jury, except in cases arising in the land or naval forces, or in the Militia, when in actual service in time of War or public danger; nor shall any person be subject for the same offence to be twice put in jeopardy of life or limb; nor shall be compelled in any criminal case to be a witness against himself, nor be deprived of life, liberty, or property, without due process of law; nor shall private property be taken for public use, without just compensation.

Art. VI

In all criminal prosecutions, the accused shall enjoy the right to a speedy and public trial, by an impartial jury of the State and district wherein the crime shall have been committed, which district shall have been previously ascertained by law, and to be informed of the nature and cause of the accusation; to be confronted with the witnesses against him; to have compulsory process for obtaining witnesses in his favor, and to have the Assistance of Counsel for his defence.

Art. VII

In Suits at common law, where the value in controversy shall exceed twenty dollars, the right of trial by jury shall be preserved, and no fact tried by a jury, shall be otherwise re-examined in any Court of the United States, than according to the rules of the common law.

Art. VIII

Excessive bail shall not be required, nor excessive fines imposed, nor cruel and unusual punishments inflicted.

Art. IX

The enumeration in the Constitution, of certain rights, shall not be construed to deny or disparage others retained by the people.

Art. X

The powers not delegated to the United States by the Constitution, nor prohibited by it to the States, are reserved to the States respectively, or to the people.

Further Amendments to the Constitution

Art. XI
Jan. 8, 1798

The Judicial power of the United States shall not be construed to extend to any suit in law or equity, commenced or prosecuted against one of the United States by Citizens of another State, or by Citizens or Subjects of any Foreign State.

Art. XII
Sept. 25, 1804

The Electors shall meet in their respective states, and vote by ballot for President and Vice-President, one of whom, at least, shall not be an inhabitant of the same state with themselves; they shall name in their ballots the person voted for as President, and in distinct ballots the person voted for as Vice-President, and they shall make distinct lists of all persons voted for as President, and of all persons voted for as Vice-

President, and of the number of votes for each, which lists they shall sign and certify, and transmit sealed to the seat of the government of the United States, directed to the President of the Senate;—The President of the Senate shall, in the presence of the Senate and House of Representatives, open all the certificates and the votes shall then be counted;—The person having the greatest number of votes for President, shall be the President, if such number be a majority of the whole number of Electors appointed; and if no person have such majority, then from the persons having the highest numbers not exceeding three on the list of those voted for as President, the House of Representatives shall choose immediately, by ballot, the President. But in choosing the President, the votes shall be taken by states, the representation from each state having one vote; a quorum for this purpose shall consist of a member or members from two-thirds of the states, and a majority of all the states shall be necessary to a choice. And if the House of Representatives shall not choose a President whenever the right of choice shall devolve upon them, before the fourth day of March next following, then the Vice-President shall act as President, as in the case of the death or other constitutional disability of the President.—The person having the greatest number of votes as Vice-President, shall be the Vice-President, if such number be a majority of the whole number of Electors appointed, and if no person have a majority, then from the two highest numbers on the list, the Senate shall choose the Vice-President; a quorum for the purpose shall consist of two-thirds of the whole number of Senators, and a majority of the whole number shall be necessary to a choice. But no person constitutionally ineligible to the office of President shall be eligible to that of Vice-President of the United States.

Art. XIII
Dec. 18, 1865

Sec. 1. Neither slavery nor involuntary servitude, except as a punishment for crime whereof the party shall have been duly convicted, shall exist within the United States, or any place subject to their jurisdiction.

Sec. 2. Congress shall have power to enforce this article by appropriate legislation.

Art. XIV
July 28, 1868

Sec. 1. All persons born or naturalized in the United States, and subject to the jurisdiction thereof, are citizens of the United States and of the State wherein they reside. No State shall make or enforce any law which shall abridge the privileges or immunities of citizens of the United States; nor shall any State deprive any person of life, liberty, or property, without due process of law; nor deny to any person within its jurisdiction the equal protection of the laws.

Sec. 2. Representatives shall be apportioned among the several States according to their respective numbers, counting the whole number of persons in each State, excluding Indians not taxed. But when the right to vote at any election for the choice of electors for President and Vice President of the United States, Representatives in Congress, the Executive and Judicial officers of a State, or the members of the Legislature thereof, is denied to any of the male inhabitants of such State, being twenty-one years of age, and citizens of the United States, or in any way abridged, except for participation in rebellion, or other crime, the basis of representation therein shall be reduced in the proportion which the number of such male citizens shall bear to the whole number of male citizens twenty-one years of age in such State.

Sec. 3. No person shall be a Senator or Representative in Congress, or elector of President and Vice President, or hold any office, civil or military, under the United States, or under any State, who, having previously taken an oath, as a member of Congress, or as an officer of the United States, or as a member of any State legislature, or as an executive or judicial officer of any State, to support the Constitution of the United States, shall have engaged in insurrection or rebellion against the same, or given aid or comfort to the enemies thereof. But Congress may by a vote of two-thirds of each House, remove such disability.

Sec. 4. The validity of the public debt of the United States, authorized by law, including debts incurred for payment of pensions and bounties for services in suppressing insurrection or rebellion, shall not be questioned. But neither the United States nor any State shall assume or pay any debt or obligation incurred in aid of insurrection or rebellion against the United States, or any claim for the loss or emancipation of any slave; but all such debts, obligations and claims shall be held illegal and void.

Sec. 5. The Congress shall have power to enforce, by appropriate legislation, the provisions of this article.

Art. XV
March 30, 1870

Sec. 1. The right of citizens of the United States to vote shall not be denied or abridged by the United States or by any State on account of race, color, or previous condition of servitude.

Sec. 2. The Congress shall have power to enforce this article by appropriate legislation.

Art. XVI
February 25, 1913

The Congress shall have power to lay and collect taxes on incomes, from whatever source derived, without apportionment among the several States and without regard to any census or enumeration.

Art. XVII
May 31, 1913

The Senate of the United States shall be composed of two senators from each State, elected by the people thereof, for six years; and each Senator shall have one vote. The electors in each State shall have the qualifications requisite for electors of the most numerous branch of the State legislature.

When vacancies happen in the representation of any State in the Senate, the executive authority of such State shall issue writs of election to fill such vacancies: *Provided*, That the legislature of any State may empower the executive thereof to make temporary appointments until the people fill the vacancies by election as the legislature may direct.

This amendment shall not be so construed as to affect the election or term of any senator chosen before it becomes valid as part of the Constitution.

Art. XVIII
January 29, 1919

After one year from the ratification of this article, the manufacture, sale, or transportation of intoxicating liquors within, the importation thereof into, or the exportation thereof from the United States and all territory subject to the jurisdiction thereof for beverage purposes is hereby prohibited.

The Congress and the several States shall have concurrent power to enforce this article by appropriate legislation.

This article shall be inoperative unless it shall have been ratified as an amendment to the Constitution by the legislatures of the several States, as provided in the Constitution, within seven years from the date of the submission thereof to the States by Congress.

Art. XIX
August 26, 1920

The right of citizens of the United States to vote shall not be denied or abridged by the United States or by any States on account of sex.

The Congress shall have power by appropriate legislation to enforce the provisions of this article.

Art. XX
February 6, 1933

Sec. 1. The terms of the President and Vice-President shall end at noon on the twentieth day of January, and the terms of Senators and Representatives at noon on the third day of January, of the years in which such terms would have ended if this article had not been ratified; and the terms of their successors shall then begin.

Sec. 2. The Congress shall assemble at least once in every year, and such meeting shall begin at noon on the third day of January, unless they shall by law appoint a different day.

Sec. 3. If, at the time fixed for the beginning of the term of the President, the President-elect shall have died, the Vice-President-elect shall become President. If a President shall not have been chosen before the time fixed for the beginning of his term, or if the President-elect shall have failed to qualify, then the Vice-President-elect shall act as President until a President shall have qualified; and the Congress may by law provide for the case wherein neither a President-elect nor a Vice-President-elect shall have qualified, declaring who shall then act as President, or the manner in which one who is to act shall be selected, and such person shall act accordingly until a President or Vice-President shall have qualified.

Sec. 4. The Congress may by law provide for the case of the death of any of the persons from whom the House of Representatives may choose a President whenever the right of choice shall have devolved upon them, and for the case of the death of any of the persons from whom the Senate may choose a Vice-President whenever the right of choice shall have devolved upon them.

Sec. 5. Sections 1 and 2 shall take effect on the 15th day of October following the ratification of this article.

Sec. 6. This article shall be inoperative unless it shall have been ratified as an amendment to the Constitution by the legislatures of three-fourths of the several States within seven years from the date of its submission.

Art. XXI
December 5, 1933

Sec. 1. The eighteenth article of amendment to the Constitution of the United States is hereby repealed . . .

Art. XXII
February 26, 1951

Sec. 1. No person shall be elected to the office of the President more than twice, and no person who has held the office of President, or acted as President for more than two years of a term to which some other person was elected President shall be elected to the office of the President more than once. But this Article shall not apply to any person holding the office of President when this Article was proposed by the Congress, and shall not prevent any person who may be holding the office of President, or acting as President, during the term within which this Article becomes operative from holding the office of President or acting as President during the remainder of such term.

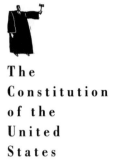

**The
Constitution
of the
United
States**

Article XXIII
March 29, 1961

SEC. 1. The District constituting the seat of Government of the United States shall appoint in such manner as the Congress may direct:

A number of electors of President and Vice-President equal to the whole number of Senators and Representatives in Congress to which the District would be entitled if it were a State, but in no event more than the least populous state; they shall be in addition to those appointed by the states, but they shall be considered, for the purposes of the election of President and Vice-President, to be electors appointed by a state; and they shall meet in the District and perform such duties as provided by the twelfth article of amendment.

SEC. 2. The Congress shall have power to enforce this article by appropriate legislation.

Article XXIV
January 24, 1964

SEC. 1. The right of citizens of the United States to vote in any primary or other election for President or Vice-President, for electors for President or Vice-President, or for Senator or Representative in Congress, shall not be denied or abridged by the United States or any stateby reason of failure to pay any poll tax or other tax.

SEC. 2. The Congress shall have power to enforce this article by appropriate legislation.

Article XXV
February 23, 1967

SEC. 1. In case of the removal of the President from office or his death or resignation, the Vice-President shall become President.

SEC. 2. Whenever there is a vacancy in the office of the Vice-President, the President shall nominate a Vice-President who shall take the office upon confirmation by a majority vote of both houses of Congress.

SEC. 3. Whenever the President transmits to the President pro tempore of the Senate and the Speaker of the House of Representatives his written declaration that he is unable to discharge the powers and duties of his office, and until he transmits to them a written declaration to the contrary, such powers and duties shall be discharged by the Vice-President as Acting President.

SEC. 4. Whenever the Vice-President and a majority of either the principal officers of the executive departments, or of such other body as Congress may by law provide, transmit to the President pro tempore of the Senate and the Speaker of the House of Representatives their written declaration that the President is unable to discharge the powers and duties of his office, the Vice-President shall immediately assume the powers and duties of the office as Acting President.

Thereafter, when the President transmits to the President pro tempore of the Senate and the Speaker of the House of Representatives his written declaration that no inability exists, he shall resume the powers and duties of his office unless the Vice-President and a majority of either the principal officers of the executive department, or of such other body as Congress may by law provide, transmit within four days to the President pro tempore of the Senate and the Speaker of the House of Representatives their written declaration that the President is unable to discharge the powers and duties of his office. Thereupon Congress shall decide the issue, assembling within 48 hours for that purpose if not in session. If the Congress, within 21 days after receipt of the latter written declaration, or, if Congress is not in session, within 21 days after Congress is required to assemble, determines by two-thirds vote of both houses that the President is unable to discharge the powers and duties of his office, the Vice-President shall continue to discharge the same as Acting President; otherwise, the President shall resume the powers and duties of his office.

Article XXVI
July 7, 1971

Sec. 1. The right of citizens of the United States, who are eighteen years of age or older, to vote shall not be denied or abridged by the United States or by any State on account of age.

Sec. 2. The Congress shall have power to enforce this article by appropriate legislation.

The
Constitution
of the
United
States

Index

Page numbers in bold text indicate the
primary article on a topic or court
case. Page numbers in italics indicate
illustrations.

A

Index

Index

Index

Index

I n d e x

Index

Index

I n d e x

Index

Index

Index

Index

Index

Military law and issues, **4:1041–1061**
Military orders affecting Japanese
    Americans, 3:576–581
Miller, Samuel F., on *Head Money
    Cases* (1884), 4:1105
Miller v. California (1973), 1:187,
    1:196–197
*Mills v. Board of Education of the
    District of Columbia,* 3:716
Miln, Mayor of New York v.,
    (1837), 4:973
Minersville School District v. Gobitis
    (1940), **1:108–111,** 1:175
Minnesota, Hodgson v., (1990),
    3:668, 3:703
Minnesota, Near v., (1931), 1:31,
    1:35–39
Minnesota state law
    gag law, 1:35–37
    Human Rights Act, 1:2, 1:23–28
    same-sex marriage, 2:348
Minor, Virginia, 3:623
Minor v. Happersett (1875), 3:614,
    3:621–627, 3:795
Minority-owned businesses. *See also*
    Reverse discrimination; specific
    minorities
    Fullilove v. Klutznick (1980),
        3:501–506
    *Metro Broadcasting, Inc. v.
        Federal Communications
        Commission* (1990), 3:507–512
    Yick Wo v. Hopkins (1886),
        3:569–575
Minority representation in government,
    3:799–800, 3:803
Minors
    abortion rights, 3:668, 3:701,
        3:703, 3:706
    contraception rights, 1:69–70,
        1:84, 3:685
    parental consent requirements,
        3:701, 3:703, 3:706
    reproductive rights, 3:667
    voting rights, 3:799, 4:889, 4:917
Miranda, Ernesto, 2:325–327
Miranda rights, 2:299, 2:327
Miranda v. Arizona (1966), 2:299,
    2:324–328, 4:958

Misdemeanors, 2:298
Mississippi University for
    Women, *3:634*
*Mississippi University for Women v.
    Hogan* (1982), 3:616, 3:630,
    3:633–639
Mississippi v. Johnson (1867), 4:865,
    4:899–904, 4:932
Missouri Compromise, 4:891–898
*Missouri Department of Health
    Director, Cruzan v.,* (1990), 1:71,
    3:516, **3:518–524,** 3:526, 3:535
Missouri ex rel. Gaines v. Canada
    (1938), 3:541
Missouri state law
    abortion law, 3:668,
        3:698–699, 3:705
    refusing medical treatment,
        3:518–524
Mitchell, Wisconsin v., (1993),
    1:248–252
Mitchell v. United States (1941), 3:583
Mitchell, Oregon v., (1970), 3:799,
    4:916–922
Mitigating evidence, 2:283
*Monell v. Department of Social
    Services* (1978), 3:594
Monopolies. *See* Trusts (commercial)
Monroe v. Pape (1961), **3:589–594**
Montgomery bus boycott, 1:13, 1:14,
    1:21, 1:192
Moore, Inez, 2:351–352
Moore v. East Cleveland (1977), 1:71,
    2:349–355
Morgan, Margaret, 3:552–556
Mormons, test of polygamy laws, 1:93,
    1:97–102
Morrison v. Olson (1988), 4:937–943
Morton, Passamaquoddy Tribe v.,
    (1975), 4:1077
Morton v. Mancari (1069), 4:1069
Mulford v. Smith (1938), 4:855
Muller v. Oregon (1908), 3:614, 4:998,
    4:1010–1016
Munn v. Illinois (1877), 4:973
Murphy, Frank, *1:171*
    Chaplinsky v. New Hampshire
        (1942), 1:172

I n d e x

Index

Index

Index

Index

Index

Index

Index

I n d e x

Index

labor standards, 4:1036–1037
legal limits, 3:614
in the military, 4:1045
voting rights, 3:621–627, *3:622, 3:624, 3:625,* 3:794–795, 4:889
Women workers, *4:1036, 4:1037*
Women's suffrage, 3:621–627, *3:622, 3:624, 3:625*
Woodson, James Tyrone, 2:266–267
Woodson v. North Carolina (1976), **2:265–269**
Woodward, Dartmouth College v., (1819), 4:822, 4:833, 4:878
Worcester v. Georgia (1832), 4:955, 4:1065, **4:1087–1087,** 4:1088–1078. *See also* Marshall Trilogy
Worcester, Samuel A., 4:1089
Works Progress Administration (WPA), 4:1033
WPA (Works Progress Administration), 4:1033

Wright, Ingraham v., (1977), **2:420–425**
Wygant v. Jackson Board of Education (1986), 3:485

Y

Yellow-dog contracts, 4:1027, 4:998, 4:999, 4:1025
Yellow journalism, 1:36
Yick Wo v. Hopkins (1886), 3:541, **3:569–575,** 3:715, 3:723
Yoder, Wisconsin v., (1972), **1:134–138**
Young, State v., (1919), 3:764
Youngberg v. Rome (1982), 3:717

Z

Zablocki v. Redhail (1978), 1:69
Zenger, John Peter, 1:64
Zoning ordinances, 2:351, 3:745, 4:976